SEVEN THUNDERS
Vol. II and III

The Rest of the Story

Ronald C. Ware

Table of Contents

Introduction vii

Volume II

Chapter 1 A Struggling Slave 10
Chapter 2 Living in Fear 23
Chapter 3 Called to be a Messenger 38
Chapter 4 Four Horses of Apocalypse 46
Chapter 5 The Great Flood 61
Chapter 6 Where Judgment Must Begin 68
Chapter 7 The Four Beasts of Daniel 72
Chapter 8 The Little Horn 83
Chapter 9 Changing of the Times 88
Chapter 10 Counting Days to the Cross 97
Chapter 11 Only Sign would be Given 111
Chapter 12 Easter or the Lord's Passover 123
Chapter 13 Sabbath to Sunday 138
Chapter 14 A Warning to Christians 148
Chapter 15 Study in Isaiah 168
Chapter 16 The Last Supper 181
Chapter 17 Two Different Plans 189
Chapter 18 Identifying Strange Woman 204
Chapter 19 The Leopard with Big Feet 218
Chapter 20 The Scarlet Coloured Beast 233
Chapter 21 Destruction of the Whore 243
Chapter 22 First Look into My Future 257

Chapter 23 Second Look into My Future 269
Chapter 24 Third Look into My Future 277

Volume III
Chapter 25 Searching for a Refuge..285
Chapter 26 Traveling with Paul 296
Chapter 27 About our Faith..313
Chapter 28 Water Baptism...333
Chapter 29 Baptism in Holy Ghost..352
Chapter 30 Peter's Visit to a Gentile...371
Chapter 31 Instructions from Paul 379
Chapter 32 Shepherds become Judges..394
Chapter 33 How to Receive Divine Power.................................406
Chapter 34 Remaining in Upper Room 438
Chapter 35 The Jealousy of Esther 447
Chapter 36 The Engrafted Word 454
Chapter 37 Loving God How?..467
Chapter 38 Final Instructions...480

Introduction

Perhaps some would say that the book stores are filled with religious books and why are we supposed to believe that your book is any different than the rest?

To this I reply, that it has been said that the best advertisement is by word of mouth. I do ask then, that you do pay attention to what others will say, concerning this message, for it contains a wake up call for all of America.

The hour is late and the hands on the nuclear clock are very close to midnight. In a little while, the nuclear winds will begin to blow and the radio-active rain will fall upon Christians and sinners alike.

I know that a great many people will say, Oh, Not So, We will soon be taken out of this world for our Lord is coming for his church.

To them I reply, I do know for sure that our Lord does not love some of us, more than he loves others for it would mean that the promises of his word are not true. If we be followers of Christ, then we should certainly know that his word is truth. I certainly do not believe that he loves the people of this current generation more than he loved his own disciples. Did he not choose them, even as he has chosen the Christians of our time? Is there anyone who does claim that they did choose Jesus, before our Lord did choose them?

In the gospel of Matthew, Jesus had this to say to his disciples.

Matthew 20:22 But Jesus answered and said, Ye know not what ye ask. Are ye able to drink of the cup that I shall drink of,

and be baptized with the baptism that I am baptized with? They say unto him, We are able.

Could it be that a great many Christians of this day and age are able but not willing to drink from the same cup as Jesus? If we would look back at history we would learn that the disciples of Jesus did indeed, drink from the same cup as their Lord and Master.

Therefore, because Solomon has informed us that history does seem to repeat it's self, and the pages of history do tell us of what happened to so very many of God's chosen people during the dark ages and the Roman reign of terror. I do say unto you, in the days ahead, many will have their faith tested by the fire, and they will learn whether or not it is strong enough to endure.

I do invite all Christians and all who are students of the Bible, to read from this book and do try to prove me wrong, according to what is written in your Bibles. I do not have any doubt but what many of you will become very angry with me, for it has always been so, for those who have been called to deliver messages from on high.

I now address myself to all who do not believe upon our Lord, Jesus Christ. Even those who are college students with much learning, who do believe they know more than what is written in the Bible. Come, and take up this book and learn from what is written here, in easy to understand language. Perhaps you think that mankind is so intelligent that he can solve almost any problem, or find a solution for any situation.

Let me just ask you, Did you really believe that mankind would create a huge stockpile of nuclear weapons, and then never use them? It is like saying to a small child, you can have many toys, but they must be kept in the closet, for you are never to play with them. What will that small child do, when no one is looking and they be given the opportunity?

Have you ever been to a theater to watch a live performance? I want us all to know that during the past decade and even before, the stage of this world has been set and the actors are now taking their places. In a little while, the last act is about to begin.

Perhaps I need to rephrase what I just said. I said that around this world there are many silos, and they do contain many huge nuclear missiles. At the same time, beneath the surface of the oceans of this world, there are a great many nuclear submarines, and they too, are carrying nuclear missiles. In a moments time, the warheads are all loaded and the missiles are made ready for what they were designed to do.

Come, learn of the mighty angel whose face is as bright as the sun. Who placed one foot on land and the other on the sea and cried out with a mighty voice, as the roar of many lions, and then listen, for the voices of the seven thunders will soon utter their voices, telling this world, what is done is done. Almighty God is not mocked, for he has paid the people who have trampled on his holy commandments the wages they are due.

I say then to all who do not believe, Come, and let us reason together. Prove me wrong, if you think that you can.

To those of you who do recognize I do come in truth, God's holy Word does provide us with a great many instructions for how we are to prepare for what lies ahead. I have labored diligently to share with you God's instructions and I know there are many blessings for those who do take hold of them and do them.

Paul often said that he did not want the people he did write letters to, to be ignorant. It is written in our Bibles that God's people do perish because of a lack of knowledge. I do beg of you, please do not choose to be ignorant, but learn what shortly must come to pass. Search diligently for the truth and the truth will set you free. Learn so that you may help others and if you happen to be able to help many, and do help them, great will be your reward.

A servant of Christ,
Ronald C Ware

Chapter 1 A Struggling Slave

⤳⤳⤳

I cried unto the Lord with my voice; I cried unto the Lord with my voice; And I said, "Dear God up in heaven. If you really are God and if you can hear my voice, please listen to me and what I have to say. I know that I am only a no good sinner and I know that I do not have any right to be talking to you but there is no where else for me to go and there is no one else who will listen to me. Please. dear God up in heaven, have mercy upon me, even though I am nothing but an ordinary sinner."

"My foot is caught in a trap and it is a trap that I set myself. I cannot get free from this trap and I have struggled and tried many times and it does not seem to matter how hard I have tried, for I am still caught in it. It will cause my death and I know this for sure for I have witnessed what happened to others who were not able to get free from this very same trap."

My mother, whom you know, warned me about the dangers of using alcohol and tobacco long ago, but I laughed at her and I did not pay any attention to her warning. I allowed alcohol and tobacco to become my friends when I was young and they have been my constant companions for many years. It is only now and during the last ten years that I have become aware that my former friends have turned against me and are trying to kill me. Slowly but surely they are destroying me and I know they will cause my death unless I am able to get free from this trap.

My heart is so heavy I cannot even describe how deep the hurt is for it is almost more than I can bear. I love my dear wife with all of my heart and I certainly do not want to hurt her. I know that she will be hurt when I die, and I fear that it will be a hurt she will have to endure the rest of her life. Dear God up in heaven, please believe me when I tell you that I do not want to hurt my dear wife, for her life has been hard enough and she does not deserve to be hurt this way.

Again I ask that you forgive me for coming to you this way dear God, for I am fully aware that I have sinned against you all the days of my life and I have no right to ask favors of you. However, my dear mother knew you and she told me all about you whenever she could and I know that she told you all of her troubles almost every day. It is because of what she told me about you that I now come to you, seeking your help in delivering me from my situation and from this deadly trap in which I find myself. Please dear God, will you help me now, for I do not want to die and I am afraid, and my heart is breaking and I do not know what to do.

Much to my surprise a voice began to speak to me. I could not see the one who was speaking but I could hear his voice and it was real and not something from my own imagination. Not only could I hear his voice but I could feel his presence and so I came to think about the owner of this voice as being the "invisible presence."

This voice said unto me "There is no need for your heart to be filled with sorrow for you only need to turn to me and I will give you rest."

At the sound of his voice and afterwards as I thought about the meaning of what he said, a blanket of peace came as a cloud and settled around me and I felt peace deep down in my soul. This blanket of peace remained with me even when I went to bed and when I awoke in the morning, the memory of what had happened was still fresh in my mind. I wish that I could tell you that I did as the voice suggested and that I turned to God and that everything was fine from then on, but that is not what happened.

Within a few days, my life had returned to normal and my foot was still caught firmly in the trap of alcoholism. I continued to travel down the alcohol road to death and though there were brief encounters with sobriety, for the most part my life was on a downward spiral and my own self pity I tried to keep hidden in my heart. However, my sorrow was so great that it was very hard to conceal unless I consumed large quantities of alcohol which enabled me to become an actor.

The problem I often encountered when I allowed myself to become an actor is that I found it difficult to determine who I really was and what I was pretending to be. I could go all day and all night playing the role of being a happy and successful person who is enjoying life to the max. Sooner or later, I would find myself bent over the toilet and heaving my guts out and so sick that I could hardly stand up. This is when a certain amount of reality came into my life and would drive the actor in me away. This was a time that I would have preferred to avoid but it seemed to be inevitable for I could not stay intoxicated forever and still function. This is when I would enter into sobriety and I would have to face the reality of my situation.

Quite often the reality of my situation was more than I could bear and so I would cry again unto the Lord and explain to him how I was hurting and how I did not know what to do. Again the voice of the "invisible presence" came unto me and informed me there was no need for my heart to be filled with sorrow for if I would but give my burdens to him, he would carry them for me.

I suppose that at this time I was in need of wise counsel for I needed to seek out someone who knew about this invisible presence and who knew and could instruct me about how I was to turn to him and what this meant. Having been an independent operator for the greatest part of my life, I continued to live my life my own way which meant that I continued on my downward spiral that would lead to my untimely death.

The voice of the Lord came to me on at least three different occasions and each time it was the same. Each time he instructed me that all I needed to do to be delivered from my situation was to turn to him. I would point out that it was necessary that I do so of my own free will, for he would not force me to do anything.

It is to my shame that I must say that I always found myself back where I started with my foot still caught securely in the trap of alcoholic bondage. What is more, when I found myself having to deal with reality, I would cry unto the Lord but it was as if he could not hear my voice any more and he did not answer me. It was like he had given me several chances to turn to him, but I had not done so and I had used up all of my chances. I cried unto him quite a few different times with my heart heavy and with the cloud of alcoholic depression almost more than I could bear, but he did not come to me nor did he answer my voice.

Several months passed and I had gotten to the point where I seemed to be resigned to my fate. I knew that I was as good as in hell for I had been given the instruction for how I could be set free from my situation but I had chosen to continue my love affair with the bottle. My love affair with the one who was certainly intent upon killing me, and yet I could not break free from the trap which held me. What is more, deep down inside I knew that I had rejected the love of the one who really did care for me, for I had rejected the instruction of my Creator, which is my heavenly Father.

And so it was one dark and rainy night that I sat alone at the old oak table, with a full glass of whiskey in my hand and watched the rain drops as they hit against the window pane and trickled down. As I watched the rain drops trickling down the window they eventually disappeared into the darkness.

I thought about how my short life would soon be over and how I, like the rain drops was on my way down to the darkness of death.

A great wave of self pity came sweeping over me and I felt extremely sorry for myself because I knew beyond any doubt that the alcohol I had already consumed was destroying my body and my mind and that death was inevitable. I did not know at that time that self pity is just as destructive in an invisible way as alcohol is in a physical way.

Perhaps it was because my situation seemed to be so hopeless, having been given the opportunity to accept salvation, but not being totally aware of how to receive it, always finding myself staring into a toilet with vomit and blood. It did appear to me that I had progressed down the alcohol road to where I was now beyond the hope of salvation, for the voice of the "invisible presence," no longer would answer me when I called.

As I sat there at the old oak table with a glass of whiskey in my hand from out of the darkness of my despair, came evil thoughts and I invited them into my mind and allowed them to dwell there. I considered that I had one foot in hell already so what did it matter if an evil thought or two took up residence in my mind, I thought to myself. Perhaps I was in hell already and the evil thoughts were little messengers of what was yet to come.

Suddenly another thought entered into my mind. I could remember how my mother had taught me when I was very young that I was not to look upon any evil, nor was I to speak any evil, and I was not even supposed to think any evil. In other words, it was completely wrong to invite evil thoughts into my mind and allow them to linger there.

My mother believed that God gave us the power to deny entry to any evil thoughts so that they were not even allowed to enter into our minds in the first place. She also believed that should we happen to find any evil thoughts in our minds that in the name of Jesus we were to command them to leave and they would have to obey, it is was simple as that.

I did not have any doubt that this always worked for my mother for she was a God fearing woman who spent much time down on her knees talking to God. Even so, it was not the same for me, for whenever I tried very hard not to think about a given subject, my mind would not cooperate with me and the very thing I did not want to think about would then be the thing I thought about the most.

I then thought about the voice of the "invisible presence" and how it came to me when I cried out to God and told him all about my troubles, that first time. How he had spoken to me on several different occasions always telling me that I could be free from my alcoholic bondage if I would but turn to him. I knew for sure that God is real and that my mother knew what she was doing when she got down on her knees and talked to God.

Some of my friends had suggested that my mother was a religious fanatic for her belief in God was something she lived and she was always telling people how wonderful it was to be a Christian.

I know now, that they did not understand because they did not know God and in fact, many of them did not believe in God. This was probably because their parents did not believe in God and they followed in their parents footsteps. I knew that God was real for he had spoken to me on several different occasions and I was very sure that it was not a product of my imagination.

As I thought about what the voice of the "invisible presence" had said to me, it came to me that he was also aware of the evil thoughts I had been thinking and had allowed to linger in my mind. I further realized that he know every detail of my evil thoughts and there was not one that was hidden from him. My knowledge that this was true brought shame to my mind and as I sat there at my old oak table, my shame became multiplied unto me and I became engulfed in it.

As I sat there with a full glass of whiskey in my hand I became aware that I was not alone for an invisible presence had entered into the room where I was sitting. It was slightly different than it had been on previous occasions for this was the presence of a convicting spirit and I knew then, deep down in my soul that I had been convicted and that I was guilty before Almighty God. I had never been more guilty in my entire life and my shame and my guilt possessed my whole being.

The voice of this invisible presence, this spirit of conviction began to speak to me in a very firm way. The voice did not contain anger but it was the voice of a very loving Father who had come to the end of his patience. It was also the voice of complete authority and I was fully aware that it was.

The voice then said unto me "You have now come to a very important place in your life. If you ever take another drink of alcohol, I will have no more to do with you forever. Do you understand what this means?"

At first, I wanted to crawl under the table and try to hide myself from this spirit of conviction. However, I was also aware that it would not do any good for I knew that I could not hide from it. Therefore, I sat there with my hand wrapped around my glass and I became absolutely still, like a piece of wood and I listened very closely to the words that were spoken unto me.

Somehow in my mind I regarded the drinking of hard liquor as serious drinking but I had always thought of beer as not being really serious but more of a matter of being social.

In a very small and timid voice I asked the "invisible presence" while I realized that drinking whiskey was a very serious thing, would it be alright for me to stop off at the tavern and have a few beers with my friends? Would it be alright as long as I did not drink to the point of intoxication but only drank a few in order to make friendly conversation?

There was a long moment of complete silence as I waited for the invisible presence to reply to my question. He spoke again to me with the voice of complete authority and he did issue me an ultimatum.

"If you ever allow so much as even one drop of alcohol to escape past your lips and enter into your mouth, you will be cast into the darkness of outer space where you will remain forever alone and without hope." Do you understand what this means?

I sat there at the table, motionless, too afraid to even move. The invisible presence of the spirit of conviction did not depart right away but remained with me and did cause me to understand better, the meaning of what he said to me. I will go further and say that in a way, he allowed me to experience in some small degree what complete separation from God is like, and to come to a deeper understanding about where the lost will spend eternity.

Surely, some of you have experienced the heart break of splitting up with your girl friend or boy friend. Many have experienced the tragedy of divorce and they know about the deep down hurt in the soul that is far greater than any physical pain. Still others have experienced what it is like to lose a child and know what it is like to have a void in your heart that not even time can heal. Perhaps there arc a few who have been rejected by their parents and know they will carry the emotional scars for all of their lives.

What you do not know is the tremendous sorrow you will experience on the day when the books will be opened and you find that your name is not written down in the Lamb's book of life. You do not know how you will feel when you discover that the very same heavenly Father who has loved you all the days of your life, has now rejected you forever.

My pitifully small vocabulary cannot describe the great sorrow that enveloped me as I sat at the old oak table and God allowed me to experience in some small degree what total and eternal separation from God feels like. If we were to take all of the sorrow filled experiences we have already mentioned and then multiplied them by at least a thousand, you might have some idea of what eternal separation from God will be like for the millions who will have refused to turn to God.

I had always had the idea that hell was a very hot place in the middle of the earth where all of my friends and I would go and where we would be shoveling coal for all of eternity. Instead, I had just received knowledge from the very same God who created this universe in the first place, and he caused me to know that those who are lost will spend eternity in complete darkness, alone and without hope. How very different was this knowledge compared to what I had been lead to believe.

The invisible presence stayed with me until I had experienced the great sorrow of eternal separation and then it departed from the room as suddenly as it had come.

I sat at the table weeping for my sorrow was so great I did not know what else to do. Slowly, the sorrow began to weaken but in it's place I was invaded by a great and terrible fear. I would call it, the fear of God, for I knew very well that God did mean what he said. I knew for sure that at that very moment that I was very close to being cast into hell for all of eternity.

I looked down at my hand and it was still wrapped around a full glass of whiskey. The truth of my situation caused my fear to be multiplied and the glass of whiskey became something I greatly despised. I found the strength to get up out of my chair and even though my knees were weak, I walked over to the kitchen sink and poured the glass of whiskey down the drain.

In this way, I poured a very large portion of my life down the drain too, and I never drank another drop of alcohol ever again, not even till this day.

I suppose that it would only seem natural for one to think that from that time on I would have become a Christian and would live a good Christian life. I wish I could say that I did but I must be honest with you and that is not what happened. It is true that from that moment on I never took another drink of alcohol for I was very sure of what would happen to me if I did. However, I still lived my life my own way and my way at that time was not God's way.

I earned my living for many years as a fisherman, and I owned and operated my own small fishing vessel. I became used to being the boss and the one who made all decisions pertaining to the operation of the fishing vessel. I did not always follow the crowd so to speak, but quite often I chose to fish in areas that were not popular with many fishermen.

To sum up what I am trying to say is that I did it my way and my independent method extended to many of the other areas of my life as well. What I have called being independent some would say that I was set in my ways while others would say that I was just plain stubborn. I do not doubt that this was a true description of me, but I want you to know that this was the result of many years of having to make all of the decisions. Perhaps the percentage of good decisions versus bad ones does contribute to how stubborn and set in one's ways they do become.

During the weeks and months that passed following the ultimatum I received from God, fear became my constant companion. I was very much afraid that something would cause me to have a weak moment and that I would return to the bar room someday and take one more drink of whiskey. Perhaps a friend would offer me a beer at a moment when my desire for one was quite strong and I would be tempted beyond my ability to resist.

It was for this reason that I began to stay away from my friends and I spent most of my time either alone or with my wife. I lived from day to day, finding many ways to stay busy and my body began to heal and my health to improve after having suffered so much abuse from the effects of alcohol.

After about a year had passed, my fear was somewhat diminished for I felt my life was under control and that I need not worry quite so much about not having the will power to abstain from alcohol. At the same time I fully realized that the power to abstain from alcohol did not come from me but was only because God loved me enough to give me this power as a gift. Therefore, the much better health I was experiencing was also a gift from God who loves and cares for me.

The Christmas season was drawing near and so we purchased a video recorder and began to record the movies on television that.

were about the life of Jesus. I was thankful in my heart and I found that I wanted to say thank you to God, but I did not know how.

In addition to the movies about Christ we also began to listen to what I call the Sunday sermons.

Because there were so many of them and there were times when they were on at the same time on different channels and so we began to tape these Sunday sermons and then we listened to them when it was more convenient for us.

My wife and I were both interested in knowing more about God and his only begotten Son, whose name is Jesus. At that time we could have began attending church but I had no idea of which one was the right one for us. I felt like perhaps we should listen to the people on television and maybe after awhile we would have a better idea of where we should go. I knew we could just look for the same church my mother had gone to, but I decided that I wanted to learn a little more about the other churches and what they believed first.

After a while, I became so comfortable with taping the Sunday sermons as well as the movies and the special programs that I forgot all about attending church. It was so much more convenient to sit at home and push buttons and then I could choose from quite a variety of religious denominations, as well as different speakers and programs. However, deep down in my soul there was a hunger that I could not deny and all of the religious programs on television could not satisfy.

One night I had a strange dream and it was a dream that came from the same "invisible presence" that had spoken to me on previous occasions. In my dream, as I watched television the news announced that Jesus, who was crucified, had now returned to the earth to claim his kingdom and there would now be peace on earth.

It seemed as though all people everywhere were weary of so many wars and so much fighting and killing, and so this news of the return of Jesus was most welcome. It was reported that Jesus had returned at a time when he was not expected and so the people of the world were not prepared for his sudden arrival. However, now that they knew he had arrived from heaven, every country on earth was preparing a huge celebration in honor of the new world leader.

The well known news commentator went on to say that a huge parade was about to begin in New York City and Jesus was there now. The religious leaders of the world had come as quickly as they could to be here for this special occasion. In addition, there were also kings and queens, and presidents and premiers, and all the leaders of the world, for they were all here to pay respect to the only begotten Son of God.

In the first volume of this work I told about this dream in detail. A few people who I talked with mistakenly attached a great importance to who the people were that I did observe at this huge parade. It seemed as though they wanted me to assure them that the religious leaders of their religion or sect were present at this parade. I want to make very clear to you the identity of who the people were at this parade are not at all important. What did happen to me is what is important about this dream.

First, the many religious leaders of the world proceeded down the parade route, riding in big fancy convertibles and waving to the crowd.

They were followed by the kings and queens and presidents and premiers, some who looked a tad bit uncomfortable while trying to maintain their dignity. These were followed by the cars carrying congressmen and statesmen and governors and other government officials and the crowds would often cheer when they did see the person whom they had probably voted for.

Along the parade route there were vendors selling popcorn and souvenirs of this most historic parade in history and I could hear them calling out as they advertised their merchandise. Then there were police men on motorcycles patrolling back and forth, warning the people to move back and to make room for the marching bands of which there was practically no end.

The view point of the camera looking down the parade route revealed there was quite a large space or gap in the parade. The crowds of people were quite noisy as they were calling back and forth to each other and making comments about the parade. Suddenly a silence came over all the people and I noticed people climbing up on top of cars and whatever they could in order to better see what was coming down the street.

Off in the distance was the car that was carrying Jesus, and though I could see his figure sitting in the car, it was still too far off to make out the details of his face. The cameras then shifted to the crowds of people lining the streets. They were able to catch the great anticipation on the faces of those who were waiting to look upon the face of the Lamb of God.

As the car bearing Jesus passed by them, their anticipation changed and many faces reflected the glory of the Lord, and their joy was unspeakable for I do not have the words to describe it. Tears came to their eyes and I do not think there was a dry eye to be found anywhere.

The cameras then shifted back to the car bearing Jesus as it proceeded down the street in our direction. It was much closer now and I felt my heart start to beat faster for I was soon going to be able to look upon the holy face of the one who had rescued me from certain death. The one who is known as the Savior and the Prince of Peace.

As my eyes were focused on his car the cameras began to get blurry and then the television screen became completely blank for the space of a minute or so. At this time, the sound was also distorted and I could not understand anything that was being said. I was very disappointed and there was nothing I could do.

Suddenly, the sound was restored but the picture was not. The voice said we are extremely sorry for this temporary interruption in service. Almost as soon as he announced this the picture was restored and I could now see the car bearing Jesus getting smaller in the distance as it had already passed by our vantage point.

I felt both disappointment and then frustration because I was unable to do anything to change my situation. I had allowed my television set to reveal unto me the holy face of Jesus but it had failed me due to a technical difficulty.

I had been so close that I could have practically reached out and touched his garment but, as it were, I had to settle for just a glimpse of his silhouette in the distance as he approached and again in the distance as he departed. My disappointment changed to anger and then to a deep sorrow. This had been a once in a life time opportunity and because I had depended on my television I was denied this memory to surpass all memories.

My heart was filled with sorrow and disappointment and so I began to cry. I am sure that my pillow was wet from my tears and it was probably the sound of my sobbing that caused me to awake from my troubled sleep. I lay there and a feeling of relief came sweeping over me as I realized that it had all been a dream and there was not any reason for me to feel sorrowful.

Suddenly I became aware that I was in the presence of the Holy Spirit and he said unto me, "You will have to do more than watch television if you are ever to look upon my holy face."

Chapter 2 Living in Fear

⚜

It was because of what the Holy Spirit had spoken to me I now knew beyond any doubt that the voice of the invisible presence had really been the voice of Jesus all the time. Somehow, this knowledge made me feel good inside and it was like I had a secret that I wanted to share with everybody and I could not for the fear that they would not understand or believe me. I could hardly blame them for it did not seem reasonable for the Holy Spirit to communicate with an ordinary sinner like me. Yet, I knew for sure that he had and no one could take that truth from me.

My mind then turned to the meaning of what the Holy Spirit had spoken to me and it became very clear to me that I must do more than what I was doing. Again, at this point I should have sought out wise counsel that could have advised me of what was expected of me. I believe that it was because of my independent life style that I did not seek counsel but did my best to figure it out for myself.

First, I knew that my wife and I could begin attending church but I really did not know where to start. There were so many different churches and I knew that if I were to ask the people who attended them, it is likely they would all tell me that their church was better than all the rest of them. From time to time some people knocked on my door and then informed me that they were from the only true church. Now to be truthful with you, I could not see anything about them that suggested to me that they were any different than the rest.

I know that some would ask why didn't I just return to the church of my youth, the church my mother attended? I thought about it and I knew beyond any doubt that my mother knew God and lived a Godly life. However, I believed this was because of her commitment to God and did not mean that her church was without error.

This was not the reason why I did not choose her church for It had to do with some of the early teaching I received in that church for they taught certain things I did not and could not believe.

For instance, they taught that an angry God would one day cast all bad little boys and girls, and all thieves and liars and murderers and people like Hitler into hell. The hell they believed in was a huge lake of fire where the fate of all who were cast there is to suffer in the flames forever.

I reasoned in my own mind that the God they knew was unable to tell the difference between the sins of a young boy struggling with the problems of growing up in Bellingham Washington and the sins of a Hitler who was responsible for the death of millions of Jews. This was most difficult for me to understand for I believed in a God that was intelligent enough to see a difference between ordinary young people and world terrorists and murderers and their kind.

My thoughts turned to my mother and I wondered what she would have advised me to do, if she were still alive. I knew that she attended church fairly regularly through out her life but during her last ten years as her health failed, so did her church attendance.

There were two other weapons in her arsenal that she used in her battle to overcome the evil of this world. There was the fact that she did regularly each day take all of her burdens to her Lord in prayer. In fact I once overheard some ladies talking about my mother at the small church where she attended and they described her as being a "faithful prayer warrior."

I thought about this but it did not seem to be the answer for me. I have already shared with you how the Holy Spirit did communicate with me on those occasions that I have mentioned. There were a few times when I wanted to talk to God and I did try, but it was like he did not hear me. Other than those times when I cried unto the Lord from the depths of my deepest despair, it did not appear to me that the Lord wanted to communicate with me. I could hardly blame him for I was still an ordinary sinner and I could not truthfully say that I had turned to him, for I was still living my life my own way and not God's way.

The other weapon in my mothers arsenal was her Bible. She spent many hours studying her Bible and as her eyes were failing toward the end of her life she would read with the benefit of a magnifying glass.

I can remember her once saying to me "Son, I know that you think that you are smart and that there is nothing I can tell you, but I want you to know that all of the knowledge you will ever need to know to reach heaven is contained in God's holy book. All of the knowledge and all of the wisdom that is contained in all of the books that have ever been written is not as much as is contained in my Bible."

I thought about what she said to me so long ago and I decided that perhaps she would have advised me at this time to begin reading the Bible. I really was not sure of which church I should attend and I really did not know how to pray, and so it seemed to be the best choice I could make.

A few weeks after I received the strange dream, I finally found myself alone with the time to sit down and begin reading God's own word, the Holy Bible. I thought about how my mother had spent many hours studying the well worn pages of her Bible. I could remember that she was always seeking for the scriptures that would reveal unto her, the United States in prophecy. No doubt it was for this reason she often read from the pages of the Revelation. In addition she spent a good deal of time in one book of the prophets or another, always searching but never seeming to find what she was searching for.

I thought about how there could be no doubt that the Holy Spirit had made it very clear to me that I must do more than watch television and push buttons to be put right with God. Seeing as how it was obviously God's will that I begin reading His Holy Word, I thought I might begin reading from the last book of the Bible, the Revelation which had captured so much of my mothers time and attention.

I was about to begin when a thought came to me that perhaps I should pray to God and ask him to help me to understand what I was about to read, for I did believe in my mind that with God, all things are possible. I did bow my head and I asked "Dear God up in heaven, since I believe that it is your will that I begin reading your holy book, I ask you now 0 God, to open up my mind and my eyes and my ears that I might understand the mysteries that are hidden in your word."

I remained silent for a long moment, not knowing how to end this one sided conversation with God. Then from the depths of my memory, I could hear my mothers voice as she concluded her prayers and then I said "All of these things I do ask in the holy name of the Lord, Jesus Christ. Amen."

Without any further delay, I took up my Bible and I began to read from the book of Revelation. I do not claim that I understood everything I read, but I could tell that somehow there was a difference in my understanding. It was like my mind was now open to understanding and the meaning of each sentence was much clearer. I continued to read along with my intention being to read the entire book of Revelation without stopping.

I found chapter nine very interesting and mysterious and I suspected that it contained knowledge that was pertinent to this present time, but I did not have the key to unlock and possess that knowledge.

I was about to go on to chapter ten when I suddenly became aware that I was in the presence of the Holy Spirit. My first reaction was one of respectful silence, for I waited for the Holy Spirit to speak to me, just as he had on those previous occasions that I have shared with you. However, the Holy Spirit did not say anything to me, and so I felt that it was his will that I continue to read chapter ten.

In a very small voice I said, "help me 0 Lord, to understand what it is, that you want me know." And then I began to read from chapter ten, and the Lord was with me.

Revelation 10:1, And I saw another mighty angel come down from heaven, clothed with a cloud: and a rainbow was upon his head, and his face was as it were the sun, and his feet as pillars of fire:

And he had in his hand a little book open: and he set his right foot upon the sea and his left foot on the earth,

And cried with a loud voice, as when a lion roareth: and when he had cried, seven thunders uttered their voices.

And when the seven thunders had uttered their voices, I was about to write: and I heard a voice from heaven saying unto me, Seal up those things which the seven thunders uttered, and write them not.

I will now share with you the knowledge I was given, concerning the mystery of these things that are mentioned in the first four verses. The first verse begins with "And I saw another mighty angel come down from heaven, clothed with a cloud." The Holy Spirit caused my mind to travel back in time to when I was a very small boy attending a movie in Everett Washington. They showed what was called a news reel, and the news was that our government had been working in the desert of New Mexico on a secret new and terrible weapon. That terrible weapon was what would be known as the "atomic bomb."

The news reel then showed a group of men who were crouched behind some kind of barrier as they were about to observe first hand the blast of the atomic bomb. They were all required to wear very special protective glasses, because the center of the blast was like looking into the sun.

We did not have to wait very long and then the bomb went off. It as a sight that was burned forever into my memory, for not only was the center of the explosion a giant fireball, just like the sun, there as also a huge mushroom cloud rising up above the earth. In time, I came to always associate this distinctive mushroom cloud with an atomic explosion.

As I sat at my table, with my Bible open before me, I realized that two of the descriptions that were given in the first verse had taken place within my life time. I truly understood the meaning of the face as it were the sun and that it was clothed with a cloud, for the meaning was very clear that this was speaking of the coming of the atomic age.

However, I must confess that the other things that were mentioned remained a mystery for a little while longer. I knew that their true meaning should be within my grasp if only I could open up my mind to see a little deeper into what John, the disciple of Jesus was trying to describe as he saw it in this vision. I read the first four verses over and over and then slowly, it began to come to me.

I focused my attention on the two feet that were as pillars of fire. We must not think that they were pillars of fire but that they were AS pillars of fire. Surely, I thought to myself, I must have seen these two pillars of fire if they are a part of the sequence of the coming of the atomic age. I began to think that the pillars could also be columns of fire and then I thought about those times that I watched a guided missile being launched as it was shown on television.

I then read the second verse again and I noticed that the mighty angel then placed his two feet that were as pillars of fire, one on land and the other on water. I realized that these verses were describing what has come into reality within my life time, for this is speaking of guided missiles that are based on land as well as on sea.

At the time of my discovery, both the United States and the Soviet Union did possess many nuclear powered submarines that were armed with many mighty nuclear missiles. This was the explanation of the foot that was placed on the sea.

As far as the foot that was placed on land, surely you must be aware that across the United States as well as across Europe and perhaps elsewhere, there are many mighty nuclear missiles contained in silos. It is true that we might have reduced their numbers these past few years but I believe that it is a fact that they still do exist.

The rainbow that is mentioned in verse one remained a mystery for a little longer and I continued to think about it. At first, nothing I came up with seemed to make sense and I realized that perhaps I was allowing my mind to think in too broad of a way. Just what does the rainbow have to do with guided missiles and only guided missiles?

I soon realized that the rainbow is the symbol of the trajectory of the large intercontinental missiles. They can be launched in a vertical manner from one continent, travel across the ocean and then hit their target on a different continent.

The rainbow then indicates that these verses are not talking about short range missiles that might be launched from a jet aircraft and seek out their target traveling in a horizontal manner. The sign of the rainbow does insure us that these verses are speaking of very large and destructive intercontinental missiles and their trajectory is like a half moon arc.

My mind began to think about the time of these things. The coming of the atomic age in 1944 or 1945. Certainly the month of August in 1945 could be considered an important date for what happened at Hiroshima was written in the pages of history forever.

Perhaps we were somewhat limited in our delivery system at that time, for those two very important bombs "fat man and little boy" had been delivered by a pair of B-29s. As our technology progressed, so did our delivery system for it lead to our present day guided missile arsenal which can destroy any city in the world on very short notice.

At this time we shall pass over verses 5,6, and 7, but we might examine them later for their meaning. We shall go directly to verses 8,9 and 10.

Revelation 10:8, And the voice which I heard from heaven spake unto me again, and said, Go and take the little book which is open in the hand of the angel which standeth upon the sea and upon the earth.

And I went unto the angel, and said unto him, Give me the little book. And he said unto me. Take it and eat it up; and it shall make thy belly bitter, but it shall be in thy mouth sweet as honey.

And I took the little book out of the angels hand, and ate it up; and it was in my mouth sweet as honey: and as soon as I had eaten it, my belly was bitter.

I will share with you the meaning of these verses even as it was given to me. First of all, the book the angel held was small for it did not contain a great amount of knowledge. Neither did it contain anything that was extremely complicated or difficult to understand. As I have already shared with you, it contained the knowledge that marked the coming of the atomic age. When John took the book from the angel and ate it simply means that he read it and did understand what was written there. He said this knowledge would be at first, sweet in the mouth but would turn to bitterness in the stomach.

When I was a little boy, living in Everett, I was very seldom allowed to attend any movies and when I was allowed, it was only when I was accompanied by my older siblings. There was another rule in our home and that was the reading of funny books was absolutely forbidden. My mother did not want me to fill my mind with such foolishness for she wanted me to read more nourishing material that would benefit my education.

There was a barber shop several blocks away from where we lived on Wetmore Ave. Probably at least once or twice a month I would visit this barber shop and my reasons for doing so were two fold. First, I was raised in a home that was dominated by females as my dad had died when I was very young. I longed to listen to men talk about things that were interesting to men, for all I ever heard at home was a bunch of chatter coming from my sisters who thought they knew everything.

Second, there was a very large selection of comic books at the barber shop and so it was very pleasant for me to stop off and read the funny books while listening to men discuss those things which are important to men.

I can remember hearing a man say with great authority, "there will never ever be another war, for we have fought the war that will end all wars." Almost immediately, the barber asked him to explain just what he was talking about.

He said that "no one and I mean absolutely no one will dare fight us after what has happened." He went on to say that it was well known that the Japanese were the type of people who would never give up easily for many of them would have rather died than give up. However, the bomb that was dropped on Hiroshima and again on Nagasaki was so terrible that they were forced to admit they were completely defeated and did immediately sign the peace treaty."

Several other men joined into the conversation and they all did agree that the United States was the heavy weight champion of the world.

It was because we were the only ones with the bomb, and that did seem to insure that the world would now enter into a time of peace for the whole world was weary of war.

Those men did seem to know what they were talking about for we were about to enter into a time of prosperity. There were many victory parades across the nation and the bands played with gusto as pretty girls twirled their batons and our fighting men came marching home.

It was often said that "the bomb" our most terrible weapon of war was responsible for the war ending much sooner than was expected. I want for you to think about those times if you can and remember how very happy we all were because the war was finally over. Surely you will agree, this knowledge that was attached to the coming of the atomic age was very sweet in the mouth. The rumor that there would never be another war seemed to be the frosting on the cake.

As some time passed and people everywhere were adjusting to the changing economic conditions, we became aware that perhaps all was not as well as it first seemed. This was the time when the victors would divide the spoils of war and many conferences and meetings were held. Such names as Pottsdam and Yalta came up in the conversation at the dinner table and gradually an uneasiness crept over many Americans and perhaps the English as well.

Winston Churchill was still a strong voice but our beloved Franklin Roosevelt was gone and in his place was a tough little man by the name of Truman. However, Truman and the very popular General MacArthur did not always agree on our foreign policy and many Americans were confused and did not know what to think.

Some of our military leaders did not like Stalin and I heard it said that he was not to be trusted and that he was not really our friend. We were about to enter into the cold war, and while some were still living in the after glow of victory, others were preparing for trouble and in time this would lead to an arms race.

The news arrived that we were not the only one with "the bomb" for we learned that the people who had become our enemies were also building bombs. In retaliation we began to build more and bigger bombs and we also worked night and day to improve our delivery capability which lead to the development of our guided missile system on both land and sea.

A great fear began to pierce the hearts of many Americans for they were greatly afraid that what had been done to the Japanese would now be done unto us. As a child I learned that our government had created as a matter of defense what they called the D.E.W. Line, which stood for distant early warning system or so I was told. Through out the public school system air raid drills became a normal practice and little men selling survival shelters came knocking on our doors. Whether or not to invest in one became a frequent conversation at the dinner table and little children were afraid.

The younger generation of many countries through out the world began to resent what those nations who were regarded as super powers were doing, for it soon became apparent that the entire world was covered by the nuclear shadow of so many weapons of great and terrible destructive force. Many young people began to rebel and to demonstrate and protest for no one in the whole world was safe from the destructive weapons which were controlled by only a few.

I want you to think about this and perhaps you will agree that this is the time when the knowledge that was at first sweet in the mouth has now turned completely bitter in the stomachs of sane people everywhere. Please do be aware that these scriptures pertaining to what was once sweet and what has become bitter has now been fulfilled.

I want you to think about everything that has been said and if you do understand what these verses are describing and if some of the mystery they do contain has now been revealed unto you, we shall proceed on, for there is more knowledge to be gained. There is a sequence of events that we need to study for they reveal what shortly must come to pass.

Let us return to the second verse and begin where it is written **Revelation 10:2, and he set his right foot upon the sea, and his left foot on the earth, and cried with a loud voice, as when a lion roareth: and when he had cried, seven thunders uttered their voices.**

First, it was necessary that many large intercontinental nuclear missiles be prepared and put in their places on both land and sea, in order for this prophecy to begin. Of course, we know that the missiles have been prepared and ready for a long time now. Even many years.

The next step in the sequence is when the mighty messenger (atomic age) is to cry out in a loud voice, and then John compares this loud voice with something he has heard before, the roaring of a lion. Have you ever heard the loud roar of a full grown male lion when he is either hungry or angry?

When I was a little boy living in Everett, my older sister did take me to the zoo at Forest Park for we did not live very far from there. There were times when several lions would begin to roar and I could not tell if it was because they were hungry or if they were threatening one another. I do know that it was a most frightening sound and it caused a great amount of fear to grab a hold of me. I did not have any doubt that the lions would have gladly eaten me for their lunch or anyone else that was foolish enough to enter into their living quarters.

What is important is for us to try to understand what it was that John was trying to describe to us. Obviously, John was speaking of something he did hear and see in his vision that was given to him by his Lord Jesus. It does appear to me that the roar of a lion was the only sound that even came close to what John was trying to describe.

I think it is safe to say that John did not know anything about such things as nuclear intercontinental missiles. However, we can be sure that the one who gave this vision unto John is also the one who does know the future, and he is the same one who foretold in 31 A.D., the total destruction of Jerusalem that occurred in 70 A.D.

There is one point here that I want to make and that is I believe that the noise that John heard in his vision was not like the sound of a single lion but perhaps the sound made by a whole pride of lions. I do not believe that it is the sound of only one missile taking off but is actually the sound of many missiles as they begin to roar very loudly as they begin to lift off of their launch pads. Be quiet and listen, perhaps you can hear them too.

Revelation 10:3, and cried with a loud voice, as when a lion roareth, and when he had cried, seven thunders uttered their voices.

My first thought as perhaps these verses were speaking of only seven nuclear missiles for the sound of thunder off in the distance is the sound that is made when the missiles strike their targets. Surely, this is not too difficult to understand. First there is the sound of the loud roar as the missile rises up into the sky and begins speeding towards the target. Then there is the loud ka-boom, or explosion, a sound much like the sound of thunder when the missile does fulfill it's mission.

It was only after giving it much study that I came to understand that the number seven when used symbolically does not always mean or is limited to seven in number. It is the symbolic number of completion. In other words, instead of thinking there were only seven guided missiles that were launched, in John's vision, it would be better for us to understand that this is referring to a complete number of missiles. In the same way, instead of thinking there were only seven thunders who replied to the loud roar the missiles made during take off, there was a complete number of thunders which did reply. I say again, the number seven as it is used in these verses is not to be taken literally but is used in the symbolic sense. Whether or not you do agree with me, I do hope that you do understand what I am trying to say.

Complete in what way, you might be wondering? It simply means that a complete number of missiles did lift off and began speeding toward their targets. When they did arrive at their targets, the seven thunders did utter their voices.

What did they say, you might be wondering? They said and we can be sure of this, that the job they were given to do was completed and the destruction of their targets was complete. In other words, the message that was uttered when the seven thunders did speak did tell the news that their intended target was completely and utterly destroyed.

Let us take another look at the sequence of events that are foretold by our Lord Jesus Christ in a vision and given unto John to be placed in his book of Revelation. First, there was the coming of the atomic age and we all know what happened at Hiroshima. Time went on and then the angel placed one foot on the land and the other on the sea. We certainly do know that these things did take place quite a while ago.

Since that time, there has been much trouble in many different parts of the world but there has not been a major confrontation between any of the super powers which would lead us into a nuclear world war three. However, there is one thing we can absolutely be sure of and that is that there is a day coming when many large missiles will be launched and the destruction they will cause on that day that is coming will be far greater than we even know.

Verses five and six do inform us that the time is coming when time as we know it today will come to an end. In other words, it will be the end of this age and the time to enter into eternity will have come.

To increase our understanding of these verses we need to turn to the twenty-second chapter of Revelation and examine what is said in verses 10 and 11.

Revelation 22:10, And he saith unto me, Seal not the sayings of the prophecy of this book: for the time is at hand.

He that is unjust, let him be unjust still: and he which is filthy, let him be filthy still: and he that is righteous, let him be righteous still: and he that is holy, let him be holy still.

And then in verse twelve we hear the words that were spoken by Jesus.

Revelation 22:12, And behold, I come quickly; and my reward is with me, to give every man according as his work shall be. I am Alpha and Omega, the beginning and the end, the first and the last.

In other words, the very same Jesus who gave this vision of future events unto John in the first place is saying that the time is very near when everyone shall be paid the wages they have coming. I want for you to think about what kind of wages you will receive on that day that is coming?

We need to return once more to the tenth chapter of the Revelation and examine what is said in verse number seven.

Revelation 10:7, But in the days of the voice of the seventh angel, when he shall begin to sound, the mystery of God should be finished, as he hath declared to his servants the prophets.

First I want to point out that the seventh angel and the angel that is mentioned in verse one, another mighty angel, are not the same.

To come to a better understanding of the seventh angel, we would need to study the first six angels and while there is no doubt a good thing to do, now is not the time for there are other things I want to discuss. As I have shared with you the knowledge that was given unto me, you must be aware that the hour is late and the time is near when all of these things will come to pass. It is possible that the seventh angel began to blow his trumpet with the coming of the atomic age, but many of God's shepherds have been sleepy and they have failed to warn the people. Believe me, I would not say such a thing if it were not so.

I want us to take one more look at what is mentioned in the seventh verse. Notice where it states that the mystery of God should be finished, as he hath declared to his servants the prophets. The footnote in my Bible substitutes "hidden truths" for the word mystery. What this is saying to us is that if we want to learn more about the great and terrible day that is close at hand, we can learn about it by studying what has been written in the books of the prophets.

I now want to ask you a question and I want you to answer it as truthfully as you can. As I have shared the knowledge that as given unto me concerning the meaning of these verses in the tenth chapter of Revelation, are you able to see what they are trying to portray? Can you understand that they are describing a time when many large intercontinental nuclear missiles will lift off and begin speeding toward their targets?

It is a picture of the final result when they do reach their targets for John described it as being the voices of seven thunders. John was not allowed to write down what they said and yet God has commanded me to share with you the knowledge I was given.

I know some people whose minds are dull and they will say that it is too hard to understand. Some will only see those things they want to see and they are completely blind to the things they do not want to see. Many people have been blinded by their religious knowledge for they believe that they already know all there is to know. Therefore, there is nothing they can learn and it would be a waste of their time to read this book.

I have but one more question to ask you, and that is how do you think that John came by this vision in the year of about 96 A.D. on the Island of Patmos. I want for you to think about the conditions that John was living in during that period of time and then compare it with what is described in a way that we can understand if we will only allow our minds to be open.

I thought about it a great deal and I came to the conclusion that the Holy Bible is a very supernatural book for it contained all of this knowledge for hundreds and hundreds of years but it was not available to us because of our ignorance. However, when we examine both history and our current technology we should be able to understand that these prophecies are for the time in which we are living.

In order for John to write about such things in 96 A.D. he could only have received this knowledge from a supernatural source. How could it be otherwise?

I am sure that you have many questions that need to be answered concerning what we have just learned. It is certainly my intention to answer as many as I can but I feel that I must warn you that with knowledge comes responsibility.

Let us look at the very last verse in chapter ten of the Revelation for it reveals what that responsibility does include.

Revelation 10:11, And he said unto me, Thou must prophesy again before many peoples, and nations, and tongues, and kings.

If you have begun to understand the message that is contained in this tenth chapter of the Revelation even as I have shared with you the knowledge I was given, then you are responsible before God to share it with others. You must share it with your family and with your neighbors and whoever will listen.

Chapter 3 Called to be a Messenger

When the truth of what I had learned as it was given unto me by the Holy Spirit began to penetrate into my mind and began to register there what these verses were truly saying to me, something else happened. The very strong wall I had built around my heart began to crumble.

I read the verses over and over again and I hoped that they did not mean what I knew they really did mean. However, their true meaning did not leave me and in fact as I thought about everything that is said in the tenth chapter of the Revelation it became clearer and stronger. I knew beyond any doubt that my Bible is a supernatural book and the message I had received did not originate on this earth but came to me from the one who is sitting on the right hand of God in heaven.

I got down on my knees and with tears flowing down my face, I surrendered to God. I had been fighting and struggling to live my life my own way and without any help, but I finally had to admit that my way was not good and God's way is perfect. I had to admit that I was a common and ordinary sinner and my sins were so filthy that I was in great need of cleansing. Only the blood of Jesus is able to take away our sins and for this I will be forever thankful.

There is a point I want to make and that is the fact that I had believed in God for many years. However, I had not surrendered at the foot of the cross and I continued to live my life my own way. I did not allow the Holy Spirit to be the boss and so I was still lost in my sins.

There are a great many people today who have been lead to believe that all they have to do is believe in God and believe in Jesus and they will be saved no matter what. I am saying that this is not true for we must believe to the point that we are willing to surrender our own will, in order that the Holy Spirit can take up residence in our heart and lead us down the very narrow path that leads to salvation.

Many will ask what! Do you mean that we are saved by our works? No, I do not mean that we are saved by our works. I just want you to be aware that unless we first surrender, we can not be born again. If we are not born again neither will we be saved for Jesus made it very clear that we must be born again.

It was when I became born again that the Holy Spirit came into my heart to dwell. It is true that I had a lot of bad habits and ways that were not pleasing to God, but it was at the point of surrender that the remodeling work began. Praise God.

I want to be very brief about what happened next. I began to read the Bible and I did not stop until I had read it from cover to cover. I knew then, what will happen when the seven thunders shall utter their voices for the Bible made it very plain to me. This knowledge became a heavy burden and I tried to share my knowledge with others but I was not well received.

The people who do not know God and who have not been born again were not at all interested in hearing what I had to say, for they were only interested in their own pursuit of pleasure and worldly riches.

By the same token, those people who claimed to be Christians did not seem to be interested either, for most of them seemed to think they already knew all there was to know and they were simply not interested in listening to anyone as common and ordinary as myself. Since I did not seem to fit the mold they had built concerning what they believed a Christian should look and talk like, they simply dismissed me as being some sort of crack pot who was deceived and they believed that I did not have any idea of what I was talking about.

I soon came to be sick and tired of people making fun of me and ridiculing me for trying to share with them the truth of God's word.

I decided that I would just keep my knowledge to myself for no one took me seriously. It was at this point that I began to travel down the wrong road and one that leads away from God and into the darkness of this world.

I do not want you to think that I returned to my former sinful way of life for I certainly did not do that. I knew that there was nothing there for me, but neither did I feel like enduring the rejection I felt from sinners and Christians alike. Perhaps I was a little like a man along time ago that was supposed to go to Nineveh and deliver a message from God, but he was reluctant to do so.

Instead he tried to run away from God so that he would not have to deliver it and that is what I did, for I too, tried to run away from the truth.

However, within a years time, I came to realize that I was making a very serious mistake for I realized that I could not survive without God. God finally came to me and allowed me to see how very foolish I had been for no one can hide from God for he can find us no matter where we try to hide. It is necessary for me to repent once more for my sin of running away and God's tender mercy and grace through the blood of Jesus did restore me once more in to his divine presence.

At that time, I was called by my Lord to be a servant and I was given a job to do. "You must tell them about the day when the seven thunders will utter their voices and you must tell them about me" the voice of the Holy Spirit did speak to me. It as at this time that the knowledge was given to me that I should write a book for I would be able to reach more people via the written page than I would by the spoken word.

This high calling was what lead to the first volume of this work. I am aware that volume two is long over due and that is why I am anxious to finish this work and speed it on it's way as soon as possible. It is not my intention to speak further about myself for I want to share with you the truth I have been given as much as it is possible. This truth can be found in God's Holy Word.

Therefore, at this time I shall insist that if you do not already own a Bible that you do acquire one.

Everyone should own their very own Bible for I consider it's value to be beyond measure. I now own many different Bibles but the one I use the most and has become a very dear friend to me is my old King James Bible and it is what we might call a regular King James Version. There is one called the New King James Version but mine is the old one that has been in print for many of years.

When I first began to read the Bible I found the language of the old King James Version to be difficult to understand. It was for that reason that I borrowed from my younger brother a modern English version.

It does not make any difference to me which version you choose for that is a choice you will have to make for your self. If you are able to read and understand the old King James Version then that is the one I do recommend. If you should happen to find the old King James Version too difficult, I hope that you will choose one that is easy to read and understand and you can graduate to a more difficult version later, should you need to.

It is absolutely necessary for you to obtain your very own Bible at this time if you are ever to learn from a supernatural source about those things we must prepare for. It will be your duty to look up each and every scripture I mention in your very own Bible so that the "Living Word" can speak to you personally from the pages of your own Bible.

It is also necessary so that you can make sure that the things I say are written in the Bible and that I do not twist or distort their true meaning for there are many today who do.

In the 24th chapter of Matthew and at the 10th verse Jesus said "And many false prophets shall rise and shall deceive many." I do believe that what Jesus said does apply to the time in which we are living for I see and hear false prophets through out the Christian community. What Jesus said has come true for there are a great many people today who have been deceived by these false teachers and false prophets.

It is for this reason that I do insist that you do not think of me as being a prophet. It is true that I have come to you, bringing to you a message from God, but that message can be found in the pages of your very own Bible. Therefore, I would prefer that you think of me as being a servant and a messenger and we shall allow the Word of God to do the prophesying.

I now want us to turn in our Bibles to the book of Ecclesiastes where we shall try to grasp a great truth as it has been recorded by the wise old king.

Ecclesiastes 1:9, The thing that hath been, is that which shall be; and that which is done is that which shall be done: and there is no new thing under the sun.

It is with this key that we are able to come to a better understanding of prophecy. What Solomon has said in other words is that history does seem to repeat it's self. Perhaps you will recall that someone else once said that "if we fail to learn from history, then we are doomed to repeat it." If you were to read your Bible from cover to cover you would learn that Israel never seemed to learn from history for they repeated the same mistakes, over and over again.

We shall now examine something Jesus said to his disciples that does seem to verify that history does repeat it's self. Please do be aware that the words spoken by Jesus were in a private conversation with his disciples. Let us begin at

Matthew 24: 3, And as he sat upon the mount of Olives, the disciples came unto him privately, saying, Tell us, when shall these things be? and what shall be the sign of thy coming, and of the end of the world?

Jesus answered them by giving a rather long and detailed account of things that would happen. Many of the things Jesus described did take place during their life time and to be more specific, when Jerusalem was completely destroyed by the armies of Rome in 70 A.D. However, the things that Jesus continued to speak of did not end at Jerusalem in 70 A.D. but did extend far into the future and even to the time of his second coming. The part we are looking for is found in verses 36 and 37

Matthew 24: 36-37, But of that day and hour knoweth no man, no, not the angels of heaven, but my Father only.

But as the days of Noah were, so shall also the coming of the Son of man be.

There are two great truths contained in these two verses and I want us to take a hold of both of them. First, no man or woman knows exactly when Jesus shall return and neither do they know exactly what day the seven thunders will utter their voices. Every now and then we hear of someone who does claim that they have had a divine revelation and they then predict the time of the second coming of Christ or the end of the world. Either way, we can be sure that they are false prophets for what they claim is in direct disagreement with the Word of God.

In order that we come to a more complete understanding of the second truth I want for us to turn to the gospel of Luke and to the seventeenth chapter.

Luke 17:26-30, And as it was in the days of Noah, so shall it be also in the days of the Son of man. They did eat, they drank, they married wives, they were given in marriage, until the day that Noah entered into the ark, and the flood came, and destroyed them all.

Likewise also as it was in the days of Lot; they did eat, they drank, they bought, they sold, they planted, they builded; But the same day that Lot went out of Sodom it rained fire and brimstone from heaven and destroyed them all.

Even thus shall it be in the day when the Son of man is revealed.

Jesus gave us these two different examples of how history is about to repeat it's self. If we are observant we should be aware that there are some differences between what happened in Noah's day and what took place at Sodom and Gomorrah. In Noah's day the flood covered the earth and destroyed all flesh except for the animals and people who escaped by entering into the ark. I believe that it is important that only eight people, Noah and his wife and his three sons and their wives were saved.

The account that is given in the story of the destruction of Sodom and Gomorrah informed us that fire and brimstone rained down from heaven, and destroyed them all. Of course, Lot, his wife and his two daughters did escape from those sinful cities but something did happen to Lot's wife on their way to safety. We shall examine this story later on, but for now I want for us to grasp the truth of the way these two different stories are the same.

In verse 27 it does say that the flood came and destroyed them all. In verse 29 it does say that it rained fire and brimstone from heaven, and destroyed them all. Jesus has informed us through his word that it will be the same again, when he returns. The voice of the seven thunders when they utter their voices will say the same thing, for they will say that the destruction is complete and the people will be destroyed.

In verse 27 it states that in Noah's day, they did eat, they drank, they married wives, they were given in marriage, until the day that Noah entered into the ark and the flood came, and destroyed them all. In verse 28 it states that they did eat, they drank, they bought, they sold, they planted, they builded: verse 29 But the same day that Lot went out of Sodom it rained fire and brimstone from heaven and destroyed them all.

Let us picture if we can, what life was like just before these great catastrophes came upon them. I can imagine that there were great wedding ceremonies, and much feasting and celebration. The people were probably not concerned with anything that Noah said, nor did they fear the wrath of God.

The Bible states quite clearly that they were eating and drinking and because it will be the same in our day, I can imagine that the restaurants and the taverns will be very busy as usual. In our bigger cities there are drinking places that are filled to over flowing each day as people stop in after work for a few drinks. There are many expensive restaurants where people are waiting in line to even get in the door. In the same manner, I believe that in the large gambling casinos the dice will be rattling in their cups. The roulette wheels will be spinning and the long legged ladies will be strolling back and forth crying out "Keno, Keno."

I can imagine that when the day arrives, within the stock exchange and elsewhere it will be business as usual. People will be buying and selling and they will give no thought that by the signs of the times we can tell that the end is near.

The scripture also states that they planted and they builded. My mind turns to those vast acreage where hundreds and hundreds of acres of wheat are grown. Perhaps we should include those areas where many fresh vegetables are grown. I can imagine that on the day when many nuclear missiles will take to the skies, the men who are busy with planting will be up very early as they prepare to plant the fields which supply us with our daily bread. Because we do not know the time, perhaps the harvest workers will be laboring many hours each day, bringing in the harvest of what was planted in the spring. I can picture many people preparing for work as usual, with no idea that a day of death is close at hand.

In the same way, the scripture mentions that they were building. Again I can imagine all of the workers going to work, creating many miles of pavement across the land as huge sky scrapers continue to be built in our cities. Hotels and motels and restaurants and hospitals and schools will be being built when that day comes upon us.

We must take hold of why Jesus gave this description of the way it was just before the flood and again just before the destruction of Sodom and Gomorrah. Was he not informing us that everything will be as usual and no one will be prepared for the sudden destruction that is about to come?

The people were completely unaware of what was about to befall them. They were so intent upon living their own lives in pursuit of their personal wealth and pleasure that they did not pay any attention to the warning given by either Noah or Lot. Jesus has said that it will be the same way again and because Jesus said it, we know that it is true.

Jesus has said that he is the Alpha and Omega, the beginning and the end. If we think about what this means we should understand that Jesus knew what the end would be, even at the very beginning. Therefore, we can be sure that history will repeat it's self. The question we should be wondering, Is there anything we can do ?

Chapter 4 Four Horses of Apocalypse

Ecclesiastes 1:18, For in much wisdom is much grief: and he that increaseth knowledge increaseth sorrow.

I have brought to your attention this observation of King Solomon, and feel that I must warn you that I do intend to increase your knowledge concerning the day when the seven thunders shall utter their voices. In order to do so, we shall take another look at the day when the voice of seven thunders shall speak from a little different angle. We will find this different perspective in the 6th chapter of the Revelation.

The verses we are about to read tell us about the four horses of the apocalypse. If it were possible, I would ask that you forget everything that you have every heard concerning the meaning of these verses. I realize that over many years a great many comments have been made concerning these four horses and their riders. Because this is so, it will be very hard for many to view them with an open mind, for many think they already know all about them, because they agree with the comments made by certain authors and religious commentators. Even so, I am going to ask that you allow your mind to be as open as though you are now seeing these four horses for the very first time.

Revelation 6:1, And I saw when the Lamb opened one of the seals, and I heard, as it were the noise of thunder, one of the four beasts saying, Come and see.

2 And I saw, and behold a white horse: and he that sat on him had a bow; and a crown was given unto him: and he went forth conquering, and to conquer.

3 And when he had opened the second seal, I heard a second beast say come and see.

4 And there went out another horse that was red: and power was given to him that sat there-on to take peace from the earth, and that they should kill one another: and there was given unto him a great sword.

5 And when he had opened the third seal, I heard the third beast say, Come and see. And I beheld, and lo a black horse; and he that sat on him had a pair of balances in his hand.

6 And I heard a voice in the midst of the four beasts say, A measure of wheat for a penny, and three measures of barley for a penny; and see thou hurt not the oil and the wine.

7 And when he had opened the fourth seal, I heard the voice of the fourth beast say, come and see.

8 And I looked, and behold a pale horse: and his name that sat on him was Death, and Hell followed with him. And power was given unto them over the fourth part of the earth, to kill with sword, and with hunger, and with death, and with the beasts of the earth.

Let us examine these verses one at a time. First of all, the first verse mentions there were four beasts. These four beasts are not to be confused with the four horses for they are completely different. I believe that the translators did err when they decided to call these four beings "beasts." To get a better idea of what they were truly like we need to go back to the fourth chapter which does give a description of them.

Revelation 4:6-9, And before the throne there was a sea of glass like unto crystal: and in the midst of the throne. and round about the throne, were four beasts full of eyes before and behind. And the first beast was like a lion, and the second beast like a calf, and the third beast had a face as a man, and the fourth beast was like a flying eagle.

8 And the four beasts had each of them six wings about him; and they were full of eyes within: and they rest not day and night

saying, Holy, holy, holy, Lord God Almighty, which was, and is to come.

John's description of their appearance is so strange that it is difficult to form an opinion as to what they really looked like. However, we can see in verse 8 that these four beings do worship God both day and night. Therefore, I feel like it is not proper to call them beasts. I think that it would be much better if we thought of them as being "heavenly beings," for that is what they are. In this account given by John, they are the ones who say unto him "Come and see."

There are two levels of understanding of the meaning of these four horses and their riders. At the first level we shall see that they are given a numerical order and do form a cycle. This cycle has been repeated over and over again, ever since time began.

The second level of understanding does apply to what will take place when the voices of the seven thunders do utter their voices. We shall examine them both.

In the second verse it mentions a white horse and we are told that it's rider did have a bow; and also that a crown was given unto him. He went forth conquering and to conquer.

Keeping in mind that the white horse is the first horse of a sequence, we shall find the key to understanding this first horse in the Gospel of John and in the first chapter. Please do not harden your mind to what we are about to learn.

John 1:1-2, In the beginning was the Word and the Word was with God, and the Word was God. The same was in the beginning with God.

We learn at verse 14 that the word was made flesh and we realize that this is speaking of our Lord, Jesus Christ. However, for a very long time and through out the history of the old testament, there was the Word of God and it is with us, even now. We shall see how this does apply to the first horse which was white.

In the beginning in Genesis, the Word of God which was also spoken by God, did come to Adam and Eve in the garden of Eden and did inform them of what was right in the eyes of God. then read of their fall from grace and their departure from the garden of Eden.

Then we learn that the Word of God did speak to Cain and did warn him that if he failed to do what was good in the eyes of God that sin as knocking at the door of his heart. We then learned that Cain, being angry and jealous did slay his brother Abel. Please do be aware that in both cases, the white horse and it's rider were present for they are symbolic of the Word of God, which does express the righteousness of God.

There are several different scriptures in the old testament which does inform us that God does have a bow and that he does shoot arrows that are to prick a man's conscience. There are also scriptures that reveal unto us that Jesus has received a crown of righteousness. However, in order to be brief, I just want to bring to your attention that I believe that the white horse does represent the Word of God and that it does inform mankind of the knowledge of what is right in the eyes of God.

Then the red horse and it's rider came upon the earth. I believe they represent mankind's rebellion against the white horse and it's rider. The red horse is the symbol of rebellion against God and against God's righteousness. We notice that they were given the power to take peace from the earth.

We then must ask the question, "Was there once peace on earth?" I certainly do believe that before Eve was tempted by the serpent that there was complete harmony and peace within the garden of Eden. It was there that the Word of God did communicate with Adam and Eve, and did inform them of what they were to do and what they were forbidden by God to do. I believe that living under those conditions and having communication with God that their lives were very peaceful and good and they lacked nothing.

Then came the serpent which lead to the temptation of Eve. Adam failed in his responsibility and they both disobeyed the Word of God which had been spoken unto them. Their disobedience allowed the red horse and it's rider to enter and it has been with us ever since. The red horse and it's rider represent rebellion against the Word of God and against the righteousness of God.

We shall now return to the book of Genesis and attempt to increase our understanding of the red horse as it relates to the story of Cain and Abel.

Genesis 4.1-7, And Adam knew Eve his wife; and she conceived, and bare Cain, and said, I have gotten a man from the Lord. verse 2, **And she again bare his brother Abel, and Abel was a keeper of sheep, but Cain was a tiller of the ground.**

3 And in the process of time it came to pass, that Cain brought of the fruit of the ground an offering unto the Lord.

4 And Abel, he also brought of the firstlings of his flock and the fat thereof. And the Lord had respect unto Abel and his offering: verse 5, **But unto Cain and to his offering he had not respect. And Cain was very wroth, and his countenance fell.**

6 And the Lord said unto Cain, Why art thou wroth? and why is thou countenance fallen?

7 If thou doest well, shalt thou not be accepted? and if thou doest not well, sin lieth at the door. And unto thee shall be his desire, and thou shalt rule over him.

Let us picture two brothers living in the same land, one was a gardener and the other raised and tended his sheep. Verse 3 does inform us that in the process of time it came to pass, that the older of the two brothers decided to offer an offering to the Lord. I believe that it is very important that we be aware of what kind of offering this offering probably was. From what is said in verse three it is most likely that this was an offering of thanksgiving and it was also a free will offering. I say this for there was nothing said that would indicate that it was required or commanded.

As to what was offered verse 3 simply states that Cain did bring an offering from the fruit of the ground. Verse four is a little more descriptive for it informs us that Abel did bring an offering of the firstlings of his flock. This is one of those places where we must learn by observing what was missing from Cain's offering. The scriptures do not say that his offering was from the first fruits and so we may assume that it was from just any fruit. The great truth of this matter is that God will not accept an offering of just any fruit.

God is still the same today, and there are many who offer to God, far less than their best. I know of some who only attend church once in a while, and I know others who can never arrive at church at the time the service is scheduled to begin. Still others, wear their very best clothes when they go someplace with their friends, but put on their old clothes when they go to church, claiming that they are more comfortable. I see these things through the eyes of an observer and not a judge. These are all examples of how some people fail to offer their best to God.

In contrast, I can remember watching some videos of people attending churches in the Caribbean. They were very poor people by our standards and could not afford many of the luxuries that are common here. I can remember all of the smiling little faces of the children, wearing their very best clothes and their hair combed to perfection, with little ribbons carefully in place.

The adults too, were wearing their very best clothes and attending church each week was the high point of their lives. They spent a great deal of time in preparation in getting them selves ready and with their children also for they were joyful that they were going to the house of the Lord to be with their King. Their Kings name is Jesus and they were very happy to be able to sings songs of praise and worship.

Oh how I wish that people who live in the land of abundance would show the same enthusiasm when it comes to preparing for and attending church. They seem to be ignorant that the way we are now will affect the way we will be, for all of eternity.

Let us return to Cain's offering and the fact that something was wrong with it in the eyes of God. There are a great many religious teachers who claim that it was because Abel's offering required the spilling of blood, and that Cain's offering was lacking because it was of fruit and not of animals, and therefore did lack the spilling of blood.

The apostle Paul had something to say that is of interest
1st Thessalonians 5:21, Prove all things; hold fast that which is good.

There is a scripture in the book of Hebrews that does explain about why the shedding of blood was so important.

Hebrews 9:22, And almost all things are by the law purged with blood; and without shedding of blood is no remission of sin.

We know that this verse does speak the truth, therefore we must hold fast to it and not forget it.

Of course, we are now aware that our Lord, Jesus Christ, through the shedding of his innocent blood did make an offering and atonement for us, once and for all. Therefore, there is now no need for the shedding of any more blood for Jesus has paid the debt we owe in full.

We must now wonder, was there anything said that would indicate that Cain's offering was an offering for sin? I say no, for I do not believe this was an offering for sin by what is said and what is not said. Let us examine what was said one more time. Genesis 4 and verse three begins "And in process of time it came to pass, that Cain brought of the fruit of the ground an offering unto the Lord." There is nothing to indicate that this offering was anything more than a free will offering and a offering of thanksgiving. Not one word was given that would suggest that this was a sin offering with the requirement of the shedding of blood. If we close our minds as so many people do, and claim that the only thing missing from Cain's offering was the blood, then we will never learn the real reason God did not have respect for it.

I have come to the conclusion that Cain's offering was made of just any fruit, for nothing is said that would indicate that anything other than just any fruit was used. On the other hand, the scripture does indicate that Abel's offering was from the firstlings of his flock. In other words, it was an offering from the very best that Able owned. We must not forget the end result for it is written that God had respect unto Able and to his offering. But unto Cain and to his offering he had not respect.

To further show why I do not believe this was a sacrifice for sin we need to examine what is said in verse seven.

If thou doest well shalt thou not be accepted? and if thou doest not well, sin lieth at the door, and unto thee shall be his desire, and thou shalt rule over him.

We can see by what is said in this verse that Cain was somewhat ignorant about sin. If he were not, then why did God take the trouble to issue to him this very important warning concerning the nature of sin.

I believe that God was well aware that in his heart he was very angry with his brother and wanted to kill him. This is why God informed him that he was not to give in to this desire but was to take control over it.

We must ask, Where was sin when Cain did make his offering from just any fruit? It is because we are aware that just any fruit is not acceptable unto God, that by his own word, sin was knocking at Cain's door. Therefore, this offering could not have been a sin offering.

If we believe that the reason God did not accept Cain's offering is because it did not involve the shedding of blood, then we fail to understand that God will not accept anything from us that is less than our best.

The devil rejoices when we are unable to understand this truth, and we see many Christians today who continue to offer to God, far less than their best. It is written in God's word that many are called but few are chosen. I have no doubt that is this one of the reasons why this is so.

We must now return to the four horses of the Revelation. Are you able to understand that the red horse and it's rider were there on the day when Cain slew his brother Abel? Can you see that it is now riding through out the land, encouraging people everywhere to rebel against the righteousness of God's Holy Word ?

We must now examine the black horse and it's rider for they are the one's who are rapidly approaching as the day of seven thunders draw nigh.

Revelation 6:5, And when he had opened the third seal, I heard the third beast say, Come and see. And I beheld, and lo a black horse; and he that sat on him had a pair of balances in his hand.

The black horse and it's rider is symbolic of God's judgment. God's judgment always follows man's rebellion against God and against the righteousness of His Holy Word.

If we were to examine the total history of Israel throughout the Bible we would learn that time after time they did rebel against God. We would also learn that time after time, God did bring his judgment against them. It has always been this way.

Of course, there are other examples given of God pronouncing judgment against people and it was not always Israel. In the days of

Noah God did bring judgment against all the people except for Noah and his family. Later on, a sinful situation developed and I believe the people of Sodom and Gomorrah were Gentiles for Israel had not been born. Nineveh which was spared in Jonah's day was eventually destroyed, and it was inhabited by Gentiles.

I am sure that you have probably seen at one time or another a statute of a blindfolded woman holding in her hand a set of balance scales. They can sometimes be found in the hallways of county court-houses and sometimes within the court rooms they are displayed.

Perhaps the rider of the black horse does resemble this blind folded lady, for the judgment of God is not partial when judgment is passed against the people who have rebelled against God. However, keep in mind that while the judge is the one who pronounces the sentence or determines what the wages will be, he is not the one who carries out the sentence. The punishment (wages) is performed (paid) by another branch of the government.

Let us first return to Genesis and listen in as God pronounces his judgment against those who did rebel against him and His Holy Word at the garden of Eden. If we are observant and able to see into the shadows we should notice that in a symbolic sense, the black horse and it's rider are there.

Let us take up the story not at the beginning but after the rebellion had set in and after their transgression against God's Holy Word had already taken place.

Genesis 3:8, And they heard the voice of the Lord God walking in the garden in the cool of the day: and Adam and his wife hid themselves from the presence of the Lord God amongst the trees of the garden.

9 And the Lord God called unto Adam, and said unto him, Where art thou?

10 And he said, I heard thy voice in the garden, and I was afraid, because I was naked; and I hid myself.

11 And he said, Who told thee that thou wast naked? Hast thou eaten of the tree, whereof I commanded thee that thou shouldest not eat?

12 And the man said, The woman whom thou gavest to be with me, she gave me of the tree and I did eat.

13 And the Lord God said unto the woman, What is this that thou hast done? And the woman said, The serpent beguiled me, and I did eat.

I first want to bring to our attention the situation as it must have been. They were living in a very beautiful and perhaps magnificent garden where every kind of tasty and good fruit did grow.

I believe that there was an abundance of good food to eat and in the necessities of life they did not lack a thing. What is more, God came down and did walk in the garden during the cool part of the day and did communicate with them.

And they in turn, were blessed tremendously by God's presence and words can not express how perfect and carefree their lives must have been. God gave unto them the job of caring for his beautiful garden and in return, he supplied their every need, so that they did not lack a thing.

It was during this perfect situation that temptation did enter into their lives. Perhaps it has always been this way. So often we do not appreciate what we have until the time comes when we no longer have it. It is only then, that we truly begin to see and understand how foolish we are.

I would also bring your attention to the one who did originally employ what is known as "passing the buck." I want you to notice how right away he wants to place a large portion of the blame on the woman. In fact, he does carry it a bit further and wants God to assume a portion of the blame also because God did give him the woman in the first place.

Of course, the woman, following Adams lead did place the blame on the serpent. Let us listen as God does pass sentence on all who were involved in this rebellion in the garden.

Genesis 3:14, And the Lord God said unto the serpent, Because thou hast done this, thou art cursed above all cattle, and above every beast of the field; upon thy belly shalt thou go, and dust shalt thou eat all the days of thy life.

15 And I will put enmity between thee and the woman, and between thy seed and her seed; it shall bruise thy head, and thou shalt bruise his heel.

16 Unto the woman he said, I will greatly multiply thy sorrow and thy conception; in sorrow thou shalt bring forth children and thy desire shall be to thy husband, and he shall rule over thee.

17-19 And unto Adam he said, Because thou hast hearkened unto the voice of thy wife, and hast eaten of the tree, of which I commanded thee, saying Thou shalt not eat of it: cursed is the ground for thy sake; in sorrow shalt thou eat of it all the days of thy life; Thorns also and thistles shall it bring forth to thee; and thou shalt eat the herb of the field.

In the sweat of thy face shalt thou eat bread, till thou return unto the ground; for out of it wast thou taken: for dust thou art, and unto dust shalt thou return.

As I have already said, I believe the black horse and it's rider with the set of balance scales in his hand is symbolic of the one who judges when mankind rebels against God. I want us to notice that there were three different individuals involved in this rebellion against the righteousness of God's word. The deeds or transgressions of each one was weighed separately on the balance scales and then each one was paid exactly the wages that was due them.

Let us examine what happened to Cain, after he allowed his anger to become so great that he murdered his brother.

Genesis 4:9-15, And the Lord said unto Cain, Where is thy brother? And he said, I know not: Am I my brothers keeper?

And he said, What hast thou done? the voice of thy brother's blood crieth unto me from the ground. And now art thou cursed from the earth, which hath opened her mouth to receive thy brother's blood from thy hand;

When thou tillest the ground, it shall not henceforth yield unto thee her strength; a fugitive and a vagabond shalt thou be in the earth,

And Cain said unto the Lord, my punishment is greater than I can bear. Behold, thou hast driven me out this day from the face of the earth; and from thy face shall I be hid; and

I shall be a fugitive and a vagabond in the earth; and it shall come to pass, that everyone that findeth me shall slay me.

And the Lord said unto him, Therefore whosoever slayeth Cain, vengeance shall be taken on him sevenfold. And the Lord set a mark upon Cain, lest any finding him should kill him.

Once more, we see that the things that were done by Cain were weighed on the balance scale and then he did receive the wages he had coming. Not only was Cain guilty of killing his brother, he attempted to hide his body and cover up the evidence of his terrible crime. Then to add to what had already taken place, when God did ask him about where his brother was he tried to lie to God and claim that he didn't know.

If he were to be tried for his crimes in some of our states there is no doubt that he would have received the death sentence. However, he was tried in the very highest court of all and when he learned of his sentence he cried out, "My punishment is greater than I can bear."

It is most likely that Cain did live out his life in misery and sorrow, for he was a marked man, and everyone knew who he was and what he had done. I doubt that he had many friends and yet the record does show that he got married and had children. I want to make very clear to you that I do not question the punishment that he received for God can see what we are not able to see.

The point I do want to make once more, the deeds that were done by an individual were weighed upon the balance scale and then the wages he was owed was paid to him. There is a difference when it is the sins of a group of people that are being weighed, such as it was in the days of Noah. In this case they did receive the death sentence and God did bring the flood to carry out or to pay them what they were owed. In the case of Adam and Eve and again in the case of Cain it does not appear that the sacrificial system was in place. Once God did judge them for what they had done, the sentence was immutable. There was no provision made for them to sacrifice an animal and then be restored to their former relationship with God. It is plain that Cain was banned for the rest of his life from the presence of God and I do not believe that most people today even begin to understand how severe that penalty really was.

I believe that if he were able to do so, Cain would have purchased an animal and would have offered a sacrifice for his sins, rather than live out his life as a marked man, a fugitive and vagabond. However, once the black horse and it's rider have weighed the deeds that have been done and the wages have been determined, the payment will be made and of this we can be sure.

In order to increase our knowledge concerning when animal sacrifices were first instituted we need to listen to the instructions God did give to Noah, and we find them in chapter seven.

Genesis 7:1-2, And the Lord said unto Noah, Come thou and all thy house into the ark; for thee have I seen righteous before me in this generation.

Of every clean beast thou shalt take to thee by sevens, the male and his female: and of the beasts that are not clean by two, the male and his female.

I would point out that if we had very carefully studied everything that was written leading to this point in time, we should be aware that Noah and his family were vegetarians. Therefore, the reason for the clean animals to be taken into the ark by sevens is that they were to be more plentiful for they would be needed for sacrifices.

Genesis 8:20, And Noah builded an altar unto the Lord; and took of every clean beast, and of every clean fowl, and offered burnt offerings on the altar.

I do believe that following the flood, people began to eat flesh and the sacrificial system was put in place. I believe that if we were to fully study the scriptures they would support what I have said. However, this would lead us away from the knowledge we are trying to attain, regarding the four horses of the apocalypse.

Let us be aware of the function of the white horse as it first came into the garden of Eden. Did not the Word of God come to Adam and Eve and inform them of what they were to do? Did not the Word of God make it very clear what they were forbidden to do?

Did not the Word of God also come to Cain and warn him that sin was at the door? Did not the Word of God instruct Cain that he was to rule over sin and not let sin have dominion over him?

Again I say, the rider of the white horse was given a bow so that his arrows could prick the conscience of mankind and speak to their hearts. He was given a crown because it was a crown of righteousness and God's word does express and inform people of the righteousness of God.

The red horse and it's rider were given a sword and the power to take peace from the earth. When Adam and Eve did willfully disobey God, and were forced to leave the garden, did they lose their peace?

When Cain did willfully disobey God and did murder his brother did he ever again receive the peace that comes from being in God's presence? I believe that the red horse and it's rider with a sword does cause anger to well up within a person and to multiply. I believe that if it is not controlled it can increase to the point that people do commit murder. Surely it is not hard to understand how the red horse has taken peace from the earth.

The black horse must always follow the red horse for rebellion against God and against His Holy Word will be judged as surely and as long as God is God.

Let us now return to the sixth chapter of the Revelation and let us put the past behind us and look to the future. We shall try to increase our understanding of how these horses do relate to the day that is coming, the day when the voices of seven thunders shall deliver their message that the destruction is complete.

As I have said, we can hear the black horse and it's rider approaching and we know that it is close at hand. Wait! I hear a voice speaking, what is it saying?

Revelation 6:6, And I heard a voice in the midst of the four beasts say, A measure of wheat for a penny, and three measures of barley for a penny; and see thou hurt not the oil and the wine.

An observant person might say that this is saying that wheat is worth three times what barley is worth. I do not think that this is what is important. What I believe this verse is saying to us is that the one with the balance scale has weighed the deeds that people have done and their value has been determined. However, the voice then instructs the ones who are about to pay the wages, be sure that you do not hurt the oil and the wine. This is really quite simple for the wine is symbolic for all of those people whose sins have been covered by the blood of Jesus. The voice is instructing the angels who are to pay the wages, to go ahead with paying the people what they have coming but let no harm come to those who have the blood of the lamb over the door post of their hearts.

The oil as it is used in this verse is used symbolically to represent those of God's people who have received the anointing of the Holy Spirit. Who are they, you might wonder?

Let us turn to the 4th chapter of Paul's letter to the Ephesians and I will show you some of them.

Keep in mind that Paul is speaking about something Jesus did do.

Ephesians 4:11-12, And he gave some, apostles; and some, prophets; and some evangelists; and some, pastors and teachers; For the perfecting of the saints, for the work of the ministry, for the edifying of the body of Christ:

These are some of the ones who have received the anointing of the Holy Spirit, but I do not believe that it is limited to just them. There are also missionaries and people at the hospital who minister unto the sick and the dying and many more.

There is one thing I want to make clear to you, the ones who have received the anointing by the Holy Spirit do know who they are for the Holy Spirit has revealed himself unto them.

Chapter 5 The Great Flood

Revelation 6:7-8, And when he had opened the fourth seal, I heard the voice of the fourth beast say, come and see.

And I looked and behold a pale horse: and his name that sat on him was Death, and Hell followed with him. And power was given unto them over the fourth part of the earth, to kill with the sword, and with hunger, and with death, and with the beasts of the earth.

As the black horse and it's rider with the set of balance scales held in his hand do represent God's judicial system, then the pale horse and it's rider whose name is Death must represent God's penal system. The one with the balance scales has weighed the deeds that people have done and then a voice from heaven cries out, pay them what they have coming but be sure that you do not hurt the ones who are covered by the blood of Jesus or his anointed ones.

I would like to bring to your attention that death in this verse does receive a capital D. The reason is simply that these verses are not speaking of a little bit of death, such as occurs on our freeways everyday. It is talking about a time when Death shall rule supreme over the land and it shall be everywhere.

I am sure that Jesus wanted us to have some idea of what it would be like and so in the 17th chapter of Luke he gave us two examples of what it will be like. In the first example he said that it would be as it were in the days of Noah.

I want for us to try to imagine what that must have been like. First there must have been those individuals with a quick wit and a sharp tongue. "What do you think you are building there Noah? Expecting it to rain, so you think you have to build a boat. Ha ha.

Have you been talking to your God again Noah? Ha ha, The God you claim is real but nobody can see. Ha ha. Well, keep up the good work Noah, and when you talk to your God again, tell him hello for me. Ha ha. Ha ha.

Now I can imagine that this went on for a long time and it was probably harder for Noah's sons and their gives than it was for Noah. After all, Noah knew God personally and God did communicate with him. I would think that Noah's faith in God was very strong and I believe that he certainly did recognize that God's ways are high above mans ways. However, I am sure that there must have been many times when the sons felt very uncomfortable being on the receiving end of much worldly scorn. There must have been times when their gives were more than a little embarrassed when exposed to public ridicule but did not say anything or complain, for fear of causing trouble within the family.

Then came the gathering of the animals and I can imagine for the people of the land that it was much like a circus. They laughed and they scoffed and they continued to live in their usual sinful way. Do you remember the description Jesus gave us when he said they were getting married and giving, in marriage, eating and drinking without any worry about what was to come. He said it will be the same way this time.

This continued till the time that all of the animals were safely in the ark and then Noah and his family entered into the ark and God shut the door.

And then the rain began to fall. Now prior to this time the Bible informs us that the earth was watered by dew and the people had never seen rain before. It must have been quite a surprise, and I can not help but think of how little puppies act the first time they experience snow. Perhaps the people ran back and forth, splashing in the puddles and playing like little children.

However, as the rain continued to fall, so did the waters continue to rise. All of a sudden it wasn't funny anymore, and the people were forced to seek higher ground. Then as the waters continued to rise even higher, it became most fearful for it was becoming increasingly difficult to find any ground high enough to escape from the water.

I can imagine that some gathered outside the door of the Ark and called out to Noah, "Open the door Noah. We didn't mean to make fun of you, for we were only kidding. Open the door Noah, and let us come in."

Of course, God had closed the door and no man could open it. Finally it reached so high that it hid the tallest tree and covered the highest mountain. Picture what it would be like to be either sailing or flying over the ocean and then come across thousands and thousands of people trying to tread water without so much as one life preserver.

There they are, no land in sight, and they are almost exhausted by all of their effort to stay afloat. Perhaps it was a little like the sinking of the Titanic when so many people were forced to enter the water. It is not a pretty sight for we all know what the outcome must be. In a little while, they will all be dead, and it is sad because they could have entered into the ark, while the door was open, had they wanted to. Again I say, it will be the same way this time for God has provided a place of safety but few there will be that will enter into that safe place.

In the second example that Jesus gave, fire and brimstone fell on the cities of Sodom and Gomorrah and destroyed them all. Perhaps this example is a bit closer to what will happen this time, for we know that God will not cause a flood to destroy the earth again.

Yet, I know that for many, death will not come as swift as it did in the two examples that have been given. Perhaps this is why Hell, with a capital H is following the pale horse, for Hell is waiting to receive the souls of those who have rebelled against His Holy Word. What is more, Hell will now be here on earth, for a while and it is written that some will receive only a few stripes while others will receive many. With the coming of the pale horse and Hell following behind, it is time for the great tribulation to begin.

There are some people who do not like me to use the word Hell, for they do not believe in hell.

They claim that the grave would be a far better word and that the original translators did err when they used the word hell instead of Hades. I believe the word Hell with a capital H is the right word to be used in these verses. It is not speaking of the grave for the truth of the matter is there will not be nearly enough survivors to bury all of the dead. The land will be literally filled with the dead and the smell of rotting flesh shall fill the land. Notice what Jesus said about this subject in

Matthew 24:28, For wheresoever the carcase is, there will the eagles (vultures) be gathered.

I am sure that Jesus knows very well what he was talking about. It does not sound like they will be buried with a proper funeral and all but that they will be scattered here and there and everywhere and the scavengers have been invited to a great feast, to feed upon the flesh of those who have rebelled against God's most Holy Word and used the Lord's holy name in a vain or profane way for they will not be found without guilt before Almighty God.

There is another word Jesus used to describe hell and that is Gehenna. It was located in the valley of Hinnom and it was a place where Pagan sacrifices were once made. Later, King Josiah defiled it by making it a garbage dump where fires were kept burning continually to consume the garbage and the flesh of dead and rotting animals.

It was a dirty and smelly and unpleasant place and it was a place where the worm dieth not, and where flies did lay their eggs in the rotting carcases of dead animals. We can be sure that it was similar to what it will be like, when the pale horse reigns supreme over the land that has been destroyed by the nuclear missiles.

I now want to bring our attention to. that part of the verse that states that,

And power as given unto them over the fourth part of the earth, to kill with sword, and with hunger, and with death, and with the beasts of the earth.

The first thing I want us to take. a hold of in this verse is that the area of God's judgment at this particular time will cover a fourth of the earth. I will go a bit further and suggest to you that this one quarter is speaking of one continent. Do not forget what we have already learned about the missiles that will be involved in this event. In a little while we shall see if the scriptures will reveal unto us which continent is going to receive judgment from God.

I want to take a moment to discuss the way that death will come during the time of the pale horse. Of course, many will die from the initial attack of missiles, just as many people died at Hiroshima. However, I want to bring to your attention what will take place afterward.

Notice that the scripture states the power to kill with sword. The sword is used in a symbolic sense and is not limited to swords or even to knives of any kind. This must include all of the weapons or at least most of them that are known to man.

Perhaps at one time it would have been limited to bow and arrows and spears and swords but now must include pistols and revolvers and rifles and shotguns and assault weapons. It is because there will be a lack of food that people will be willing to murder even their neighbors in order to attain their food. Some people will stop at nothing in order to survive.

The second way that death will come to the land is through famine and starvation. We shall learn that the other nations will do nothing to help the people who have suffered a missile attack for their hearts shall be against them. The land will be hurt in such a way that nothing will grow. The food supply shall disappear and man and animal alike shall starve to death.

The third way that death will come is by disease and sickness. There will be no hospitals and no more drug stores and there will be out breaks of radiation sickness and the medicine to treat such illness will be in short supply. There will also be outbreaks of other contagious diseases and the pain and suffering will be so great that many will welcome death 'when it comes.

The fourth way that death will come will be by animals. Perhaps the dogs that are now man's best friends might turn against him in this time of great trouble.

Imagine if you can, what it will be like for those who are so sick and so weak they can hardly move, waiting for the angel of death to mercifully take them away from their suffering. Suddenly, they are surrounded by a pack of dogs that are completely mad because of their hunger. The lead dog approaches and then suddenly they all attack their victim and do rip the flesh from off their bones. In some cases the end will come quick but in others it might come quite slow.

What if they are attack by only one dog, and that dog does proceed to feed upon their leg without administering death first.

Of course, there will be death by bears and cougars and other critters that are capable of killing people but I think they will be outnumbered by the packs of hungry dogs.

In the area where I live there are no leash laws and dogs run loose and use other peoples yards for their toilet. Each day I see many dogs that lay peacefully beside the mailbox, waiting for their masters to come home. However, once in a while I have observed these very same dogs as they begin to run in a pack. Their attitude is a great deal different when they begin doing this.

A couple of years ago, not far from where I live a man was walking through the neighbor hood on foot, searching for a certain address. Suddenly he was attacked by a pack of about five or six dogs. The biggest dog did knock him down and immediately the smaller dogs began to chew on him. He struggled to his feet only to be knocked down again, and his situation was becoming serious. It was obvious that the dogs enjoyed what they were doing for they were very aggressive.

There was snow on the ground and a neighbor man who was preparing to shovel his walk heard the commotion and came to the mans rescue. He was able to beat the dogs off of the man with his shovel and a little neighbor boy helped him, armed with a broom.

These dogs were not a pack of wild dogs roaming the countryside, but were well known neighborhood dogs and it was not hard to locate their owners. The smaller ones were just as vicious as the larger one, once the man as down.

The larger dog which was the leader was not a Rottweiler or a Pitbull or some other breed of dog known for their aggressive behavior. It was just an ordinary black Lab with a bad attitude.

The owners of these dogs were shocked and I even heard some that claimed that the man, who was a stranger in the neighborhood must have done something to provoke such an attack. Have you ever heard it said, "Not my dog? My dog would not do anything like that."

I have used this example so that you might have a better idea of how death will come to the people who have rebelled against God's Holy Word.

There is another question some people might be wondering. Just how long is the tribulation supposed to last. Some will say seven years while others claim that at the end of three and one half years something is supposed to happen. I urge you to use caution when, listening to such people for I do not believe they truly know what they are saying.

I know that we can depend upon the truth that Jesus shared with us, concerning how long it will last.

Matthew 24: 21-22, For then shall be great tribulation, such as was not since the beginning of the world to this time, no, nor ever shall be.

And except those days should be shortened, there should no flesh be saved; but for the elect's sake those days shall be shortened.

I know that many people might want to argue with me and say that Jesus was talking about what happened at Jerusalem in 70 A.D. Let us not forget the wisdom of Solomon who told us that history does repeat it's self. Let us not forget that Jesus said it would be as it were in the days of Noah and again that it would be like it was when God destroyed sinful Sodom and Gomorrah.

I shall let them be doubtful but I am very sure that what Jesus said concerning the shortening of days does apply to the great tribulation that follows the day the seven thunders do utter their voices.

There are still others who claim that the "elect" that is mentioned in these verses is speaking of the Jewish people. This is certainly not true. Jesus was speaking of his very own people meaning the ones who have chosen to follow him. The ones who have surrendered to God at the foot of the cross. The ones who have genuinely repented of their sins and have been born again. Who have accepted Jesus Christ as their Savior and have allowed him to be their Lord by obeying His Holy Word.

We who have been redeemed by the blood of the lamb are the elect and chosen of God and we do not know how long the tribulation will last for it is not given unto us to know. Instead, we are to pray for our faith to be strong so that we might endure until the end.

Chapter 6 Where Judgment Must Begin

❧

Now that you have been introduced to the four horses of the apocalypse and are aware of how they do form a cycle that has been repeated over and over again through out history, we can go on to the next step. Of course, we are aware that the rider of the black horse has already weighed the deeds of this current generation and has determined that the wages to be paid in a very short while is death for those whose sins are not covered by the blood of the lamb.

By this time, I expect that you have acquired your very own Bible and have been reading these verses from it, line by line. If you have not, then I do advise you to put this book down and do not waste your time trying to understand it. The message I have to deliver will not make any sense to you, if you fail to read these verses from your own Bible for it is the easiest way for you to receive the Living Word. It is my hope that the Living Word will speak to you in your mind, and in your heart, just as it has spoken unto me.

I want to share with you a Biblical account of a group of Christians whom the apostles Paul and Silas did visit during the early days of Christianity.

Acts 17:10, And the brethern immediately sent away Paul and Silas by night unto Berea: who coming thither went into the synagogue of the Jews.

11 These were more noble than those in Thessalonica, in that they received the word with all readiness of mind, and searched the scriptures daily, whether those things were so.

This is how I want it to be for you. I want you to receive the Word of God with an open mind. At the same time, I want you to be extremely critical of everything I do say, and I want for you to search the scriptures daily to see if they do say what I claim they do say.

Remember that Jesus did warn us that in the last days there would be many false prophets and false teachers. There are a great many today, who have perverted and twisted the true meaning of the scriptures to the point we have many different denominations each teaching something a little different than the rest. The end result of all of this twisting of the truth is confusion and the Bible informs us that God is not the author of confusion.

If the Christians of these latter days were more like the Christians of Berea, in that they did search the scriptures daily, to see if what their pastors and teachers were telling them was true according to the Word of God, I do not believe there would be any need for so many different denominations.

God's own man, the prophet Isaiah will now share with us some knowledge that will be useful to us, as we begin to search for which one quarter of the earth over which the fourth horse of the apocalypse will soon reign.

Isaiah 28:9, Whom shall he teach knowledge? and whom shall he make to understand doctrine? them that are weaned from the milk, and drawn from the breasts.

10 For precept must be upon precept, precept upon precept; line upon line, line upon line; here a little, and there a little.

I realize that we are not all the same age as it does apply to understanding the meaning of scriptures. Some are more mature in the Word of God, while others we think of as being "babes" in Christ. The portion of these scriptures I want for us to take a hold of, is where it says "here a little and there a little." We shall not find all of the knowledge we are searching for in one place in the Bible but we must search the scriptures daily, and we will find what we are searching for, but we will find a little here and a little there.

Let us listen as Peter, who was one of the twelve disciples does provide us with some very important knowledge concerning the judgment of God in these latter days.

69

1st Peter 4:17, For the time is come that judgment must begin at the house of God: and if it first begin at us, what shall the end be of them that obey not the gospel of God?

18 And if the righteous scarcely be saved, where shall the ungodly and the sinner appear?

The fisher of men, Peter has made it easier for us to find what we are searching for. He has informed us of a Godly principle and that is God's judgment must begin at the house of God. Therefore, it does seem perfectly logical that we need to find where the house of God is located and then we can determine which continent or which one fourth part of the earth will be host to the pale horse and it's rider whose name is Death..

Now some would assume that the temple of God was located in Jerusalem and we can be sure that Peter as well aware of where it was located. However, God's judgment did come against Jerusalem in 70A.D. and till this day, the temple has never been rebuilt. We must then ask, is this the house of God that Peter was referring to, or did he mean something entirely different? Therefore, our search must continue.

I realize that perhaps millions of people believe that the house of God is now the Vatican, and of course, we all know that it is located in Rome. The question we must ask is can this be confirmed by the scriptures. Is Rome the place where the judgment of God will soon begin? I think not.

The apostle Paul had something to say to the Christian church at Corinth concerning the information we are looking for.

1st Corinthians 3:16-17, Know ye not that ye are the temple of God, and that the Spirit of God dwelleth in you ?

If any man defile the temple of God, him shall God destroy; for the temple of God is holy, which temple ye are.

Let us not forget that Peter said that judgment must begin at the house of God. We can be sure that this Godly principle is still the same for God is still the same. God will not bring judgment upon the nations of the East and far East where Pagan religion does prevail, before he brings judgment upon that nation which does claim to be of God and to be blessed by God.

70

In fact, even our coins speak the words "In God we trust." If we truly do place our trust in God then we should also trust that God will keep his word and he will judge us before he judges any other nation. After all, if we truly are a Godly nation that places our trust in God, we should have no fear, should we?

On the other hand, if we are not truly a Godly nation but are merely pretending to be, we probably do have a great deal to fear. Remember, the Word of God is true and the name of the one who does ride the pale horse is Death. The area where the pale horse shall have power is a fourth of the earth. My Lord has called me to deliver this message to you; and he did not call me to deliver it to a foreign country.

Chapter 7 The Four Beasts of Daniel

I believe that during the time when Paul as a world traveler, preaching the gospel of Christ, and visiting many churches, there were many who did trouble the churches with strange doctrines. I have no doubt but what some must have claimed to be the risen Christ, and did seek to drag men after themselves. Let us now listen to these words of warning from our brother Paul as he does address these things in his second letter to the Thessalonians.

2nd Thessalonians 2:1, Now we beseech you, brethern, by the coming of our Lord Jesus Christ, and by our gathering together unto him,

2 That ye be not soon shaken in mind, or be troubled, neither by spirit, nor by word, nor by letter as from us, as that the day of Christ is at hand.

3 Let no man deceive you by any means: for that day shall not come, except there come a falling away first, and that man of sin be revealed, the son of perdition.

According to the footnote in my King James Bible, Paul did write this letter about A.D. 54. Paul has mentioned two things that are very important to our search for the truth. Looking back at history we must first establish when the man of sin was revealed. When we have done that we must then learn about the falling away, that Paul has mentioned. The prophet Daniel will increase our knowledge on these two subjects.

In our quest to learn more about the future, we shall again return to the past, and what we shall learn will prove once again, that God does know all about the future. We shall turn to the seventh chapter of Daniel and learn of a strange dream that was more than a dream, for it was a vision of what would come to pass.

1 In the first year of Belshazzar king of Babylon Daniel had a dream and visions of his head upon his bed. Then he wrote the dream and told the sum of the matters.

2 Daniel spake and said, behold the four winds of heaven strove upon the great sea.

3 And four great beasts came up from the sea, diverse one from another.

4 The first was like a lion and had eagle's wings, I beheld till the wings thereof were plucked, and it was lifted up from the earth; and made stand upon the feet and a man's heart was given to it.

Those who have traveled down this same road do all seem to agree that this first beast that was like a lion, did represent the Babylonian Empire. Even as the lion is regarded as the king of beasts, so was the Babylonian Empire the king of all empires. With Nebuchadnezzar as it's leader, the mighty armies of the golden empire had subdued Assyria, Phoenicia, Judea, Egypt, and Arabia. These mighty conquests must have had a great affect on the king's self esteem and he became obsessed with his own greatness.

Let us listen as King Nebuchadnezzar does say....

Daniel 4:30, The king spake, and said, Is not this great Babylon, that I have built for the house of the kingdom by the might of my power, and for the honour of my majesty?

Perhaps his pride and his vanity came up before God and it was a little more than God would tolerate. Have you not heard it said? Pride goeth before a fall. So we see that God did decide that it was time to humble the king and the scriptures do tell of how this did take place.

Daniel 4:31, While the word was in the king's mouth, there fell a voice from heaven saying, 0 king Nebuchadnezzar, to thee it is spoken; the kingdom is departed thee.

32 And they shall drive thee from men, and thy dwelling shall be with the beasts of the field: they shall make thee to eat grass as oxen, and seven times (years) shall pass over thee, until

thou know that the most High ruleth in the kingdom of men, and giveth it to whomsoever he will.

I do hope that this does explain to us about the wings that were plucked in verse 4 of chapter 7. Not only did the king lose his throne, he lost his mind and ability to reason as well. However, as a part of God's plan, the end result was the conversion of King Nebuchadnezzar.

Let us listen and learn how a new heart was given to the first beast of Daniel chapter 7.

34 And at the end of the days, I Nebuchadnezzar lifted up mine eyes unto heaven, and mine understanding returned unto me, and I blessed the most High, and I praised and honoured him that liveth for ever, whose dominion, and his kingdom is from generation to generation:

35 And all the inhabitants of the earth are reputed as nothing: and he doeth according to his will in the army of heaven, and among the inhabitants of the earth: and none can stay his hand, or say unto him, What doest thou?

So we can see that the 1st beast of Daniel chapter 7 is speaking of the Babylonian Empire and of the conversion of King Nebuchadnezzar.

We can also see that the wings of a fowl can represent how very quickly the power to rule can escape from the ruler and fly away if God does so choose. We shall now examine the second beast.

5 And behold another beast, a second, like to a bear, and it raised up itself on one side, and it had three ribs in the mouth of it between the teeth of it: and they said unto it, Arise, devour much flesh.

The first beast was like a lion and of course, the lion is king of beasts and supreme over all other beasts. The bear, while it certainly is a predator to be feared, did not match the speed nor the strength of the Lion. There is no doubt that the bear represented the Medo-Persian Empire, which was less in every way than the Babylonian Empire, when Nebuchadnezzar was king and conqueror.

The scripture mentions that the bear raised up on one side, and this seems to be speaking of a lop sided bear. This could mean that the people of Persia and the Medes were not evenly matched, hence the bear was higher on one side. Chapter eight speaks of a ram with one horn higher than the other, and this is also speaking of the Medo-Persian Empire, for the scripture does say so very plainly.

The three ribs that were in the mouth of the bear probably represent the three provinces that made up the Babylonian kingdom. They were Babylon, Lydia and Egypt. I do not doubt but what the bear did consume much flesh during this period of time.

6 After this I beheld, and lo another, like a leopard, which had upon the back of it four wings of a fowl; the beast had also four heads; and dominion was given to it.

This third beast like a leopard with wings does seem to represent the Grecian Empire under Alexander the great. The leopard is a very agile animal that often takes it prey through hiding on a tree limb, and then swiftly falling upon it's prey in ambush like fashion.

The wings might represent great speed, for it did not take the kingdom of Alexander very long to conquer all the armies of the world, and the pages of history do tell us of his cunning, and his use of surprise and speed, against his adversaries. In a way, speed does tell the story of his life for as quickly was his rise to power, so did his life's end come quickly for he died from sickness at the age of thirty-two.

Following his death, his empire was divided into four parts, which we believe were symbolized by the four heads. Each head probably represented a general within the Grecian kingdom. The pages of history do inform us that Cassander ruled over Greece, while Lysimachus ruled over that part of the world known as Asia Minor. Seleucus ruled over Syria and Babylon, and Ptolmey ruled over Egypt.

7 After this I saw in the night visions, and behold a fourth beast, dreadful and terrible, and strong exceedingly; it devoured and brake in pieces, and stamped the residue with the feet of it: and it was diverse from all the beasts that were before it; and it had ten horns.

Again, the commentaries I do have all agree that this fourth beast does represent the Roman Empire. The description that it was dreadful and terrible and exceedingly strong do match what we know about the Roman Empire. It was indeed diverse from the beasts that preceded it, and so was the government of Rome much different than any of the others.

Even though many of the leaders of Rome were certainly educated, and yet, they seemed to rule through terrorism and brute force without mercy. I have read that along the Appian Way, the great road that lead into Rome, there were many crosses where the bodies of criminals were left hanging as a warning to all who entered into the city. Things being as they were, a person must have been very careful about what they said, regarding the government of Rome, lest they too, ended up hanging on a cross.

In this vision given unto Daniel, it does not seem to indicate the Roman Empire at any given time during the long reign of the Emperors, but seems to show the passing of time. As we come to the end of verse seven we notice that this very powerful beast had ten horns. I have mentioned the passing of time, for we shall soon see that these horns did not appear until in the latter years of the Roman Empire.

Let us listen to Daniel as he does describe the things he did see in this strange vision.

8 I considered the horns, and, behold, there came up among them another little horn, before whom there were three of the first horns plucked by the roots: and, behold, in this horn were eyes like the eyes of man, and a mouth speaking great things.

Because we are only looking at these verses to establish a foundation upon which we can build, so that I may share with you the truth, even as others have shared it with me, we shall jump ahead to verse 15.

15 I Daniel was grieved in my spirit in the midst of my body, and the visions of my head troubled me.

16 I came near unto one of them that stood by, (an angel) and asked him the truth of all this. So he told me, and made me know the interpretation of the things.

I want us to pause a moment and notice that when Daniel did ask the angel about these things, what did take place? Notice that the angel did make Daniel know the meaning of these things, for this is what the scripture does say. Daniel was made to know and in turn, Daniel does write these things down so that we might know.

17 These great beasts, which are four, are four kings, which shall arise out of the earth.

18 But the saints of the most High shall take the kingdom, and possess the kingdom for ever, even for ever and ever.

19 Then I would know the truth of the fourth beast, which was diverse from all the others, exceeding dreadful, whose teeth were of iron, and his nails of brass; which devoured, brake in pieces, and stamped the residue with his feet;

We have already learned that the four beasts do represent four great empires. I do believe that an empire is not a single nation, but is made up of several different nations or groups of people. Most of the people who have written commentaries on the book of Daniel all do agree that these four empires were the Babylonian Empire, the Medo-Persian Empire, the Grecian Empire of Alexander the great, and the long lasting and powerful, Roman Empire.

I want us to notice that with the end of the nineteenth verse, Daniel now changes the subject slightly and begins to talk about the ten horns and also about the eleventh horn.

20 And of the ten horns that were in his head, and of the other which came up, and before whom three fell; even of that horn that had eyes, and a mouth that spake great things, whose look was more stout than his fellows.

21 I beheld, and the same horn (eleventh horn) made war with the saints, and prevailed against them;

I believe it is possible this war that was waged against the saints did take place through out the dark ages. Notice that in verse twenty-one that the same horn, which is the eleventh horn, did prevail against the saints.

The saints that are mentioned here, are not the ones who would be appointed by a religious system, but is speaking of saints as those spoken of in the book of Acts. These saints are also of the church that Jesus said he would build and the gates of hell would not prevail against it.

We are given a description of these saints in the 14th chapter of the Revelation.

verse 12 Here is the patience of the saints: here are they that keep the commandments of God, and the faith of Jesus.

I want us to be aware that they keep the commandments of God, rather than the commandments of religious men, and because they do, they are the true followers of Christ. Our Lord Jesus Christ was a commandment keeper and the Word of God does say that he was. This person, the eleventh horn, who would appear as the supreme religious authority, was not a friend of Christians but was actually, by the description we have been provided, the enemy of the faithful followers of Christ.

We shall now listen as the angel continues to explain these things to Daniel.

23 Thus he said, The fourth beast shall be the fourth kingdom (future in Daniel's time) upon earth, which shall be diverse from all kingdoms, and shall devour the whole earth, and shall tread it down, and break it in pieces.

24 And the ten horns out of this kingdom are ten kings that shall arise: and another shall rise after them: and he shall be diverse from the first, and he shall subdue three kings.

And now we shall learn more about what is written in the pages of history, concerning these ten kings and their kingdoms. Actually, the pages of history does not speak of them exactly as kings, but as Gothic tribes. Of course, it goes without saying that each of these tribes did have a leader or a type of king which ruled over them.

As the very foundations of the Roman Empire began to weaken and to crumble, there were already some very fierce people from the north, who were organized into groups of fighting men, some as savage as wolves, hunting in packs for whom they might devour.

My mind goes back to the war of the kings in Abraham's time, and we can see that in some ways, mankind did not change very much. It was much the same when the great armies of the Roman Empire begin to disperse, for when law and order did fail, then the world did return to the law of the jungle. The age old philosophy of might makes right did at times, prevail during this time of the fall of the Roman Empire.

We are told that in the year of 376, a great group of people known as the Visigoths, did begin arriving within the territory of the Roman Empire, and they did not all come at once, but did trickle in over many years of time.

The Visigoths were not alone for there were other tribes, searching for a better life, much as the immigrants who came to America. They took up residence, where ever they could make a living and for many, it was a matter of survival.

The Roman historian, Macchiavelli, did write that the Roman Empire was divided among the various Gothic tribes. I believe that if we count them we will find that we can identify ten of these tribes. In addition to the Visigoths, there were the Vandals, the Ostrogoths, the Lombards, the Franks, the Huns, the Burgundians, the Heruli, The Suevi, and the Anglo-Saxons.

These tribes were the people who would become the nations of Europe and if we were to search, I am sure that we could find many groups of people whose roots could be traced back to these Gothic tribes, that did claim the territory of the Roman Empire, and much more.

There is one thing I do want to make clear to you. I do not share these events of the past with you as one who is a judge of history. However, if we are to know the truth, then we should be aware that the religions that do exist in this world have played a very important part in shaping history. Therefore, we must look back at history coldly, and clearly, and without passion nor prejudice, much like research scientists studying life under a micro-scope.

I say this for the scriptures have very clearly said that the eleventh horn would wage a war against the saints of the most high God. We should then at least suspect, that this eleventh horn is a prominent figure, who is also a very powerful religious leader.

We see then, the ten horns did represent ten tribes which did eventually claim the territory of the Roman Empire. The eleventh horn does represent a religious figure who would come up, or rise to power, at the same time, when the Roman Empire was divided among the ten Gothic tribes.

We shall do our best to identify this eleventh horn, by what has been said in the Word of God. First, we must remember that it did come from out of the fourth beast which did represent the Roman Empire. This very clearly means that the eleventh horn would also be Roman.

It had the eyes and the mouth of a man. This seems to mean that it is speaking of a man, or the office of a man, who would rise to power. At first, it was the little horn, but later Daniel described it as "whose look was more stout, than his fellows." This could only mean that it had more power and authority than any of the ten horns. It goes without saying, that the description does seem to speak of a powerful religious leader of Roman origin.

I must confess that I do not know very much about religion during this period of time. However, I do remember that in the struggle for power, the churches, which all claimed to be of Christ, even though they did cling to those things which were Pagan, were divided into two parts. There were the eastern churches which claimed to be orthodox, and then there were the western churches which did claim to have the power to change times and laws. It does seem, that the little eleventh horn, which rapidly became more stout than any of the ten horns is speaking of the Bishop of the western churches.

The twenty-fourth verse informed us that the eleventh horn would subdue three of the ten horns, and verse eight said that he would pluck up three horns by the roots. We must allow the pages of history to reveal unto us, whether or not this did happen, as it was foretold to Daniel.

It is a rather long story and would take a long time to tell if we were to examine all of the details of the removal of three of the ten tribes. However, keep in mind that there must have been competition between these tribes as they did divide the territory among themselves.

Even though these ten tribes have been described as uncivilized, they were not without religion, for the pages of history do speak of this. It has been said that the Visigoths did practice a form of religion known as Arianism, and so they have been described as Arian Visigoths.

It could be that it was for this reason the eleventh horn did consider them a threat to his religious supremacy, for he was not tolerant of other religions.

The eleventh horn, the leader of the western churches did seek the help of the last Roman emperor, who was Justinian, and with his authority and power, two of the ten tribes were removed. The

Vandals were exterminated in 534, and the power of the Ostrogoths was broken in 538. Earlier, the emperor Zeno had entered into a treaty with the leader of the Ostrogths, which treaty did result in the eradication of the kingdom of the Heruls in 493.

It is when we search for the truth, and are able to do so without passion nor prejudice, but truly do accept what has happened in history, that we can see that three of the ten horns were plucked up and removed before the face of the eleventh horn.

What is more, we can also see that according to history, when the Arian Ostrogoths were defeated and their power broken, it enabled the eleventh horn to swiftly rise to power. We are told that this did take place in the year of 538, and from this time on, the eleventh horn's rise to power proceeded quite swiftly.

I do hope that we can all see that the fourth beast, which was the old Roman Empire, was replaced by a larger and more powerful governing body. I am speaking of the Roman religious empire, which is a very unique power, in that it maintains it's status as a political entity, and an advisor of nations, while it continues to claim supreme religious authority, over much of the world, even now at this present time.

I have heard it said, that no one has all the truth. I certainly do agree with this statement, and especially when it comes to knowing what will take place in the future. However, the information of what has happened in the past is available to all who are willing to search for it. This is why I am going to give you a small amount of home work to do.

I want you to visit your public library as soon as it is convenient and I want for you to find the answer to these questions.

First, I want you to consult the history books or encyclopedia of your choice and learn about the first beast which many do believe represented the Babylonian Empire. See if you can find out why God used the lion as the symbol of this very wealthy empire.

Second, you will recall that the bear had three ribs in it's mouth. See if you can find out if the Babylonian Empire was indeed, made up of three provinces, just as I have said.

The third thing I do ask is that you study the Medo-Persian Empire and find out why the bear was lop-sided. Surely, the pages of history should supply you with this information.

Then do look up and learn a little about Alexander the great. Much has been written of him, and of his brilliant conquest of the world. Then find out if his kingdom was divided between four of his officers, and then also consider the third beast, the leopard with wings and four heads.

Finally, I want you to study the fall of the Roman Empire and search for the ten Gothic tribes, to see if they do appear in the pages of history. I especially want for you to verify the part about the three tribes that were removed, and notice the date of when these things took place. See if these things happened as the leader of the western churches was rising to power. Also, try to find out if he had anything to do, with why they were removed.

When you are finished with your search for this information, be sure and write down in your notes the date, when each of these events did take place. Then notice that the date when Daniel did receive this knowledge through his dream was when Belshazar was king of Babylon in 553 B.C.

Chapter 8 The Little Horn

I now want us to return to the seventh chapter of Daniel and to the 25th verse. Now that the foundation is almost finished, it is this 25th verse that does contain the information we have been searching for.

25 And he (eleventh horn) shall speak great words against the most High, and shall wear out the saints of the most High, and think to change times and laws: and they shall be given into his hand until a time and times and the dividing of times.

By now I do hope that we are all aware that the bishop of Rome did become the highly exalted leader of the Roman religion, and to be specific, I am speaking of the one that is known the world over as the Pope. When we do examine these prophecies we should be able to see that they do not speak of just one man, but rather a series of men. We call this the Papacy. Also, we have come to believe that the Roman Pagan Empire, with it's many emperors was replaced by the Roman Papal Empire, and now there is a long list of the Popes who have held this high office.

We must ask, What are the great words the little horn would speak against the most high? Well, to make it very short, among other claims, he does claim papal infallibility. This is a doctrine of Roman religion. In it, he does claim to be equal to God, for in reality, only God is infallible, for there is no man without spot or blemish, in the eyes of God.

How about this wearing out of the saints of God? I ask that you consider Joan of Arc, and be aware of what happened to her, at the hands of those who served the little horn. When her body was consumed by the fire, there could not have been much left of her. Surely then, her body was worn out or used up, or just plain destroyed. This was an example of the wearing out of the saints.

If we were to visit the public library, we could find many books that would speak to us concerning this dark period of history. There are books that speak of the "burning Years," when thousands of people were burned to death at the stake. Although more in some places than others, it was possible where ever the kingdoms of this world did lend their power to the head of Roman religion.

Many were burned to death for what they believed, and then there were some that were burned to death because of what they refused to believe. And it is possible that some were burned to death because someone did desire to own that person's possessions, and did bring false accusations against them.

I do suggest that you search for a rather small book the title of which is John Foxe's book of Martyr's. It is written by a man who did live during the time when many good Christian men and women were put to death because they refused to accept the doctrines of Roman religion. It is a book that does make us realize how very easy it has been for us, who live in the land of religious freedom and with liberty. It was not always so for our ancestors who came here from Europe.

I do not believe that any of us would have enjoyed living in England during the reign of Mary, the daughter of Henry the eighth, who did earn for herself a descriptive nickname.

The verse them mentions that the little horn would seek to change times and laws and that the power to do so would be given unto him. The verse also mentions that the power to do so was for a limited amount of time. This changing of the times is what we are going to talk about next. When we are finished with that, we shall learn of how the law was changed.

Notice that the scripture does say, "think" to change the times and the laws. In reality, we can not change what is already past. However, the little horn was successful in convincing many that the times were changed, even though in reality, they could not be changed because they were already past history.

In regard to the limited amount of time that is mentioned in this verse. We who study the Bible do believe that a "time" is speaking of one year, or three hundred and sixty days. When time becomes plural, such as in "times," we believe that this is speaking of two more years of 360 days each.

When the Bible mentions the "dividing of time" we believe this is speaking of less than one year and to be more specific, we believe this is speaking of one half of one year, or one hundred and eighty days. When we add them altogether, we come up with the sum of twelve hundred and sixty.

When we use the Biblical formula for understanding prophetic time that is given in the fourth chapter of Ezekiel, we learn that one day can be the symbol of one year. Therefore, it should be fairly easy to understand that a time, and times, and the dividing of time, is speaking of a period of time of twelve hundred and sixty years. This figure does seem to agree with several other scriptures that do speak of this same amount of time. In Revelation 13:5 this period of time is described as 42 months and in Revelation 12:6 as 1260 days. We believe these verses are speaking of the same period of time as spoken of in Daniel seven and verse twenty-five.

We must not forget that the scripture we have just read in the seventh chapter of Daniel did speak of the limited amount of time the eleventh horn would have the power to change both times and laws. So then, we shall try to determine when the eleventh horn first received this power.

Looking to those who have already traveled down this very same road, we notice that some have placed the date of 538 as the year when the eleventh horn first received the power to change times and laws. Why this year, we must all be wondering?

For a very long time, the structure of the government of the Roman Empire had prevented the leader of the western churches, in that none of the emperors of Rome were willing to share their authority with a religious figure. We must not forget that each of them claimed to be divine, for it went with the territory, and to allow a religious leader to share their authority, was to admit they were not what they claimed to be. However, as the foundations of the Roman Empire began to crumble, so did the power and the authority of the emperor's begin to wane. At the same time, the number of Arian Ostrogoths had continued to increase to the point they were a force to be feared. It is reported that they were most powerful through out Italy, and did pose a great threat to the Pope, for he could not gain in power as long as they were opposed to him.

It was for this reason the Pope did seek the help of Justinian, whose seat of power was no longer in Rome but had been moved to Constantinople (Istanbul) during the reign of Constantine. In one of the last display's of power, the armies of Rome did come against the Vandals, completely wiping them out, in 534. A few years later, The force of the Empire came against the fighting forces of the Arian Ostrogoths and did defeat them in 538, to the point they disappeared from history.

This was the year that the power of the Arian Ostrogoths was broken, and the last hindrance in the way of the eleventh horn was now removed. He was now free to institute many religious laws and also to employ the civil authorities to enforce them. His power did begin to spread and of course, there was the religious crusades to make sure that it did. During this time, religion was not voluntary but was mandatory.

As he gained in power, there were religious tribunals put in place, as well as the various inquisitions which did earn themselves a place in the religious history of the world.

I do suggest that you examine "Ridley's History of the World," which will supply you with much information, concerning what did happen during the dark ages, Of course, there are a great many books available in the library that do also speak of the history of religion and how it affected the history of the world.

I would also point out that during this blackest of times, often. the most feared people through out the land were the religious leaders. If you have read the story of Joan of Arc you should be aware of the method in which religious law was enforced. It was simply because there was no separation of church from state, that the civil authorities did carry out the sentence pronounced by the religious courts.

The date that is given as the end of the eleventh horn's reign of power is 1798. What happened that particular year, to bring to an end, the power of the eleventh horn, you might be pondering?

History does inform us that the government of France did have a quarrel with the government of the Vatican. Just exactly what the reasons for this disagreement was, can be found by those who search for it in the pages of history. What the record does show was that the elderly Pope was taken prisoner and did become ill and died, in a tower in Valence France, where he was being held and the year was 1798.

It was reported that several of the newspapers in various different cities of the world had headlines which announced, "Power of Papacy finally broken."

Of course, the power of the Papacy was diminished considerably with the arrival of the reformation.

However, the reformation did not exactly take place over night, but over a much longer period of time. If we were to set an exact time for the eleventh horn to have lost his power to rule over others with force, I find that the date of 1798 does seem to be reasonable, and I can find no reason to dispute it. I do ask you to count the number of years from 538 to 1798. What a strange coincidence.

I would bring to your attention that even as a great multitude of people were being put to death at the hands of those who did serve the Roman religious system, the prayers of their loved ones came together in protest. Their faithful prayers of protest did enter into the holy place, and God did hear their prayers. I say this, for the prayer of William Tyndale was one of many thousands, that cried out to the Lord, that justice be done.

The power of Roman religion to rule religiously and by force was finally broken. Those people who did live by faith were free to return to the truth of God's word and to live their lives according to that truth. It is rather surprising, but the great majority of Christians did seem to prefer the doctrines of the dark ages and traditions with roots in Paganism, to the truth contained in God's Holy Word. It remains this way, even now, and the lessons of history seem to be completely forgotten.

I do want us to be aware that the church that Jesus is still building did continue to keep the commandments of God and did reject the times that were changed by Rome.

Chapter 9 Changing of the Times

We shall now search for the meaning of the changing of the times. We notice that times is plural, and so we will address three of those times that we believe were changed by the eleventh horn, of Daniel chapter seven.

The first one might or might not be in the numerical order of when they were changed, but we shall now study when the birth of our Lord Jesus Christ did take place, according to the Word of God. I consider this to be a very elementary study, and one that young adults should be taught in their Bible classes.

The passage of scripture we are about to read is very special and I do hope that it will mean as much to you, as it does to me.

Luke 1:26, And in the sixth month the angel Gabriel was sent from God unto a city of Galilee, named Nazareth,

27 To a virgin espoused to a man whose name was Joseph, of the house of David; and the virgin's name was Mary.

28 And the angel came in unto her, and said, Hail, thou that art highly favoured, the Lord is with thee: blessed art thou among women.

29 And when she saw him, she was troubled at his saying, and cast in her mind what manner of salutation this should be.

30 And the angel said unto her, Fear not, Mary: for thou hast found favour with God.

31 And, behold, thou shalt conceive in thy womb, and bring forth a son, and shalt call his name JESUS.

32 He shall be great, and shall be called the Son of the Highest: and the Lord God shall give unto him the throne of his father David.

33 And he shall reign over the house of Jacob for ever; and of his kingdom there shall be no end.

I rather doubt that Mary, a young Hebrew maid, a daughter of Israel, engaged to be married to Joseph, truly did understand the magnitude of what the angel was saying to her. Verse 29 does say she was troubled, because of what the angel had said. Even so, she does seem to be rather courageous, and instead of being frightened into silence, she does speak up and does ask the angel this rather important question.

34 Then said Mary unto the angel, How shall this be, seeing I know not a man?

35 And the angel answered and said unto her, The Holy Ghost shall come upon thee, and the power of the Highest shall over-shadow thee: therefore also the holy thing which shall be born of thee shall be called the Son of God.

36 And, behold, thy cousin Elisabeth, she hath also conceived a son in her old age: and this is the sixth month with her, who was called barren.

37 For with God nothing shall be impossible.

38 And Mary said, Behold the handmaid of the Lord; be it unto me according to thy word. And the angel departed from her.

Notice that Mary did not protest or argue like so many young girls would. Perhaps it was because of her strong faith and her religious knowledge, but her attitude was so very positive. "If it is the Lord's will, and surely it must be, then let this thing happen to me, and I will not fear," is what she seemed to be saying.

39 And Mary arose in those days, and went into the hill country with haste, into a city of Juda;

40 and entered into the house of Zacharias, and saluted Elisabeth.

I want us to notice the very beginning of this verse. It does clearly say that Mary, arose in those days. We must ask, in what days did Mary arise. I believe it is speaking of the early days of her pregnancy. In other words, even though it does not appear that much time has passed, Mary is now with child.

41 And it came to pass, that, when Elisabeth heard the salutation of Mary, the babe leaped in her womb; and Elisabeth was filled with the Holy Ghost:

42 And she spake out with a loud voice, and said, Blessed art thou among women, and blessed is the fruit of thy womb.

43 And whence is this to me, that the mother of my Lord should come to me?

44 For, lo, as soon as the voice of thy salutation sounded in mine ears, the babe leaped in my womb for joy.

45 And blessed is she that believed: for there shall be a performance of those things which were told her from the Lord.

It is because Elisabeth was filled with the Holy Ghost at this special time, that she did receive super-natural knowledge from God. This is how she does know these things which she does say to Mary. Mary then does reply to her

46 And Mary said, My soul doth magnify the Lord.

47 And my spirit hath rejoiced in God my Savior.

48 For he hath regarded the low estate of his handmaiden: for, behold, from henceforth all generations shall call me blessed.

Mary does say quite a bit more and then we notice that Mary does decide to stay with Elisabeth through the rest of her pregnancy. I believe this is so, because we have been told that Elisabeth was six months in to her pregnancy When Mary first came to visit her. Verse 56 does inform us that Mary did abide with her three more months.

I believe the important thing we do want to establish here, is that not very much time had elapsed, from when Mary first received the news from the angel, and when she went to the hill country to visit Elisabeth. The angel did inform Mary that Elisabeth was six months along when he did speak to her, but we do not know exactly how much time passed, before Mary became pregnant. However, the scriptures have informed us that she stayed with Elisabeth about three months, and then she returned home.

The next verse does clearly say that when Elisabeth's full time came, that she should be delivered, she brought forth a son. We must remember that the angel did say Elisabeth was in her sixth month and this was before Mary became pregnant. Mary stayed with Elisabeth about three months and six and three make nine.

The point of all this, is simply that when Elisabeth did give birth to her son John, Mary was three months along. With this little bit of information we should be able to determine fairly close the birth date of our Lord Jesus. It would seem that what we need to do is determine just when John was born, if that be possible.

We shall now turn to the gospel of Luke, chapter one and verse five, and we shall find a part of the information we are searching for.

Luke 1:5, There was in the days of Herod, the king of Judea, a certain priest named Zacharias, of the course of Abia: and his wife was of the daughters of Aaron, and her name was Elisabeth.

6 And they were both righteous before God, walking in all the commandments and ordinances of the Lord blameless.

7 And they had no child, because that Elisabeth was barren, and both were now well stricken in years.

8 And it came to pass, that while he executed the priest's office before God in the order of his course,

9 According to the custom of the priest's office, his lot was to burn incense when he went into the temple of the Lord.

We have learned that Zacharias and Elisabeth did not have any children, and that the time had come for Zacharias to fulfill his priestly duties in the order of his course. The fifth verse informed us that his course was the course of Abia.

We shall now turn to 1st Chronicles twenty-four, and verse nineteen, and we shall learn about the courses. We find all the priestly courses listed by number in this verse and they total twenty-four in number. We also find that because Zacharia was of the course of Abia or Abijah, it is the eighth course and we find this information in verse ten.

Next, we must take the twenty-four priestly courses and divide them into the twelve months of the Jewish year. Of course, we soon realize that each course lasted for about two seeks.

To arrive at the time of Zachariah's course, we first must understand that the first month of the Jewish year began very near what would be the first of April according to our modern calendar. It does appear the first two courses were in April and the third and fourth courses were in May. The fifth and sixth courses were in June, and the seventh and eighth courses were in July.

To be more specific, the eighth course would be during the last two weeks of July, and this is not at all difficult to figure.

Now that we are aware of when it was that Zacharias was performing his priestly duties in the temple, let us return to our study in the gospel of Luke.

10 And the whole multitude of the people were praying without (outside) at the time of incense.

11 And there appeared unto him (Zacharias) an angel of the Lord standing on the right side of the altar of incense.

12 And when Zacharias saw him, he was troubled, and fear fell upon him.

13 But the angel said unto him, Fear not, Zacharias: for thy prayer is heard; and thy wife Elisabeth shall bear thee a son, and thou shalt call his name John.

14 And thou shalt have joy and gladness; and many shall rejoice at his birth.

15 For he shall be great in the sight of the Lord, and shall drink neither wine nor strong drink; and he shall be filled with the Holy Ghost, even from his mother's womb.

16 And many of the children of Israel shall he turn to the Lord their God.

17 And he shall go before him in the spirit and power of Elias, to turn the hearts of the fathers to the children, and the disobedient to the wisdom of the just; to make ready a people prepared for the Lord.

This is a fairly awesome thing the angel is saying to Zacharias, and it is a lot of information to take hold of, in such a short amount of time. I am sure that Zacharias probably had several questions he wanted to ask the angel, but he did manage to ask him one.

18 And Zacharias said unto the angel, Whereby shall I know this? for I am an old man, and my wife well stricken in years.

19 And the angel answering said unto him, I am Gabriel, that stand in the presence of God; and am sent to speak unto thee, and to show thee these glad tidings.

20 And, behold, thou shalt be dumb, and not able to speak, until the day that these things shall be performed, because thou believest not my words, which shall be fulfilled in their season.

21 And the people waited for Zacharias, and marveled that he tarried so long in the temple.

22 And when he came out, he could not speak unto them: and they perceived that he had seen a vision: for he beckoned unto them, and remained speechless.

23 And it came to pass, that, as soon as the days of his ministration were accomplished, he departed to his own house.

24 And after those days his wife Elisabeth conceived

We must remember that Zacharias was of the priestly course of Abia, which was the eighth course. We then notice that the Jewish calendar begins very near the first of April, on our current day calendar. Having divided the twenty-four priestly courses into the twelve months of the year, we determined that the eighth course as the last two weeks of July. We can be sure that Elisabeth did not become pregnant until the first week of August, for in the verse we just read it does sound like she became pregnant soon after Zacharias returned home.

This is where some people begin to count using their fingers. When we count the nine months of her pregnancy, counting from the first week of August, we arrive at the month of April, and this was when John the Baptist was born. Most likely very near the first week, for we are not trying to pinpoint the date, but to come fairly close.

From what we have already learned, and that Mary was three months along when John was born, then it is fairly easy to understand that our Lord Jesus Christ was born very near six months later. Counting six months from the first week of April, we arrive at the month of October. I do invite you to double check everything we have learned, and the method we have used. You can even count on your own fingers to see if you come up with the same answer.

There is a man I know, a very dear man of God, who has spent a great deal of time studying the birth of Christ. I might add that according to his on testimony, he gave his heart to the Lord and received the baptism in the Holy Ghost in 1929. It is his opinion, after very carefully examining the calendar that was used in Israel at that time, that Jesus was most likely born on the first day of the feast of tabernacles, which would have been on October fourth of our modern calendar.

I now must ask you this question. Was there anything difficult about the method we used to establish the birth date of our Lord, Jesus Christ, as being in October, and the time of the fall harvest? If we have found there was nothing difficult in finding the true Biblical date of Jesus' birth, then why do not more people and especially Christians speak of it? After all, most of the pastors of our Christian churches did attend college and did have to gain a degree, so why don't they tell their congregations about the true date as established by the scriptures, instead of December 25th? Could it be, that they are not interested in the truth but do prefer to remain with the established Christian traditions?

The next thing I want us all to know and that is there is no record that any of the disciples of Christ ever celebrated the date of his birth. Jesus did not leave instructions for how his birth was to be celebrated for a very good reason.

He simply did not want those who do know him well to become involved in celebrating Pagan festivals, for surely, he knew that this was what certain religious leaders would do.

I do not want to become involved in explaining every Pagan aspect of the Christmas celebration, but just about everything about Christmas has Pagan roots.

Of course, the birth of Christ was truly a wonderful and blessed event, but in no way was the birth of Christ a part of the winter solstice festival that had been celebrated by the Pagans for countless centuries, before Jesus was born.

If we were to go to the library and search for the information we could find all kinds of interesting bits of knowledge concerning mistletoe and wreathes from evergreen trees and ancient Christmas traditions of Europe and the world. I have no doubt that we could find enough material to fill a book, but I do not intend to do that.

Almost every year at Christmas time I find an article in the newspaper, written by someone who is greatly opposed to Christianity, who does claim that the Christians of the past were thieves, for they did steal the Pagan's time of celebration and did attach the name of Jesus to it. If we do listen to these claims and then begin to investigate them, we might find there is a great deal of truth in what these people have said.

First, I want to remind everyone that we must look at these things as if we were scientists looking at tiny one celled animals under a microscope. The words come to mind as clearly and coldly as ice, and without prejudice nor passion. I am fully aware that many people get very angry When ever anyone mentions anything that might demean their favorite holiday of Christmas.

Let us then focus our attention on the scripture that foretold that the little horn would not remain little, and would seek to change times and laws, and it would be permitted to do so.

It is because we can now figure out for ourselves when Jesus was born, within a week or so, that we should have established within our mind that Jesus was born in October. Then the question before us should be, who changed the date to December and why did they change it?

In the first place, we must be aware that this change could not have been made without ignorance, for the great majority of the people were ignorant of the Word of God. The only Bibles in print belonged to churches and they did not let anyone that came along read them. In this way, people were probably encouraged to leave the reading and the interpreting of scripture to those who were officers of the church. We can be sure that a great many very dear Christians simply placed their faith in the religious leaders, for they had no reason to doubt them.

It does seem to me that one of the main reasons to move the birth date of Christ to coincide with the time of the winter solstice festival, was really to make this mid sinter celebration acceptable to Christians. Perhaps there was also some thought as to the conversion of the Pagans, for it was probably easier to convince them to begin attending church if they did not need to give up their former times of celebration. In this way, telling the truth became of lower priority, for increasing the numbers of converts far out weighed the importance of telling the truth, or so they must have thought. In this regard, the will of religious men, seeking to prove their authority, did place their will above God's divine will, and did convince a great many people to believe a lie.

I now ask that we consider the origin of the word "Christmas." Do you suppose that once upon a time it was really two words, like in the Christ mass? Surely, we must consider the name of this celebration to determine who it was, that changed the times. Do you suppose it is possible if we were to truly search for the origin of the Christmas celebration, we would find that it is a gift to this world from the Roman religious system? I ask this because we do know the prophecy that the eleventh horn which was Roman, was given the power to change the times, and we now know beyond any doubt that someone with great authority did change the time of the birth of Jesus from October to the 25th of December.

If you really do want to know the answer to this question, then I do suggest that you visit the library and search diligently, and I am sure that you will find that the Christ mass was first celebrated in those churches with allegiance to Rome. If we can look at these things as clearly and coldly as ice, and without prejudice, we will admit that a very large lie has been told, for what else could we call it?

On this day you have been given a great truth concerning the birth of Christ. You can be sure that I do not intend to judge anyone, regarding the celebration of Christmas. However, do be aware that the truth is very precious to our Lord Jesus, and to his heavenly Father and what we do with the truth we have been given, is very important to him.

Jesus once said, "I am the way, the truth and the life: no man cometh unto the father, but by me." Isn't it strange that the very people that are the shepherds of our Master's flocks have rejected the truth in favor of religious and worldly tradition?

Chapter 10 Counting Days to the Cross

I now want us to re-construct the events in the life of Jesus that lead to the day of his crucifixion, and the resurrection. We shall now turn to the gospel of John and examine the life of Christ in those days that lead to the time of his death upon the cross. I want us to pay special attention to the time and to keep track of the days leading to the cross.

John 12:1, Then Jesus six days before the passover came to Bethany, where Lazarus as which had been dead, whom he raised from the dead.

2 There they made him a supper; and Martha served: but Lazarus was one of them that sat at the table with him.

I do believe this day, six days before the passover was actually Friday, the ninth day of Nisan. On this day he did eat supper with Lazarus, and it was upon this day that Mary, who was the sister of Lazarus, did anoint the feet of Jesus.

There was one disciple who complained because he would have much rather had the money the expensive perfumed ointment cost, but Jesus did have this to say.

7 Then said Jesus, Let her alone: against the day of my burying hath she kept this.

8 For the poor always ye have with you; but me ye have not always.

We shall learn that Jesus who knew very well that he had an appointment with death, had stopped off here in Bethany to visit with his friends whom he loved very much. However, the next day, he continued on his journey to Jerusalem, for he knew that this is what he was born to do.

12 On the next day (sabbath) much people that were come to the feast, when they heard that Jesus was coming to Jerusalem,

13 Took branches of palm trees, and went forth to meet him, and cried, Hosanna: Blessed is the King of Israel that cometh in the name of the Lord.

14 And Jesus, when he had found a young ass, sat thereon; as it is written,

15 Fear not, daughter of Sion: behold, thy King cometh, sitting on an ass's colt. (Zech. 9:9)

16 These things understood not his disciples at the first: for when Jesus was glorified, then remembered they that these things were written of him, and that they had done these things unto him. (Luke 18:34)

Please do remember that while this day is the sabbath day, it is also the tenth day of the month and is the day when all of the little lambs were separated from the flocks. The scriptures we have just read do indicate that from this time on, Jesus was set apart and his death was being planned.

We shall now turn to the gospel of Mark and notice that chapter eleven is describing this very same day, for it does show the day when the Lamb of God was separated to be examined by the Pharisees for blemishes. However, at the beginning of this day, he was certainly accepted by the people for many had heard of the miracle of Lazarus being raised from the dead.

Mark 11:1 And when they came nigh to Jerusalem, unto Bethphage and Bethany, at the mount of Olives, he sendeth forth two of his disciples,

2 And saith unto them, Go your way into the village over against you: and as soon as ye be entered into it, ye shall find a colt tied, whereon never man sat; loose him and bring him.

3 And if any man say unto you, Why do ye this? say that the Lord hath need of him; and straightway he will send him hither.

4 And they went their way, and found the colt tied by the door without in a place where two ways met; and they loose him.

5 And certain of them that stood there said unto them, What do ye, loosing the colt?

6 And they said unto them even as Jesus commanded: and they let them go.

7 And they brought the colt to Jesus, and cast their garments on him: and he sat upon him.

8 And many spread their garments in the way: and others cut down branches off the trees, and strewed them in the way.

9 And they that went before, and they that followed, cried, saying Hosanna; Blessed is he that cometh in the name of the Lord:

10 Blessed be the kingdom of our father David, that cometh in the name of the Lord: Hosanna in the highest.

I want us all to make a note of how popular Jesus was at this time with many people coming to meet him and to greet him and make him feel welcome.

I now want us to underline this next verse for it is very important to our understanding of these days.

11 And Jesus entered into Jerusalem, and into the temple: and when he had looked round about upon all things, and now the eventide was come, he went out unto Bethany with the twelve.

I want us to be aware that all of these things did happen on the tenth day of the month and that it was also the weekly sabbath day. Notice that Jesus was well received by a great many people and then he continued to ride the colt into Jerusalem. He then went to the temple and looked at the evidence of what had been taking place there, and then left for Bethany where he would spend the night.

The question that should be on everyone's mind is why didn't Jesus cast out the money changers on this day? After all, the verse we just read did say that he did look around upon all things, and he certainly must have seen the evidence of what had been taking place within the temple on a daily basis.

The answer is simply because the money changers were not there. This was the sabbath day, and it was the custom of the Jews that they carried neither their purses, nor money on the sabbath day. In this way they removed the temptation to either buy or sell, and they did this because of their respect for the commandments of God. I believe that it is still this way today, for those people who do esteem the commandments of God very highly. There simply is no reason for them to carry money on their person on the sabbath day, for they have no intention of buying anything.

We shall now continue in our story and be aware that the next day would be Sunday, the first day of the week and the eleventh day of Nisan.

12 And on the morrow, when they were come from Bethany, he was hungry:

13 And seeing a fig tree afar off having leaves, he came, if haply he might find any thing thereon: and when he came to it, he found nothing but leaves; for the time of figs was not yet.

14 And Jesus answered and said unto it, No man eat fruit of thee hereafter for ever. And his disciples heard it.

15 And they come to Jerusalem: and Jesus went into the temple, and began to cast out them that sold and bought in the temple, and overthrew the tables of the moneychangers, and the seats of them that sold doves;

16 And would not suffer that any man should carry any vessel through the temple.

17 And he taught, saying unto them, Is it not written, My house shall be called of all nations the house of prayer? (Isaiah 56) but ye have made it a den of thieves.

18 And the scribes and chief priests heard it, and sought how they might destroy him: for they feared him, because all the people were astonished at his doctrine.

19 And when even was come, he went out of the city.

This verse brings to a close this day which I believe was Sunday, the eleventh day of Nisan. Paying attention and counting the days, we notice that verse twenty informs us that it was in the morning of the next day, which would be Monday, the twelfth day of Nisan.

20 And in the morning, as they passed by, they saw the fig tree dried up from the roots.

21 And Peter calling to remembrance saith unto him, Master behold, the fig tree which thou cursedst is withered away.

22 And Jesus answering saith unto them, Have faith in God.

23 For verily I say unto you, That whosoever shall say unto this mountain, Be thou removed, and be cast into the sea; and shall not doubt in his heart, but shall believe that those things which he saith shall come to pass; he shall have whatsoever he saith.

24 Therefore I say unto you, What things soever you desire, when ye pray, believe that ye receive them, and ye shall have them.

25 And when ye stand praying, forgive, if ye have aught against any: that your Father also which is in heaven may forgive you your trespasses.

26 But if ye do not forgive, neither will your Father which is in heaven forgive your trespasses.

It does appear by the account given in these scriptures that Monday the 12th was a very long day. Jesus did teach many things on this day and we can follow along in the scriptures clear to the end of chapter thirteen.

Chapter fourteen does begin with announcing that another day had come and we know by counting that it is speaking of Tuesday, the thirteenth day of the month.

Mark 14:1 After two days was the feast of the passover, and of unleavened bread: and the chief priests and the scribes sought how they might take him by craft, and put him to death. 2 But they said, Not on the feast day, lest there be an uproar of the people.

I realize that the description we are given, concerning what day it was can be a little confusing. Because we have been careful to not lose track of any days we can be confident that these verses do indicate that it is the thirteenth day of the month and the high day sabbath, the first day of unleavened bread is two days away, for it is always on the fifteenth day of Nisan. We find that quite often the people of that time spoke of the passover and the feast of unleavened bread, all in the same breath. However, the day that was most important to them, was the day of the feast.

These verses also inform us that the religious authorities did want very much to kill Jesus as soon as possible, but they feared killing him on the high day sabbath which was the fifteenth day of the month.

We continue through the scriptures until we come to the 12th verse which is also a little confusing.

12 And the first day of unleavened bread, when they killed the passover, his disciples said unto him, Where wilt thou that we go and prepare that thou mayest eat the passover?

This is speaking of the fourteenth day of Nisan and in the order we have been following it did come on a Wednesday. But it is speaking of the time right after sundown. Remember that according to the Jewish method of reckoning time it became Wednesday as soon as the sun did set. By the way we do reckon time, it is speaking of Tuesday evening.

We shall turn to Luke's gospel and learn of this same time as it is described by the man who was also a doctor.

Luke 22:1 Now the feast of unleavened bread drew nigh, which is called the Passover.

I want us to all realize that the feast of unleavened bread was on the fifteenth day of Nisan, but quite often they spoke of the entire time as being the Passover. In reality, it began on the tenth day of the month when they separated the lambs from the flocks and lasted through the seven days of unleavened bread, the last day being a high day sabbath, just as the first day of the feast was.

7 Then came the day of unleavened bread, when the pass-over must be killed.

Again I feel I must point out that the day when the lambs were to be killed was in the afternoon of the fourteenth day. This verse is speaking of the very first portion of the fourteenth day, which is shortly after sundown. Again I repeat myself, for I know this can be confusing, but this is speaking of very early on Tuesday evening, by the way we keep track of time.

8 And he sent Peter and John, saying Go and prepare us the passover, that we may eat.

9 And they said unto him, Where wilt thou that we prepare?

10 And he said unto them, Behold, when ye are entered into the city, there shall a man meet you, bearing a pitcher of water; follow him into the house where he entereth in.

11 And ye shall say unto the goodman of the house, The Master saith unto thee, Where is the guest chamber, where I shall eat the passover with my disciples?

12 And he shall show you a large upper room furnished: there make ready.

13 And they went, and found as he had said unto them: and they made ready the passover.

I believe it is important that we understand certain details concerning this meal which they very clearly referred to as the passover meal. It was not an ordinary passover meal, for the rest of Israel would not eat the passover lambs until very late in the afternoon about the time of sundown, on the fourteenth day. This was according to the instructions of Moses that we have already received.

This was because Jesus had an appointment with death, for he would die in the afternoon, at the same hour as the perfect little lambs were being slain. It is for this reason this passover meal with his disciples had to be eaten during the very first portion of the fourteenth day, the time we think of as Tuesday evening.

I seriously doubt that this very special meal that is the last meal Christ would eat with his disciples contained the meat of a lamb. I do believe they prepared the traditional type of food, including the bitter herbs, for it was according to the instructions given in scripture. I do not doubt but what many Jewish families today, continue to eat the same type of food made from the same recipes, for it has been handed down from one generation to the next. Even so, I do not believe that the meal eaten by Jesus and his disciples contained any meat, for you see, Jesus would become the passover lamb.

Let us turn once again to the gospel of John and we shall take up the story at verse thirteen. Listen closely to what is said in this first verse.

John 13:1 Now before the feast of the passover, when Jesus knew that his hour was come that he should depart out of this world unto the Father, having loved his own which were in the world, he loved them unto the end.

2 And supper being ended …..

I want us to all be aware that the passover meal that Peter and John had prepared was over and they had finished eating. When we come to verse four we learn ….

4 He (Jesus) riseth from supper, and laid aside his garments; and took a towel, and girded himself.

5 After that he poureth water into a basin, and began to wash the disciple's feet, and to wipe them with the towel wherewith he was girded.

6 Then cometh he to Simon Peter: and Peter saith unto him, Lord, dost thou wash my feet?

7 Jesus answered and said unto him, What I do thou knowest not now; but thou shalt know hereafter.

I want us to pause a moment and consider what Jesus said to Peter. If it was just a matter of washing Peter's feet in the physical sense, so they would be clean, then Peter would not have a hard time understanding. However, because Jesus informed him that later he would understand, then we must be aware that the washing of the feet by one who was his teacher and master had to contain a very deep spiritual significance. It is rather obvious that Peter was rather ignorant of spiritual matters judging by what he said next.

8 Peter saith unto him, Thou shalt never wash my feet. Jesus answered him, If I wash thee not, thou hast no part with me.

9 Simon Peter saith unto him, Lord, not my feet only, but also my hands and my head.

10 Jesus saith to him, He that is washed needeth not save to wash his feet, but is clean every chit: and ye are clean, but not all.

11 For he knew who should betray him; therefore said he, Ye are not all clean.

By what Jesus has said we can see that the purpose of the foot washing was not for physical cleansing.

12 So after he had washed their feet, and taken his garments and was set down again, he said, Know ye what I have done to you?

13 Ye call me Master and Lord: and ye say well; for I am.

14 If I then, your Lord and Master, have washed your feet; ye also ought to wash one another's feet.

15 For I have given you an example, that ye should do as I have done to you.

16 Verily, verily, I say unto you, The servant is not greater than his Lord; neither he that is sent greater than he that sent him.

17 If ye know these things, happy are ye if ye do them.

I want all of us who will soon become the saints of the great tribulation to hear these words spoken by our Lord and Savior and hear them well. The purpose of the foot dashing is to give us the proper attitude so that we might partake of the emblems, as we should. There are many today who call themselves Christians but only a few who are willing to place their trust in these words spoken by Jesus and follow our Lord's instructions.

According to the way we keep time, this Tuesday evening was a very long night. Jesus had much to say to his disciples and we can read and study the 14th, 15th and 16th chapters of John concerning the things that Jesus did teach his disciples in his final hours.

The 17th chapter of John contains the very beautiful prayer of Jesus, as he prays for his disciples and for you and me as well. There is one thing in our Lord's prayer that I do want to bring to your attention,

John 17:15 I pray not that thou shouldest take them out of the world, but that thou shouldest keep them from the evil.

16 They are not of the world, even as I am not of the world.

17 Sanctify them through thy truth: thy word is truth.

18 As thou hast sent me into the world, even so have I sent them into the world.

19 And for their sakes I sanctify myself, that they also might be sanctified through the truth.

20 Neither pray I for these alone, but for them also which shall believe on me through their word;

21 That they all may be one; as thou, Father, art in me, and I in thee, that the world may believe that thou hast sent me.

I want to bring to your attention that the one thing Jesus did not pray for was an early rapture of his church. Instead, he prayed that his heavenly Father should keep us safe from evil. Yet, it is quite popular these days to preach and teach the very thing that Jesus did not and would not pray for.

Then notice verse seventeen. It quite clearly does state that we are to be sanctified (set apart) by the truth of God's word. Yet, as we are learning, perhaps the majority of Christians today greatly prefer tradition to truth.

Chapter eighteen begins with .....

1 When Jesus had spoken these words, he went forth with his disciples over the brook Cedron, where was a garden, into which he entered, and his disciples.

It was here that Judas betrayed him and it was from here, and on this very same night, that he was taken away by the soldiers and the Jewish authorities. It was also on this very same night that his disciples denied that they even knew him, and we can not help but think of how Peter must have felt when he heard the rooster crowing. I believe that by the time that Peter heard the rooster crow it must have been very early in the morning.

The account given in the gospel of Luke does have this to say about this particular event.

Luke 22:54 Then took they him, (Jesus) and led him, and brought him into the high priest's house. And Peter followed afar off. 55 And when they had kindled a fire in the midst of the hall, and were set down together, Peter sat down among them.

56 But a certain maid beheld him as he sat by the fire, and earnestly looked upon him, and said, This man was also with him.

57 And he denied him, saying, Woman, I know him not.

58 And after a little while another saw him, and said, Thou art also of them. And Peter said, Man, I am not.

59 And about the space of one hour after another confidently affirmed, saying, Of a truth this fellow also was with him: for he is a Galilaean.

60 And Peter said, Man, I know not what thou sayest. And immediately, while he yet spake, the cock crew.

61 And the Lord turned, and looked upon Peter, and Peter remembered the word of the Lord, how he had said unto him, Before the cock crow, thou shalt deny me thrice.

62 And Peter went out, and wept bitterly.

It is my very sincere hope that none of us would experience the shame that Peter felt at that moment, as Jesus looked into his eyes. Yet, it almost goes without saying that sooner or later, most Christians will experience in some degree how Peter must have felt, and so I warn you now to guard against that day.

I am reminded that our purpose in this study is to learn about the time frame of the crucifixion and the resurrection and it is so easy to become side tracked. We must return to the gospel of John and the eighteenth chapter.

To speed things up, we notice in verse 28 that it was very early in the morning when the Jewish religious authorities did bring Jesus unto the hall of judgment to appear before Pontius Pilate. Of course, we all know that even though Pilate would find that Jesus had not done anything worthy of death, he gave in to the Jewish religious leaders and sentenced Jesus to death by crucifixion.

The time table that the scriptures plainly show is that this day which was Wednesday the fourteenth, the day of preparation for the high day sabbath, the very day when the little lambs were to be killed. The wheels of government which normally turn ever so slow, began to turn very fast. Of course, we do remember that the Jewish religious authorities were concerned, because they did not wish to start a riot by having Jesus executed on the high day sabbath of unleavened bread. Therefore, it seems as though they insisted that the death sentence be carried out by the Romans as soon as possible.

The scriptures inform us that shortly after appearing before Pilate, Jesus was forced to bear his own cross, and he did so with a great deal of difficulty. We are told in one account that a certain man then helped him to bring his cross to Calvary, and Jesus was nailed to it at nine o clock in the morning.

The scriptures also inform us that at noon, the sky became very dark and the darkness did prevail through out the region. At three in the afternoon, Jesus died, and the scriptures of the Hebrew Bible that foretold of the coming and the death of the Messiah were fulfilled. We must never forget that Jesus said "it is finished" and we realize that through the shedding of his blood, the old covenant came to an end and a new one in Christ Jesus was established.

We then examined what took place following his death and do understand that his body was placed in the sepulchre between three in the afternoon and sundown. I have set the time as being near five but want to make it clear that this is just an estimate, for we do not know the exact time. What we do know is that when the sun went down, it became the high day sabbath of unleavened bread, and the body of Jesus was lying in the tomb. We also know that the two women who loved Jesus were there, to see where and how they placed the body, for the scriptures do bear witness of this.

Let us listen to the account given in Matthew's gospel for perhaps it can increase our knowledge concerning what did take place. We shall take up the story when the time was even, and it is speaking of soon after Jesus had died.

Matthew 27:57 When the even was come, there came a rich man of Arimathaea, named Joseph, who also himself was Jesus' disciple:

58 He went to Pilate, and begged the body of Jesus. Then Pilate commanded the body to be delivered.

59 And when Joseph had taken the body, he wrapped it in a clean linen cloth,

60 And laid it in his own new tomb, which he had hewn out in the rock: and he rolled a great stone to the door of the sepulchre, and departed.

61 And there was Mary Magdalene, and the other Mary, sitting over against the sepulchre.

By this account as well as the others we see that the two Marys were there when the body of Jesus was placed in the tomb.

And now, we shall learn a little more that we have not previously discussed.

62 Now the next day, that followed the day of the preparation, (Thursday) the chief priests and Pharisees came together unto Pilate,

63 Saying, Sir, we remember that the deceiver said, while he was yet alive, After three days I will rise again.

64 Command therefore that the sepulchre be made sure until the third day, lest his disciples come by night, and steal him away, and say unto the people, He is risen from the dead: so the last error shall be worse than the first.

65 Pilate said unto them, Ye have a watch: go your way, make it as sure as ye can.

66 So they went, and made the sepulchre sure, sealing the stone and setting a watch.

I want us to realize that from that time on, I believe there were at least two Roman soldiers guarding the tomb for the remainder of the three days and three nights. In addition, there as a seal placed on the door that would be broken if anyone attempted to open it and gain entry into the tomb.

In reviewing what we have just learned, by carefully counting the days to the cross, we now know that our Lord's last supper did take place after sundown on Tuesday evening, and according to Jewish time it was the beginning of the fourteenth day of Nisan.

After supper was ended Jesus did wash his disciple's feet and then after a little time had passed, they left for the garden of Gethsemane. Here it was where Judas betrayed him, and then he was taken captive to the high priest's house and that is where Peter denied that ha even knew him.

From there they took him before Pontius Pilate and there he was condemned to die on the cross, even though Pilate could find no fault in him. Let us listen to the account given in the Gospel of John.

John 19:1, Then Pilate therefore took Jesus and scourged him. (Jesus received thirty-nine stripes)

2 And the soldiers platted a crown of thorns, and put it on his head, and they put on him a purple robe.

3 And said, Hail, King of the Jews! and they smote him with their hands.

4 Pilate therefore went forth again, and saith unto them, Behold, I bring him forth to you, that ye may know that I find no fault in him.

5 Then came Jesus forth, wearing the crown of thorns, and the purple robe. And Pilate saith unto them, Behold the man!

6 When the chief priests therefore and officers saw him, they cried out, saying Crucify, crucify him. Pilate saith unto them, Take ye him, and crucify him: for I find no fault in him.

Moving down to verse 14

14 And it was the preparation of the passover, and about the sixth hour, and he saith unto the Jews, Behold your King!

15 But they cried out, Away with him, crucify him. Pilate saith unto them, Shall I crucify your King? The chief priests answered, We have no King but Caesar.

16 Then delivered he him therefore unto them to be crucified. And they took Jesus and lead him away.

17 And he bearing his cross went forth into a place called the place of a skull, which is called in Hebrew Golgotha.

18 Where they crucified him, and two other with him, on either side one, and Jesus in the midst.

This brings to and end our counting of the days leading to the cross but remember that this day was the preparation day of the high sabbath of unleavened bread, which day was the fourteenth day of Nisan.

Chapter 11 Only Sign Would be Given

꧁

The 28th chapter of Matthew begins with....
Matthew 28:1 In the end of the sabbath, as it began to dawn toward the first day of the week, came Mary Magdalene and the other Mary to see the sepulchre.

We must first establish why they came to the sepulchre late in the afternoon of the sabbath day. The scripture does tell us very plainly that they came to see the sepulchre. First, they were well aware that there was a very large stone closing the entrance to the tomb. Second, they were also aware that the tomb had been sealed and a guard placed there to insure that no one gained entry into the tomb. The third reason they came late on the sabbath day was that they were aware that the three days and three nights were actually over, when the sun went down.

Let us examine how much time had passed since Jesus' body was first placed in the tomb. Joseph and Nicodemus had placed his body in the tomb, just before sundown on the day of preparation which was late Wednesday afternoon, the 14th day of Nisan. The next day was Thursday, the high day sabbath of unleavened bread. When the time came to be just before sundown, Jesus had been in the tomb for one night and one day. Of course, this amount of time is also twenty-four hours.

Then came Friday, and it too, was the day of preparation, for it preceded the weekly seventh day sabbath. On Friday, just before sundown Jesus had been in the tomb for two nights and two days, or a total of forty-eight hours.

Now the next day was the weekly sabbath and the two Marys were quite able to count the hours that Jesus was in the heart of the earth. They knew very well that just before sundown would mark the end of the three days and three nights that Jesus had prophesied, and I can well imagine they were more than a little anxious to see what was going to happen.

Let us think about what we would have done, had we been there and knew what they knew. Do you suppose that we would have been curious and that we would have gone to the tomb just as soon as the three days and three nights were past? I think this visit was to satisfy their curiosity for we notice that it does not mention they brought their spices on this visit.

Let us look once more and find out what happened next.

2 And, behold, there was a great earthquake: for the angel of the Lord descended from heaven, and came and rolled back the stone from the door and sat upon it.

3 His countenance was like lightning, and his raiment white as snow:

4 And for fear of him the keepers (guards) did shake, and became as dead men.

5 And the angel answered and said unto the women, Fear not ye: for I know that ye seek Jesus, which was crucified.

6 He is not here: for he is risen, as he said. Come, see the place where the Lord lay.

7 And go quickly, and tell his disciples that he is risen from the dead; and, behold, he goeth before you into Galilee; there shall ye see him: lo, I have told you.

8 And they departed quickly from the sepulchre with fear and great joy; and did run to bring his disciples word.

9 And as they went to tell his disciples, behold, Jesus met them, saying, All hail. And they came and held him by the feet, and worshipped him.

10 Then Jesus said unto them, Be not afraid: go tell my brethren that they go into Galilee, and there shall they see me.

I am afraid that this is the end of the account given in Matthew, as far as the women telling the disciples is concerned. Matthew is strangely silent about the women informing the men of this event.

We then turn to the gospel of Mark who does have this to say about the women and their conversation with the angel. However, we notice that the time is at the rising of the sun.

Mark 16:6 And he (angel) saith unto them, Be not affrighted: Ye seek Jesus of Nazareth, which as crucified: he is risen: he is not here: behold the place where they laid him.

7 But go your way, tell his disciples and Peter that he goeth before you into Galilee: there shall ye see him, as he said unto you.

8 And they went out quickly, and fled from the sepulchre; for they trembled and were amazed: neither said they anything to any man; for they were afraid.

Please do notice what the women did after listening to the angel. It does quite clearly say they ran away and did not tell anyone, for they were afraid. I point this out for what does take place in verse nine must have happened some time later.

9 Now when Jesus was risen early the first day of the week, he appeared first to Mary Magdalene, out of whom he had cast seven devils.

Again, we find the comma in the wrong place. Therefore, what this verse does indicate is that Jesus, having already risen, did appear to Mary first, and it was the first day of the week.

We shall now learn what happened next.

10 And she went and told them that had been with him, as they mourned and wept.

11 And they, when they had heard that he was alive, and had been seen of her, believed not.

We are aware that the time of this visit to the disciples by Mary is on Sunday morning.

We shall turn to the gospel of Luke and learn of one more account that took place on Sunday morning. Only this time it is not Mary alone, for there are quite a few different women with her.

Luke 24:10 It was Mary Magdalene, and Joanna, and Mary the mother of James, and other women that were with them, which told these things unto the apostles.

11 And their words seemed to them as idle tales, and they believed them not.

I have used these verses to show that even though Jesus had told the disciples he would rise again on several different occasions, they still did not believe the words of Jesus, and they were not about to believe the things reported by Mary Magdalene, or any other women, as well.

The point I want to make is how very rigid and powerful and unchangeable is the unbelief of these men who were the companions of our Lord. We would think that perhaps they would consider the words that Jesus did speak to them concerning his death and resurrection. When the reports from the women did speak of the very thing that Jesus foretold, surely they should have been willing to let go of their unbelief and begin to hope that what they heard was true. The scriptures do speak of how very stubborn they were and how unwilling they were to believe those things that were foretold by their Lord and Master, and then confirmed by very devout, God fearing women.

I now want us to consider that the first visit to the tomb took place late on the sabbath day, just before sundown. The scripture in Matthew did tell us that shortly after the angel did speak to the two women, they did meet Jesus and did actually touch him and did worship him. Jesus did speak to them comforting words and did tell them what they sere to do.

We shall now gather our wits and examine what must have been the very next visit to the tomb. Let us turn to the gospel of John and notice that in this account it does sound as though Mary is alone.

John 20:1 The first day of the week cometh Mary Magdalene early, when it was yet dark, unto the sepulchre, and seeth the stone taken away from the sepulchre.

The first thing I want to mention is that it became the first day of the week, just as soon as the sun went down on sabbath afternoon. John describes the time of this visit as early, when it was yet dark. I believe that he is speaking of a time even before dawn, when it is very dark.

It has been said that it is always the darkest, just before dawn. Speaking from my own experience, having stood wheel watch through the night many times and waited for daylight to come, as we traveled to westward Alaska and the Bering Sea. Quite often the moon does set by three or four and the time just before dawn can be very dark indeed. How welcome are the first signs of light in the east, for they foretell of the coming of the sun and a new day about to begin.

I now want us to think about this very carefully and seriously consider what the scriptures do tell us. What was a women such as Mary, who had been possessed by seven demons before Jesus delivered her, doing in a graveyard among the tombs in the dark of the night? I want you to think about this and then ask yourself, would you go by yourself to the local cemetery on foot, and wander about the graves, searching for something during the darkness of night? I do believe that this was a very unusual thing to do, and it does indicate that Mary, at this time, was a very troubled woman.

I believe that the two Marys did just what Jesus told them to do, when they did see Jesus shortly after their first visit to the sepulchre. I do realize that what I am about to say is speculation and I do admit that it is. But I do ask that we consider all of these things.

At first, even though the women did experience some fear, they also had great joy, for the gospel of Matthew 28 and verse eight does speak of this. I believe that it is most likely they did go to at least one or perhaps more of the disciples that very evening and did tell them about their experiences.

I believe the men were so very powerful in their manner of unbelief that they were overwhelming and soon robbed the women of the joy in their hearts. I can imagine that within a very short time, they had attacked the credibility of the women and informed them that they had allowed their emotions to cause them to believe things that just did not happen. It is quite possible that both women then left the disciples in tears and returned home so confused they did not know what to believe.

After awhile, they probably came to the conclusion that what the men said was true, and so they began to prepare the spices they had previously purchased so they could anoint the body of Jesus on Sunday morning.

I want us to think about this a little more. They had seen with their own eyes that the stone had been rolled away from the door of the sepulchre. They could also see that the body of Jesus was not there. With their eyes they could see the angel and with their ears they could hear the words spoken by the angel. Later, their eyes did behold Jesus and with their ears they did hear the words Jesus did speak to them. And then, in just a few moments after having heard the discouraging words of unbelief expressed by the very men who did know Jesus better than anyone else, they gave up all that they had experienced.

I now say unto you, my dear brothers and sisters, our faith and our belief must be greater than the unbelief we shall encounter as we go to fulfill our great commission. What I am saying is that there are many religious teachers and preachers who refuse to believe the words of Jesus, as they do apply to the three days and three nights. They continue to teach a Friday crucifixion and a Sunday resurrection and the Word of God has revealed to us that this is against the sign that Jesus did give.

Let us remember these words that Jesus did speak to his Father in heaven.

John 17:17, Sanctify them through the truth: thy word is truth.

18 As thou hast sent me into the world, even so have I sent them into the world.

19 And for their sakes I sanctify myself, that they also might be sanctified through the truth.

The truth of God's word as it is revealed by the three days and three nights is that Jesus was crucified on Wednesday, the day of preparation for the high sabbath, and was resurrected shortly before sundown on the seventh day of the week. All of the accounts that are given in the four gospels do show that by Sunday morning, the tomb was empty, for it was empty before the sun went down on the sabbath day. Jesus did arise from the dead, exactly when he said he would.

We must now remember the prophecy given in Daniel who foretold that the eleventh horn would seek to change times and laws, and into his hand it would be given. The teaching of the Sunday resurrection is one of the false doctrines which was introduced very early in the history of Christianity. Of course, only the religious authorities had Bibles, and the people just had to accept their words and interpretation of scriptures.

Even now, there are pastors who claim to know Jesus very well, and yet they continue to teach the false doctrines that have been handed down from one generation to another. In this way they do show the same kind of unbelief that was once displayed by the disciples. They simply do not believe nor do they teach the words spoken by Jesus, but do cling to the religious traditions of the dark ages.

It is my hope that our faith and our belief in God's Holy Word will be much stronger than is their unbelief, so that we will not cave in and go along with the false doctrines that are being taught from the pulpits through out America. I do hope that we will take a stand for truth and will share the truth of God's word with all who are able to receive it.

We must now take one more look at the time table of visits to the tomb, for what really happened should be much clearer now. The first visit as it is reported in the gospel of Matthew did take place late on the afternoon of the sabbath, just before sundown. I believe that everything happened just as it is described and we do remember that Jesus did tell the women they were to inform the disciples that they did see him.

We are not told, but I do believe the women did do exactly as Jesus had told them to do. However, they encountered such strong unbelief and sharp criticism to the point their hearts were torn, and they returned home in tears so confused they did not know what to believe. I believe that Mary was so troubled that she could not sleep and so she slipped away in the dark of the night and came once more to the tomb, just as it is reported in the gospel of John. I believe she was so confused she came once more to verify the very things she did witness on her first visit.

On this visit she does encounter both Simon Peter and John, who I believe she did see earlier in the evening. It might have well been these two disciples who robbed these two women of their joy, they did receive when Jesus did speak to them.

This is also a strange time for Peter and John to show up in the graveyard, for we must remember that the gospel of John has described the time as very early while it was yet dark. We must ask, why didn't Peter and John just wait until sunrise to visit the tomb, for it does seem to be the most natural thing to do.

I believe the answer is that even though they must have attacked the credibility of the women as to what they really did see, deep Within their minds and hearts they were troubled too, and decided to come to the sepulchre to see if the women had been telling the truth about their experiences earlier that evening. This is the only reason I can think of that would explain their presence there, during the darkest part of the night.

According to the scriptures in the 20th chapter of John, after seeing Mary, both men did run to the sepulchre and did enter in, and did look at the empty grave clothes that Jesus left behind when he arose. What is interesting is that it does sound like the empty grave clothes must have looked a little like a cocoon, for I do not believe Jesus needed to unwind them to escape from them.

Verse eight does inform us that when they did look upon these things that the other disciple, whom I believe to be John, did believe. We can not help but notice that the scripture does not say that Peter believed at this time, and I am reminded that Peter was a very stubborn and impetuous man.

Verse nine does inform us that they knew not the scripture, that Jesus would be killed and would rise again. Even so, We do know that Jesus had told them of these things on quite a few different occasions, including all that Jesus had taught them at the last supper. It should be very plain to us that the disciples simply refused to believe the things Jesus had told them, and did not believe them until later, and perhaps much later and long after the resurrection.

John 20:9, For as yet they knew not the scripture, that he must rise again from the dead.

10 Then the disciples went away again unto their own home.

I want us all to notice that the two disciples did leave the graveyard and did return home. I believe the reason they did so, was because the hour was very early, and it might well have been quite a while before sunrise. I say this for the scriptures do show that quite a few people did visit the tomb at sunrise or shortly after.

Shortly after they left, Mary does once more encounter Jesus and does listen as Jesus does give her instructions. Mary does obey the instructions and we learn of this in verse eighteen.

18 Mary Magdalene came and told the disciples that she had seen the Lord, and that he had spoken these things unto her.

Notice that we are not told just when it was that she did inform them of this. I say this for I believe that she returned home and was able to join the company of the other women who then returned to the sepulchre to see these things for them selves, at the time of the rising of the sun.

I believe that the account given in Matthew does show the first visit to the tomb as being late on the sabbath day. I do believe that the account given in the gospel of John does show that the second visit to the tomb did occur very early on Sunday morning, while it was yet dark, and perhaps long before sunrise.

I do believe that the accounts given in both Mark and Luke are speaking of the same visit. Of course, if we have followed these events closely, this is the third visit for Mary Magdalene. Let us examine these two accounts and notice the similarities contained in both.

Mark 16:1 And when the sabbath was past, Mary Magdalene, and Mary the mother of James, and Salome, had bought sweet spices, that they might come and anoint him.

2 And very early in the morning the first day of the week, they came unto the sepulchre at the rising of the sun.

In Luke's gospel we learn of basically the same things except there are other women with them. Notice the time is very early in the morning, which makes me think that this is speaking of the same occurrence recorded in the gospel of Mark.

Luke 24:1 Now upon the first day of the week, very early in the morning, they came unto the sepulchre, bringing the spices which they had prepared, and certain others with them.

Notice that Mark has also mentioned the spices as did Luke. Notice also the time of day and this leaves me to conclude that both accounts are of the same visit and that Mary Magdalene is present in both of them.

We have learned of three different visits to the tomb of Jesus and perhaps we all know more about these things now, than we ever knew before. It is extremely important that we understand that the Word of God does not teach a Sunday resurrection, for it would mean that Jesus did make false statements about the three days and three nights on several different occasions. Of course, we do know that Jesus would not lie about such a thing and that the truth is available for those who search for it. Did not Jesus say "Seek, and ye shall find?"

We must now consider the three accounts that all took place on Sunday morning. The gospel of Matthew does show that the discovery of the empty tomb did first take place late on the sabbath day, but there are few today that are able to accept, what is clearly written in the Word of God.

Further more, it was late on the sabbath that there was an earthquake and an angel rolled the large stone away from the door of the sepulchre. In the other three accounts, the stone was already removed when they did arrive upon the scene. I do hope that we can all understand this means that the accounts given in Mark, Luke and John do agree and do not contradict the account given in the gospel of Matthew. Let us keep in mind that by sunrise on Sunday morning, all of these accounts do testify of an empty tomb.

Now we must return to the prophesy given by our Lord Jesus. He very definitely said that he would be in the heart of the earth for three days and three nights. Therefore, it should be easy to understand that the resurrection would take place at the same time of day as when his body was first laid to rest.

We have already established that the time of his burial would be between the time that he died at three in the afternoon, to sometime shortly before sundown at six P.M. I have estimated that time to be in the vicinity of five o clock, but of course it could have been a little sooner or a little later, we really can not be sure.

Because we now know that the resurrection could not have occurred on Sunday morning, we must then look to the nearest time it could have occurred. Again, after having examined the evidence we have been given, it would seem to have taken place very near five o clock in the afternoon of the sabbath day.

Counting back three days and three nights from five P.M. on sabbath, we arrive at the time of his burial, and that being on Wednesday afternoon. Of course, this is also consistent with the prophecy given in the book of Daniel.

Daniel 9:26 And after three score and two weeks shall Messiah be cut off, but not for himself: and the people of the prince (army of Rome) that shall come shall destroy the city and the sanctuary; and the end thereof shall be with a flood, and unto the end of the war desolations are determined.

Notice that this verse written by the prophet Daniel did foretell that the Messiah would be cut off (killed), but not for himself. He then foretells of the complete destruction of Jerusalem and the temple of God at the hands of the Roman armies, which did take place in 70 A.D.

This next verse again speaks of Jesus.

27 And he shall confirm the covenant with many for one week: and in the midst of the week he shall cause the sacrifice and the oblation to cease

We realize this verse is speaking in prophetic language, and yet, we find that Jesus was executed in the middle of the week. When Jesus died on the cross, we are told that the veil within the temple was torn in two, which does clearly indicate the end of the need for the daily sacrifices and Levitical priesthood, for the way into the Holy of Holies was now made manifest, Jesus having become our high priest.

In looking back at all we have learned that Jesus was not born in December and certainly not at the time of the winter solstice, but was born at the time of harvest.

We also learned that Jesus was not crucified on Friday, as so many people believe but was crucified on the Jewish preparation day on the fourteenth day of Nisan. In the year that Jesus was sacrificed for our sins that day fell on a Wednesday.

Learning from the lesson of three days and three nights, we learned that the resurrection did take place just before sundown, late on the sabbath day which day is Saturday.

Let us remember how we followed the scriptures and counted the exact number of days to the cross, beginning on the ninth day of Nisan and concluding of the fourteenth day of Nisan when Jesus was crucified.

We then went to the day of discovery, which was early on Sunday morning, and counted backward from Sundown on Saturday, three days and three nights and came to the same exact day of crucifixion. We know that the Word of God is true and must realize that someone has told a lie regarding these times.

Chapter 12 Easter or the Lord's Passover

Daniel 7:25 And he (eleventh horn) shall speak great words against the most High, and shall wear out the saints of the most High, and think to change times and laws: and they shall be given into his hand until a time and times and the dividing of time.

From where Daniel stood, it must have been most difficult looking forward to the future and trying to understand these mysterious things. However, from where we stand, we have the advantage of hind sight and can search through the pages of history which do tell us how these things did come to pass.

We have learned that the time of our Lord's birth was moved from October to the 25th of December, which had been a time of Pagan celebration, long before Jesus was born. We can not help but ask, was this done in order to confuse Christians, or to pacify and please Pagans? If we but think about it we should be able to discern that it was not the will of God for God is truth and the roots of the Christ Mass are firmly fastened to a lie.

We have now learned how the time of our Lord's resurrection was changed from late on the sabbath day to early on the Sunday morning. However, there is much more to this story, for the time of the resurrection was also moved from three days after the passover, to Easter Sunday. There is more that we do need to know about this.

The first thing we must do is establish just what or who is Easter. Can this word or name be found in the Bible.

The answer is yes, it does appear in my King James Bible, but it really should not be there. We shall find it in the 12th chapter of the Acts and please be aware that it does not appear in the original manuscripts. Therefore, we must assume that it is an error of the translators. Of course, by the year of 1600, the doctrine of Easter was firmly established in most Christian churches.

Acts 12:1, Now about that time Herod the king stretched forth his hands to vex certain of the church.

2 And he killed James the brother of John with the sword.

3 And because he saw it pleased the Jews, he proceeded further to take Peter also. (Then were the days of unleavened bread)

4 And when he had apprehended him, he put him in prison, and delivered him to four quaternions of soldiers to keep him; intending after Easter to bring him forth to the people.

5 Peter therefore was kept in prison: but prayer was made without ceasing of the church unto God for him.

It is an easy matter to look this up in Strong's concordance and we find the original word was "pascha." In 1st Corinthians five and verse seven we find the same word "pascha" and it is translated as passover. It should be easy for us to understand that because it was the time of unleavened bread, the translation in Acts should be "after passover."

In order that we increase our knowledge concerning the changing of the times, we need to learn a little more about Easter and how it did enter into the early Christian churches.

First of all, where does the word or name Easter come from? We find that it is an Anglo-Saxon word perhaps at one time being Eastre, or Eoster, and German, Ostern. We also find it was possibly derived from Eostre, or Ostara, who was the Anglo-Saxon goddess of spring.

I have before me a Webster's dictionary that does have this to say about Easter. "The prehistoric name of a pagan spring festival." Of course the dictionary does tell how it is also a very special time for Christians, but we already know that it is. What we are trying to learn is how the time of the death and resurrection of our Lord Jesus

Christ came to be associated with the time of a prehistoric Pagan spring festival.

The first thing I want us to grasp is that there isn't any place within the scriptures where we are given instructions for celebrating the birth of Christ. In other words, Christmas became the gift of the Roman religious system, but it did not come from God's Holy Word. We find the same is true concerning the resurrection of Christ, for the scriptures do not instruct us as to the celebration of the resurrection.

However, Jesus, on his last night with his disciples did make it very clear how they were to commemorate his death. First, Jesus made it very clear that it was his desire that his disciples should continue in the foot washing, which was not to wash away dirt.

John 13:14 If I then, your Lord and Master, have washed your feet; ye also ought to wash one another's feet.

15 For I have given you an example, that ye should do as I have done to you.

16 Verily, verily, I say unto you, The servant is not greater than his Lord; neither he that is sent than he that sent him.

17 If ye know these things, happy are ye if ye do them.

These instructions should be very clear to all who do truly love Jesus and do want to please him. In Luke's gospel Jesus also said....

Luke 22:19 And he took bread, and gave thanks, and brake it, and gave unto them, saying, This is my body which is given for you: this do in remembrance of me.

We can easily understand that within these instructions, it was certainly his desire that we continue in these things as a very beautiful memorial of what Jesus did for us. However, we must not forget what a memorial is and not try to make it into something it is not.

Again, let me remind us that the Word of God is completely silent regarding the celebration of the birth of Christ and is equally silent regarding the celebration of the resurrection. Let us then be aware that our righteous and holy God does know all things and there is a reason for this silence.

I believe that it was about the year of 60 A.D. when Paul did warn us of the grievous wolves that would enter in and not spare the flocks. Peter also warned us of religious people who would twist the Word of God, even unto their on destruction. They were not alone for John in his epistles did tell us of people who were once in the church that had departed from them. People who did not accept that Jesus was truly the Son of God.

Jude who was also the Lord's brother did have some very strong things to say about certain people within the churches. Among other things, Jude did say this describing some within the church

Jude 16 These are murmurers, complainers, walking after their own lusts; and their mouth speaketh great swelling words, having men's persons in admiration because of advantage.

The point I want to make is that it should be clear according to the scriptures that there would come division within the churches and the pages of history do verify that this was so. I now bring to our attention that within the first one hundred years of Christianity we can find there was differences between the Eastern orthodox churches and the leadership of the western churches, that was based in Rome.

It is reported that the Eastern churches did cling to a different time of our Lord's death and did observe the resurrection at a time different than Rome.

The question is now before us, is when do we observe a memorial? I believe we should all agree that the most common time to observe a memorial is on the date or anniversary of whatever it is that we are to remember. We observe a person's birthday on the date they were born. We observe a wedding anniversary on the date they were married. These are both examples of when we should observe a memorial.

We shall now listen to what the apostle Paul had to say to the Christians at Corinth regarding time.

1st Corinthians 11:23 For I have received of the Lord that which also I delivered unto you, That the Lord Jesus the same night in which he was betrayed took bread.

24 And when he had given thanks, he brake it, and said, Take, eat: this is my body, which is broken for you: this do in remembrance of me.

I want us all to notice that Paul made it very clear that Jesus did say these things the very same night he was betrayed, which according to Jewish method of reckoning time was the 14th day of Nisan. However, we must not forget that Paul said it was the same night. He did not say it was morning nor did he call it "the Lord's breakfast." He did very clearly say that he did deliver unto the Christians at Corinth, which he received from the Lord, that the same night he was betrayed did brake bread.

My point is that it is reported that the churches of the Eastern division did cling to the date of the passover and did reject the time of the Pagan spring festival called Easter.

The pages of history do inform us that the churches of the western division in obedience to the authority in Rome, did observe this same memorial on Sunday. However, the eastern churches did observe it at the time of the Jewish passover, and the passover came on a different day each year.

It does seem to me by way of common sense, the reason most likely given for limiting this memorial day celebration to Sunday, was that they were probably teaching a Sunday resurrection at even this early date. However as we well know, the resurrection did not occur on Sunday, but late on sabbath afternoon, just before sundown.

I feel that I must point out to you that there are two kinds of memorials spoken of in the scriptures. First, there is the seventh day sabbath, and it is a memorial of creation and especially of the example that God set before us for us to follow. God has spoken very clearly that we are to rest from our work, just as he rested from his. In this way, the seventh day is a memorial given to us, for all time.

Going back to the time of Moses we shall learn of a different kind of memorial, for God did have this to say concerning the passover.

Exodus 12:14 And this day shall be unto you for a memorial; and ye shall keep it a feast to the Lord throughout your generations; ye shall keep it a feast by an ordinance for ever.

The word "forever," as it is used in this verse can be a little missleading. I believe that to the end of the age, would be more appropriate. It should be clear that when Jesus said, just before he died, "it is finished," he became the pascal lamb, and there was no more need for any more lambs to be slaughtered. He paid the price for our sins in full, and in the book of Hebrews it is written, "once and for all."

Therefore, it is rather important that we understand that on the same night that Jesus was betrayed he instituted a new ceremony that we call the Lord's passover, for this is what Jesus called it in Luke 22. The apostle Paul, when addressing the Corinthian church many years later spoke of it as the Lord's supper. Let us be aware that the part that we observe, including the foot cashing did take place after the meal had been eaten.

Looking once more to the pages of history, we are told that quite a few Christians in the western churches did choose to remember their Lord's death at the time of the passover. However, it is reported that they were stigmatized as being heretics and were ridiculed and mocked by those who did prefer Sunday as the day of celebration.

It has been suggested that this division within the church was a source of trouble and that the leader of the western churches, Pope Pius the 1st, c. 147 did bring an end to this by firmly establishing that the memorial service must be held on "the Lord's day" which they believed to be Sunday.

His successor was Anicetus, and we are told that he remained firm as to limiting the celebration to Easter Sunday. During this time there was the man known as Polycarp, and he was the very respected Bishop of Smyrna, and he paid Anicetus a visit in 159 A D. His purpose was to convince the bishop of Rome to return to the time of the passover and to follow the same formula to establish the correct time, as did the Eastern Orthodox churches. We are told that he failed in his mission for the supreme authority of the western division greatly preferred Easter Sunday as the time of celebration and refused to change the time. As we can see, the leadership of the Roman churches were not interested in promoting truth, but insisted on clinging to their Pagan ways.

What I consider to be rather strange is the fact that the Eastern Orthodox churches do share the same basic doctrines as does the Roman brand of religion and yet they do disagree with the times that were established by the Roman leaders. Even till this very day, they do not agree and they do celebrate many important dates at a completely different time.

What is even more strange is that the Protestant churches of America, for the most part, do celebrate the times that were first established by Roman religion, even though their basic doctrines are completely different.

I do not know exactly when the Lord's last supper memorial service was changed to become the central theme of the mass, We will learn more about the mass a little later for it is a very important doctrine of the Roman religious system.

It does appear that by the year of 325, the changing of the time of the resurrection was confirmed by the religious authorities who formed the Nicene council. From that time on the time of the resurrection would be changed to one certain Sunday and would be called by the name Easter, which was more acceptable to the Pagan gentiles than was the Biblical name, "passover," which as considered to be Jewish.

This did not show honor for our Lord and Savior in any way, but did show respect for the Pagan goddess of spring and her fertility rites. The pre-historic spring festival named Easter must have included the gathering of colored and decorated eggs and a feast containing food that no religious Jew, including the disciple Peter, would have eaten.

What is so very interesting about the Nicene council, which met in 325 is that it was called for by a man by the name of Constantine, who was the emperor of Rome. What is more, it is reported that he did preside over this meeting of the religious authorities and we can be sure that he did have a great influence on their decisions.

The first thing we should know about Constantine is that he did claim to be divine and to be a god. This was true of all of the emperors, for it was just a part of the territory that came with being emperor of the Roman Empire. I have no doubt but what he was used to getting his own way and he had a great many people to help him enforce his will on others. I do not believe it made any difference whether the matter was civil or of a religious nature for the will of the emperor was always right. It does seem to me that men who are given total power most often are inflicted with a disease of the mind, wherein they often believe they are immortal and their judgments infallible.

I have no doubt but what the will of Constantine was done at the council of Nicaea, for who would dare to express an opinion that was contrary to the views held by the Emperor of Rome? Surely, those who found favor with the Emperor had a great advantage over those who did not agree with the supreme authority of the empire. I think this must have been especially so with the leaders of the churches, for it certainly helped to have the authority of the Roman government on their side when it came to creating and enforcing religious laws.

In order that we come to a better understanding of these things we need to go back a few years to the year 321. Again, history does reveal that on March seventh of that year, Constantine did issue the following edict.

Let all judges, and all city people, and all tradesmen rest on the venerable day of the Sun. But let those dwelling in the country freely and with full liberty attend to the culture of their fields, since it frequently happens that no other day is so fit for the sowing of grains or the planting of vines; hence the favorable time should not be allowed to pass lest the provisions of heaven be lost.

"Given the seventh of March, Crispus and Constantine being consuls, each for the second time." Codex Justin, lib. 3 tit. 12, 1, 2.

I want us to realize that as far as we can tell, this was the very first Sunday law, and it came from a man who was a Pagan emperor and not from God, nor from God's Holy Word. There is no where in the entire Word of God that we can find such a commandment. The commandments of God very clearly say that we are to set aside the seventh day of the week, while the Roman emperor proclaims that the first day of the week, that day being the venerable day of the sun, should be set aside. I do hope that it is clear to all that the two laws are in direct opposition to each other.

Having copied the edict of Constantine from the pages of history, word for word, I want us to notice that it does not mention the will of God, nor his only begotten Son, our Lord Jesus Christ, anywhere. It should be very clear to us that Constantine, at this point in time wanted to force everyone except farmers to yield and to conform to his own religious ways which involved Pagan worship of the sun God.

There is nothing said here to indicate that Constantine was concerned with a Sunday morning resurrection, nor that he cared about the commandments of God. His choice of words do show that his only concern was forcing his religious will upon others and just what his true religious convictions were must have been a little confusing at times.

When we consider the fact that Constantine in issuing this edict does reveal his partiality to Sun worshippers, then it should come as no surprise that the council of Nicaea with Constantine presiding, did form the religious law, changing the time of the observance of the death and resurrection of Christ to Friday and Easter Sunday. Of course, the various leaders of the churches did help by twisting, the Word of God in order to teach a Friday crucifixion and a Sunday resurrection. There is a aide spread belief that Constantine was the first Christian emperor and of course, he was greatly admired by all who did conform to the Roman religious system. We must therefore ask the question, "Was Constantine ever converted from his Pagan religion to become a follower of Christ?"

Rather than answer that question, I would prefer that you search through the pages of history and learn about what happened to certain members of the family of Constantine. His first marriage was to Minervina, and she bore him a son they named Crispus. His second wife, Fausta bore him three daughters and three sons. We are told that Crispus became an outstanding soldier and was a son that his father could be proud of.

In 326, the year following the council of Nicaea, and long after Constantine was supposedly converted to Christianity, it is reported he had his son Crispus put to death. Shortly thereafter, his wife Fausta was also put to death and we are told that both his son and his second wife were executed, or murdered, on the order of Constantine.

I can imagine that you are probably wondering why would a good Christian man such as Constantine give the order to have his family members put to death? The story behind these deaths contain all of the sordid details that are popular with so many writer's today. If you want to learn of these things then I do advise you to search for these details in the pages of history, for I do not feel like repeating them.

Perhaps you will also learn of the death of his nephew Licinius, who was flogged to death at the order of Constantine and also others whose lives were taken because they did offend the emperor in one way or another. Because these things did happen after he was supposedly converted we must ask, Was Constantine truly a born again Christian, or was he one in name only?

The Word of God does have this to say regarding those who do commit the sin of murder. Surely, in a court of law, the one who gives the order is as guilty as the one who does the actual killing.

1st John 3:15 Whosoever hateth his brother, (or son or wife) is a murderer: and ye know that no murderer hath eternal life abiding in him.

Was Constantine truly a Christian emperor as so many do claim? I say we must allow the Word of God to be the judge.

We are told that Constantine once had a dream, or a vision, and that he saw a cross which did appear against a background of the setting sun. It has been said that from this time on, he was converted to Christianity and while it makes for a good story, the historical facts of his life seem to refute this claim.

The story also goes that he did receive the knowledge that this scene was to appear upon the royal banners of Rome, when they went into battle against their enemies and they would have the victory. Of course, the cross was already the symbol of the cruel method of execution used by Rome and it was well known through out the world. I believe it was used from the beginning of the Empire and several hundred years before Jesus was born.

As the new religion of Christianity began to spread through out the world, the cross very quickly became the main symbol of that religion, for Christians everywhere did identify with what Jesus had done for this world, having died upon a cross. Even so, I am sure that many people did fear this symbol because of the purpose and way Rome did use the cross, as a very cruel means of execution and a tool of terrorism.

What I want us to understand is that the cross imposed against the setting sun does appear to be the combining of two religions. Surely, as a banner on the battlefield, to gain the acceptance of Christians while maintaining the emblem of the setting sun to please the Pagans for it would lead both into the battle. It must have occurred to Constantine that by mingling and mixing those dates which were important to the Pagans with those certain events that were important to the Christians, he could bring many people together and the Empire would be made stronger. What better way to bring unity to the Empire than to cause them to all celebrate their different festivals on the same dates. Also, what better way to make things that were clearly Pagan acceptable to those who claimed to be followers of Christ.

I can not help but think what a terrible abomination to God it must have been, to love this world so much that he gave his only begotten Son, and to have the world care so little, that they changed the name of that time from Passover to Pagan Easter, in honor of the ancient spring festival.

I do want us to learn what the Word of God does have to say regarding the mixing of other religions with the worship of Jehovah. Of course, what ever is said would also apply to Jesus, for we know that Jesus is seated at the right hand of his Father in heaven.

Surely, we all remember that Aaron had two sons that did place strange fire upon the altar of God. The sons of Aaron were a part of the Levitical priesthood which was a symbol of the five fold ministry of the new covenant.

We believe that the strange fire was the symbol of other forms or ways of worship that God had not commanded and he struck them both dead, beside the altar. Let us pay close attention to what Moses did say to his brother, for Aaron was understandably unhappy about his sons deaths.

Leviticus 10:1 And Nadab and Abihu, the sons of Aaron, took either of them his censer, and put fire therein, and put incense thereon, and offered strange fire before the Lord, which he commanded them not.

2 And there went out fire from the Lord, and devoured them, and they died before the Lord.

3 Then Moses said unto Aaron, This is it that the Lord spake, saying, I will be sanctified (set apart) in them that come nigh me,

and before all the people I will be glorified. And Aaron held his peace.

It certainly does appear that the mixing of other religions with Pagan doctrines and forms of worship would not be tolerated by a completely righteous and holy God, during the time of Moses, and of course, God is still the same today.

The word sanctified means to be set apart. Because God is still the same today as he always was, then we who draw close to him must always set him apart from other gods and all forms of Pagan worship. This is just as true and important today, as it was when Nadab and Abihu were struck dead beside the altar.

Moving to the time of Jeremiah, we find these instructions given in the tenth chapter. Keeping in mind that the children of Israel were to be taken as slaves to the land of Babylon because they had turned away from God; but even in their captivity God still loved them and cared about them.

Jeremiah 10:1, Hear ye the word which the Lord speaketh unto you, 0 house of Israel.

2 Thus saith the Lord, Learn not the way of the heathen...

I do hope that we understand that the heathen were people who did not know Jehovah God, nor did they have a relationship with him. They were simply the Gentile people living in Babylon and they were ignorant concerning the will of Jehovah God.

I believe that I should bring it to our attention that ancient Babylon was the birth place of almost all Pagan religion. Perhaps you can remember they were attempting to build the tower of Babel, which was a symbol of man made religion and attempting to find the way of heaven (eternal life) without conforming to God's will. We are told that God decided to give them different languages to speak that they might not understand one another. Even today, the words babel and babble mean to speak with confusion. At that time, they were scattered across the face of the earth and we can still find bits and pieces of their religion everywhere.

With this in mind, we can see that God loved his people so much that he told them to not learn the ways of the heathen while they were in captivity in Babylon. Surely, the worshipping of the Sun and the ancient spring festivals of fertility were all a part of the ways of the heathen. Even though the name Easter is an Anglo-Saxon word, this type of worship is common to many people of this earth and is not limited to the people of Anglo-Saxon descent.

What then should we say about the early church leaders which sought to incorporate many of the heathen ways into the teachings of the church? When the church leaders did prefer the ways of the heathen to the ways of God, they were following in the footsteps of Nadab and Abihu, and surely we have not forgotten what happened to them.

When Anicetus refused to listen to the teaching of Polycarp, was he being a follower of Christ or did he reveal that he did prefer the ways of the heathens or Pagans? When Constantine gave his edict concerning the setting aside of the venerable day of the Sun, was he being a follower of Christ, or was he opposed to that Word of God which once proceeded from the mouth of God? (ten commandments)

When we arrive at the council of Nicaea, and learn that the observance of Easter became the law of the church, was that governing body following Christ, or was it consenting to the Pagan practices of the past?

I would point out that in order to truly become a Christian, we must be willing to give up our former way of life in order that we become born again. Once we have established that we are willing to die to self, then we are instructed that we must take up our cross and follow Jesus.

I say this, for though at times it did appear that Constantine did favor the Christian religion, he never ever did fully give up his Pagan ways, and thus, he did encourage the church leaders to form a religion of compromise and error. The evidence of Pagan Sun Worship can still be found in the statutes and art work on display at the Vatican.

I now want us to consider the prophecy given unto Daniel concerning the eleventh horn which would seek to change both the times and the law. We have learned about the time when Jesus was really born and do realize that the date of December 25th is important concerning the ways of the Pagans.

We have also learned that Jesus was in the heart of the earth for three days and for three nights and did arise late on the seventh day of the week, shortly before sundown. However, we also learned that the Nicene council did decide in 325 that the time of the resurrection was moved from the Biblical time of the passover, to the Pagan time of celebration of the ancient spring festival, Easter.

I now want us to focus on that part of the prophecy that speaks of changing the law. What law would be changed by the eleventh horn, you might be pondering? I do believe this is speaking of the changing of God's law, the ten commandments.

Perhaps we are also aware that God's law is in heaven and the power to change it there was not given to the eleventh horn, even though he does claim to have this power. To better understand how God's law would be changed we must consider where God does desire that his law be written. It is because we have now become the temple of God, that God does want to place His most Holy Word in our hearts and in our minds and he wants it to remain there for all of eternity. I would point out that because this is so, that Satan, above everything else does want to place his word in our hearts and the hearts of all mankind. In that way, when the judgment comes, he will claim that all who have received his word, instead of God's most Holy Word, do belong to him.

All of those people who do claim that they are not under the law, and have refused to allow the Holy Spirit to write God's law in their hearts and minds, are without law. Satan is not overly concerned with these people, for their rejection of God's law does mean they do not follow Christ, but insist upon doing their own thing. We can be sure that Satan does rejoice because of their rebellion and is aware that lawless people do choose the way of darkness rather than the way of our Lord's marvelous light.

I must also point out that because Satan is very clever and subtle, he knows that all he has to do is substitute just one of his laws for one of God's laws, and his goal, will have been accomplished. He does know this for Satan is very familiar with the scriptures and he is very much aware of the truth they do contain. We can be sure that he is aware that James did write

James 2:10, For whosoever shall keep the whole law, and yet offend in one point, he is guilty of all.

In his sermon on the mount, Jesus made it quite clear that he had come not to abolish the law, but to magnify it. Therefore, let us understand that whosoever has rejected even one of God's precious commandments has in fact, rejected them all.

Also be aware that all who seek to improve upon the commandments of God, have in reality rejected the commandments of God. God has made it very clear that we must not add to or subtract from His most Holy Word. We must now consider the edict of Constantine and how the church leaders did adopt the law of Rome and did make it the law of the church. By now we must all be aware that the leaders of the western churches were in direct violation of God's word and would eventually receive the promises of God, concerning their disobedience.

I now remind you of the cycle of the four horses of the apocalypse. Rebellion against God and against the commandments of God has always brought the judgment of God. Jesus has informed us in Matthew 24 that it will be as it was in the days of Noah and again, in Luke 17, like what happened when Sodom and Gomorrah were destroyed.

Chapter 13 Sabbath to Sunday

The prophecy in Daniel concerning the eleventh horn, did say that he would seek to change the times and the law, and then it also mentioned that he would wage a war against the saints and would actually prevail against them and wear them out. I then used the account of a very courageous women by the name of "Joan of Arc" as an example of how the eleventh horn would wear out the saints.

The pages of history do inform us that Pope Eugene IV (1431-47) condemned Joan of Arc to be burned alive for being a witch. It should be very clear to us that when this sentence was carried out and this very dear woman, (a teenager) did perish in the flames, because it was the will of the Pope.

I believe it is also interesting that according to what is written, in the year of 1919, the man of Rome, Pope Benedict IV, declared Joan of Arc to be a "saint." I have mentioned this to reveal that there are many contrasts within the Papacy for quite often the different Popes did not agree upon many religious matters. Of course, this does not say much for the Roman doctrine of Papal infallibility.

The pages of history tell of the time when Pope Stephen VI (896-897) brought former Pope Formosus (891-896) to trial. What makes this story so bizarre is the fact that Pope Formosus had been dead for eight months. Never the less, his rotting body was brought forth from the tomb, dressed in priestly robes and made to sit upon a throne.

As his trial proceeded he could not say as much as one word in order to defend himself against the accusations brought against him by the new Pope, and so he was soon found to be guilty as charged. His robes were ripped off, his ring finger hacked off, and his body was thrown into the street. His body was then dragged through the streets of Rome behind a cart and was then finally cast into the river.

However, the river was not to be the final resting place for this Pope, for a Monk managed to retrieve the body, and it was later buried with full honors in St. Peters under the approval of the next Pope.

I do not speak of these things in order to ridicule anyone's religion. I speak of these things because they are recorded in the pages of history and I believe that it is absolutely necessary that we learn something about what has happened in the past. I say this, for the wise old king did inform us that what has happened in the past will happen again and it is the key to understanding much prophecy.

Our purpose has been to identify the little or eleventh horn that did become a mighty world power, and I do think that what is written in history has positively identified him.

As far as changing the times is concerned, we must ask who it was, that is responsible for changing the date of our Lord's birth and moving it to coincide with the date of the Pagan Saturnalia festival of ancient times, and then giving it the name of Christ-mass?

We then must ask who is responsible for changing the time of our Lord's death from late on Wednesday and then moving it to Friday? Who is also responsible for changing the time of our Lord's resurrection from late on the sabbath day to early on Sunday morning? To this we must add, who then was responsible for moving the time of the Lord's death and resurrection to the weekend of the ancient Pagan spring festival known as Easter?

When we have the answer to these questions, then we must answer just one more. Who or what was responsible for changing the sabbath to Sunday? I believe the Word of God that is contained in our Bibles has made it abundantly clear that God created the seventh day holy in the very beginning, and that he did rest from all his labor on the seventh day. When he gave the commandments to Moses at

Mount Sinai, he commanded his people to follow his example and to remember and keep, the seventh day holy.

He also made it very clear that only the seventh day was to be sanctified for he said "Six days shalt thou labor." It does seem that there are a great many people who do not agree with God and are in direct opposition to his commandments. What is more, not only are they opposed to the commandments of God, they do not approve of the life that Jesus lived without sin, for Jesus lived his life in perfect obedience to his Father's holy will. This means that Jesus did labor on the first day of the week and did rest upon the seventh day.

I believe that during the time when Paul was a world traveler, preaching the gospel of Christ, and visiting many churches, there were many who did trouble the churches with strange doctrines. I have no doubt but that some must have claimed to be the risen Christ, and did seek to draw men after them selves. Let us now listen to these words of warning from our brother Paul as he does address these things in his second letter to the Thessalonians.

2nd Thessalonians 2:1 Now we beseech you, brethern, by the coming of our Lord Jesus Christ, and by our gathering together unto him,

2 That ye be not soon shaken in mind, or be troubled, neither by spirit, nor by word, nor by letter as from us, as that the day of Christ is at hand.

3 Let no man deceive you by any means: for that day shall not come, except there come a falling away first, and that man of sin be revealed, the son of perdition.

According to the footnote in my King James Bible, Paul did write this letter about A.D. 54. Paul has mentioned two things that are very important to our search for the truth. Looking back at history we must first establish when the man of sin was revealed. When we have done that we must then learn about the falling away, that Paul has mentioned. The prophet Daniel has increased our knowledge on these two subjects.

By now, it should be obvious that the falling away first began to happen a long time ago. I am sure that we can all remember that the time that the little horn would wield his power to change times and laws would be for 1260 years. We have already established this time to probably be from 538 until 1798.

Even though Constantine did certainly have much to do with changing the times and the law at an earlier date, Later the rulers of Roman religion adopted those changes and did seek to have their religious laws enforced by the civil authorities.

Remembering the words of Daniel that three of the horns would be plucked up by the roots before the face of the little eleventh horn. When this was finally fulfilled in the year of 538, it allowed the supreme ruler of Roman religion to expand and to grow very powerful. During this time, there were many nations that did bow down to the man seated upon the throne in Rome, and did enforce his religious will upon others. I do not have any reason to doubt the time of the 1260 years that we previously identified.

Of course, after many were tortured and burned to death at the stake, for resisting Roman religion, they and their families cried out in protest and their cries were heard even in heaven. This brought about that event that is called the reformation, but it was slow in coming and many suffered great persecution because of the evil and wicked ways of those in power.

Needless to say, there would not have been a reformation if there were not a great need for religious reform, for history does tell the story of how some religious rulers became intoxicated with their own great power.

I must also point out that the Papacy and the various different religious councils did adopt the edict of Constantine and did create the religious law of Sunday observance. which was strictly enforced by the civil authorities. What is more, they absolutely forbid anyone to observe the seventh day of the week as commanded in the law of God. As I have already said, this very clearly does mean that they were in direct opposition to God's Holy Word. The records do show that they did punish people for obeying God, and we can be sure that many were put to death because they refused to obey the great beast of false religion.

We must now move along to the time when people from Europe first began immigrating to this country, many of them seeking freedom from oppressive religion. I am aware that at first it was as though they in turn became authoritative and did try to enforce their religious will upon others. The witch trials of early America do come to my mind as just one of the examples of religious superstition and ignorance.

Eventually, our founding fathers of this nation did try to insure that we would be a nation of religious freedom and not one of religious oppression. However, even at this late date, there are little towns and communities through out our land where certain people do their very best to enforce their religious will upon others in the form of Sunday laws. When ever we do come across a place where these Sunday laws are still on the books, we realize that the beast of false religion is still with us.

During the time that has passed since we first gained our independence, Christians everywhere throughout these United States have been free to study the Word of God and have been free to return to the truth of God's word. However, the great majority of Christians did not choose to return to the truth but did prefer their religious traditions, many of which were handed down from the dark ages.

When given the truth concerning such things as Christmas and Easter and the fourth commandment of God, they do say that they are not saved by their works but by God's grace, and in this way, they have rejected God's most Holy Word.

Many of them claim that it does not make any difference as to which days they do observe the birth and the death and resurrection, for as long as they love God and do attend church once in a while, they will be saved.

Of course, Jesus said "If you love me, keep my commandments," and it should be easy to understand that the way we do show our love is by our obedience to his word. However, they are simply not interested in obeying God, for they would much rather follow their own rules when it comes to matters of religion.

The bottom line of what I am trying to say, is that the falling away that Paul is speaking of, first took place hundreds of years ago, and does certainly continue until this very day. The evidence of the falling away is the rejection of one or more of God's commandments. If we have rejected even one of God's commandments, it is as though we have rejected them all. This is what has brought God's judgment in the past.

Paul then said that it would be necessary for the man of sin to be revealed, and he called him the son of perdition.

I believe that we need to allow the Bible to give us the definition of sin. John, the disciple of Jesus said it quite plainly so that all might be easily able to understand.

1st John 3:4, Whosoever committeth sin transgresseth also the law: for sin is the transgression of the law.

Therefore we must ask, what man or series of men, or office of man, has caused the most people to transgress God's holy law? The answer is quite simple, for it is that man who has forbidden millions of people through out the ages to observe the fourth commandment of God's law, and has replaced it with his own law, which was first introduced by a Pagan emperor. In other words, the Papacy has continued to esteem the commandment of Constantine over the commandments of Almighty God and has convinced a great multitude of people to do the same.

Is it a sin, to fail to keep the sabbath day holy, some might ask? The scriptures we have just read have made it very plain that it is. Of course, we do live in the land of religious freedom and no one should force anyone to observe anything against their own will, even the restrictions placed on businesses on Sunday, for it is very clearly an example of religion by force.

The apostle Paul said as much in his letter to the Colossians.

Colossians 2:16, Let no man therefore judge you in meat, or in drink, or in respect of an holy day, or of the new moon, or of the sabbath days.

When we do think about the meaning of this verse, we should be able to see that people who want the civil authorities to help them enforce their religious will upon others in the form of Sunday laws, are greatly opposed to the full meaning of this verse. We, as Christian men and women should not be judging others in this regard but we must be aware that God will judge us all, even including those who insist upon trampling on his fourth commandment.

Having now allowed the Word of God to reveal unto us both the falling away, as well as the man of sin, let us continue to listen as Paul delivers his description of the man of sin in Thessalonians.

2nd Thessalonians 2:4, Who opposeth and exalteth himself above all that is called God, or that is worshipped; so that he as God sitteth in the temple of God, showing himself that he is God.

We must ask, has the man in Rome, who does near a crown and does sit upon a throne as a highly exalted ruler, been consistently opposed to the fourth commandment of God? We already know that from the time of Constantine until this very day, the Papacy has demanded that Sunday be observed. In the first place, his crown is known as the triple tiara and it supposedly symbolizes that the Pope is supreme ruler in three different places, at the same time. He claims as his jurisdiction all of heaven, all of earth, and even does preside over the lower regions known as hell or Hades. In this way and by his crown, the triple tiara, he does exalt himself above all that is called God.

It is because he does claim to be equal with God in all matters of religion, and because he does claim to be the Vicar of Christ, we can see that the temple in Rome is his temple and he does claim to be as God. Notice that he does not claim to be God, but he most certainly does claim to be as God.

When Paul wrote his letters to the Thessalonians he was certainly aware that they would be first read by the Roman authorities. It is for this reason that he has chosen his words most carefully. He did want the people the letter was intended for to understand it, but for much of it to remain hidden from the Romans.

5 Remember ye not, that, when I was yet with you, I told you these things?

6 And now ye know what withholdeth that he might be revealed in his time.

7 For the mystery of iniquity (lawlessness) doth already work: only he who now letteth will let, until he be taken out of the way.

It should be obvious that Paul had told them about these very same things in a previous conversation. He them mentions that what withholdeth will be revealed in his time. It does appear here, that Paul was saying that the Emperor of the Roman Empire did allow evil to prevail through out the Roman Empire, but that the Emperor must be removed to make way for the really evil and wicked one to take his place on the throne. At that time, his wickedness would be revealed to all who truly do love the Lord, and I do believe that it was.

As an alternative to the removing of the Emperor, picture if you can that it was decided that both the Emperor and the Pope could rule at the same time. Perhaps they could have both had their thrones placed side by side, and the Emperor could have ruled on matters pertaining to the Empire while the Pope could have ruled on matters of religion.

If we truly do understand how having great power and authority does affect the minds of men, we would realize that the two thrones placed side by side could never be.

The mystery of iniquity could be speaking of an authority that was opposed to the will of God, and yet claimed to be righteous. We might think of it as a form of self righteousness. I have no doubt but what Paul was referring to the Emperor of Rome who did claim to be divine, which is about as self righteous as one can imagine.

The phrase, he who now letteth will let, has lost much of it's original meaning when it was translated to English. The word "let" is an old English word that means to hinder. This should read that he who does now hinder, shall continue to hinder until he be taken out of the way.

What I believe Paul was speaking of was actually the fall and the decline of the Roman Empire. Of course, he could have only received this knowledge of the future by the means of the Holy Spirit. In other words, the Papacy could not rise to be a great power as long as the mighty Roman Empire was in power, for the Emperor simply would not have allowed the competition, nor would he have shared his glory.

We must not forget the prophecy in Daniel regarding the three horns that would be plucked up by their roots. Once the three horns were removed, it made it possible for the little horn through religious persuasion and influence to become more firmly established.

However, it was necessary for the Roman Empire to fall, in order for the Papacy to rise.

My only point in examining these scriptures was to make sure that you do know about the falling away and to allow the Word of God to identify the man of sin. There are a great many people, even many millions who believe the man of sin is really a very good man, a man of peace. They do not believe that it matters that this very religious man is in direct opposition to the fourth commandment of God, for so are they. Therefore let us go to verse ten.

10 And with all deceivableness of unrighteousness in them that perish; because they received not the love of the truth, that they might be saved.

11 And for this cause God shall send them strong delusion, that they should believe a lie.

There are a great many people today who might well seem to be very dear Christians, who in fact do cling to and believe the traditional lies that did originate within the Roman religious system. It is rather sad, but these people do place a higher value on the commandment of Constantine than they do the commandments of God and do trample God's holy sabbath day under their feet, refusing to sanctify it, as God commanded.

I am reminded of something Paul did say in his letter to the Romans.

Romans 3:31, Do we then make void the law through faith? God forbid: yea, we establish the law.

The law that Paul as speaking of as not the law of Rome but as the law of God. Yet, we can clearly see that the law of God was made null and void by the Roman religious system, and was replaced by the religious law of Rome, and then enforced by the civil authorities.

From the time of the reformation until this very day, the sons and daughters of those who once protested have been free to return to the law of God as it is written in His Holy Word, but they have not done so. Instead, they have chosen of their own free will to continue in the law of the Roman religion, and many have enacted Sunday laws in an effort to force others to bow down to the religious will of Rome.

In a little while, we shall inherit the promises of God, and I want us all to remember what happened to those Israelites who did provoke God to such great anger during the forty years they were in the wilderness. Do you remember what it was, that did cause them to murmur and complain against God? If you have forgotten I do suggest that you examine the 20th chapter of Ezekiel one more time to refresh your memory.

Chapter 14 A Warning to Christians

These are the words of King Solomon, the wise old king, who did contribute to us, three of the books of the Hebrew bible.

Ecclesiastes 1:9, The thing that hath been, it is that which shall be; and that which is done is that which shall be done: and there is no new thing under the sun.

If we will allow our minds to dwell upon the meaning of these words, we should be able to understand that King Solomon is telling us that history does repeat it's self. If we want to understand what the future will be, then we need to return to history and learn the lessons of the past. This, we shall soon do.

We shall now dig a little deeper in the scriptures and we shall increase our knowledge as to why God will soon pour out his wrath upon this earth. In our search for this information we shall also learn what the reason was, for the trouble that was causing the Hebrew Christian converts to even consider the rejection of Christ, and the return to the old covenant and the laws of Moses. They were in great danger then, even as the people of this nation are today, and the author of the letter to the Hebrews does issue unto them,, several very severe warnings.

Let us listen as the author of this important letter does begin with a comparison between our Lord, Jesus Christ, and Moses.

Hebrews 3:1, Wherefore, holy brethren, partakers of the heavenly calling, consider the Apostle and High Priest of our profession, Christ Jesus.

2 Who was faithful to him that appointed him, as also Moses was faithful in all his house.

3 For this man was counted worthy of more glory than Moses, in as much as he who hath builded the house hath more honour than the house.

4 For every house is builded by some man; but he that built all things is God.

5 And Moses verily as faithful in all his house, as a servant, for a testimony of those things which were to be spoken after;

6 But Christ as a son over his own house; whose house are we, if we hold fast the confidence and the rejoicing of the hope firm unto the end.

Let us examine this warning, for surely that is what it is. In verse six, he has said that we are the Lord's house, or the dwelling place of the Holy Spirit, provided we hold fast and not let go, of the confidence of our hope of eternal life in Christ Jesus, all of the way to the end of our mortal life.

The reason for this warning should be obvious, for the very thing the Hebrew Christians were considering, was to let go of their confidence in Christ and a return to the sacrificial system of animal sacrifices, according to the laws of Moses.

The author of this letter does continue in his warning, but now he does begin to expand it, so that we might come to understand a little more of the reason for it.

7 Wherefore (as the Holy Ghost saith, Today if ye will hear his voice,

8 Harden not your hearts, as in the provocation, in the day of temptation in the wilderness:

9 When your fathers tempted me, proved me, and saw my works forty years.

10 Wherefore I was grieved with that generation, and said, they do always err in their heart; and they have not known my ways.

11 So I sware in my wrath, they shall not enter into my rest.)

By the way or method he does express himself, he seems to imply that in some way, these Hebrew Christians are following in the example of those Hebrews whom God did bring forth out of Egypt.

He has said that "Today, that is, this very day, if you hear the voice of the Lord speaking to you, do not harden your heart to that voice. Whatever that voice is telling you to do, then obey it, and do not delay.

He then mentions the provocation, in the day of temptation in the wilderness. This is speaking of the time, during the forty years they wandered about in the wilderness, when they often set conditions for God to meet, much as Jacob did. In other words, they did tempt God by always demanding that God really prove that he is God, usually by performing some miracle.

Verse nine does say... "When your fathers tempted me, proved me, and saw my works for forty years.." During these forty years, God did perform many miracles and did provide for them, all through this time. One that we are all familiar with is, that God did perform a mighty miracle by the parting of the Red sea, and then delivering them from the hand of the Pharaoh and his army, and did bring them out from being slaves in Egyptian bondage. How very quickly they did seem to forget the sting of the whip, and did begin to grumble and complain about having to live in God's perfect ways, instead of the ways of slavery and bondage, in Egypt.

If they had truly loved God, they would not have erred in their heart, and as we have already learned, love that is real does produce obedience, or to put it another way, a desire to please. If they had loved God, they would have rejoiced and been glad they were no longer forced to labor seven days a week under the whip of Egyptian bondage.

In a way, this is a picture of many Christians today. God has delivered them from being slaves to sin, wherein they once served sin and were in bondage to alcohol, or drugs, and tobacco, as well as the carnal desires of this flesh. However, after a while they begin to mumble and to complain because they prefer the way of sin and bondage to the liberty of being free from sin, in Christ Jesus. Almost always, they do reject Christ and do return to their old sinful ways, because they do err in their hearts.

In verse 10 the author does inform us that God was grieved with that generation of Hebrews, whom he lead out of Egypt, from being slaves in bondage. He then said they did always err in their heart. This simply means that they did fail to love God, and they did not perceive God as being their loving heavenly Father, but as a powerful ruler over them, that they greatly resented.

The last part of this verse does say... "they have not known my ways." In other words, they simply refused to keep his commandments, for the commandments of God do reveal unto us the way that God does want us to, live. Is it not the same today? for there are many people who call themselves Christians, but who refuse to keep the commandments of God.

Verse eleven does say that God was angry and he did say that those people who had erred in their hearts, (failed to love God) and refused to keep his commandments, that he would not allow them to enter into his rest. This is a very serious thing, for it speaks of not receiving the gift of eternal life.

We know that the Word of God does inform us that for those people who do truly love God, there remains a rest for them, when their mortal life on earth is done. But for those who do not love God and do rebel against His Holy Word, there shall be no rest.

These verses are speaking of the rest that we are to enter, when our natural, mortal life has come to an end. I want us all to grasp how very serious is this warning, for he is warning these Hebrew Christians they are in danger of following in the same error as their ancestors. We know they were not allowed to enter into the promised land but did all die in the wilderness. Their children, twenty years of age and younger, that were born in the wilderness were allowed to enter the promised land but those older than that were held accountable unto God and they all died in the wilderness, except for two, Caleb and Joshua.

I do say unto all of us, it is very important that we do know God's ways and do walk in them, for that which happened so long ago, can happen once more. It is true that we are no longer under the laws of Moses but our holy and righteous God remaineth the same through out all ages, and the same is so of his commandments. There are many who are ignorant and do not know God. However, there are those who do know the commandments of God and do refuse to walk in them. The time is near when they will receive what they have coming to them, for their deeds have been weighed by the one who rides the black horse.

It does appear that the writer of the letter to the Hebrew Christians is warning them, that what did happen to their ancient ancestors, who died in the wilderness, and were not allowed to enter into the promised land, could happen to them also. To make this very clear, it is plain that their salvation was in jeopardy.

What we need to do is determine just why this was so. Of course, we are aware that they were considering returning to the religion of their ancestors, but we must try to find out why? We are also aware that to reject Christ, is to reject God's one and only plan of salvation, but there seems to be much more to this warning that we need to learn.

12 Take heed, brethren, lest there be in any of you an evil heart of unbelief, in departing from the living God.

13 But exhort one another daily, while it is called today; lest any of you be hardened through the deceitfulness of sin.

14 For we are made partakers of Christ, if we hold the beginning of our confidence stedfast unto the end;

15 While it is said, Today if ye will hear his voice, harden not your hearts, as in the provocation.

16 For some, when they had heard, did provoke: howbeit not all that came out of Egypt by Moses.

17 But with whom was he grieved forty years? was it not with them that had sinned, whose carcases fell in the wilderness?

18 And to whom sware he that they should not enter into his rest, but to them that believed not?

19 So we see that they could not enter in because of unbelief.

In issuing this warning, the writer has gone back more than fifteen hundred years to the Exodus, and compared the sins of these Hebrew Christians with the sins of their ancient ancestors, whom Moses did lead out of Egypt.

I do want us to notice that he has clearly said, They did not enter into the promised land because of their unbelief. I do not believe that we can fully understand the reasons for this warning, unless we are more able to understand the details of their ancestor's unbelief.

In the 20th chapter of Ezekiel we will find the information we need to gain a better understanding of the nature of their unbelief.

Ezekiel 20:5, And say unto them, Thus saith the Lord God; In the day when I chose Israel, and lifted up mine hand unto Jacob, and made myself known unto them in the land of Egypt, when I lifted up mine hand unto them, saying, I am the Lord your God; 6 In that day I lifted up mine hand unto them, to bring them forth of the land of Egypt into a land that I had espied for them, flowing with milk and honey, which is the glory of all lands:

10 Wherefore, I caused them to go forth out of the land of Egypt, and brought them into the wilderness.

11 And I gave them my statutes, and showed them my judgments, which if a man do, he shall even live in them. (a way of life)

12 Moreover also I gave them my sabbaths, to be a sign between me and them, that they might know that I am the Lord that sanctify them (set apart).

Before we can go on, we must increase our understanding of this last verse. Our mighty God, speaking through the prophet Ezekiel has informed us that he gave unto the children of Israel a sign. This sign was the visible evidence that God had entered into a covenant agreement with these people. He quite clearly has said that he did give them his sabbaths (plural) to be the visible evidence for all to see, that he had set them apart from the worldly and religious people around them.

Now as to this matter of sabbaths (plural) we need to divide into two parts. First, there is the weekly sabbath day that is an important part of God's commandments. This day God made holy and sanctified it, and the Bible does have this to say about the seventh day, which is the sabbath of the Lord.

Genesis 2:2, And on the seventh day God ended his work which he had made; and he rested on the seventh day from all his work which he had made.

153

3 And God blessed the seventh day, and sanctified it: (set it apart) because that in it he had rested from all his work which God created and made.

In addition to the weekly sabbath day, which is an important part of the ten commandments there were also the seven annual holy days which. are a part of the laws of Moses. I mention this, for though the covenant that God made with Israel at the time of Moses was limited in time, the commandments of God are not limited but are the will of God forever. Lest we forget, it was this Word of God, that was with God in the beginning.

Ezekiel 20:13, But the house of Israel rebelled against me in the wilderness: they walked not in my statutes, and they despised my judgments, which if a man do, he shall even live in them; and my sabbaths they greatly polluted: then I said, I would pour out my fury upon them in the wilderness, to consume them.

14 But I wrought for my name's sake that it should not be polluted before the heathen, in whose sight I brought them out.

15 Yet also I lifted up my hand unto them in the wilderness, that I would not bring them into the land which I had given them, flowing with milk and honey, which is the glory of all lands;

16 Because they despised my judgments, and walked not in my statutes, but polluted my sabbaths; for their heart went after their idols.

17 Never the less mine eye spared them from destroying them, neither did I make an end of them in the wilderness.

18 But I said unto their children in the wilderness, Walk ye not in the statutes of your fathers, neither observe their judgments, nor defile yourselves with their idols:

19 I am the Lord your God: walk in my statutes, and keep my judgments and do them;

20 And hallow my sabbaths; and they shall be a sign (visible evidence) between me and you, that ye may know that I am the Lord your God.

We shall now return to our study beginning at the fourth chapter of Hebrews. Having examined what is said in the 20th chapter of Ezekiel, we should now be aware what it was that the children of Israel did that provoked God to anger, kindling his great wrath. The scripture does reveal they refused to live in God's ways, and did not keep his commandments. Also, in rebellion they refused to keep his sabbaths holy and did pollute them by doing their on things, and ignoring the will of God, completely.

The warning letter to the Hebrews, almost fifteen hundred years later inform us that these Hebrew Christians were in danger of following in the footsteps of their ancient ancestors, who did always err in their heart. To look once more at the 19th verse of chapter 3.

19 So we see that they could not enter in because of unbelief.

In what way, did they not believe, you might be wondering? They simply did not believe that God would punish them for their disobedience, and rebellion against his government and his holy law. They believed that they could continue to live in sin, and that God did love them so much that they would be saved anyway. They did not believe that God would keep his word and not allow them to enter into the promised land, just because they insisted upon polluting his holy sabbath days, and did use them for their own purposes, instead of his.

We shall now continue in the fourth chapter to see if we can learn more about the error of these Hebrew Christians.

Hebrews 4:1, Let us therefore fear, lest, a promise being left us of entering into his rest, any of you should seem to come short of it.

I want to point out there are teachers today who do teach that it is impossible to come short of salvation, for we will all be saved no matter what. Once saved, always saved, they do claim. However, this doctrine is totally false, and the reason we are to fear is that this verse does inform us that it is possible to come short of, or not receive God's one and only plan of salvation. Remember this, this warning was given to these Hebrew Christians who had once accepted Jesus as their Savior, just as many people have in our present time..

2 For unto us was the gospel preached, as well as unto them: but the word preached did not profit them, not being mixed with faith in them that heard it.

3 For we which have believed do enter into rest, as he said, as I have sworn in my wrath, if they shall enter into my rest:

although the works were finished from the foundation of the world.

The first thing, we must notice is that the Word of God we hear must be mixed together with our faith. If it is not mixed with faith, then it will not profit us.

The next thing I want us to notice is the first line of verse three. "For we which have believed do enter into rest," is speaking of having believed in the past, do enter, which is present. This is something the letter writer was doing at the time of this letter. This rest of which he is speaking, is something that was finished and in place at the time of creation. This rest, that was present, is speaking of the seventh day, which was created holy and was blessed by God, because he rested from his work, setting an example for all mankind to follow.

However, the ancient Hebrews did rebel against God in the wilderness, and refused to rest from their work on the seventh day sabbath. It should be clear that they insisted upon doing their on thing, instead of obeying the God who loved them.

God made it very clear to us, that this is why he became so angry with them, and did not allow them to enter into his promised land. God will not allow rebellion against him and His Holy Word to remain in his presence, and it was for this reason that Lucifer and a third of the angels were cast out of heaven.

Let us pay close attention to these next two verses, so that we might be sure of what they mean.

4 For he spake in a certain place of the seventh day on this wise, And God did rest the seventh day from all his works.

5 And in this place again, If they shall enter into my rest.

It should be very clear that when Jesus was baptized by John, even though he was without sin, he was baptized to fulfill all righteousness and to set the example for us to follow.

It should also be perfectly clear to all Christians, as it was to those Hebrews who walked by faith, that when God rested upon the seventh day, he did so to set the example for us to follow.

Then to make it perfectly clear, to even those whose minds were dull, God did command this very same thing when he spoke to the children of Israel, as it is recorded in the 20th chapter of Exodus.

Then, lest anyone be dull of hearing and have a tendency to forget, God did write this commandment with the others, upon tablets of stone, which were then placed in the ark of the covenant. It should be very clear to all of us who believe in God, that his will regarding the sabbath day has not changed in any way, and is the same today.

I now bring to our attention that the 4th verse is speaking of the importance of observing the fourth commandment. However, the 5th verse is speaking of the rest we all want to receive when our natural and mortal life comes to an end. It should be obvious that if we want to receive the gift of eternal life, or enter into the rest that God has provided, then we must not rebel against God and do rest from all of our work on the seventh day of the week, just as God did rest in the beginning.

There are two things I want to make perfectly clear to you. The first one is those early Hebrews whom God brought out of Egypt, did rebel against God and greatly polluted his sabbaths, for the scriptures do say this is so.

The second thing, is that their rebellion kindled God's great wrath, and he did not allow them to enter into the promised land, for they died in the wilderness. In other words, they did reap what they sewed.

We shall see that the 6th verse is speaking of the rest we hope to enter when our natural life is over.

6 Seeing therefore it remaineth that some must enter therein, and they to whom it was first preached entered not in because of unbelief.

I do hope that you have been able to grasp how very important this warning is, for most Christians today are either not aware of it, or have chosen to ignore it altogether. The writer of this important letter did issue this warning to Christians and it does apply to us today, just as much as it did to them during the early days of Christianity.

However, there remains something of a mystery concerning why this warning was issued to these Hebrew Christians. First, if they were to return to the Jewish religion, then there would be no reason to warn them about failing to keep the sabbath. To return to the old covenant, would mean that they had rejected the sacrifice that Jesus became on our behalf, and therefore, they had also rejected God's one and only plan of salvation.

Secondly, the Jewish religion certainly did teach the observance of the fourth commandment, so then why was the author making this comparison between them and their ancient ancestors who did rebel against the commandments?

I believe there is only one answer, when everything has been considered. The writer of this letter has told them that they must hold fast their confidence in Christ Jesus. After he has laid down this foundation, he then informs them, that they must not make the same mistake as did those children of Israel in the wilderness. When we did search for the reasons for God's wrath at the time of the provocation, we found that the polluting of the sabbath was always mentioned. As we did proceed on, we found by what was said, that this seemed to be the main issue of this warning.

Therefore, we should be able to see that what was troubling these Hebrew Christians was that Pagan Gentiles had invaded the church they attended, and were teaching very false doctrine. I believe that one of their goals was to change the way the church did believe, in order to bring in their Pagan times of celebration and festivals.

This is what Paul did have to say to the churches.

Acts 20:28, Take heed therefore unto yourselves, and to all the flock, over the which the Holy Ghost hath made you overseers, to feed the church of God, which he hath purchased with his own blood.

29 For I know this, that after my departing shall grievous wolves enter in among you, not sparing the flock.

It does appear that some of these grievous wolves had entered into the church of the Hebrews and had convinced many that they should no longer observe the fourth commandment. If we are alert as to why this was so, it appears that they wanted to change the day of rest and worship to another day, which was more acceptable to the new Christians with a Pagan background. I do not doubt but what this change in the day of worship had caused these Hebrew Christians much grief and concern. It is possible that they were so troubled that they were considering going back to their old religion, for they were aware of the promises of God concerning the sabbath. They simply did not want to give them up, for it was something they had believed in and cherished all of their lives.

It is possible that they could not understand how God could make these promises through his prophets, long after Moses time, and then cancel them because of what Jesus did at Calvary. If those who did promote the changing of the sabbath to another day were right, then it would mean that God does not remain the same, but does change his mind from time to time. How very disturbing this must have been.

Let us examine one of the promises they did not want to give up.

Isaiah 58:13 If thou turn away they foot from the sabbath, from doing thy pleasure on my holy day; and call the sabbath a delight, the holy of the Lord, honourable; and shalt honour him, not doing thine own ways, nor finding thine own pleasure, nor speaking thine own words:

14 Then shalt thou delight thyself in the Lord; and I will cause thee to ride upon the high places of the earth, and feed thee with the heritage of Jacob thy father: for the mouth of the Lord hath spoken it.

When I allow my mind to dwell upon this 14th verse I am reminded of that beautiful song we sing," Just a closer walk with thee." This verse does inform us of how we may have that closer walk, for when we delight ourselves in our Lord and his ways that are so deep we can not measure, then he is with us and will help us in the trials of this life. God does not expect us to be delighted in his sabbath, if it were not first a delight to God. When we examine such a glorious promise from God, it is not at all difficult to understand why they might not want to give up their holy sabbath day with the blessings of God.

However the warning they did receive from the writer of this letter does say they were to continue in Christ, and they were to continue in the commandments of God, including the sabbath commandment. To fail to do so, was to place their salvation in great jeopardy. We shall now continue on to the 7th verse.

7 Again, he limiteth a certain day, saying in David, Today, after so long a time; as it is said, Today if ye hear his voice, harden not your hearts.

The day that is limited is today. Today is the day of our salvation, if we do not harden our hearts to the voice of our Lord, but today is limited. How is today limited, you might be wondering? God has provided us with a picture in the book of Genesis.

Genesis 6:3, And the Lord said, My spirit shall not always strive with man …..

In other words, God has been very patient with the people of this nation, but the time is near, when they will be judged and they shall receive the wages that are due them. Today, while it is yet today, the door of salvation is open, but when the day of judgment comes, that door will be closed and no man will be able to open it.

The picture God gave to us, is the one of Noah and the ark. In the seventh chapter of Genesis we read

Genesis 7:4, For yet seven days, and I will cause it to rain upon the earth forty days and forty nights; and every living substance that I have made will I destroy from off the face of the earth.

It does sound like during this time, as the animals were being loaded, the door of the ark, which was the door of their salvation was open. Those who did choose to, could have entered in. Of course, those who did not enter in, did perish in the flood. It should be clear that this was the time when salvation was available, while it was yet, Today.

When the door was closed, then salvation was no longer available and it had become the day of judgment. Therefore, the day or time of our salvation is limited. When we get to the 16th verse we learn

16 And they went in, went in male and female of all flesh, as God had commanded him: and the Lord shut him in.

When God shut the door, no man could open it, and the day of salvation had come to an end. It then became the day of God's judgment and the time of salvation was past.

We must not forget that the writer of the letter to the Hebrews was reminding these Hebrew-Christians of that, which they should have already known. The warning is that Today is limited, and that they must not harden their hearts as those ancient Hebrews did while they were in the wilderness.

It is rather strange, for if we mention the commandments of God to Christians today, we usually do not get much re-action, accept some will say they certainly do approve of them, while others will inform us they are no longer under the law. However, if we mention the fourth commandment and that we are to remember the sabbath day to keep it holy, we can detect a hardening of their hearts almost immediately.

We shall go on to the 8th verse and it is one that has caused much controversy.

8 For if Jesus had given them rest, then would he not afterward have spoken of another day.

It does seem as though before I can explain about the true meaning of this verse, I must first explain about the controversy. The person that is mentioned in the King James Version is Jesus, and rightfully so. However, most modern versions do place the name of Joshua here, for they do not like the meaning of this verse as it was written in the King James Version, and have taken it up on them selves to change it.

I do intend to show you beyond any doubt, that the name that should be written here, is none other than the name of our Lord Jesus Christ. I ask us now to think about this and may we be reasonable. If we believe the name that does belong in this verse is Joshua, then the meaning of this verse does not make any sense at all. Joshua has nothing to do, whatsoever, with the subject matter at hand.

The warning the Hebrew Christians did receive was concerning the weekly sabbath day, as well as remaining in Christ and not returning to the old covenant which had expired. We should not forget that from the cross, Jesus cried out, "it is finished"

A comparison was made, in the third chapter of Hebrews, regarding the sin and error of those who rebelled against God in the wilderness, but this did not involve Joshua, for Joshua did enter into the promised land. If we place the name of Joshua in this 8th verse, it would seem to imply that if Joshua had given them rest, then he would have spoken of another day of rest. This simply does not make sense for it would mean that God had given to Joshua the authority to change the day that God both blessed and sanctified, at the time of creation, because he rested upon this day.

We must ask the question, "Did God rest because he was tired?" How very foolish this all is. Of course not, for God is not like mankind, but did rest to set an example for us to follow. It was for our benefit, but we must not forget that it was and is God's will. To say, if Joshua had given them rest, would he not afterward have spoken of another day? simply does not fit into the logic of what has been said.

However, as the author originally intended, to say if Jesus had given them rest, does make a great deal of sense, as we shall see. Instead of giving his disciples rest, Jesus gave his disciples a great amount of work to do in the form of the great commission, which is recorded in the 28th chapter of the gospel of Matthew.

We then must ask the question, "Did Jesus change the sabbath to another day?" This 8th verse does tell us very plainly that he did not. The eighth verse does mention the word "afterward." We must ask, after what? I realize that it probably means that if Jesus had given us another day to rest, then after he had given it, he would have also given us instructions about how to observe it.

However, the word afterward could also apply to after the resurrection. According to the record we have been given, Jesus was seen of men for forty days following the resurrection, but all during this time, never once did he mention that the sabbath had been changed to another day. Now we would think, that if Jesus had wanted for the sabbath to be changed to another day, he would have given his disciples instructions regarding this change. We can be very sure that there are no such instructions within the Word of God.

However, the scripture does inform us that Jesus loved his heavenly father and always obeyed him, even to his death upon the cross. It is when we really do know Jesus, we realize that he would never advise us to do anything against his Father's holy will. To do so would be contrary to the two great commandments we received from our Lord and Savior. His first great commandment was that we are to love his heavenly Father with all that we are, our whole being. So then, it is because we do know Jesus that we realize that he never, ever, did change the sabbath to another day, for he could not do so, without first rebelling against his Father's most Holy Word.

My mind goes back to what Jesus said concerning the sabbath day, to his disciples. They were having a private conversation and Jesus did warn them of how they must run for their lives, speaking of the great destruction of Jerusalem, which would take place about 37 years in the future. I say this, for looking back, this conversation took place in A.D.33, and the complete destruction of Jerusalem came in A.D. 70, at the hands of the Roman army.

Jesus did have this to say....

Matthew 24:19 And woe unto them that are with child, and to them that give suck in those days!

20 But pray ye that your flight be not in winter, neither on the sabbath day:

We can be sure that this warning regarding Jesus' concern for nursing mothers and that their flight would not be in the winter, or on the sabbath day was intended for the ears of his disciples. They in turn would warn the people who would listen to them preach the gospel.

In other words, it does show that Jesus was well aware that Christians would still be observing the fourth commandment, long after his resurrection. Therefore, it should be obvious that Jesus did not change the sabbath day to another day.

Now to return to the book of Hebrews. If we leave the name of Jesus in this verse just as it appears in the King James Version then it makes good sense. If we do change the name to Joshua it does not make any sense at all.

I do submit unto you that the only one who has been given the power to change a day, is the one who created the day in the first place. Our brother Paul does have this to say about our Lord Jesus Christ.

Colossians 1:16, For by him were all things created, that are in heaven, and that are in earth, visible and invisible, whether they be thrones, or dominions, or principalities, or powers: all things were created by him and for him.

It should be clear that neither Moses nor Joshua, had the power, nor the authority to change the sabbath to another day. In the interest of making this abundantly clear, let us turn to the book of Joshua, and listen as Joshua does have this to say.

Joshua 1:13, Remember the word which Moses the servant of the Lord commanded you saying, The Lord your God hath given you rest, and hath given you this land.

163

15 Until the Lord have given your brethern rest, as he hath given you, and they also have possessed the land which the Lord your God giveth thee: then ye shall return unto the land of your possession, and enjoy it, which Moses the Lord's servant gave you on this side Jordan toward the sunrising.

Notice who Joshua did say had given them rest. Very clearly, it was not Joshua, nor does it imply that Joshua was supposed to give them rest. I have read every word of the book of Joshua and it does not suggest, nor imply that Joshua was supposed to give them rest, for very clearly, only their Lord could give them spiritual rest.

As for physical rest, that is something we must do ourselves, for it is a commandment of God, that we rest from our work on the seventh day. To make this clear, only the one who created the day in the first place, has the power and the authority to change the day. According to what is written in my King James Version, Jesus did not change the sabbath day to another day.

The scriptures do mention Today, but this is speaking of the time of salvation which is limited. Today, has no affect on the permanence of the sabbath day, for the commandments of God are immutable and are forever.

There is one thing I do want us to know. If Jesus did not change the sabbath day to Sunday, then who did? We have already found the answer in Daniel seven and twenty-five.

A Great Treasure

I now want us to consider what happens when we elect a new president. One of the first things a new president must do, is select the men and women of his cabinet, which will help him to lead and guide this nation for the next four years. It is a very serious thing, for how well the president can do his job is greatly affected by how those he has chosen do their jobs. It is for this reason, that the president does weigh very carefully, the skills and ability of each person, for he himself, will be judged by how well they do, and the end result will be written in the pages of history.

I want us now to return to a time long ago, when a certain very important man was faced with an enormous undertaking, one that would change people's lives for hundreds of years to come. The man was James, the king of England, and the thing of great importance, was the translating of the Holy Scriptures into a more accurate and readable version, for the English speaking people of the world.

We are told that James, himself, was a student of the Bible and had a love for God's Holy Word. In the year of 1604 James did appoint 54 of the very best men he could find in all of England to begin the work of producing a more accurate and easy to read Bible. Of course, I am speaking of what would be known as the King James Version, and it would bless more people on this earth, than we are able to count. It goes without saying, the results of the labor of those 54 men, came to be the most read and most important book that was ever produced in the English language, for all time.

These men were scholars from such places as Oxford, and Cambridge, and many were active within the church that did then prevail through out England. They were educated men and many were religious men, devoted to truth and the job they were to do. We can be sure that the King did choose them rather carefully, for their work would bear his name, and even the reputation of all of England was in their hands.

If my memory serves me correctly, I believe the 54 men were divided into six groups of nine people each. These six groups were to each work independently of each other, but when they came together to examine each other's translation, they all had to agree. It was believed that this was necessary to insure that no one would bend or twist the meaning of the scriptures to satisfy the dogmas of their particular church, or religious beliefs.

Also, they were advised that their work was not to be a completely new translation, but was to be an improved version of the Bible that was so widely accepted at that time, namely, The Bishop's Bible.

In addition to the Bishop's Bible, they were instructed to make use of five of the English versions then in use in the churches. These five were the Tyndale's Bible, Matthew's Bible, the Genevan Bible, the Great Bible, and the Coverdale's Bible. Now in addition to these early Bibles, we are told they also consulted Luther's Bible, which must have been a German translation. Also, there were French, Italian, Spanish, Latin and Greek versions available to consult as needed.

The greatest fear, when one mentions a new translation of the Bible, is that in some way the work will be affected by the religious views of the translators. That they will interpret certain passages of scriptures according to the doctrines that they were taught, and might bend or alter the truth of the original manuscripts. A good example of what I am talking about is the changing of the name Jesus to Joshua, in the modern versions of this late hour. Of course, I do realize the root word for both is the same, and that is why the logic of what is being said, must be considered.

The point I want to make here, is that without any doubt, the King James Version has been accepted by more Christians and more churches than any Bible in history, and even though the different denominations religious views might differ greatly, they do agree that the King James Version has served them well, and is overall, the most accurate of all Bibles, while retaining the poetic language in which it was written.

The first King James Versions were made available in the year of 1611. The one I have been reading from carries a date of 1986, and even though it has been improved, since it was first printed in 1611, it still uses the name of Jesus in this 8th verse of the fourth chapter of Hebrews. The reason it is still there, after this many years have passed, is because there are still men and women of God who know that the name of Jesus is the name that the author of this letter did originally intend to be there.

Let us now look at this passage of scripture as it does appear in the King James Version.

Hebrews 4:7, Again, he limiteth a certain day, saying in David, (Psalms) Today, after so long a time; as it is said, Today if ye will hear his voice, harden not your hearts.

8 For if Jesus had given them rest, then would he not afterward have spoken of another day.

9 There remaineth therefore a rest to the people of God.

10 For he that is entered into his rest, he also hath ceased from his own works, as God did from his.

11 Let us labour therefore to enter into that rest, lest any man fail after the same example of unbelief.

We can easily understand that in six days, God did create all that was made, and then, on the seventh day, God set the example for us to follow. It is a picture of the life we live, here on earth. The six days do represent all of the work we shall ever do in our natural life, and then, when our life is over, we do look forward to the promise we were given.

We should be able to see that the weekly sabbath day rest is a picture of the greater rest that is yet to come.

On that day, we do rest from our work and do focus our attention on heavenly things, for that is the way it will be, when our natural life here, is over.

I would bring to your attention that there were many people to whom we should always be grateful for the effort they made to help us to each have the Bible for our very own. One such man was William Tyndale who devoted his life to bring to as many people as possible, the truth of God's own word. The pages of history do tell us that this brave man was apprehended in 1535 and tried for heresy. He was then strangled and in October of 1536 his body was burned at the stake. It is reported that his last words were a prayer when he cried out, "Lord, open the King of England's eyes!"

From time to time, as I read and study my King James Version, I think about the fact that God did hear the prayer of this courageous and dedicated man and did answer his prayer. I consider not just my own King James Bible, but also a multitude of witnesses, to be the evidence that our God did answer William Tyndale's prayer and did give to us, a great treasure for all time. May we never forget the many courageous men and women who gave their lives and shed their blood, so that we today may possess this great treasure of God's Holy Word.

I must also ask you to consider this ..... If God became so very angry with the children of Israel in the wilderness, because they refused to obey God and refused to keep his sabbath day holy, is it not the same today? Has God changed in any way?

Just think of all of the people who call themselves Christians, and yet they simply have rejected the fourth commandment and have chosen to obey the commandment of a man instead and history does show that he was a murderer of his own family.

Chapter 15 Study in Isaiah

ᴄᴣᴣᴄ

There is a saying I first heard from one who was my teacher for quite a few years. I do not say that he originated it, for he might well have heard it spoken by someone else. Never the less, it is a saying that does require some thought.

"As goes the family, so goes the church. As goes the church, so goes the nation."

I do want you to consider the meaning and ways this saying might be true. While you are giving this some thought, we shall listen to something Paul did say to all of us, but especially to those whom God has called to preach the Gospel.

1st Corinthians 14:3 But he that prophesieth (preaches) speaketh unto men to edification, and exhortation, and comfort.

I am sure that as many men called by God have sought the will of God, down on their knees, to determine the message they should deliver unto the congregation, that God did lay it upon their hearts a message of exhortation that his children needed. Even though God did give them the message to deliver, quite often it was not well received by the congregation.

There must have been times when the leaders of the church did call for a meeting of the church board. The subject of the meeting might have been that the new pastor was not working out quite as well as they had expected, and so it was decided that they would seek to replace him with yet another pastor.

The great majority of the people responsible for the way the church was being managed, did insist that the sermons should be pleasing and should make people feel comfortable and glad that they did attend the service.

It is true that Paul did clearly say that we should speak to edification, but he also said for the purpose of exhortation and comfort. We can not have a steady diet of just one, for then the body of Christ will become lacking in the other areas needed for maturity. In other words, from time to time, a small child does need to be corrected and so does the body of Christ within the churches.

However, in these last days there are many churches where the job the pastor must do is make people feel good about them selves and attending church and he must become skillful at saying just the right words needed to entertain and pacify them. How true were the words of Paul when he said they would gather to them selves, teachers having itching ears. That they would rather hear fables than they would hear the truth of God's word.

Once again we think about that saying "As goes the family, so goes the church. As goes the church, so goes the nation." All too often the direction of the church is not decided by the men whom God has called to be the pastor of the church, but is decided by those who do contribute the most money, or have a high social standing. I want you to know my dear brothers and sisters, This is not right and this is not the way things should be.

Yes, it is true that we do need to have church boards and they do serve a very important purpose. They are to insure that the church does not become a one man show and begin to resemble a cult with a cult leader. And we know there is safety in a multitude of counselors. However, they should not dictate to the pastor, what his sermons must be, as long as the sermons do not contradict the Word of God. In other words, the sermon should be a message from God and from God's Holy Word and if it is, it will vary from time to time, as needed.

As I sit at my desk, and prepare this message, I am not under the authority of the church board but I am and will be held responsible for every word I do write by my Lord Jesus Christ. Therefore, I must warn you that this portion of this message is not for edification but is to reveal unto you, the truth of God's word that you might not have heard in church. There are few pastors today, who would be willing to risk their jobs in order to tell you these things.

We shall find within the letter to the Hebrews the following description of our Bibles.

Hebrews 4:12, For the word of God is quick, and powerful, and sharper than any two edged sword, piercing even to the dividing asunder of soul and spirit, and of the joints and marrow, and is a discerner of the thoughts and intents of the heart.

Because we know this verse is absolutely true, we shall now take up our Bibles, our two edged swords, and we shall cut swiftly and deeply, even to the heart of this matter. However I must warn you, even your heart might be pierced at this time.

The prophet Isaiah is one of the most respected prophets and this is true for both Jewish people and Christians. I have read that there were quite a few copies of his book found within the Dead Sea scrolls. It should be obvious that the religious sect that was responsible for hiding them at Qumran did hold his book in very high esteem.

Among Christians, the prophet Isaiah came to be known as the Messianic prophet. This is because his writings do contain more prophecy concerning the coming of the Messiah than any other. Of course, these prophecies were fulfilled in our Lord, Jesus Christ and this truth is recognized by born again Christians but not recognized by those of the Jewish faith.

Within my King James Version there are little crowns placed next to the verses in the old testament that do speak of Jesus. The 53rd chapter of Isaiah does contain but 12 verses and there is a little crown beside each verse. I want us to examine these verses, for they are a foundation that will help increase our understanding of the fore knowledge of our Creator.

Isaiah 53:1, Who hath believed our report? and to whom is the arm of the Lord revealed?

2 For he shall grow up before him as a tender plant, and as a root out of a dry ground: he hath no form of comeliness; and when we shall see him, there is no beauty that we should desire him.

3 He is despised and rejected of men; a man of sorrows, and acquainted with grief: and we hid as it were our faces from him; he was despised, and we esteemed him not.

4 Surely he hath borne our griefs, and carried our sorrows: yet we did esteem him stricken, smitten of God, and afflicted.

5 But he was wounded for our transgressions, he was bruised for our iniquities: the chastisement of our peace was upon him; and with his stripes we are healed.

6 All we like sheep have gone astray; we have turned every one to his own way, and the Lord hath laid on him the iniquity of us all.

7 He was oppressed, and he was afflicted, yet he opened not his mouth: he is brought as a lamb to the slaughter, and as a sheep before her shearers is dumb, so he openeth not his mouth.

8 He was taken from prison and from judgment: and who shall declare his generation? for he was cut off out of the land of the living: for the transgression of my people he was stricken.

9 And he made his grave with the wicked, and with the rich in his death; because he had done no violence, neither was there any deceit in his mouth.

10 Yet it pleased the Lord to bruise him; he hath put him to grief: when thou shalt make his soul an offering for sin, he shall see his seed, he shall prolong his days, and the pleasure of the Lord shall prosper in his hand.

11 He shall see the travail of his soul, and shall be satisfied: by his knowledge shall my righteous servant justify many; for he shall bear their iniquities.

12 Therefore will I divide him a portion with the great, and he shall divide the spoil with the strong; because he hath poured out his soul unto death: and he was numbered with the transgressors; and he bare the sin of many, and made intercession for the transgressors.

Isaiah or his scribe had a talent for writing and I believe that the Holy Spirit, as it came upon him, did even give him the very beautiful and accurate words to write, describing in great detail our Lord and Savior who was sacrificed for our sins and for our rebellion against God. I want us all to take hold of the fact that this 53rd chapter was written about 712 B.C. How absolutely positive are these verses that do reveal unto us, the fore knowledge of our holy God.

A great many people are certainly aware of these prophecies that foretold of the crucifixion of Christ, and it is surprising that more people do not seem to take hold of the fact that they do prove beyond any doubt that God did know all about the future when these words were first recorded by the prophet Isaiah, over seven hundred years before our Lord Jesus Christ was born.

What many people and even those who do study the Bible fail to realize, is that the future foretold by the prophet Isaiah did not end at the cross. Isaiah did have some things to say regarding the age of the Christian religion and some that are very important to us who are living in these last days. According to the date given in my Bible, the 56th chapter of Isaiah was written about 698 B.C. However, as we shall soon see, much of the scriptures could have a double application for it does contain instructions for believers in Isaiah's time but more importantly, does have some things to say concerning this current generation.

Because some of these things are hard and difficult to understand, I have no doubt but what we should pray and ask God to increase our ability to understand these things.

Oh heavenly Father, hallow be thy name. We come before thee this day, 0 Lord, asking that our eyes be opened that we might see, and that our ears be made to hear, so that we might better understand the deeper truths that are hidden within your word. We do thank you for the truth dear Lord, and do pray that we will receive It this very day. We ask all things in the holy name of our Lord, Jesus Christ, Amen.

It is because I want us all to grasp as much truth as we possibly can, we shall take these verses one at a time and examine them for their meaning.

Isaiah 56:1, Thus saith the Lord, Keep ye judgment, and do justice: for my salvation is near to come, and my righteousness to be revealed.

This desire of God is a continuous one, for God has always wanted mankind to do what is right in his eyes. To obey his judgments and be just in all things is just as important today as it was when Isaiah did record these verses.

I do want us to notice that he has said, that his salvation was near and that his righteousness to be revealed. We must "When did the salvation of mankind come to the world and when was the righteousness of God revealed unto his people?"

The old man named Simeon, who came to the temple on the eighth day of Jesus' life had this to say.

Luke 2:27, And he came by the Spirit into the temple: and when the parents brought in the child Jesus, to do for him after the custom of the law,

28 Then took he him (Jesus) up in his arms, and blessed God, and said,

29 Lord, now lettest thou thy servant depart in peace, according to thy word;

30 For mine eyes have seen thy salvation,

31 Which thou hast prepared before the face of all people;

It should be clear that Isaiah, by the power of the Holy Spirit was speaking of the very same salvation. I do hope that we all understand by first reading the 53rd chapter, that before Jesus gave his life for our sins, there was a debt that was owed. I would also point out that it was a debt that was impossible for us to pay, except we do know Paul did clearly say that the wages of sin is death. This verse in Isaiah 56 is very clearly speaking of the time when Jesus would come and lay down his life for his friends and his enemies alike.

When he said, "my righteousness to be revealed" what was he talking about? I do hope that we can all see that this is speaking of the completely righteous life that Jesus did live, for Jesus alone was without sin. In this way, the righteousness of God was revealed in the life that Jesus did live.

2 Blessed is the man that doeth this, and the son of man that layeth hold on it; that keepeth the sabbath from polluting it, and keepeth his hand from doing any evil.

The will of God is just the same today, as when these words were first recorded by Isaiah. God does not change, and we should be able to understand that his instructions and promises in regard to the sabbath remains the same through out all ages. Only the devil would try to tell you any different. I believe this verse is also speaking of Jesus who set the example for all of us to follow in obeying the fourth commandment and did no evil.

3 Neither let the son of the stranger, (Gentile) that hath joined himself to the Lord, speak saying, The Lord hath utterly separated me from his people: neither let the eunuch say, Behold, I am a dry tree.

4 For thus saith the Lord unto the eunuchs that keep my sabbaths, and choose the things that please me, and take hold of my covenant;

5 Even unto them will I give in mine house and within my walls a place and a name better than of sons and of daughters: I will give them an everlasting name, that shall not be cut off.

In the first case, the stranger or Gentile, under the terms of the old covenant, it was required they all be circumcised or else they could not be accepted by the Israelites, and would not be accepted by God. However, God does have a promise for the Gentiles and we shall learn of it in verse six.

Let us then pay attention to verse five as it relates to the eunuchs who could not produce children naturally. God has promised them something better than sons and daughters and in fact he has promised them an everlasting name that shall not be cut off. Of course, this is speaking of the gift of eternal life and we do already know that there is only one way that we can receive it.

I must point out that to both the eunuchs and the strangers (Gentiles) that there are certain conditions that must be met in order to receive these promises.

These conditions are made clear in the sixth verse.

6 Also the sons of the stranger, that join themselves to the Lord, to serve him, and to love the name of the Lord, to be his servants, every one that keepeth the sabbath from polluting it, and taketh hold of my covenant;

7 Even them will I bring to my holy mountain, and make them joyful in my house of prayer: their burnt offerings and their sacrifices shall be accepted upon mine altar; for mine house shall be called an house of prayer for all people.

174

I want us to study the conditions of these promises very carefully. The eunuchs and the Gentiles must join them selves to the Lord, to serve him and to love the name of the Lord, and they are to observe the fourth commandment. During the time of the old covenant, the house of the Lord certainly was not called a house of prayer for all people, for under the terms of the old covenant, there were certain restrictions placed upon who could become a Jew. Therefore, we should be able to understand that in order for these promises to be fulfilled, it could only happen under the new covenant. In verse six we see that it includes everyone that keepeth the sabbath from polluting it, and take hold of my covenant. This is speaking of the covenant that is written with the blood of Jesus and when we take hold of this covenant, we do repent of our sins and do accept Jesus Christ as our Savior and allow him to be our Lord.

I realize that there are many who do have a hard time accepting this truth, so we shall go to the next verse which does verify that it is so.

8 The Lord God which gathereth the outcasts of Israel saith, Yet will I gather others to him, beside those that are gathered unto him.

First I want us to realize that within Israel, the true believers were few in number. There were many who claimed to be God's chosen people, but only a few who were actually converted in their hearts and did their best to live their lives in obedience to God's holy will. I believe this small minority was often shunned by the religious establishment, just as the prophets were. I believe that the "outcasts" of Israel is speaking of the small minority of people who did truly love God with all of their hearts.

Notice then, that to this small number of outcasts, he will add others, and gather them to himself. It should be very easy to see that this is speaking of the age of the Christian church and of the great commission to go into all the world and preach the Gospel unto every creature.

Before we go any further, I do want you to review all that we have read so far in Isaiah 56 and take notice how very important the fourth commandment is to God.

Keeping the sabbath day holy and not polluting it does bind all of these verses together, and it should be clear that this is a condition that is to be met during the age of the Christian religion.

The next verse is very important and we must set it aside and find some other verses to help us to better understand it.

9 All ye beasts of the field, come to devour, yea, all ye beasts in the forest.

It should be very clear that this is speaking of a day of God's judgment and it does go with the very things that Isaiah did describe in earlier chapters. What does make it unique is that in these verses, it is not speaking of under the old covenant, but of the time that is described in the previous verse. I am absolutely sure that this verse is speaking of what will take place shortly after the day of seven thunders does occur.

Jesus did have this to say, regarding this same time

Matthew 24:28, For wheresoever the carcass is, there will the eagles be gathered together.

Luke 17:37, Wheresoever the body is, thither will the eagles be gathered together.

The land where Christians dwell will be filled with death, and the carnivorous animals and the vultures will feast upon the dead bodies of animals and humans alike.

We shall now look once more to the book of Revelation and keep in mind that the things contained in this book were given to John to write down by our Lord Jesus Christ who announced that he is both the alpha and omega. The beginning and the end.

Revelation 6:8 And I looked, and behold a pale horse: and his name that sat on him was Death, and Hell followed with him.

And power was given unto them over the fourth part of the earth, to kill with sword, and with hunger, and with death, and with the beasts of the earth.

I do hope that we can all understand that the ninth verse of Isaiah is speaking of the very same things that Jesus did speak of both in Matthew 24 and Luke 17 and again in the book of Revelation. Animals and or fowls feasting upon dead bodies are common to all of these scriptures.

Let us move on in our study in Isaiah and see if we can learn why this strange ninth verse does appear in this chapter. Let us not forget that verse eight did inform us beyond any doubt that it is speaking of a time when God would gather others to him, beside the outcasts of Israel.

In others words, during the time of Christianity.

10 His watchmen are blind: they are all ignorant, they are all dumb dogs, they cannot bark: sleeping, lying down, loving to slumber.

11 Yea, they are greedy dogs which can never have enough, and they are shepherds that cannot understand: they all look to their gain, from his quarter.

I must point out that the word shepherd and pastor do come from the same word (*poimen*) in Greek. These verses are describing the pastors of many Christian churches during these latter days. Please do keep in mind that this is not my words but are the words of the prophet Isaiah. He is the very same man who did write the very beautiful words describing Jesus we read in the 53rd chapter.

Just who are these pastors, you are probably wondering? If we will but cling to our spiritual understanding, this last verse will identify them, beyond any doubt.

12 Come ye, say they, I will fetch wine, and we will fill ourselves with strong drink, and to-morrow shall be as this day, and much more abundant.

The wine that is mentioned here is the wine that is used in the mass. It is fermented wine and to use such wine as being symbolic of the pure blood of Jesus is an abomination, to say the least. If we were to study this subject, we would learn that at our Lord's last supper, they did drink from the fruit of the vine, which is very pure grape juice. I realize that many religious men will not agree, for they prefer fermented wine, but never the less, I do remain firm in my belief. I have thoroughly studied this subject, and know that even as Jesus was without sin, so must the fruit of the vine remain pure and without fermentation, in order to be the true symbol of the blood of Christ.

When the scripture in Isaiah 56 does mention "we will fill ourselves with strong drink" it is not speaking of alcoholic drink, but is symbolic and is speaking of a strong and intoxicating religious doctrine. It is foretelling of a time when certain religious leaders would form a new religious doctrine that is known as the doctrine of transubstantiation. I do realize that it is rather a big word, and it is a very important word, for it is the main foundation stone upon which the many Roman churches, as well as others, through out the world, do sit.

If we were to fully examine the beliefs of those courageous men and women who did participate in bringing to us the reformation, we would find that just about all of them did have one thing in common. That is they all completely rejected the false doctrine of transubstantiation, for they did recognize it to be contrary to the Word of God and a form of robbery.

Looking back to the early days of Christianity, I can imagine that many of the church leaders were impressed by the complete power demonstrated by the emperors of Rome. I believe this was especially the case during the time when Constantine claimed to have been converted to the Christian religion, even though he quite openly did cling to many things that were of Pagan origin. Perhaps some were even a little jealous of his total power during the time when he did preside over the meeting of religious leaders at the Nicene council.

It does appear that Constantine became the role model they tried very hard to copy, when they did form the high office of the Papacy. Even though they did claim that Peter was the first Pope, in reality we can not find any substance to this claim, for it is very easy to see the resemblance between the various popes and the Roman emperors. They did dress alike, they did speak alike and did both sit upon a throne as highly exalted rulers and did even share the same title.

It was in the year of 63 B.C. when Julius Caesar was officially recognized as the "Pontifex Maximus." This did mean that he was the supreme ruler over all of the Roman Empire, but also that he was the divine head of the religion of Rome, which did originate in Babylon. Of course, the mystery religion of Babylon and later of Rome was very clearly Pagan during the reign of Julius Caesar when he did assume this title.

It does seem a bit strange that the leaders of the Roman brand of Christianity would cling to this title, which was so obviously Pagan in it's origin.

Perhaps it was because they wanted the fullness of the power that went with this Pagan title, for a great many people over hundreds of years were forced to bow and to worship the one who did claim to be the Pontifex Maximus.

In contrast, we find in Acts 10 that Peter would not allow the centurion, nor the people at his home to bow down and worship at his feet.

Acts 10:24, And the morrow after they entered into Caesarea. And Cornelius waited for them, and had called together his kinsmen and near friends.

25 And as Peter was coming in, Cornelius met him, and fell down at his feet, and worshipped him.

26 But Peter took him up, saying, Stand up; I myself also am a man.

I believe these verses certainly do make it very clear that the many Popes do not follow this example set by Peter, but follow the example set by the Caesars, for they insist that they be worshipped as God. Of course, they do sit in their temple, wearing the clothing and crown of a divine ruler, showing the whole world that they are as God, and are not mere men, as Peter did claim to be.

In order to gain the power of the Roman emperors, the religious leaders must have thought long and hard in order to devise a plan. Of course, it should not be too hard to understand that ignorance would become a tool in their hands. They soon began to take steps to insure that people would remain ignorant by taking control of written material, as much as possible. Much later in time this would lead to the burning of many books, including Bibles, and in this way, they did help create the darkness of the dark ages. Surely, we are all aware that the main reason for the darkness of the dark ages was the suppression of knowledge.

Peter did warn us of people who would "wrest" or twist the Word of God, even to their own destruction. How very strange it is, that the very people that Peter did warn us of, are the ones who claim that Peter was the founder and head of their church. I say it is strange for even though they do make this claim, they do not in any way follow Peter.

Peter was a follower of Christ, and they are opposed to the way Jesus lived. Jesus lived in complete obedience to the commandments of God, his Father but they do reject those same commandments and do prefer the commandments of Constantine.

Even today, they do esteem Sunday very high as a day of worship, but the seventh day, the day that God blessed and set aside as a day of rest and worship, they despise and treat as common.

Chapter 16 The Last Supper

Now to increase our understanding of how they formed their false doctrine concerning the wine used at every service, we must go to the gospel of Matthew and learn of how they did twist and distort the true meaning of God's Holy Word.

Matthew 16:13, When Jesus came to the coasts of Caesarea Philippi, he asked his disciples, saying, whom do men say that I the son of man am?

14 And they said, Some say thou art John the Baptist: some Elias; and others, Jeremiah or one of the prophets.

15 He saith unto them, But whom say ye that I am?

16 And Simon Peter answered and said,

Thou art the Christ, the Son of the living God.

17 And Jesus answered and said unto him, Blessed art thou, Simon Barjona: for flesh and blood hath not revealed it unto thee, but my Father which is in heaven.

18 And I say also unto thee, That thou art Peter, and upon this rock I will build my church; and the gates of hell shall not prevail against it.

The very first thing we must do, is establish just what the rock really is, that Jesus did speak of. When Jesus said "Thou art Peter," (petros, a small stone) he did not mean to imply that somehow Peter was a rock, (petra, a massive rock) for the rock is symbolic of something firm and solid and the starting place to build a foundation.

The rock that Jesus was speaking of is the solid rock (petras) of his true identity. Jesus was saying that he would build his church on the solid truth that he was truly the Christ, the anointed one and the Son of the living God. His identity is an immutable truth and cannot be changed. Therefore, it is the rock and a very solid rock, and the church that Jesus is continuing to build, is built on this solid truth.

If we believe that Jesus chose to build his church upon Peter and that he was the solid rock of the foundation for his church, then we are all in trouble. Even on the same night that Jesus was betrayed, Peter did reveal how unstable he was by denying three times that he even knew Jesus. What is more, in doing so he very clearly revealed that he was also a liar, for what else could we call what he did?

Even so, we know that Jesus was able to see beyond that night and knew that Peter would become a fisher of men and a pillar of the church, symbolically speaking, in time to come. However, in this regard, so were the other apostles for they were chosen and given the duty of going forth to establish churches in Judea and Samaria and through out the whole earth.

Let us now listen to another man who helped to establish many churches through out Asia Minor and beyond. Of course, I am speaking of that world traveler and evangelist and apostle, Paul, who did contribute so much to our new testament by the letters he did write.

Ephesians 2:19, Now therefore ye are no more strangers and foreigners, but fellow-citizens with the saints, and of the household of God;

20 And are built upon the foundation of the apostles and prophets, Jesus Christ himself being the chief corner stone;

I hope by studying this verse that we can understand that Paul believed the Christian church was built upon the foundation of the writings of the old testament prophets, and upon the teaching and preaching of the twelve apostles, and that our Lord Jesus Christ was and is the chief corner and most important stone. Of course, Peter is included in this foundation, but we must not think for one moment that he is the entire foundation. If we do believe that Jesus did build his church upon Peter and only Peter, then it does go against every thing that Jesus did teach, including the lesson of the foot washing at the last supper.

Let us look to what happened as it is recorded in the gospel of Mark.

Mark 10:35, And James and John, the sons of Zebedee, come unto him, saying, Master, we would that thou shouldest do for us whatsoever we desire.

36 And he said unto them, What would ye that I should do for you?

37 They said unto him, Grant unto us that we may sit, one on thy right hand, and the other on thy left hand, in thy glory.

38 But Jesus said unto them, Ye know not what ye ask: can ye drink of the cup that I drink of? and be baptized with the baptism that I am baptized with?

39 And they said unto him, We can. And Jesus said unto them, Ye shall indeed drink of the cup that I drink of; and with the baptism that I am baptized withal shall ye be baptized.

40 But to sit on my right hand and on my left hand is not mine to give; but it shall be given to them (plural) for whom it is prepared.

I want for us to consider both what they were asking and the answer that Jesus did give to them. Of course, the custom of the times and in that part of the world was for the second in command to sit at the right hand of the king, and the next in rank to sit upon the left.

Now if Jesus had really chosen to build his church upon Peter as the leaders of Roman religion do claim, then Jesus would have told them at this time, that the place on his right was reserved for Peter and the place on the left was to remain vacant. Of course, Jesus did not say this, for it certainly was not his intention to build his church upon mortal men with feet of clay but on himself, the Messiah and true Son of God. Let us listen as Jesus continued to address this subject.

41 And when the ten heard it, they began to be much displeased with James and John.

42 But Jesus called them to him, and saith unto them, Ye know that they which are accounted to rule over the Gentiles exercise lordship over them; and their great ones exercise authority upon them.

43 But so shall it not be among you: but whosoever will be great among you, shall be your minister;

44 And whosoever of you will be the chiefest, shall be servant of all.

He did not say that one of them would sit upon a throne as the highly exalted ruler over them. Jesus did not say that one of them would wear a man made crown like a king. He did not say that people would bow down and kiss the hands and feet of the one who wore the crown. What he did very clearly say is that not one of them would be exalted or rule over the others, for they were to all be servants of one another. This is also the lesson that was taught at our Lord's last supper.

In Galatians, our brother Paul did have this to say...

Galatians 2:7, But contrariwise, when they saw that the gospel of the uncircumcision (Gentiles) was committed unto me, as the gospel of the circumcision was unto Peter;

8 (For he that wrought effectually in Peter to the apostleship of the circumcision, (Israel) the same was mighty in me toward the Gentiles;)

I want for us to notice that even as God had called Peter to take the gospel message to the nation of Israel, so was Paul called to preach the good news to the Gentile people through out the earth. In this regard, they were even, and one was not above the other.

Paul then had this to say more, concerning these things.

9 And when James, Cephas, (Peter) and John, who seemed to be pillars (in the church), perceived the grace that was given unto me, they gave to me and Barnabas the right hand of fellow-ship; that we should go unto the heathen, (Gentiles) and they unto the circumcision. (Israel)

Surely it is not hard to understand that Peter, James and John, who seemed to be pillars of the church, were not above or more exalted than were Paul and Barnabas, for though they were given to preach the gospel to different people, they were all equal. There is more that Paul did say in this letter that we need to learn, and we must remember that it is Paul that did write these words.

14 But when I saw that they (Peter, James and John) did not walk uprightly according to the truth of the gospel, I said

unto Peter before them all, If thou being a Jew, livest after the manner of the Gentiles, and not as do the Jews, why compellest thou the Gentiles to live as do the Jews?

In this way, Paul did rebuke Peter to his face and before the other apostles, who were there. How could Paul do this, if Jesus had chosen to build his church upon Peter, as the leaders of Roman religion do claim? Don't you find this a bit strange?

I have shared these verses with you in an effort to reveal unto you the truth of God's word and to expose the false teaching that Jesus would choose to build his church upon just one of his disciples. We shall now return to the 16th chapter of the gospel of Matthew and listen as Jesus does have more to say unto Peter.

19 And I will give unto thee the keys of the kingdom of heaven:

Before we go any further, we must determine two different things. First, we must come to a better understanding of what the kingdom of heaven, really was and is, that Jesus was speaking of. In the same manner, we must determine what the keys were, that Jesus did promise to give to Peter, for it should be clear that they were not given to Peter at the time of this conversation. This conversation did precede the denial by Peter that he even knew Jesus, let alone, that he was a friend and follower of the man from Galilee they held as prisoner.

We shall now search for a little more information regarding the kingdom of heaven. In the gospel of Matthew we find....

Matthew 3:1, In those days came John the Baptist, preaching in the wilderness of Judea,

2 And saying, Repent ye: for the kingdom of heaven is at hand.

We then go to the gospel of Mark and we learn that Mark did write of this saying...

Mark 1:14, Now after that John was put in prison, Jesus came into Galilee, preaching the gospel of the kingdom of God,

15 And saying, The time is fulfilled, and the kingdom of God is at hand: repent ye, and believe the gospel.

We see then, that both John the Baptist and our Lord Jesus Christ did teach that the time of the kingdom of God and the kingdom of heaven was at hand. In other words, they were not speaking of something far off in the future, but of something that was present during the time in which they were living.

Turning to the gospel of Luke we listen to these words spoken by Jesus regarding the time of the kingdom.

Luke 16:16, The law and the prophets (old testament) were until John: since that time the kingdom of God is preached, and every man presseth into it.

It should be clear that again Jesus does speak of the kingdom as being present at that time. However, in the 18th chapter he does speak of how difficult it is, for certain people to enter into the kingdom of God.

Luke 18:24, And when Jesus saw that he was sorrowful, he said, How hardly shall they that have riches enter into the kingdom of God!

25 For it is easier for a camel to go through a needle's eye, than for a rich man to enter into the kingdom of God.

It is interesting to note that it was not impossible for a camel to enter through the eye of a needle, for this was what they called a certain type of entrance into the walled cities. It did require that the camel get down on their knees and bow down, in order to duck under the wall. In this way, it is hard for a rich man to humble himself before God, because of his personal pride.

I am sure that many are wondering if the kingdom of heaven and the kingdom of God are the same. We must ask, who is it that does live in heaven? Of course, it has always been the home of Almighty God, Jehovah. Therefore it should not be too hard to understand that the kingdom of heaven and the kingdom of God are speaking of exactly the same thing.

Most people think of it as being somewhere beyond the clouds and perhaps even beyond the atmosphere of earth. However, we shall allow the Bible, the Word of God to reveal unto us the location of the kingdom as it is important to us. Listen to these words spoken by Jesus.

Luke 17:20, And when he was demanded of the Pharisees, when the kingdom of God should come, he answered them and said, The kingdom of God cometh not with observation:

21 Neither shall they say, Lo here! or, lo there! for behold, the kingdom of God is within you.

It is very important that we understand that Jesus did tell them that they could not see the kingdom of God with human eyes. We can be sure that it is not someplace high in the sky, with Peter waiting by the pearly gates.

Notice also that Jesus said that it is not here or over there, for it is within us. This means that it is not a physical kingdom, as so many people believe, but is an invisible spiritual place, where the Holy Ghost does reside. Surely we can remember that Jesus promised us that both he and his Father would make their abode within us. When this does take place, when one does repent of their sins, the kingdom of God is within us. However, it does not exist within those who do believe but refuse to surrender to God, and refuse to repent of their sins. The kingdom of God must include the government of God and Jesus must be the one who does sit upon the throne within us.

Now that we know the true location of the kingdom of heaven and of God according to the scripture, it will be much easier to identify the keys to the kingdom.

Down through the ages, a great many people have no doubt formed the picture in their minds of Saint Peter waiting by the pearly gates of heaven, having the keys in his hand, and the authority to decide who does enter in and who is barred from entry. Many stories have been told that have painted this picture of Peter and the keys.

Perhaps this was the picture that did exist within the minds of some of the early church leaders, and they might have become jealous of Peter, because they did believe that Jesus did choose to bestow this great gift on him alone. I believe that they did seek to have complete power over the people and they saw the keys to the kingdom as the means to gain that power.

If we were to go to the 2nd chapter of The Acts we would soon learn about the day of Pentecost, when those to whom the promise was given, did receive the power from on high.

When Peter did receive the baptism in the Holy Ghost, he also received the keys that Jesus did promise him.

Perhaps we can remember that Peter did preach the gospel message that day with such conviction that it did produce this response from the people.

Acts 2:37, Now when they heard this, they were pricked in their heart, and said unto Peter and to the rest of the apostles, Men and brethern, what shall we do?

38 Then Peter said unto them, Repent, and be baptized every one of you in the name of Jesus Christ for the remission of sins, and ye shall receive the gift of the Holy Ghost.

To this we must ask, What is the gift of the Holy Ghost? The answer is fairly simple for the gift of the Holy Ghost is the same as the gift of God as Paul did explain in his letter to the Romans. Paul did say that the wages of sin is death but the gift of God is eternal life. In order to receive this gift, one must be born again.

Surely, we can remember that Jesus did say unto Nicodemus that unless a person become born again, they could not see, nor understand, nor enter into the kingdom of God. The born again experience is absolutely essential to salvation, but it was something the leaders of Roman religion did not understand.

The keys to the kingdom that Jesus gave unto Peter was the anointing of the Holy Spirit, which enabled Peter to preach with super natural power and his preaching did bear much fruit.

41 Then they that gladly received his word were baptized: and the same day there were added unto them about three thousand souls.

So we can see that Peter did use his keys that day, which was the anointing of the Holy Ghost to preach super naturally and the doorway into the hearts of three thousand Jews were opened by the salvation message. The keys that opened their hearts was Peter's very anointed preaching with conviction. They are not the keys to the pearly gates of heaven, but are the keys that open the hearts of ordinary sinners, and cause them to repent of their sins.

Chapter 17 Two Different Plans

We need to come to a better understanding of the keys to the kingdom, as it is taught by the Roman brand of religion.

We can be sure that the early church leaders did search through out the scriptures, looking for a way in which they could find the keys that Jesus promised to give unto Peter. Their goal must have been to seize them and wrest them away from Peter, any way they could, for they saw the keys to the kingdom as the means to gain power over all people.

After much searching for a way to gain their goal, they must have come to realize that our salvation does depend upon the blood that Jesus shed for us. Therefore, it does appear that they came to the conclusion that the keys they were searching for, were in the blood of Jesus, and they must find a way to become the ones in control of the blood of Jesus. I say this, for I even have a book in my possession, written by a person of Roman religion, that does clearly state in the title that "The Keys Are of This Blood."

I know beyond any doubt that if Jesus did not shed his blood for us, there could not be any salvation, for only the blood of a perfect sacrifice, that is without sin, could pay the price of the debt of our sins. Surely it is not at all difficult to understand that Jesus became our scapegoat when he died for our sins. Even so, as Jesus hung upon the cross and just before he died, he said "It is finished." We can be very sure that following his death there would be no more need for any more blood to be shed. The scriptures do inform us that he died once and for all, the price of our sins was paid in full.

We can be very sure that the keys that Jesus gave unto Peter were not in the blood, as so many people do believe. One of the claims of Roman religion is that their priests and only their priests do have the power to change the elements of bread and wine into the flesh and blood of Christ, during the mass ritual. We must ask, is there any where to be found in the scriptures, that would indicate there is a need for the wine to be changed into the blood and the bread into flesh? This ritual seems to imply that what Jesus did for us was not enough, and there is more that must be done by the priests.

The position of Roman religion is summed up in the catholic encyclopedia, in this manner.

" In the celebration of the Holy Mass, the bread and wine are changed into the body and blood of Christ. It is called transubstantiation, for in the Sacrament of the Eucharist the substance of bread and wine do not remain, but the entire substance of bread is changed into the body of Christ, and the entire substance of wine is changed into his blood, the species or outward semblance of bread and wine alone remaining."

I do want us to think about this claim and for us to realize how very contrary and unacceptable it really is. I also want us to consider how much such a teaching actually disagrees with scripture, for the consumption of human flesh and the drinking of blood is certainly forbidden in God's Holy Word. We can be very sure that Jesus could never advocate such a thing for it would mean that he was in direct opposition to the Word of God. To partake of the flesh and blood of Jesus in the literal sense, by eating the flesh and drinking the blood would be to engage in the act of cannibalism, which of course, our Lord and Savior would never ask us to do.

Let us now examine the scripture in the gospel of Matthew and try to discern the real meaning of what Jesus said.

Matthew 26:26, And as they were eating, Jesus took bread, and blessed it, and brake it, and gave it to the disciples, and said, Take, eat; this is my body.

27 And he took the cup, and gave thanks, and gave it to them, saying, Drink ye all of it;

28 For this is my blood of the new testament, which is shed for many for the remission of sins.

We must consider these verses very carefully. When Jesus said, "take and eat, this is my body," it could only mean that he was speaking of the bread as being the symbol of his body. Jesus was alive and well, and he was certainly living in his real body when he said these words. It should not be too difficult to understand that he did not mean it to be taken literally, for it is obvious that his words can only be properly understood in a figurative sense.

When Jesus said, "Drink ye all of it; for this is my blood of the new testament, which is shed for many for the remission of sins," he actually meant that the fruit of the vine, which was in the cup was symbolic of his blood. At the time that Jesus did say these things, his blood was in his body and flowing through his veins. Therefore, we should be able to understand that he was speaking of what would happen to him in the near future and he was speaking in a figurative sense.

To take these same scriptures and give them a literal meaning, when it was very clearly meant symbolically, is to twist and distort the true meaning of the Word of God. It certainly does not require someone with a college degree to discern the symbolic meaning of what Jesus did say, for it should be obvious to anyone with common sense.

There cannot be any doubt but what the purpose of twisting the meaning of these verses really was, for it was to manufacture their own keys to the kingdom of heaven. If the keys to the kingdom were really literal keys, then Saint Peter must have become rather weary from waiting so long for the resurrection. However, if we find they were spiritual keys, then when Peter died, they would return to our Lord Jesus, seated at the right hand of his Father, and he could give them to whosoever he did choose.

Doesn't it seem kind of strange that God would leave our salvation in the hands of religious men, and not in the hands of our risen Savior?

As we shall see, the plan of Roman religion does leave God completely out of it. I say this for they claim that each Pope in succession has inherited the keys from the previous Pope, and they seem to be completely ignorant of the fact that once Jesus shed his blood, it was finished and there is no more need for more blood. The blood that Jesus shed was quite enough, for all time.

The claim of Roman religion is that they are the only ones who can change the wine into the blood of Jesus, and do claim they are the only ones who can change the bread into the flesh and body of Christ. In this way, they claim that salvation of souls is in their hands and only in their hands. They would have us to believe that no one can enter into the kingdom of heaven without their permission.

Jesus does not have anything to say about it, for they do claim to be the Vicars of Christ, which does mean they are the religious men who have replaced Christ and are now fulfilling his duties here on earth. Because so many Popes have believed they really did have this power, they became intoxicated by it and were deceived by their own invention.

Men such as Martin Luther and others of Roman religion, who had the opportunity to study the scriptures realized what a terrible and false doctrine was the main foundation stone upon which the Roman church does sit. A great many dear men and women were tortured and burned to death at the stake, because they spoke out against this false doctrine, and would not repent.

It is my guess that more people died from opposing this particular doctrine than any other. However, this was not the only reason, for we must not forget what happened to Joan of Arc, and why the Pope sentenced her to such a cruel death.

In the gospel of John and in the tenth chapter, Jesus did use a parable to increase some people's knowledge, while the deeper meaning remained hidden from others.

John 10:6, This parable spake Jesus unto them: but they understood not what things they were which he spake unto them.

7 Then said Jesus unto them again, Verily, verily, I say unto you, I am the door of the sheep.

8 All that ever came before me are thieves and robbers: but the sheep did not hear them.

9 I am the door: by me if any man enter in, he shall be saved, and shall go in and out, and find pasture.

I do hope that we all understand Jesus has informed us in the Word of God, that he is the door of our salvation. In the gospel of John, Thomas did ask Jesus this question, and Jesus did answer him.

John 14:5, Thomas saith unto him, Lord, we know not whither thou goest; and how can we know the way?

6 Jesus saith unto him, I am the way, the truth, and the life: no man cometh unto the Father, but by me.

Notice that Jesus did not inform Thomas that he was to stay on the good side of Peter, for only Peter had the keys to the kingdom, and only Peter could give him permission to find the way to follow Jesus to where he was going. If Peter was to become the way and the gate keeper as taught by Roman religion, would not Jesus have advised Thomas accordingly? The reason Jesus did not do this is because it is not true.

Another scripture comes to my mind and it is the one about the death of Lazarus. The scriptures do inform us that Lazarus was very ill and Jesus had been asked to come and to heal him. However, Jesus did not come right away and when he did come, he learned that his friend had died.

John 11:1, Now a certain man was sick, named Lazarus, of Bethany, the town of Mary and her sister Martha.

5 Now Jesus loved Martha, and her sister, and Lazarus.

6 When he had heard therefore that he was sick, he abode two days still in the same place where he was.

20 Then Martha, as soon as she heard that Jesus was coming, went and met him: but Mary sat still in the house.

21 Then said Martha unto Jesus, Lord, if thou hadst been here, my brother had not died.

22 But I know, that even now, whatsoever thou wilt ask of God, God will give it thee.

23 Jesus saith unto her, Thy brother shall rise again.

24 Martha saith unto him, I know that he shall rise again in the resurrection at the last day.

25 Jesus said unto her, I am the resurrection, and the life: he that believeth in me, though he were dead, yet shall he live:

26 And whosoever liveth and believeth in me shall never die. Believest thou this?

27 She saith unto him, Yea Lord: I believe that thou art the Christ, the Son of God, which should come into the world.

We should be able to see from these verses that for Peter to have become the gate keeper of heaven, that it has become a little more complicated. If we are to take these things literal, then we need to consider them more carefully.

The thing we need to understand that if these things be literal, it is important that in order to enter in through the pearly gates of heaven, one must first have risen from the dead. When Jesus said that he is the resurrection and the life, it should be very plain that there is a need for a resurrection, for one can not enter into the literal kingdom, unless they first be resurrected from the dead.

We must ask the question, "Did Peter have the power of the resurrection and was he able to pass this power down to the leaders of the Roman religion, to the Popes, one after another?" Let us become aware of what the apostle Paul had to say regarding the resurrection.

1st Thessalonians 4:16, For the Lord himself shall descend from heaven with a shout, with the voice of the arch-angel, and with the trump of God: and the dead in Christ shall rise first.

In light of what this verse does clearly say, it does appear that the dead in Christ, once they are risen from the dead, still need to approach Peter at the pearly gates and gain his permission to enter into heaven? Oh what utter foolishness has been invented by greedy men seeking to gain power over people who are ignorant concerning the Word of God.

Let us look further to the scriptures. In the Revelation we find Jesus saying this to John.

Revelation 1:17, Fear not; I am the first and the last:

18 I am he that liveth, and was dead; and behold, I am alive for evermore, Amen; and have the keys of hell (the grave) and of death.

I do want to be sure that you understand that it is Jesus and Jesus alone that has the keys of hell (the grave) and of death. It was never given to Peter, nor was it passed down from one Pope to the next.

This power of death and over death, and of the grave and the resurrection from the grave belongs to the Lamb that is worthy and his name is Jesus.

To this knowledge we must add this verse that was addressed to the church of Philadelphia. (brotherly love)

Revelation 3:6 He that hath an ear, let him hear what the Spirit saith unto the churches.

7 And to the angel of the church in Philadelphia write; These things saith he that is holy, he that is true, he that hath the key of David, he that openeth, and no man shutteth; and shutteth, and no man openeth.

Here we are to see who truly does have the keys to eternal life. Jesus is the one that is holy and the one that is true. Jesus is the one who has never told a lie and he is the only one.

Even at this time, as I sit at my desk and place my thoughts on paper which I hope will soon be delivered unto you, the door of salvation is open wide, and whosoever will come, is welcome to come to the cross of our Lord, Jesus Christ, and to lay their burdens down. I have tried to make it very clear that God's one and only plan of salvation does not exclude anyone, for it is for all people of all races.

It is important that we realize that the door of our salvation is open, and no man can close it, or deny unto us the love of God and deny unto us, that we enter in through the door that still remains open. Our salvation is in the hand of our Lord Jesus, and in his hands alone, for he is the author and the finisher of our faith.

In the same way, on that day when many missiles do begin to lift up from either the sea or from their land based launch pads, the door of salvation will be closed by the hand of Almighty God, and in that day, just as Jesus has informed us, no man will be able to open it. Not the pastor nor the priest, and not even the highly exalted leader of Roman religion, for Jesus has said that no man will be able to open it.

Beneath his priestly robes and under his funny looking hat, the Pope is just a man, and even with all of his power over people which they have given him, he remains just a man and a rather frail man at that. I say this for he is a man who has been deceived by the lies of those who have preceded him and will himself be held accountable for the lies he does teach.

So we can certainly see that God has only one plan for our salvation and that plan has been revealed unto us in the Word of God. Roman religion has a completely different plan and it cannot be found in the Bible, for it is not contained in the Word of God. Therefore, we must think of it as the plan of salvation according to religious men, for they are the ones who are the author of it. In no way can we claim that Jesus is the author of Roman religion, for it is completely contrary to the Word of God.

I want us to examine these next verses for they are important for us to better understand God's one and only plan.

Hebrews 10:9, Then said he, (Jesus) Lo, I come to do thy will, O God. He taketh away the first, (covenant) that he may establish the second. (covenant)

10 By the which will we are sanctified (set apart) through the offering of the body of Jesus Christ once for all.

11 And every priest standeth daily ministering and offering oftentimes the same sacrifices, which can never take away sins,

12 But this man (Jesus), after he had offered one sacrifice for sins for ever, sat down on the right hand of God.

I want us to notice that according to these verses that Jesus offered one sacrifice for sins forever. Therefore we must ask, why then, is there a need for more blood?

According to the Roman plan, when ever the so called miracle of changing the bread into the flesh of Jesus, and the changing of the wine they do drink, into the blood of Jesus, they do show that, of necessity, that they have sacrificed Jesus each time this ritual is performed. Each time the mass is repeated, they do symbolically crucify Jesus again, for the bread must become flesh and the wine turned into blood, for it is in this way they do claim to have the keys of heaven.

We must try to understand their purpose in claiming this. It is because they do realize that it is by the precious blood of Jesus that does cleanse us from our sins. They claim that they are the only ones who can cleanse us from our sins for they claim that they are the only ones that can change ordinary wine into the blood of Jesus. In this way they do continue to nail Jesus to the cross again and again and again. It is a doctrine of endless repetition and in reality, it does not accomplish anything, for it is completely contrary to God's one and only plan of salvation.

The Bible does reveal unto us, that Jesus instituted a new ritual and memorial service on the same night that he was betrayed. We call this service the Lord's supper and some call it the Lord's passover, but what is most important is that we realize that it is a memorial service, and is not a means of salvation.

Let us turn to the eleventh chapter of 1st Corinthians and learn more about this in this letter written by Paul.

1st Corinthians 11:24, And when he had given thanks, he brake it (the bread) and said, Take, eat: this is my body, which is broken for you: this do in remembrance of me.

This very clearly indicates that this is to be a memorial.

25 After the same manner also he took the cup, when he had supped, saying, This cup is the new testament in my blood: this do ye, as oft as ye drink it, in remembrance of me.

26 For as often as ye eat this bread, and drink this cup, ye do show the Lord's death till he come.

The first thing I want to bring to our attention is that the Lord did break the bread, and of course, this was unleavened bread. This is made without any leavening and does resemble pie crust in that it is rather brittle and easily broken.

We find that this is not the bread that is most often used in the churches that practice Roman religion, for they do use a small round wafer and it is not broken in the manner and example that Jesus did set before us. I have been told that the round wafers do resemble the ancient sun discs that were used in religious rituals of the Babylonian mystery religions.

Also, we are told twice in these verses that these things are to be done as a memorial of the Lord's death. Again I say, this memorial is not a means of salvation: rather it is in memory of what Jesus did do for us, so that we could become as one with the Father. It is a service for those who have repented of their sins and have become born again. It is not a service for those who want to be saved, nor is it a way in which anyone will be saved. It is very clearly a memorial service for those who have already accepted Jesus as their Savior and have made him their Lord.

There is a warning concerning this in these next few verses.

27 Wherefore whosoever shall eat this bread, and drink this cup of the Lord, unworthily, shall be guilty of the body and blood of the Lord.

28 But let a man examine himself, and so let him eat of that bread, and drink of that cup.

29 For he that eateth and drinketh unworthily, eateth and drinketh damnation to himself, not discerning the Lord's body.

30 For this cause many are weak and sickly among you, and many sleep. (dead)

I do hope that these verses do make it abundantly clear that the memorial service of the Lord's supper is not for those who are not yet born again, but is reserved for those who have already surrendered to God at the cross of our Lord Jesus Christ.

The next question that comes up is just how often should we have this special memorial service. We are aware that those who practice Roman religion do partake of the emblems of the sacrament at every service, but how often should the rest of us take part in the Lord's supper.

In verse 25 we see these instruction given by our Lord Jesus who said, "As oft as ye drink it, in remembrance of me." Again, in verse 26, For as often as ye eat this bread, and drink this cup, ye do show the Lord's death till he come. We see the word "often" and it has confused many.

Let us think of each of your children's birthdays and be aware that it is common to observe them as memorials, do we not? It is also the common practice to observe these birth days but once a year.

I want us to think for a moment what would likely be the result if we decided to observe the children's birthdays quarterly or even once a month. I say this for some churches do observe the Lord's last supper on a quarterly basis, and some even on a monthly basis and some, but once a year.

Surely, it is most likely that if we were to observe the children's birthdays more than once a year, and even on a quarterly basis, it is probable that after a while it would become very routine and could even become boring for the child. I believe this is the reason that most memorials such as birthdays and wedding anniversaries are celebrated but once a year, for in that way, they are very special and do remain precious to us.

I want us to focus on the word often as it does refer to the Lord's last supper memorial service. In the 9th chapter of Hebrews we shall find that same word as it is used in conjunction with what Jesus did at Calvary.

Hebrews 9:24, For Christ is not entered into the holy places made with hands, which are the figures of the true; but into heaven itself, now to appear in the presence of God for us:

25 Nor yet that he should offer himself often, as the high priest entereth into the holy place every year with blood of others;

26 For then must he often have suffered since the foundation of the world: but now once in the end of the world hath he appeared to put away sin by the sacrifice of himself.

We must now ask the question, "How often did the priest enter into the Holy of Holies to make an atonement for the sins of Israel?" The answer is but once a year and on the day that is well known among the Jewish people as Yom Kippur, the day of atonement.

Please do keep track of the word often, for the way it is used in these verses we can easily see that it means but once a year. This should make it very clear that according to God's time table, a memorial service should be held but once a year. To have a memorial service more than once a year, is to diminish it's true meaning, and cause it to become routine.

We must not forget that the main purpose of increasing our knowledge concerning the beautiful memorial service that was given unto us by our Lord Jesus, is to identify the religious men that Isaiah did write about. Let us return to the scriptures of Isaiah 56 and hope these verses will become more clear to our understanding.

Starting at verse nine, we see the future foretold, for Isaiah is speaking of the very same thing Jesus foretold in Matthew 24. That is Jesus did foretell that the time will come before he returns, that the eagles and vultures who feast on flesh, will be gathered where ever there is a dead body. In other words, it will be the time that is foretold in the Revelation, when the pale horse and it's rider whose name is Death, will dwell through out the land. Of course, Hell will accompany Death, for it is the time of God's judgment.

Isaiah 56:9, All ye beasts of the field, come to devour, yea, all ye beasts in the forest.

I want us to recall that saying I first received from my pastor. "As goes the family, so goes the church, as goes the church, so goes the nation." I want us to think about this as we look at the description of the religious leaders that are leading this nation into the judgment and great tribulation.

10 His watchmen are blind: they are all ignorant, they are all dumb dogs, they cannot bark; sleeping, lying down, loving to slumber.

11 Yea, they are greedy dogs which can never have enough, and they are shepherds (pastors) that cannot understand: they all look to their own way, every one for his gain from his quarter.

In verses ten and eleven we are given a description of these religious leaders who are leading our nation into the judgment. However, it is the twelfth verse that does give us the information to identify them beyond any doubt.

12 Come ye, say they, I will fetch wine, and we will fill ourselves with strong drink; (religious doctrine) and to-morrow shall be as this day, and much more abundant.

There is no point in discussing who it is that does use wine at every service, for we already do know about this. In the same way, those people who are able to discern spiritual things, it should be apparent that the strong drink mentioned in this verse is speaking of the strong religious doctrine of transubstantiation.

Now I fully realize that many will not be able to understand these things and it is possible that it is because they are following the men who are described in verses ten and eleven. The Word of God has informed us they are all ignorant and cannot understand. However, I do hope that you will be able to understand these things and be able to see how they are speaking of conditions within the Christian community at this present time.

I now want us to focus our minds on the last part of the last verse. It does quite clearly say that these people do claim that "tomorrow shall be as this day."

The first thing we must establish is that this is speaking of two days that are next to each other in numerical sequence. This is really very simple and only a person who is confused would try to make this more complicated than it needs to be. This verse mentions "this day" and then it speaks of to-morrow, and we already know that it is speaking of the time just before the judgment.

In order we determine which day tom-morrow is, we must first establish which day is "this day." The entire chapter from verse one through verse seven does inform us of how very important it is to God that his people continue to keep his sabbath day holy. Now we know beyond any doubt that the weekly sabbath which was created holy by Almighty God in the beginning is the seventh day. On our modern day calendars the seventh day is given the name Saturday.

The day that follows Saturday, is the day that is called Sunday, and it is the first day of the week. The commandments of God very clearly command us to remember **the** seventh day, **not a** seventh day, and to keep it holy.

As we have learned, for it is written in the pages of history, the Roman emperor whose name was Constantine did issue an edict that all of the people of Rome except for farmers were to set the first day of the week aside and were to work on the seventh day.

Now to make this verse even more clear to those who are having a hard time understanding what this means, I want us to look once more at this verse only this time we will insert the days this verse is speaking of.

12 Come ye, say they, (priests and pastors) I will fetch wine, and we will fill ourselves with strong religious doctrine. And Sunday, shall be as the seventh day sabbath, and much more abundant.

The last part where the sleepy shepherds and pastors do claim that Sunday shall be as the sabbath day and more abundant, they are saying that it is a better day to worship God, than is the day that God created for rest and worship.

It should not be at all hard for us to understand that these verses are speaking of the very days in which we are living, for today, the great majority of Christian leaders do claim that Sunday is a better day to worship God, than is the day created and chosen of

God. However, in doing so, they do reveal they are the ones who are described in verses ten and eleven.

I must also point out that it is not necessary for a religious leader to embrace both of these religious doctrines in order to be a leader who is leading this nation into judgment. We can be very sure that the Word of God is true, and if a pastor or a priest does cling to and teach by example, either one of these two false doctrines, then they are the ones that are described here.

I do suppose that most of us have always considered the Catholic churches to be much different than the various different Protestant churches. As we can see in God's Holy Word, He has taken both of them and brought them together as one. The reason this is so is because both of them do cling very tightly to their Babylonian doctrines and refuse to let go of them. Both of these doctrines were strictly enforced by the Rulers of Roman religion during the 1260 year reign of the beast and many were burned to death at the stake.

Peter does have something to say that should be of interest to all of us.

1st Peter 1:19, We have also a more sure word of prophecy; whereunto ye do well that ye take heed, as unto a light that shineth in a dark place, until the day dawn, and the day star arise in your hearts;

20 Knowing this first, that no prophecy of the scripture is of any private interpretation.

I want you to be aware that the knowledge contained in these verses are not my own private interpretation of the scriptures. These verses are written in your Bibles as well as mine. The meaning of these verses is available to all, but not all will be able to understand them, because they do follow the sleepy shepherds, and it is possible that they do believe a lie. The apostle Paul did have this to say, regarding those people who prefer to continue in their religious tradition, rather than obey the truth of God's Holy Word.

2nd Thessalonians 2:10, And with all deceivableness of unrighteousness in them that perish; because they received not the love of the truth, that they might be saved.

11 And for this cause God shall send them strong delusion, that they should believe a lie.

I must point out the people that Paul is speaking of are not ungodly people, who do not believe in God. He is speaking of religious people who do not love the truth. Many of these people do know that the sabbath of the Lord is not Sunday, but do continue in Sunday for they consider it to be more established as well as convenient.

In this way, they do use the Lord's day, the seventh day sabbath to do whatever they do choose, such as shopping and cleaning, and yard work as well as recreation and then do attend church on Sunday. In this way, they place their own desires first and God is second, and they have found many reasons in which they justify what they do.

I have tried to talk with many of these people and have explained to them how God feels about this, but they have turned their backs on me and are deaf to all that I say. Down through the ages, God has sent them many messengers warning them about their false doctrines but they refused to listen to them.

Chapter 18 Identifying Strange Woman

I want us to remember the four horses of the apocalypse and their riders. We must apply what we have learned to the verses of Isaiah 56.

We should be able to see that the first horse which was white, representing the Word of God does apply from verse one through verse eight, for they do speak of the will of God for his chosen people.

Verses ten and eleven and twelve do show us the second horse, which is red, did arrive and does show us that these people are in rebellion against God's Holy Word.

We can not see the black horse but we can be sure that he was already there and did judge those people who rebelled against Almighty God. I say this for verse nine does show us that the Pale horse has arrived and Almighty God has invited the beasts of the field as well as the beasts of the forests to feed upon the flesh of those people who have rebelled against him.

The Bible does clearly show that to rebel against God's Holy Word is the same as rebellion against God himself. Such rebellion is sin, and the apostle Paul did inform us in the book of Romans that the wages of sin is death.

The verses we have studied in Isaiah 56 does speak of "sleepy shepherds and shepherds do have flocks. It is because we do live in the land of religious freedom, we must also include them with their leaders because the rider of the black horse will judge them all.

What I am saying is that no one forced them to accept the false doctrines that have kindled the wrath of Almighty God. They could have walked out any time they wanted to, and perhaps began searching for the truth of God's Holy Word. Therefore let us be aware that both the leaders and their congregations are included in the great rebellion against God's Holy Word.

Now if there be any other people who do cling to these two false doctrines, we must include them with the sleepy shepherds and the men who are continuously fetching the wine for their weekly services and their congregations. Together they do form a rather mysterious Bible person. That mysterious person is spoken of in the book of Revelation and is named "The WHORE of BABYLON."

I do not doubt but what many people might be angry with me for what I have said. Some would shout at me and say "How dare you say such a thing about the very dear people of the churches of America? Through out the whole world, the Christian churches of America are the most respected and do contribute to so many worthy causes like feeding the orphans in many third world countries.

To all of these people I do reply, maybe there is something you seem to be forgetting. I am not the judge for the judge is the one who rides the black horse. I am only a messenger, called by my Lord to deliver this message to as many as can receive it. If you find that you are not satisfied with this message in anyway, I do suggest that you get in touch with the one who has called me to be a messenger and complain to him.

When we do consider the two different false doctrines that are mentioned in Isaiah 56, the pages of history does clearly show that both of these doctrines were enforced by the rulers of Roman religion. Why then does the Bible speak of the Whore of Babylon.

I want us to learn of something Peter said while he was in prison in Rome and shortly before his death. It is believed by Bible scholars that both of Peter's letters were written from prison and Peter was aware that his time was limited.

As he does bring his first letter to a close he does say

1st Peter 5:13 "The church that is at Babylon, elected together with you, saluteth you; and so doth Marcus my son."

Again, most Bible scholars do not believe that Peter was talking about a church that was at the geographic location of Babylon, for Babylon was completely destroyed many hundreds of years earlier. What they do believe was that Peter was very much aware that this letter would be read by the Roman authorities and he did not want to bring their attention to the Christian church that was already established at Rome.

Therefore, he did say the church that is at Babylon for the people for whom this letter was intended would know that Peter was referring to Rome.

In the same way today, we do realize that the modern day Whore of Babylon is really the Whore of Rome and it is because Rome did adopt so many of the ways of the Babylonians, we do understand why she was given this name.

There are probably other reasons such as Babylon was well known for it's great wealth and the way they displayed it. Of course, the whole world is aware that the United States is a very wealthy nation and uses her wealth to influence many nations to do things her way.

I am sure that our omnipotent God did not want to alarm the Rulers of Roman religion who also does influence nations, by placing their name in the book of Revelation. Those who truly do study the Bible know very well the symbolic meaning of Babylon, just as the people did who Peter wrote this letter to.

In a little while we shall allow the seventeenth chapter of Revelation to provide us with a description of the Whore of Babylon. In this description we will find the whore is seated on a scarlet colored beast and the beast does have seven heads and ten horns. These verses have puzzled Bible scholars down through the centuries but at this late hour we should be able to understand these things.

Daniel chapter seven told us of the little horn which would gain power over much of the world for 1260 years and it is the same religious kingdom that did rise from the ashes of the fallen Roman Empire. It is this beast with the little horn as it's highly exalted leader that did wage war against the saints of the most high God. The very same one that sentenced so many of God's children to death by burning; even the teenager whose name was "Joan of Arc."

Let us examine once more the scripture in Daniel that gave us a description of the little horn (the Papacy).

Daniel 7:25 And he shall speak great words against the most high and shall wear out the saints of the most high, and think to change times and laws: until a time and times and the dividing of time.

Again, we do believe that a time (singular) is speaking of one year. The verse then mentions and times, (plural) and we believe this is speaking of two more years. The final portion of this verse speaks of the dividing of time, and we believe this to be speaking of one half of a year. When we add them altogether we have a total of three and one half years, or we could say 42 months or to break it down into days we would have a total of 1260 days. Applying the Bible formula of a day for a year we do arrive at the time of 1260 years.

I realize we did speak of this earlier but I want to be certain that you have not forgotten it, because it will be important as we begin to study scriptures in the book of Revelation.

Before we go any further I feel I should say a little prayer for I feel in need of help from a divine source.

Our heavenly Father which art in heaven. Hallow be thy name. I have come before thee this day to make my request known to thee. I ask of thee dear Lord, may I be a workman, approved unto thee, that I might rightfully divide thy word of truth. I ask this 0 Heavenly Father, because the scriptures we are about to examine have puzzled and confused even the most educated scholars down through the centuries. Therefore I do ask, may I be able to explain them in such a way that many will be able to understand them and know the truth they contain. For it is written that the Truth is able to set us free.

Thou knowest that I am just a common man, and what I ask would seem to be impossible, but we know the scriptures have informed us that with you in control, nothing is impossible. In this way, I do place my trust in thee, 0 Heavenly Father and do thank you Lord, for the abundance of faith thou hast bestowed upon me.

We do ask all of these things in the holy and precious name of our Savior, our Lord Jesus Christ. Amen.

I ask you now to open your bible to the 1st chapter of the book of Revelation, I want you to understand that my Lord has given me the meaning of some of the scriptures in this book but in no way do I claim to understand every mystery that has been written in these chapters. He made very clear to me what the future will soon be but if I want to know everything then I will have to study like everyone else. I do not believe that God does give to anyone all of the answers but just enough to do what God has called them to do.

In the public library thee are many volumes written on the strange and rather mysterious book of Revelation. A few of the writers have made the comment that John, who wrote this book while he was in exile on the island of Patmos did surely write about things that were in the future.

Even though this does sounds good but is not exactly correct. Beginning at the 9th verse .....

Revelation 1:9, I John, who also am your brother, and companion in tribulation, and in the kingdom and patience of Jesus Christ, was in the isle that is called Patmos, for the word of God, and for the testimony of Jesus Christ.

10 I was in the Spirit on the Lord's day, and heard behind me a great voice, as of a trumpet,

11 Saying, I am Alpha and Omega, the first and the last: and what thou seest, write in a book and send it unto the seven churches which are in Asia; unto Ephesus, and unto Smyrna, and unto Pergamos, and unto Thyatira, and unto Sardis, and unto Philadelphia, and unto Laodicea.

12 And I turned to see the voice that spake with me. And being turned, I saw seven golden candlesticks;

13 And in the midst of the seven candlesticks one like unto the Son of man, clothed with a garment down to the foot, and girt about the paps with a golden girdle.

14 His head and his hairs were white like wool, as white as snow; and his eyes were as a flame of fire;

15 And his feet like unto fine brass, as if they burned in a furnace; and his voice as the sound of many waters.

16 And he had in his right hand seven stars; and out of his mouth went a two edged sword: and his countenance was as the sun shineth in his strength.

17 And when I saw him, I fell at his feet as dead. And he laid his right hand upon me, saying unto me, Fear not; I am the first and the last.

18 I am he that liveth, and was dead; and behold, I am alive for evermore, Amen; and have the keys of hell and of death.

19 Write the things which thou hast seen, and the things which are, and the things which shall be hereafter.

It does appear to me by what is written in this 19th verse, that John was told to do more than just write about the future. He was told he was to write about three different things. My point is simply if John did write about things he did see in a vision, they could have been things in the past as well as in the future. Therefore let us expand our thinking capability and not limit ourselves by what some men have said.

I also want us to notice that in verse 10 John did inform us that he was in the Spirit on the Lord's day. I doubt very much that John would have been able to describe to us in such fine detail the things he did see that day except he was in the Spirit.

As much as it is possible I am going to ask that we all put on our spiritual glasses as we do study portions of scripture in Revelation. It is very much a spiritual book and if we only examine these things with our fleshly eyes, it is likely we will not be able to understand them.

It is like the explanation I shared with you for the four horses of the apocalypse. With our normal vision we would never be able to see these horses and their riders, for they would be invisible. It is when we do look at them through spiritual eyes that not only are we able to see them, but do better understand the part each one plays, even as it is recorded in the pages of history.

Moving on to chapter 12, we are given a view of things that have happened on earth but we are given them with a heavenly perspective. I will try to explain them as we go along, even though my ability to do so is limited.

Revelation 12:1, And there appeared a great wonder in heaven; a woman clothed with the sun, and the moon under her feet, and upon her head a crown of twelve stars.

This is a woman we have already learned about in the gospel of Luke. This young woman is a virgin, and the clothing she does wear does imply that she has found favor with God.

The twelve stars in her crown show us that she is a Hebrew woman and the twelve stars do represent the twelve tribes of Israel.

12:2 And she being with child cried, travailing in birth, and pained to be delivered.

The Gospel of Matthew does repeat the prophecy given by Isaiah in chapter seven and verse twenty-three of his book. Matthew 1:23 Behold, a virgin shall be with child, and they shall bring forth a son, and they shall call his name Emmanuel, which being interpreted is, God with us.

The prophet Isaiah, writing about 698 B.C. did have this to say

Isaiah 66:7, Before she travailed, she brought forth; before her pain came, she was delivered of a man child.

8 Who hath heard such a thing? Shall the earth be made to bring forth in one day? or shall a nation be born at once ? for as soon as Zion travailed, she brought forth her children.

Isaiah does speak of more than just Mary. He does speak of the birth of the Christian church, the one that Jesus continues to build.

Revelation 12:3, And there appeared another wonder in heaven; and behold a great red dragon, having seven heads and ten horns, and seven crowns upon his heads.

4 And his tail drew the third part of the stars of heaven, and did cast them to the earth: and the dragon stood before the woman which was ready to be delivered, for to devour her child as soon as it was born.

I want us to focus our attention on "the great red dragon." First we notice that this is a wonder in heaven. I believe this means that these things are highly unusual.

Next and very important we are informed that the dragon did have seven heads and ten horns. I want us to cling to this description for it will become increasingly more important as we go along and will help us to identify the beast upon which the whore is seated.

Then with it's tail, it did cause a third of the stars of heaven to be cast down to the earth. Most people are familiar in some way of the story that is taught that the devil was once an angel in heaven, and because this certain angel did rebel against God, he was able to persuade a third of the angels of heaven to join with him in rebellion. It is because rebellion against God is sin and God cannot stand to be in the presence of sin, that God did cast them out of heaven and down to this earth.

My wife and I have visited churches that did add to what the Bible has to say about this and were teaching that this angel was named Lucifer (Light Bearer) and that he was the most beautiful angel in all of heaven. They did continue that this angel was filled with pride and vanity and became jealous of God.

Isaiah did have some things to say about the king of Babylon, which was Nebuchadnezzar.

Isaiah 14:4, That thou shalt take up this proverb against the King of Babylon, and say, How hath the oppressor ceased! the golden city ceased!

9 Hell from beneath is moved for thee to meet thee at thy coming: it stirreth up the dead for thee, even all the chief ones of the earth: it hath raised up from their thrones all the kings of the nations.

10 All they shall speak and say unto thee, Art thou become like unto us?

11 Thy pomp is brought down to the grave, and the noise of thy viols: the worm is spread under thee, and the worms cover thee.

12 How art thou fallen from heaven, 0 Lucifer, son of the morning! how art thou cut down to the ground, which didst weaken the nations.

I feel I must point out these are things Isaiah did say about King Nebuchadnezzar. Lucifer, meaning most likely shining light is a name that was given to the morning star, which did appear just before dawn, foretelling the arrival of another day. Isaiah does then say

13 For thou halt said, I will ascend into heaven. I will exalt my throne above the stars of God; I will sit upon the mount of the congregation, in the sides of the north.

14 I will ascend above the heights of the clouds; I will be like the most high.

Notice how very similar this description is when compared to the description Paul gave of the man of sin in second Thessalonians chapter 2.

4 Who opposeth and exalteth himself above all that is called God, or that is worshipped; so he as God sitteth in the temple of God, showing himself that he is God.

I think it is obvious that in both cases the one who did sit on the throne that is within the hearts of these two different men is Satan. Never the less, the question remains was Satan once an angel named Lucifer? I have studied all of the scriptures we are given on this subject and find that some teachers seem to be in error and are teaching for doctrine things which are not in the original scriptures but do add to them.

Still others, being somewhat skeptic, would ask me just when did this rebellion in heaven take place. Was this something that happened prior to Creation?

If I was to use my imagination together with scripture, I would say I believe that the rebellion in heaven did take place just after the week of Creation. Perhaps some of the angels became jealous because God did make mankind in his own image.

To add to this story I could say that because the angels were on an eternal time basis and not limited by earthly time, they could see far enough into the future to see that through the sacrifice of God's only begotten Son, there would become a people (The Bride of Christ) that would be with him for all of eternity.

Perhaps they were jealous of these people and this is why the Dragon did greatly persecute the woman who was about to bear a child. Then later, after the child was born we will learn that the dragon did persecute the (woman) which is symbolic for the church (meaning people) that Jesus continues to build, or in other words, the bride of Christ.

However, there is something wrong with what I have just said. I believe it is wrong to teach for doctrine something that is a product of man's imagination. Therefore let us cling to the Word of God for it will provide us with all of the information we need. If there be some questions that are not answered and if a little mystery remains then it is as it should be for The Bible contains many mysteries and if we are to eliminate all of them we will become as the people who do claim that they already know everything. If we do claim to know everything, then there is nothing more for us to learn and we must remain just as we are.

I would rather be as Paul did describe, as one who looks through the glass darkly, not fully understanding everything at this present time. Therefore, with an open mind, we can continue on the path of enlightenment and learning something new everyday.

Returning to the fourth verse we see that the Dragon stood before the woman which was ready to be delivered, for to devour her child as soon as it was born. Let us allow the Word of God to increase our understanding of these things.

Matthew 2:13, And when they were departed (wisemen) behold, the Angel of the Lord appeareth to Joseph in a dream, saying, Arise and take the young child and his mother and flee to Egypt, and be thou there until I bring thee word: for Herod will search for the young child to destroy him.

14 When he arose, he took the young child and his mother by night, and departed into Egypt.

15 And was there until the death of Herod: that it might be fulfilled which was spoken of the Lord by the prophet, saying Out of Egypt have I called my son.

16 Then Herod, when he saw that he was mocked of the wise men, was exceeding wroth, and sent forth, and slew all of the children that were in Bethlehem, and in all the coasts thereof, from two years old and under, according to the time which he had diligently inquired of the wisemen.

17 Then was fulfilled that which was spoken by Jeremiah the prophet saying,

18 In Ramah there was a voice heard, lamentation, and weeping, and great mourning, Rachel weeping for her children, because they are not.

I want us to know that Jeremiah did prophesy this about the year of 606 B.C.

Going on to the next verse in Revelation 12

5 And she brought forth a man child, who was to rule all nations with a rod of Iron: and her child was caught up unto God, and to his throne..

There is something very important about this verse I want for us to understand. Prior to this verse, the verses we read were speaking of the young Hebrew woman who would become the mother of Jesus. However, the 5th verse informs us that she did bear a man child, and in the course of time, her son was taken up to heaven to be with God and his throne.

Let us not forget the virgin birth, the sinless life, the cruel death on the cross, the resurrection and forty-three days later...the ascension. I say forty three because the first chapter of Acts inform us that following the resurrection Jesus was seen for forty days, we do remember that he was not seen during the three days he was in the tomb. Therefore, the ascension must have taken place forty three days after the crucifixion.

What is so important if we use our spiritual understanding is that a metamorphous has taken place. The woman in the first verses was speaking of the "Mother of Christ," and the remaining verses the woman has become the church or in other words "The Bride of Christ." I do hope you will be able to understand this great truth.

6 And the woman fled into the wilderness, where she hath a place prepared of God (hiding place) that they should feed her there a thousand two hundred and three score days.

The first thing I want for us to notice is the exact amount of time she was to remain in this hiding place. Is it not for the same exact amount of time, the 1260 days (years) that was the time that power was given to the little horn who would wage war against the saints of the Most High God? according to Daniel chapter seven.

In the next few verses we have the same story repeated but a few more details are added.

7 And there was war in heaven: Michael and his angels fought against the dragon : and the dragon fought and his angels,

8 And prevailed not; neither was their place found any more in heaven.

9 And the great dragon was cast out, that old serpent, called the Devil and Satan, which deceiveth the whole world: he was cast out into the earth, and his angels were cast out with him.

The meaning of this verse is so very clear that I cannot see why any would doubt it but yet there are a few who do. I also want us to notice that the red dragon was called the Devil and Satan, and even the serpent. Perhaps it was because it was the serpent which did tempt Eve while she was in the garden that was located in the land called Eden.

10 And I heard a loud voice saying in heaven, Now is come salvation, and strength, and the kingdom of God, and the power of his Christ: for the accuser of our brethern is cast down, which accused them before our God day and night.

This verse contains good news that the time of salvation has come. Yet, it contains a warning for all of us, for Satan and his angels are continuously watching us and the lives we live, always looking for any little thing that they may use to accuse us before God.

Therefore, it is because we are living in these latter days and Satan's time is short, that we must follow very close behind our Savior, living our lives in the way that is pleasing to God.

Let us now learn the rest of the story concerning those Christians that Satan did accuse of wrong doing.

11 And they (the accused) overcame him by the blood of the Lamb, and by the word of their testimony; and they loved not their lives unto the death.

I do believe this is speaking of the very courageous men and women which were tortured and torn limb from limb, and those who were burned to death at the stake and those who were beaten to death and murdered in many different ways, because they would not give up their faith and bow down to the beast of false religion. Of course, these things did happen during the 1260 years that was the time allowed for the beast to have power to change the law and times and to wage war against the saints of the most High.

12 Therefore rejoice, ye heavens, and ye that dwell in them. Woe to the inhabiters of the earth and of the sea! for the Devil is coming down unto you, having great wrath, because he knoweth that he hath but a short time.

13 And when the dragon (Satan) saw that he was cast unto the earth, he persecuted the woman which brought forth the man child.

14 And the woman (body of born again believers) were given two wings of a great eagle, that she might fly into the wilderness, into her place, where she is nourished for a time, and times, and half a time, from the face of the serpent.

We could spend much time examining every word of these verses but I do not believe it is necessary. What is important for us to realize is that for a time period of 1260 years the church that Christ continues to build was greatly persecuted. Yet, there was always a remnant that survived.

Let us not forget that thousands upon thousands went to their death at the hands of the Roman religious executioners. Even so, the church survived because it is the will of God that it should.

15 And the serpent cast out of his mouth water as a flood after the woman (bride of Christ) that he might cause her to be carried away by the flood.

This is speaking of the great persecution of the dark ages and also the actual war that was waged against many different groups of Christians during the 1260 year reign of terror.

16 And the earth helped the woman, and the earth opened her mouth, and swallowed up the flood which the dragon cast out of his mouth.

This is speaking of the reformation which was necessary or else the church of Christ would have completely perished. However, the reformation did not happen over night but did take a very long time until it was brought to completion.

17 And the dragon was wroth with the woman, and went to make war with the remnant of her seed, which keep the commandments of God, and have the testimony of Jesus Christ.

If it is possible then I do suggest that you high light this verse in your Bible so that you do not forget it. Notice that the remnant of her seed, do keep the commandments of God. To be more exact, we need to understand this remnant (small amount) of born again believers do keep the fourth commandment, which is to keep the sabbath day holy. This does reveal unto us a big difference between this remnant and the followers of the sleepy shepherds of Isaiah 56, for they all do claim that Sunday is a better day for worship than is the day that God made holy. We should be able to understand that because of this, they do not keep the commandments of God.

For this reason Satan does not wage war against them, for they already do obey the beast. What is more, they have spread their rebellion against the Word of God around the world and the beast is quite pleased with them, in this regard.

I also want for us to understand that the remnant church which do keep the commandments of God are the ones who most likely will survive the great tribulation that is ahead. The ones who have rebelled against God's Holy Word, will receive the wages they are due.

Many of the men who have written volumes on the meaning of the scriptures in the Revelation seem to agree on the identity of the red dragon.

They believe that it was this red dragon which is Satan did give it's power to the old Roman Empire.

When we take a closer look, it was the old Roman Empire which did appoint Herod to be the governor over Judea. Herod was the one who was greatly concerned by the prophecy that a baby was about to be born who would become a king over the Jewish people. Herod was the one responsible for the order for the Jewish children two years old and younger should be killed. It should be understood that when the verse mentioned that the dragon stood before the woman who was about to be delivered, it was fulfilled in Herod, and Herod gained his authority from the government of Rome.

To continue in history, it was the government of the old Roman Empire that did continue to persecute the woman (bride of Christ) in the early years of Christianity. I believe that it was during the time when Nero was the emperor there was a thing called "Nero's circus" near the Mons Vaticanus that destroyed many Christians. They were slaughtered for sport and as a means of entertainment. Surely, it is not hard to understand that the power to do so came from the great red dragon who was Satan.

What we shall learn in the next chapter is that the power of the red dragon when the old empire did crumble was then given to the religious kingdom that did arise from out of the ashes.

Chapter 19 The Leopard with Big Feet

Revelation 13:1, And I stood upon the sand of the sea, and saw a beast rise up out of the sea, having seven heads and ten horns, and upon his horns ten crowns, and upon his heads the name of blasphemy.

When John informs us he stood upon the sand of the sea, he is telling us that he could see these things from the sandy shore that borders the sea. The sea is symbolic for many people of different ethnic background and who speak many different languages. Think for a moment what the situation was when the Roman Empire was finally fallen.

History does inform us of the Gothic tribes which did invade the territory once held by the old Roman Empire. In addition to these invaders, there was already a mixture of people in that part of the world. I am sure there were remnants of the old Grecian Empire, for the scriptures do mention the people of Greece and the influence they did have upon the culture at this time.

In addition there were the Hebrew people and the Romans and Medes and many, many more. In this way, John did see this beast as it arose from this great mixture of people.

John then mentions that the beast did have seven heads and ten horns. I want us to remember that the Red Dragon which did represent the old Roman Empire, did also have seven heads and ten horns. Surely, it should not be too hard to understand that the old Roman Empire did give to this new beast, it's former power as well as it's glory in a symbolic way.

We notice that the seven heads had the name of blasphemy, (singular). Also the ten horns did have crowns which are the symbol of ten kingdoms. We shall talk of these heads and the ten horns a little later, so we put them on a shelf for now.

2 And the beast which I saw was like a leopard, and his feet were as the feet of a bear, and his mouth, as the mouth of a lion: and the dragon (old Roman Empire) gave him his power, and his seat, and great authority.

We have been given many things to discuss just in this one verse. Within many of the books that have been written on the Revelation are quite a few pictures. The picture of this beast is quite striking with an animal with the body of a leopard, the feet of a bear, a lions mouth, and seven little heads that appear to be leopard kittens. Behind the small heads are ten horns arising from this strange animal.

Not wanting to merely repeat what other writers have said about this animal, I will share some of my own opinions.

Perhaps you remember that of the four beasts in Daniel chapter seven, one was a leopard. We must ask, Is this important to understanding the beast of Revelation 13. I do not think that it is.

First and foremost, the leopard is a beast of prey, and a very capable one at that. I consider this to be important as it relates to this strange beast. As I said before, the leopard is very intelligent and is able to set up an ambush situation and does then use total surprise as a survival skill. Remember this, for I consider this to be very important.

Even as the Red Dragon does represent the old Roman Empire. this new beast that looks like a leopard does represent the Papal Roman Empire that did rise up from the same area from where the old empire was fallen.

Was the new Papal Empire very intelligent? If we were to examine the pages of history we would have to conclude that the Papal Empire was very intelligent. Even while the old empire was still in existence, the little horn was able to convince the Emperor of Rome to fight against the Arian Ostrogoths, which were the enemy of Roman religion.

What is more, the strategy of the new beast was often very carefully planned to cause both kings and queens to come to his aid and to give their power to the one who did sit on the throne in Rome. As a very intelligent predator, we find the leopard is indeed a very accurate symbol of the Roman Papal Empire.

We then look down and cannot help but notice the rather strange sight of a leopard with the feet of a bear. What could this possibly mean. Is it speaking of the bear that represented the kingdom of Persia? I do not think so.

When I was a young man and did spend much time wandering along the beaches of Westward Alaska, I did observe quite a few bears. I found them to be very interesting to watch if one did so from a safe distance.

These bears of the coastal regions of western Alaska are known as brown bears and they are very large. I believe many of the adult male bears would weigh more than a thousand pounds and a great many of the younger ones and females would weigh more than five hundred pounds.

Despite their great size and weight, these bears cam move very fast across extremely rough terrain, whenever the situation calls for speed. Let me assure that not even the fastest Olympic athlete could cover the same ground as the bear, as quickly as the bear, when the bear is in his own element. Only a fool would think he could outrun the bear, if the bear really wanted to catch him.

Having walked along the well worn paths of the bear along side of a stream, and having given this some thought, the bears feet are quite large and very strong, for they must support his great weight as well as enabling him to catch his prey. Bears of Alaska are also predators and do kill other animals to eat when the opportunity does come their way.

They are best known for catching salmon when they arrive from the ocean and begin to swim up the rivers. However, the time of the salmon run is limited and the hungry bears do feed upon moose and caribou and even dogs if they find them available.

So what we can see in the strange beast of Revelation is a leopard, (very intelligent predator) with the exceptional strength of the feet of a bear. The feet will support the weight quite easily for a leopard does not weigh as much as a bear.

I see these feet as being the very strong foundation of the old Roman Empire. Of course, this does include the architecture that was so well built that much of it still exists. To add to this, the Roman Papal Empire has also built some very enduring buildings.

However, it does imply more than buildings made of stone but must include the structure of the political base upon which Roman Catholicism does sit. From the high position of Pope, down to the many Cardinals all dressed in red, the Bishops and the great power they wield, and down to the many Priests that serve around the world. Yes, the feet of the bear are a very sturdy foundation.

Then there is the mouth of a lion. Notice that it did not say the head of a lion. I believe this is quite accurate for it means to me that the beast still retains the head of a leopard. I believe that even though the leopard is smaller in size than the lion, it is more intelligent. Indeed, it almost has to be, for often they do occupy the same territory, and they must compete for the same prey which will sustain them and their young ones.

The female lions often prowl in the darkness of night, several of them together, and do run down their prey under the cover of darkness. Female leopards also use the cover of darkness but they almost always hunt alone.

They often are able to ambush their prey, by waiting at some strategic location, but they are not limited to this method. They are very fast and can run down their prey when they need to. After they have killed their prey they often drag the carcass up into a tree, to avoid the hungry packs of hyenas, which would take it away from her.

Not so with the lions, for they are king of the territory and because they do hunt with other lions, the lions would not be threatened by hyenas or jackals or any other would be thieves of the night.

This strange leopard beast of Revelation did have the mouth of a lion. I believe this tells us that when this beast does speak, it speaks with the same great authority as do the lions.

When the animals that share the same territory with the lions, do hear the mighty roar of the lion, as they begin to prowl, they have one thing in common and that is fear. From the smallest monkey to the very large animals and the other predators, they all have great respect and fear of the king. I do not believe any of them are willing to challenge the lions supremacy.

In the same way, when the Pope did speak, through out the 1260 year reign of terror, even the kings and queens and the heads of state and other government leaders did listen. Even to this very day, great crowds gather to hear the Pope speak and the news media do inform people all around the world what the Pope did say. It is not at all hard to understand the mouth of a lion as being the symbol of the Papacy.

In the final part of this second verse we are told that the dragon gave him his power, his seat, and great authority. We must not forget that the dragon is used as the symbol of Satan, as well as the old Roman Empire, Therefore, the power of this strange beast that did arise from the sea is satanic.

Also I want us to notice that it did give to the new beast, the seat of his power which also could mean his throne. Of course, we know that the throne of the Emperors was in Rome except for a short time it was moved to Constantinople. All during the blackest period in history, the seat of the beast has been in Rome.

Now we need to talk a little about the seven heads that John did see on this strange leopard like beast with unusual big feet. If you were to search through the many volumes that have been written on this strange and rather mysterious beast, you would also find many highly unusual explanations for what people have believed these heads do represent.

I do have the notes of the one who was my teacher, who has now passed on, on this very subject. He was a very dear man of God who truly did study the scriptures through out his life. I find that I have no reason to disagree with what he believed the heads do represent. I will share with you what they might represent but I will not tell you who they represent. In this way, if you want to know more, then you can search the pages of history, just as many who have been down this road before us. After all, the purpose of a mystery is so we will have to seek knowledge, in order to solve the mystery.

These seven heads might represent each one a period of time in history, when either a nation or a group of nations (a federation) or an empire, has given their power, civil as well as military, to the one who sits upon the throne in Rome.

An example would be way back in the beginning when the old Roman Empire did support the Papacy in the defeat of the Ostrogoths. They also did enforce the religious laws of Roman religion such as the Sunday law introduced by Constantine.

There is a book that is available at most libraries the title of is "the Holy Roman Empire," by James Bruce and you might learn from it the very interesting story of how Charlemagne did come into power. It was a very important time in history for the Catholic church. It is even possible that he was one of the seven heads, but I will leave that for you to find out.

Then there was such men as Otto the great in 962 and Henry the third in 1056. Perhaps they do have a place in this great mystery. Following along in the course of time, there was Frederick I, Henry VI, Frederick II, and they were from 1152-1250. I do not say these were heads but I offer this information to you, to help you in your search of history.

Because we are given the description that these heads are also mountains, we must realize that between each mountain there must be a valley. A time when the nations withdrew their power and Roman religion was considerably weakened in it's quest to rule religiously over the entire world. Upon the death of Fredrick II, the Roman religious empire fell into such a valley and it was known as The Great Interregnum, which lasted from 1250 to 1272. I mention this for it is an example of the type of valley I am talking about.

Again, as I have said, I do not intend to solve this mystery at this time for as a messenger called by God, I am not required to. The names of these seven heads are not important to the message I am to deliver.

3 And I saw one of his heads as it were wounded to death, and his deadly wound was healed: and all the world wondered after the beast.

Most of the writers do agree what this wound was but they do not agree upon the date it occurred. The head that was wounded might be the head of power given to Roman religion when the great sword of truth, in the form of the reformation did strike it a deadly blow.

Many people believe this blow was struck by Martin Luther when he nailed his theses to the door of the church in Wittenburg. Others believe the date should be in 1648 at the treaty of Westphalia. Both the Lutherans and the Calvinists were declared free from all jurisdiction of the Pope or any Catholic, at that time. However, I believe this occurred during a period of time between mountains of power, the time being one we designated as a valley. Quite a few people who have studied these things do believe it occurred in 1797 when the Pope who had been taken captive by France died there. It is true at least one major newspaper ran the headline, "Power of Papacy finally broken." However, it is quite possible that this too, did occur during a period in the time of a valley.

I really am not certain when it was struck so I will leave it to you to solve this mystery. What I do know is that it has already occurred and that is what is important.

The same verse also told us that the wound had healed. We must ask the question, "When did the healing take place?" Some say one thing and some say another. I will share with you what I do believe regarding the healing.

There was a Jesuit priest by the name of Ribera who began the false doctrine that the anti-Christ would not appear until the end of the age. This doctrine was no doubt invented because more and more people were beginning to believe as Martin Luther, and William Tyndale and John Calvin and Sir Isaac Newton and many more did believe, that the prophecy about the anti-Christ was fulfilled in the Papacy.

The doctrine that the antichrist would not appear until the end of the age was first taught in 1585, and of course it was taught to the many people of the Catholic faith.

During the same period of time, the fathers of the reformation did teach that the prophecy was fulfilled and that the man of sin had been revealed and almost all of the reformers believed this way.

As time went by and one generation died and another one was born there came to be quite a few teachers of the Protestant faith that were very liberal in what they did believe and teach. They took hold of the false doctrine of the future anti-Christ and it wasn't very long and it was accepted by the majority of Protestant churches and is still to this very day.

Perhaps you can remember that the apostle Paul did speak of a people who did not love the truth, so God would allow them to be deceived and believe a lie. I believe the lie told by Ribera, the Jesuit is the fulfillment of this prophecy. In this way, the deadly wound was healed and the people of Protestant faith are still waiting for the coming of a future anti-Christ.

4 And they worshipped the dragon which gave power unto the beast: and they worshipped the beast, saying, Who is like unto the beast? who is able to make war with him.

I believe it is possible that this verse is speaking of the long period of time of the many religious crusades. I believe it is possible that during the time of a religious war that a great many people did bow down and worship the power that was successful in war. Surely, it must have been this way during the very short life time of Joan of Arc for she was very successful in leading the army into battle.

5 And there was given unto him a mouth (lion's mouth) speaking great things and blasphemies; and power was given unto him to continue forty and two months.

The first thing I want to bring to our attention is the time of forty and two months. Is it not the exact amount of time that Daniel said would be given to the little horn? Which we have determined to be the one highly exalted leader. Also notice that out of his mouth he did speak great things and blasphemies.

The scripture in Daniel 7 did describe the little horn as 25 And he shall speak great words against the most High

As we have already discussed, a time and times and the dividing of times is the same amount of time as 42 months. They both amount to 1260 days and when we apply the Biblical formula of a day for a year we arrive at the same amount of time 1260 years.

Surely you can remember how we learned of how the Red Dragon stood before the woman wanting to destroy her child. Then we learned of Herod who was appointed by the Roman Empire and how he gave the order to slaughter the children.

The next thing we learned is about the leopard like beast and how the dragon did give it's power to this beast. What I want us to do is view the little horn of Daniel with the leopard beast of Revelation and we should be able to see that they are speaking of almost the same thing. I say almost, because the prophecy in Daniel was concerning one particular man who would be the highly exalted ruler of a religious empire. The leopard beast of Revelation is speaking of the religious empire and the lion mouth it did receive is the same as the little horn of Daniel chapter seven.

Let us compare them to see how they are alike.

1 the little horn.. Daniel 7:25 He shall speak great words against the most high. The leopard beast Revelation 13:6 He opened his mouth in blasphemy against God.

2 The little horn.. Daniel 7:21 The little horn made war against the saints, and prevailed against them. Leopard beast Revelation 13:7 makes war with the saints, and overcomes them.

3 The little horn did arise from the ashes of the fallen Roman Empire. The leopard beast arose at the same time for the dragon, (old Roman Empire) gave him his power, his seat, and great authority. Revelation 13:2.

4 The time of the little horn was limited to a time, and times and the dividing of times which we have determined is 1260 years. The Leopard beast was given power for 42 months which is the same amount of time when we apply the formula we were given.

It should not be too hard to understand the leopard beast is speaking of the mighty religious empire that sought to rule over the entire earth. The little horn is the highly exalted ruler of that religious empire and they both lost their power to greatly persecute the true followers of Christ who keep the commandments of God, and testify of Jesus, at the same time.

10 And I beheld another beast coming up out of the earth, and he had two horns like a lamb, and spake as a dragon.

In order that we better understand these mysterious verses I believe it will help if we view these things in the chronological order in which they will come upon earth.

Let us recall that the dragon (old Roman Empire) had seven heads and ten horns. Then we can see that the Leopard beast (Vatican) also had seven heads and ten horns. As we study we will soon learn of a scarlet colored beast and it has seven heads and ten horns. The fact that all three have seven heads and ten horns is extremely important for it connects them together. It is when we first learn of these things and then we will learn of the beast like a lamb with two horns,

The lamb like beast is very near for this is speaking of a "New World Order" and people are already talking about it.

It was quite a few years ago when the Lord brought to my attention a book he wanted me to read. The name of this book is "The Keys of This Blood" and it was written by a man whose name is Malachi Martin.

Mr. Martin does tell us of a struggle for world dominion between Mikhail Gorbachev of the Soviet Union, the Capitalist West, (United States) and Pope John Paul 11. He goes on to say that these three are the only contestants that are capable of sustaining a one world form of government, though there be many who would cling to their coat tails.

On the first page of his fascinating book he declares It makes no difference whether or not we are willing, or if we are ready, for we are very much involved in an all out, no holds barred, three way global competition. He then goes on to say that it is all out, because now that it has already started there is no way anyone can call it off.

"No holds are barred, because the world and all that is in it, our way of life as individuals and as citizens of the nations, our families and our jobs; our trade and commerce and money; our educational systems and our religions and our cultures; which most of us do take for granted, All will have been powerfully and radically altered forever. No one will be exempted from its effect. No sector of our lives will remain untouched."

He then predicts that the people who are under 70 years of age will see some of the basic structure of the new world order installed. Those who are 40 and under will live under its legislative and judiciary authority and control.

What I want for us to understand is that Malachi Martin is a man who does know what he is talking about. He is described as being an eminent theologian, expert on the Catholic church, a former Jesuit and professor at the Vatican's Pontifical Biblical Institute and the author of several best selling books. He was trained in theology at Louvain. There he received his doctorates in Semitic Languages, Archaeology and Oriental History. He also studied at Oxford and at Hebrew University in Jerusalem. From 1958 to 1964 he served in Rome, where he was a close associate of the renowned Jesuit cardinal Augustin Bea and Pope John XXIII.

On the back of the cover it does say, **"Only Malachi Martin, Vatican insider and intelligence expert, could reveal the untold story behind the Vatican role in today's winner take all race against time to establish, maintain, and control the first one-world government."** It then asks these questions. **"Will America lead the way to the new world order? Is Pope John Paul II winning the battle for faith? Is the breakup of the Soviet Empire masking Gorbachev's worldwide agenda."**

So much for the big print, it is when we get inside of the book and begin to read the small print that we learn of a Polish man whose name is Karl Wojtyla and he was the Archbishop from Poland. The year was 1976 and he did give a prophetic speech in New York City, but I wonder how many really listened to what he said.

He did say **"We are standing in the face of the greatest historical confrontation humanity has gone through. A test of two thousand years of culture and Christian civilization, with all of its consequences for human dignity, individual rights and the rights of nations.**

But he chided his listeners on that September day: "Wide circles of American society and wide circles of the Christian community do not realize this fully." Even then in 1976, the man from Poland was speaking of a new world order. In 1978 this man was elected to be the Pope and his name was changed to John Paul II. Almost immediately he began to employ the strategies that would lead to victory.

If you want to learn of the struggle for a new world order and see it through the eyes of one who knew very well the goal of the Vatican, a man who was not only a very intelligent but was a remarkable writer able to describe in fine detail the things that are hidden from the general public. Go either to your book store or to the library and obtain a copy of "The Keys of This Blood" and learn of these things, just as I once did.

My copy of this book bears a copyright date of 1990. I believe it was in 91 or maybe in 92 that I first read The Keys of this Blood, and the Lord caused me to know that it was speaking of the beast that would arise from the earth with the horns of a lamb. When I am given knowledge from this supernatural source, I know I can depend on it, for he does know the future.

There is one thing I want to make very clear to you, and that is the Roman Catholic religion does dogmatically insist there can be no separation of church from state. This was how the beast through out the 1260 year reign of terror, did gain it's full power for the nations did give it the authority to rule over them religiously. The laws of Roman religion became the laws of the land and was enforced by civil authorities.

Shortly after I had finished reading this very interesting book, my wife and I were invited to a wedding in Portland Oregon. When the wedding was finished and all of the hands had been shaken, we left Portland and drove up the river and to the Tri-city area of Washington. I visited with my brother who lived there on the sabbath day and we left for home early on Sunday morning.

We came to the town which is named George and we were hungry and stopped there because of a certain restaurant which is known for the delicious breakfasts they do serve,

The weather was very warm on this Sunday morning and there were many young people wearing bathing suits and skimpy clothing and for a reason. The Columbia river is near by and so many of them were headed there for a day of fun in the sun and swimming in the river.

As I sat there waiting for our breakfast to be served I thought about the many people who would be on their way to church on Sunday morning and I wondered how very many did not go to church at all. I thought about the new world order if the Vatican did get it's way and how it would insist there be no separation of church from state. I thought about how it would insist that everyone under their authority would have to attend church on Sunday.

I tried to imagine how these many young people headed for the river with their swimming suits and inner tubes would react to a law like that.

I realized then, that the people of the United States would never, ever, accept an organization or a law that insisted it be mandatory that all attend church, let alone on Sunday morning. Therefore, because they would not accept it, it would be enforced by the civil authority, police officers of the religious state, and they might even put people in jail for failing to attend church.

As I ate my breakfast, among so many joyful and noisy, well tanned boys and girls, I thought of how there was a such a wide separation between the culture of young America and the elderly rulers of the Vatican, a bunch of grumpy old men who considered them selves worthy to judge the whole world. Young America could never be compatible with mandatory religion.

Americans love their freedom very dearly and the leaders of Roman religion do despise such freedom, for the pages of history do show that they do.

I then thought of the word that both Malachi Martin and Karl Wojtyla used which word was a confrontation. I thought of the meaning of the word and then I wondered just how much confrontation was each of them talking about. It did seem to me that there can be many different degrees of confrontation.

I decided to examine the book one more time and I did find this, the words of Malachi Martin .....

"Perhaps the world was still too immersed in the old system of nation-states, and in all the old international balance of power arrangements, to hear what Wojtyla was saying. Or perhaps Wojtyla himself was reckoned as no more than an isolated figure hailing from an isolated country that had long since been pointedly written out of the global equation. Or perhaps, after the industrial slaughter of millions of human beings in two world wars, and in 180 local wars, and after the endless terrors of nuclear brinkmanship that have marked the progress of the twentieth century, the feeling was simply that one confrontation more or less wasn't going to make much difference."

I will leave it for you to decide just what degree of confrontation they are speaking of, but I think I know how much and it is the maximum the word does imply.

I also recall the word of Mr. Martin in describing the contest using words that are used to describe a particular type of wrestling match. He very plainly said that it was to be an "all out" and "no holds barred" kind of contest. We can be sure that the rules of the Genevan Convention will not apply. Neither will any agreement concerning the use of Nuclear Missiles be in effect.

It is strange that no one seemed to be interested in this warning given to America first by Karl Wojtyla, the man from Poland and Malachi Martin, a man who certainly did know what he was talking about. Mr. Malachi Martin was a very highly educated man and he was what is called an "insider," when it came to knowing the internal affairs of the Vatican.

In contrast, I am a man with very little formal education who has spent much of my life at sea, taking my living from the water, which was not always easy. How strange it is, that I have come to you to tell you about the very same thing Mr. Martin did, and I have come by my information from a completely different source, the Holy Word of God and the Holy Spirit.

From where we now stand, we know that Malachi Martin has passed on. He did his best to issue a warning and many people did read it and then they forgot what they read. In the same way, Pope John Paul 11 has passed on and was buried with all of the honor and dignity of his high office. However, he was the one who actually began this contest and his plans will be carried out by the men who succeed him.

While Karl Wojtyla was yet in Poland he was a friend of the man there who was a cardinal. Together they spent many long hours researching the moves that would be made by both the Eastern Contestant as well as the Western one. In a way it must have been like a very high form of chess. They examined every possible move and reaction and then formed a counter move and reaction. I am sure that they did their homework well for the Vatican does not plan on coming in second in this contest.

It will indeed be an "any thing goes" type of contest and there is one thing more I want us to remember. That is that the leopard beast did lose his power in 1798 and for more than two hundred years the nations of Europe and the West have not treated the Vatican with as much respect as the rulers of Roman religion desire. Perhaps this is the reason that Pope John II took so many trips to so many different places. Sometimes to make an apology when needed but always to improve the Vatican's position as a world power.

It is as though the old leopard beast that once was and now is not, is wakening from a long sleep. It is as though it is now coming back to life, and is once more about to become the beast it once was.

Remember, the leopard being very cunning and intelligent can set up an ambush situation and then use complete surprise as a mighty weapon in it's arsenal, to win the contest.

There can be no doubt as to the winner of the contest, for the Word of God will reveal this to us.

Chapter 20 The Scarlet Coloured Beast

I see no reason to continue any further in the 13th chapter of Revelation at this time. The reason being is we must first find out about what is preventing the new two horned beast from coming up from the earth. Before we are through, we will return to the 13th chapter and learn about the 'New World Order" from a biblical perspective. Let us now go directly to the 17th chapter and receive the description of the great whore.

Revelation 17:1, And there came one of the seven angels which had the seven vials, and talked with me, saying unto me, Come hither; I will show unto thee the judgment of the great whore that sitteth on many waters.

2 With whom the kings of the earth have committed forni-cation, and the inhabitants of the earth have been made drunk with the wine of her fornication.

3 So he carried me away in the spirit into the wilderness: and I saw a woman sit upon a scarlet coloured beast, full of names of blasphemy, having seven heads and ten horns.

There was once the leopard beast with big feet, the mouth of a lion and seven heads and ten horns. However that beast was limited to 1260 years and then as we have learned, his power was taken from him in the year of 1798. Following that time till now, a time of a little more than 200 years, the rulers of Roman religion have been made to behave themselves. They were no longer allowed to burn individuals to death at the stake because they did not accept the doctrines of the Catholic church. To use the words of John, we are speaking of the time when the beast that was and is not.

The leopard beast was taken prisoner but in it's place there is a new beast and it has the same seven heads and ten horns but the colour is different. It is now a scarlet coloured beast.

According to what is written in history, by the time that the leopard like beast did lose his power in 1798, the rulers of Roman religion had earned for their brand of religion, a very bad reputation. They had been waging war against anyone who dared to disagree with them, and they had caused the death of millions over the 1260 year reign of terror.

Therefore, it was necessary for the leopard like beast to disappear, and this was done by simply clothing it in a robe of scarlet. Then showing itself to the world that Roman religion was no longer interested in conquest and ruling the world, but had become the champion of people's rights and a peace maker. All the while maintaining it's position as an advisor of kings and a builder of bridges between warring nations.

However, beneath the robe of scarlet, the scriptures will reveal that the same deadly leopard like beast still exists. In days to come, the true nature of the scarlet beast will be revealed, when the ten horns do destroy the woman with fire.

4 And the woman was arrayed in purple and scarlet colour, and decked with gold and precious stones and pearls, having a golden cup in her hand full of abominations and filthiness of her fornication.

The woman is clothed partly in purple and that is the colour of a king. In this case it is speaking of the King of Kings and his name is Immanuel, for God is with a part of her.

Then she is also clothed in scarlet and that is the colour of the beast. So we can see she is partly of Christ and she is partly of the beast of Roman religion. Is not this the same thing we learned of the sleepy shepherd of Isaiah 56. Many of them were fetching the wine to be used in their regular service and all of them believed that Sunday is a better day to worship Almighty God. Both of these doctrines are an abomination to Almighty God.

One is the doctrine of a thief, who would rob our Lord Jesus Christ of the precious blood he did pour out for the sins of everyone. The gospel of John 3:16 does say "whosoever." They do claim that the blood they do have by changing the wine into blood is limited for it is only for the people who enter through the doors of their church.

The other is a doctrine that is directly in opposition to the fourth commandment of Almighty God which he did write on tablets of stone with his very own finger. Either one of these doctrines is filthy in the eyes of God and an abomination to him. Both of these two false doctrines are both spiritual fornication and religious fornication, for they do claim that they are of Christ, but do choose the way of murderers.

5 And upon her forehead was a name written, MYSTERY, BABYLON THE GREAT, THE MOTHER OF HARLOTS AND ABOMINATIONS OF THE EARTH.

I want us to consider this mystery for a moment. Within these United States there are more than one hundred different denominations and I am not including the catholic churches. There are more than one hundred Protestant churches and each one teaches they are the one and only really right church. This amounts to great religious confusion so that a newly converted Christian does not have any idea of which church they should attend. The Bible does inform us that God is not the author of confusion so that means that someone else is.

These same number of churches have sent people all over the world and for the most part, they do teach the very same doctrine they do teach here. To be specific, they teach in every country and nation that the commandments of God are null and void and that Sunday is a much better day to worship God than is the day created by God for Holy Worship. This is why as a whole, America is the mother of many harlots, for they do claim to belong to Christ, while at the same time they do refuse to follow Christ, but do follow in the way commanded by the beast.

6 And I saw the woman drunken with the blood of the saints, and with the blood of the martyrs of Jesus: and when I saw her, I wondered with great admiration.

It is because of this verse that a great many theologians do believe the Great Whore is symbolic of the Roman brand of religion. Surely we would all agree, because of this verse and what it says, this woman cannot be these United States. I promise you that when we have reached the last verse in chapter 18 that I will explain what this verse does mean in a way we can all understand it.

7 And the angel said unto me, Wherefore didst thou marvel? I will tell thee the mystery of the woman, and of the beast that carrieth her, which hath the seven heads and ten horns.

8 The beast that thou sawest was, and is not, and shall ascend (come up) out of the bottomless pit, and go into perdition (be destroyed) : and they that dwell on the earth shall wonder, whose names were not written in the book of life from the foundation of the world, when they behold the beast that was, and is not, and yet is.

I want for us to consider the beast that was. It was the leopard beast that did rule over the kings of the earth for 1260 years. Then it lost it's power as a beast for two hundred years, and during this time it became the beast that was and is not.

As I read and studied both the Word of God and the book "The Keys Of This Blood," I learned of how the beast that is not, was very much planning on being a beast again. This explains the final two words of verse 8. It is not a beast just yet, but will become one on the day when the seven thunders do utter their voices. In that day, the woman which is riding on the beast, and prevents him from doing the things it once did such as greatly persecuting the Christians of the world, will be removed forever.

I do not know exactly when it was that the woman climbed up on the back of the scarlet coloured beast, which is the beast that was and is not, but I suspect it might have been shortly after world war two. It was a time of prosperity and the United States did begin to get involved with the affairs of other nations.

Not only was the United States the champion of religious freedom, she did encourage other nations to promote the freedom of religion. Of course, this was in direct opposition to the will of the Vatican, for the Roman rulers do despise freedom of religion. They always have, for they believe that their brand of religion does need to be enforced by the civil authorities.

9 And here is the mind which hath wisdom. The seven heads are seven mountains, (mountains of power) on which the woman, (Whore of Babylon) sitteth.

10 And there are seven kings: five are fallen, and one is (number 6,) and the other (number 7) is not yet come; and when he cometh, he must continue a short space.

11 And the beast that was, and is not, (number 6) even he is the eighth, and is of the seven, and goeth into perdition. (be destroyed)

I must confess that this puzzle is one that I have not yet fully solved in my own mind.

This being the case, I seem to be in good company, for many educated men and women were also unable to come to any agreement as to the full meaning of these mysterious verses. However, in the course of time, perhaps these things will become more visible.

12 And the ten horns which thou sawest are ten kings, which have received no kingdom as yet; but receive power as kings one hour with the beast.

I will share with you my opinion as to the identity of these ten horns when we finish verse 16. However, keep in mind the one hour that is mentioned in the 12th verse is the same amount of time mentioned in chapter 18, for the destruction of the Whore.

13 These have one mind (purpose) and shall give their power and strength unto the beast.

It is when we determine what their power consists of, we will learn more about their identity.

The 14th verse does inform us that in the course of time, both the beast, as well as the ten horn kings, will have to harvest what they have planted.

Even as they shall destroy the Whore, they themselves will eventually be destroyed by the King of Kings who is also the Lamb of God.

However, if we want to keep these things in the chronological order in which they will take place, the 14th verse belongs very near the end of this book, for much must happen before the final battle will be won.

15 And he saith unto me, The waters which thou sawest, where the Whore sitteth, are peoples, and multitudes, and nations, and tongues. (languages)

The waters that is mentioned here are symbolic for many different people from various different ethnic backgrounds. These are people from many different nations and they speak many different languages. On New Years day, I can observe via my television a great multitude of people who are gathered together in Rome to receive the message that is given each New Year by the Pope. All of these people, who symbolically are labeled as "many waters," do have one thing in common and that is the fact that they are Roman catholic.

Now there is one thing about them we should know. That is within the Roman religious system these are two different bodies to the church. Of course, there are these great amount of people who do comprise the "worshipping church."

Then there is a distinctly different group which do make up the ruling church. There is something rather unique about the ruling church and that is the fact that they are all men. Perhaps this is the reason when John did write about the beast he always did refer to it as being male.

He never once used the word female to describe the beast. In contrast, the Great Whore of Babylon is always referred to as being female.

We must ask the question, "Have you ever heard of a female Pope, or a female Bishop or Cardinal?" The Catholic church is a religion invented by men and ruled by men, and females must always remain the servants of men.

I also want us to consider that we have learned of the Great Red Dragon with seven heads and ten horns which was cast down to the earth. It did persecute the woman (the mother of Christ) and did then persecute the church that Jesus is building which we do know is the bride of Christ.

Then we learned of the leopard beast which is the Roman brand of religion, and it too, became a great persecuting power and did do many horrible things such as wage war with the saints of the most high God for 1260 years. The pages of history do show us this is so.

Then in 1798 the power to persecute was taken from the beast and the beast became the beast that was. However in such places as Ireland and again in the Philippines, there have been many fires still burning and religious persecution has never been far from them. Perhaps it is this way in other parts of the world as well.

I mention these things so that we might realize that the persecution against God's children did not come entirely from the ruling church but did include the worshipping church.

Now picture if you can, the United States with all of it's great wealth. Sitting on the back of the beast which is a great multitude of people of the catholic faith. The Great Whore using her wealth to influence nations that they must never allow the beast of the dark ages to arise again. Insisting there must always be a separation of religion from state.

The rulers of Roman religion know exactly what I am talking about and this is what lead to the speech in New York city by Karl Wojtyla in 1976, informing the United States that these conditions were surely going to be changed.

In the same way, Mr. Malachi Martin in 1990 did give us a very strong warning that a great catastrophe in the form of a head to head confrontation was about to take place. The sad thing is that no one listened.

Why, you might ask? Perhaps it was because the financial leaders who more or less decide who will become the political leaders of this great nation were busy forming their plans for Global Capitalism to extend to third world countries such as the Republic of China.

Our religious leaders, who should have been listening have been described by the Word of God as being "Sleepy Shepherds" who are ignorant, each looking for his own gain from his quarter. Why haven't the watch dogs of America sounded the alarm? I will leave you to think about that.

Way back in time we had the DEW line, which stood for distant early warning system put in place. Now at this late hour, we are too busy waging war with terrorists and are unable to realize the direction from which are greatest danger comes from.

All of this is caused by our unwillingness as a nation, to obey the very one who gave us so much wealth in the first place.

Now we will go to verse 16 and it will tell us enough about the ten horns that we will get an idea of who they are.

16 And the ten horns which thou sawest upon the beast, these shall hate the whore, and shall make her desolate and naked, and burn her with fire.

First, we notice that these ten horns which we have been told do represent ten kings, who do hate the whore which I have identified as the United States. Keeping that in mind, we go on to learn they do have the power and are capable of destroying the Whore. The verse said they would make the Woman desolate, like as in a desolate waste land.

And then they would strip her of her fine clothes leaving her naked. The verse then said they would "eat her flesh."

I do not take that to mean they would actually become cannibals but that they would completely destroy or kill as many people as possible. It should be clear they will show no mercy for their hatred of the United States is like a fire that burns within them.

The next thing we do learn of is their method of warfare. It is written, they shall burn her with fire, and it is my understanding that at this late hour this is speaking of nuclear fire. I want you to understand that it was given to me to know that the 10th chapter of Revelation, which describes in obscure words that there is a day coming when the seven thunders will utter their voices.

What they do say is, the destruction for which the missiles were intended is complete. The day of the seven thunders and the day when the Great Whore of Babylon is destroyed is one and the same.

17 For God hath put in their hearts to fulfil his will, and to agree, and give their kingdom (power) unto the beast, until the words of God shall be fulfilled.

18 And the woman which thou sawest is that great city, which reigneth over the kings of the earth.

If we want to learn more about these ten horn kings, we must remember something that was said in the 10th chapter of Revelation. I think it is very important to the information we are seeking.

The scripture did inform us in chapter 10, that another mighty angel (messenger) did come down from heaven, and this was telling us of the coming of the Atomic Age. The second verse does say

Revelation 10:2, And he had in his hand a little book open: and he set his right foot upon the sea, and his left foot on the earth.

The 1st verse did inform us that his face was as it were the sun (very bright) and his feet as pillars of fire. If we can grasp the knowledge that his feet as pillars of fire do represent nuclear missiles, and if you can remember the rainbow did inform us of what type these missiles were. (intercontinental). What I consider to be very important is where it stated that he put his right foot upon the sea.

As I shared this information with you before, this means to me that guided missiles are no longer limited to land but can be deployed from the water as well. It is toward this area that we must focus our attention.

It is true that ships of the destroyer class are equipped with missiles, but the ones I believe the Bible is referring to are the ones that are aboard the Nuclear submarines. They are capable of delivering a missile of great destructive power.

A number of years ago it was reported that a Soviet submarine did enter the waters of Puget Sound, in the state of Washington, and was able to navigate these in-land waters without being detected.

It was also reported that they were able to do so, because of some very sophisticated equipment they had purchased from the Japanese which reduced the noise level created when they are moving. Our government officials were somewhat disturbed by this, for we have our own submarine base located in Hood Canal which is West of Seattle. It was as though the Russians were trying to prove a point and they did.

Let us consider what if the ten horns on the beast which are ten kings that have received no kingdom yet, are actually ten captains of nuclear submarines. Further more, they have a complete crew which are highly trained in the use of large nuclear missiles. Perhaps these captains have been waiting very patiently for the time to come when they may fulfil the very thing they have agreed to do. Perhaps they are fueled by an intense hatred of the United States and their crews feel the same way.

Remember they are ten in number. I could imagine that four submarines could approach within a hundred miles of our East coast without much difficulty. At the very same time another four submarines could approach within a hundred miles of the West coast.

While this is being done, perhaps the two that are left could approach the soft under belly of the United states by way of the Gulf, perhaps in the vicinity between New Orleans and Texas. If their watches were synchronized, and the time was one when we least expect it, the result would be devastating.

After having given their plan for a new world order much thought, I have come to believe their intention is to kill as many people as possible. They will not be too concerned with large industrial sights as much as they will those cities of great population.

I do not have any doubt they will gain their goal, because the Word of God has foretold what is about to happen. We will learn about what the voice of Seven Thunders did speak in chapter eighteen of the Revelation.

Chapter 21 Destruction of the Whore

I find it difficult to understand how people who have come to know Jesus as their Lord and Savior can be so stubborn when it comes to following Jesus on the sabbath day. They have the Word of God to reveal unto them that Jesus did obey his heavenly Father, even to his death on the cross. Surely, they should realize that Jesus never ever failed to keep the sabbath day holy, and he then called out to all of us "Come and follow me."

In the same way, they have the pages of history to inform them where Sunday worship did originate and it is not at all hard to understand that it does not come from the Word of God. Whenever I ask them, about whether or not they do love Jesus, they assure me that they do. When I then remind them that Jesus did clearly say, "If you love me. keep my commandments" it is as though they are always seeking a loophole by which they wiggle out and claim that it is not necessary to obey the commandments of God.

I have written many words in an attempt to reveal unto you what the price will be, for those people who do claim to know God, but also claim that it is not necessary to obey God. Perhaps you have heard of the law of cause and effect? It is said that for every action, there is also a re-action. In the same way, there is a price that must be paid by all who claim to know God, but who harden their hearts toward His most Holy Word. That is our instructions for how we are to love, for they are the commandments of God that were spoken by God before they were written. It is strange how many people do not seem to realize this truth.

Through out the scriptures there are many warnings given, concerning the price of disobedience. The letter to the Hebrews contained a very strong warning concerning God's people who turned away from the fourth commandment. The 20th chapter of Ezekiel made it very plain, concerning the provocation in the wilderness. The two warnings seemed to go together, for they were warned that history would be repeated, if they insisted upon following in the example of the children of Israel in the wilderness.

Then James did inform us that if we do choose to reject even one commandment, it is the same as if we had rejected them all. I should think this is so very clear that even a small child would be able to understand it.

In his sermon on the mount, Jesus made it very clear how very important it is, that we obey God, and yet his warning seems to be completely ignored by the great majority of Christians today. They always seem to think this warning is meant for someone else and could not possibly include them. Let us listen closely to these words spoken by Jesus and take hold of how very important it is for this time in which we are living.

Matthew 7:21, Not every one that saith unto me, Lord, Lord, shall enter into the kingdom of heaven; but he that doeth the will of my Father which is in heaven.

There are many people who continue to believe that in order to enter into the kingdom of heaven, they must first be given permission by the Pope, or perhaps Saint Peter who is waiting by the pearly gates with the keys in his hand. Let me assure you that this is not what this verse is speaking of. It is speaking of doing the will of the Father and the ten commandments are the perfect will of the Father.

However, as we have just learned those people who call them selves Christians but do prefer the commandments of Constantine, are among those who refuse to do the will of the Father. They have refused to keep the seventh day sabbath holy, for the true love of God is not in them.

Jesus said in the gospel of John..

John 14:23, If a man love me, he will keep my words: and my Father will love him, and we will come unto him, and make our abode with him.

It should be very clear to us that the religious people who refuse to do the will of the Father, have neither the Father or our Lord Jesus, abiding within them, unless they may be deceived, because they do not love the truth enough to walk in it.

We must not forget that Paul in his letter to the Romans informed us that the wages of sin is death. It was John in his letter who informed us that sin is the transgression of the law. These truths are written in the Word of God and they are written for Christians so that they might avoid the mistakes that so many have made.

Let us listen once more to the words that were spoken by our Lord. Jesus Christ, as he does inform us as to what will happen to those who have hardened their hearts against the commandments of God.

Matthew 7:22, Many will say to me in that day, Lord, Lord, have we not prophesied in thy name? and in thy name have cast out devils? and in thy name done many wonderful works?

23 And then will I profess unto them, I never knew you: depart from me, ye that work iniquity.

I must point out that in order to work iniquity, it simply means the transgression of God's holy law, which law the majority of Christians today have chosen to ignore. I say this, for we can see by what they do, they do prefer the way of the Pagan to the way of our Father which art in heaven.

The 56th chapter of Isaiah has revealed unto us just who the "Whore of Babylon" is. A woman is often used as the symbol of God's church, but in this instance, the Whore of Babylon, or we could say "great woman of religious confusion" does show how God's people did allow the religious ways that were first practiced in Babylon to enter into the church of God. We find that they did seek the blessings of the Lord, but when it came to obedience, they did prefer to obey and practice the way of the Babylonian mystery religions.

If we have read the Bible, then we should be aware of how very zealous was Ezra and Nehemiah to keep the people returning from the captivity free from the religious ways of the Pagan people whom they were near during the captivity. They knew very well how important it is to God that people who worship him must worship him in spirit and in truth and not mingle in the ways and days of other religions when they do worship him.

Looking back, we can see that it was for this very thing that God did strike Uzzah dead, for he did not show respect for the ark, nor for the Holy Word of God it contained. He did place it upon an animal cart and because he was of the tribe of Levi, he was held responsible for his actions by Almighty God.

Going further back, we learned about the two sons of Aaron who placed strange fire upon the altar of God, and they both died by the altar. They too, did not follow the instructions they were given and did suffer the consequences.

All through the Word of God, we are told that God must be sanctified by those who would come near him. We must not mingle our worship of God with the Pagan customs of other religions. And yet, there are religious leaders at this time that do assure us that it is alright and it does not matter which day we worship God. Many claim they worship God every day and then do the very things that God has commanded us not to do. Is it any wonder then, that the Holy Spirit, speaking by the prophet Isaiah, did describe them as the sleepy shepherds that cannot understand?

However, in regard to those who do claim to be of Christ, it is very important that we also be followers of Christ. If we are truly followers of Christ, then the commandments of God will become our way of life, for it is certainly the way that Jesus did live his life. In the same way, when we find people who claim to belong to Christ, and yet have turned away from the commandments of God, we recognize they do not truly love God, but do love whoever they do obey. In this way, we have come to identify the great religious whore of Babylon, for it is a religious system that has turned her back on the commandments of God.

I now want us to recall that the wise men came to see Jesus, bearing gifts. As we have studied in the book of Daniel we learned that the little eleventh horn would seek to change the times and the law. At first, the observance of the times that were changed by the

Papacy were mandatory, but following the reformation then became more like gifts the beast did give to Christians and the world alike.

I want us now to think of all of the Christian churches as though together they do form a woman. In her heart and in her mind she has received the gifts from the beast and these gifts are Christmas and Easter and Sunday worship. She does cling to them very tightly and she is not about to let go of them.

However, they do reveal who she really does belong to, for she does obey her master and her master is not our Lord, Jesus Christ. Her master is the one who did give her these gifts. Jesus said "my sheep hear my voice," but she is not listening. Our loving, heavenly Creator gave to her his beautiful word which is truth in the form of our Bibles, but she has rejected the truth and does prefer to continue in her religious tradition. She will soon be taken into the judgment, and there is little we can do for her, except pray for her.

I do feel that I must point out that we have not been called to judge her, for the Word of God has revealed to us that the one who rides the black horse is the one who has been given the duty of judging her. Therefore, we must continue to warn everyone, about what is coming and tell them why, in the hope that God's people will come out of her, but we must not judge and neither should we cast stones, not even verbal ones.

I have spent much time and have written many words in trying to warn the people who do make up this religious system, but for the most part, they have chosen to ignore my pleas. It is for this reason that I shall now allow the Word of God to cry out to them in the hope that maybe, just maybe, a few might change their minds and return to the way of the Lord, their God, and love Him with all their heart and their whole being, and show their love in the way he has made known to us.

We should be able to discern from the signs of the times, for once again, the beast is rapidly rising to power and there are those who will lend their power to the one who is the leader of the beast. The beast lost his power to enforce his religious law upon the people of many nations after the reformation. Like a very patient chess player, the eleventh horn has been abiding his time, waiting for the right time to make his move. With much of the world in turmoil and so very many people tired of the violence that is brought about by war, it does appear the world is ready for a great peace maker who does promise world peace.

The Apostle Paul did have this to say in regard to this peace.

1st Thessalonians 5:1-3

1 But of the times and the seasons, brethren, ye have no need that I write unto you.

2 For yourselves know perfectly well that the day of the Lord so cometh as a thief in the night.

3 For when they shall say, Peace and safety; then sudden destruction cometh upon them, as travail upon a woman with child; and they shall not escape.

However, in regard to this peace, the beast does have a problem. There is a woman, the Whore of Babylon riding upon his back, and she has prevented the beast from acting like a beast, for quite a few years. It does appear that in order for the one who does lead the beast, the Pope, to implement his plan for one world government, also known as a New World Order, he must first remove the woman from off of the back of Roman religion.

I do realize that some of these things do seem like a mystery and so I will share with you my thoughts.

There is a book I have read, written by Malachi Martin, that tells of how there was a three way competition to see who would be able to establish a new world order. At first there were three but one did not have enough money and was eliminated from the competition. The one that dropped out was the Soviet Union. Now the contest is down to two players and one of them is that well known lady of the west who is a champion of religious freedom.

The other is a person who is most respected by many and has a reputation as being a peace maker. However in this regard, the woman of the west does also consider herself to be a peace maker.

Perhaps it is because she is very wealthy and also carries a very big stick she is hated by much of the world.

These past ten or fifteen years, the well liked man who many consider to be a peace maker, has become a world traveler, visiting many nations in an effort to win them to his side.

During this time, the lady of the west has sought to use her wealth and military might to bring peaceful solutions to those places where there was much trouble. In this way, which might be hidden from many, the competition to see who will be able to establish the new world order continues. The woman is not afraid to use her military might while the man does seem to be content to use the art of negotiation with world leaders to attain his goals.

Now, with the coming of a new millennium, the pace has quickened, for the man is getting older and does want to fulfill his life long desire within his life time.

The woman does not seem to be aware of this and so she continues as one who is in no hurry, for she is in control of much of the world's wealth and does spend much of her time planning how she can continue to have that control.

It would seem that if both sides want world peace, then surely, they could come to some sort of an agreement. I feel that I must point out that there is one area where they do not agree and it does not seem as though either side is willing to yield to the other.

The man of peace does claim to be able to bring peace to the world if certain conditions are met. He must be given complete power over all money and have one world wide currency. He must also be given complete power over all education. Thirdly, he does demand that he be given all power over matters of religion. The final demand is that he will establish world peace but there must not be any separation of church from state and his government will be religiously oriented.

At the same time, his opponent, that great woman of the west, does insist that to be truly free there must always be a separation of church from state. She does seem to remember why so many people did flee to the west, seeking religious freedom.

It seems as though this woman, who does appear to be the champion of religious freedom will never agree to bow down to the demands of the one who does insist there be no separation of church from state.

It appears to be inevitable that soon and very soon, there will be a confrontation between these two world powers.

At first glance it would not appear to be much of a contest, for the woman is rich and has great military power. In contrast, the man does seem to be so gentle and mild and does not have any military might.

If we would but look to the lessons of history, we would learn that quite a few times in the past, there was a federation of nations and they did lend their power to the office of this very same man. In fact, this is the way it was when poor Joan of Arc was sentenced to death, for there were nations which did lend their strength to the one who did sit upon the throne and did pretend to be God.

I do suggest that you visit the public library and search for the book written by Malachi Martin, the title being "The Keys of This Blood." As the title suggests, the author has a completely different understanding of the keys than I have shared with you. However, I do suggest that you read the first two pages or even the first chapter and compare the scenario he does paint with the one I have shared with you. In this way, you might learn that there are others who are aware of this very same situation.

For now, I have given unto you quite enough to think about, and it matters not whether we fully understand every little detail of how these things will come to pass.

The pages of this chapter and the words we have just read were written about fifteen years ago, shortly after I had finished reading the book "the Keys of This Blood. I believe that date was sometime in 1993. As I now sit at my desk and finish bringing this manuscript together it is December, 2006

As the scriptures of Isaiah 56 have identified the vast religious system that is about to lead this nation into the judgment, let us be aware that what we are about to read is a description of a wealthy nation and is not Rome.

Revelation 18:1, And after these things I saw another angel come down from heaven, having great power; and the earth was lightened with his glory. (nuclear power, bright as the sun)

2 And he cried mightily with a strong voice, saying Babylon the great is fallen, is fallen, and is become the habitation of devils, and the hold of every foul spirit, and a cage of every unclean and hateful bird.

3 For all nations have drunk of the wine of the wrath of her fornication, and the kings of the earth are waxed rich through the abundance of her delicacies.

4 And I heard another voice (of Jesus) from heaven, saying, Come out of her, my people, that ye be not partakers of her sins, and that ye receive not of her plagues.

I have heard that Martin Luther heard this voice speaking to him, and he came out of the religion in which he was involved. Of course, a great many people followed his example and they too, came out of Roman religion. However, it is from where we now stand, that we can see a completely different meaning which we will discuss before we are through.

Turn from your Pagan ways and walk in the truth and the light of God's Holy Word, for he loveth you more than we are even able to comprehend. If he did not love you, then why would he send you this warning?

Peter informed us that God does not want any of us to perish. Listen once more, as the voice of our Savior, who shed his blood and gave his life for us, cries out,

"Come out of her my people."

If you can hear this voice as it speaks to you from within you, please do as he says, for our loving heavenly Father is asking us to choose life instead of death.

5 For her sins have reached unto heaven, and God hath remembered her iniquities. (lawlessness)

6 Reward her even as she rewarded you, and double unto her double according to her works: in the cup which she hath filled fill to her double.

7 How much she hath glorified herself, and lived deliciously, so much torment and sorrow give her: for she saith in her heart, I sit a queen, and am no widow, and shall see no sorrow.

8 Therefore shall her plagues come in one day, death, and mourning, and famine; and she shall be utterly burned with fire: for strong is the Lord God who judgeth her.

9 And the kings of the earth, who have committed fornication and lived deliciously with her, shall bewail her, and lament for her, when they shall see the smoke of her burning,

10 Standing afar off for the fear of her torment, saying, Alas, alas that great city Babylon, that mighty city! for in one hour is thy judgment come.

11 And the merchants of the earth shall weep and mourn over her; for no man buyeth their merchandise any more:

12 The merchandise of gold, and silver, and precious stones, and of pearls, and fine linen, and purple, and silk, and scarlet, and all thyine wood, and all manner vessels of ivory, and all manner of vessels of most precious wood, and of brass, and iron, and marble,

13 And cinnamon, and odours, and ointments, and frankincense, and wine, and oil, and fine flour, and wheat, and beasts, and sheep, and horses, and chariots, and slaves, and souls of men.

14 And the fruits that thy soul lusted after are departed from thee, and all things which were dainty and goodly are departed from thee, and thou shalt find them no more at all.

15 The merchants of these things, which were made rich by her, shall stand afar off for the fear of her torment, weeping and wailing,

16 And saying Alas, alas, that great city, that was clothed in fine linen, and purple, and scarlet, and decked with gold, and precious stones, and pearls!

17 For in one hour so great riches is come to nought. And every shipmaster, and all the company in ships, and sailors, and as many as trade by sea, stood afar off,

18 And cried when they saw the smoke of her burning, saying, What city is like unto this great city!

19 And they cast dust on their heads, and cried, weeping and wailing, saying Alas, alas, that great city, wherein were made rich all that had ships in the sea by reason of her costliness! for in one hour is she made desolate.

20 Rejoice over her, thou heaven, and ye holy apostles and prophets; for God hath avenged you on her.

21 And a mighty angel took up a stone like a great millstone, and cast it into the sea, saying, Thus with violence shall that

great city Babylon be thrown down, and shall be found no more at all.

22 And the voice of harpers, and musicians, and of pipers, and trumpeters, shall be heard no more at all in thee; and no craftsman, of whatever craft he be, shall be found in thee; and the sound of a millstone shall be heard no more at all in thee;

23 And the light of a candle shall shine no more at all in thee; and the voice of the bridegroom and of the bride shall be heard no more at all in thee: for thy merchants were the great men of the earth; for by thy sorceries were all nations deceived.

24 And in her was found the blood of prophets, and of saints, and of all that were slain upon the earth.

In regard to this last verse, it would not seem to be possible that these verses could be speaking of America.

Let us once more compare it with the 6th verse of Revelation 17.

6 And I saw the woman drunken with the blood of the saints, and martyrs of Jesus: and when I saw her, I wondered with great admiration.

When John did write that he wondered it seems to imply there was something about this woman he did not understand.

He goes on to say... with great admiration. It would seem that by her appearance, as well as her reputation as being a champion of religious freedom, she was indeed, a nation to be admired. However, there is a little more we should know.

I am going to provide us with a partial list of certain events that have taken place during the rise to power of the Papacy and the reign of the leopard beast. It is very important for our understanding of these two mysterious verses.

Emperor Justinian's decree Bishop of Rome is head of all the
     holy churches and of all the priests of God . . . . 533 A.D.
Persecution of Paulicians, a Christian sect,
     under Pope Agathon . . . . 679 A.D.
Pope Constantine.....custom of kissing Pope's toe . . . . 708 A.D.
Charlemagne, son of Pepin, compels people he conquerors
     to embrace Catholic Christianity . . . . 768 A.D.
Sergius II persecutes Paulicians. . . . . 844 A.D.
Death for so called heresy very common . . . . 1046 A.D.
Leo IX first Pope to keep an army . . . . 1049 A.D.
Pope Gregory VII (Hildebrand) claims absolute dominion over all
     states of Christendom as successor to St. Peter and as Vicar of
     Christ on earth, (Vicarious Filii Dei = 666) Henry IV of Germany
     was humbled by this Pope and was required to
     stand three days barefoot in the snow for pardon . . . . . 1073 A.D.
Laity forbidden by Council of Toulouse to read Bible . . . . . 1129 A.D.
Waldenses (Lightbearers)..persecuted . . . . 1179 A.D.
Foundation of the Inquisition . . . . 1206 A.D.
Albigenses murdered by the thousands . . . . 1208 A.D.
Pope Gregory grants full persecuting power
     to Dominicans, Papal fraternity . . . . 1233 A.D.
Vaudois, a light bearing sect, persecuted in South France
     They flee to the Alps . . . . 1237 A.D.
Alexander the IV establishes the French inquisition . . . . . . 1254 A.D.
Pope John XXII persecutor of Albigenes . . . . 1316 A.D.
Pope Clement VI persecutor of Albigenses . . . . 1342 A.D.
Inquisition established in Spain . . . . 1481 A.D.
Crusade against Waldenses . . . . 1487 A.D.
Savonarola, Converted monk. tortured and
     burnt at the stake for daring to criticize the church . . . . 1498 A.D.

Table 1. Certain events that have taken place during the rise to
    power of the Papacy.

The pre- reformation light bearers crushed and silenced Lateran
  Council pronounces death of witnesses, thus there is an end of
  resistance to Papal rule and religion,
  opposers there exist no more .... 1514 A.D.
Massacres of Vaudois led by assassin monks .... 1530 A.D.
Society of Jesus (Jesuits) established to combat the
  Reformation Loyola, first "General" .... 1540 A.D.
Jesuit plot uncovered to split Protestant church
  into conflicting sects (Rome's Tactics-page 6-12) .... 1551 A.D.
Mary of England restores Roman religion.
  Ridley and Latimer and 72 others burnt at stake ...... 1555 A.D.
Protestants of Calabria slaughtered .... 1560 A.D.
Wars with Huguenots begin .... 1562 A.D.
Terror of Inquisition in Spain .... 1563 A.D.
Duke of Alva slaughters 18,000 Protestants
  in less than six years .... 1566 A.D.
St. Bartholomew's day .60,000 Protestants murdered. Worst massacre
  of the Papacy. Pope celebrates the event by having a
  special medal cast honoring the great slaughter ... . 1572 A.D.
20,000 Protestants killed in Magdeburg .... 1585 A.D.
Romish conspiracy in Ireland and 40,000 Protestants
  persecuted and murdered .... 1641 A.D.
Revocation of the Edict of Nantes followed by wholesale persecution
  and murders. 400,000 Protestants flee to other lands and many
  of them seek refuge in America .... 1685 A.D.

Taken from notes prepared by Pastor E. L. Saunders.

Table 1 (continued). Certain events that have taken place during
  the rise to power of the Papacy.

  This is just a partial list but it contains enough information so
that you will understand what comes next.
  Let us now turn to Jeremiah 51 and be aware that Jeremiah was
foretelling the destruction of ancient Babylon. He does say this...
  **49 As Babylon hath caused the slain of Israel to fall, so at
Babylon shall fall the slain of all the earth.**

It should not be hard to understand that the slain of all the earth did not die at Babylon. Yet this verse does say that Babylon did slay God's chosen people, Israel. It was for this reason that God has held them accountable for all that have been slain on earth.

The sixth verse of Revelation 17 does say .....

And I saw the woman drunken with the blood of the saints, and with the blood of the martyrs of Jesus:

And Revelation chapter eighteen does say at verse....

24 And in her was found the blood of prophets, and of saints, and of all that were slain upon the earth.

I now address myself to the "sleepy shepherds and to all of the priests who are busy fetching the wine. as well as to all who live in America and do follow them. It is because you have rejected the fourth commandment of Almighty God, and have replaced it with the commandment of Rome. Which commandment came from out of the mouth of the beast.

And because you have even rejected the life that was without sin, that our Lord Jesus Christ did lay down for you....for Jesus always remembered to keep the sabbath day holy.

Because you did choose to obey the commandment of Roman religion and did esteem it over the commandments of God, then be aware that all of the blood of God's children who died during Rome's reign of terror, because they would not give up the commandments of God, nor bow to the authority of Roman religion, is now on your hands. You have chosen to live your lives according to the way of murderers who slaughtered God's children and you will be held accountable for all who have died for Christ.

The words of a wise old king

Ecclesiastes 1:15, For in much wisdom is much grief: and he that increaseth knowledge increaseth sorrow.

On this day, I find it is my own sorrow that has been increased, for it is greatly multiplied.

America whom I love so very much, I do weep for thee. My tears are so many it is difficult for me to continue.

I say to you, behold, the Black Horse is here now, and the Pale Horse is just over the horizon and the one who is the rider; his name is DEATH.

Chapter 22 First Look into My Future

ᘓᘍᘏ

There are a few more things I want for you to understand about the day when the "voice of seven thunders" do announce the news that the missiles have done what they were intended to do. The destruction of America is complete and the will of Almighty God has been done.

We can learn a little more by turning to Revelation 16

Revelation 16:19, And the great city was divided into three parts, and the cities of the nations fell: and great Babylon came in remembrance before God, to give unto her the cup of the wine of the fierceness of his wrath.

The great city this verse is speaking of is North America, for it is indeed, divided into three parts. They are the United States, Canada, and Mexico. All three of these nations will experience the fierceness of God's wrath in days to come.

Why Canada, you might be wondering? Not far from where I live, there is a large white structure located near the Canadian border crossing at Blaine Washington. It is called the "Peace Arch," and it was placed there as a monument, of the peace that exists between the two nations.

Across the arch are the words "Children of a Common Mother." I do believe this is speaking of England as being the mother of both nations. At this present time there are a great many people living in this area, who come from all over the world.

Therefore, I want us to realize it is because the judgment of God must begin with the house of God, that we must focus on the people of the Christian religion. These people in Canada have committed the same kind of spiritual fornication as well as religious fornication as did the people of these United States.

The cup of God's wrath when it is poured out on the United states will not stop at the Canadian border. It will cross over the border as a flood, and the nations of the world will learn that our God does keep his promises. The cities of Canada will be destroyed and the land of great beauty will become a desolate waste land.

When we speak of our neighbor to the south, God is not at all pleased with Mexico. The reason this is so is a little different than it is for the United States and Canada.

Mexico has a great deal more wealth within it's borders than most people are even aware of. Even so, those who are wealthy have done nothing to help the poor of that nation. A great many people have lived their lives and raised their families in such poverty that they are continuously on the borderline of starvation.

Our loving heavenly Father is very patient, but the cries of hungry children and their parents have reached into heaven, and God's wrath has been kindled against Mexico. During the time of trouble that lies ahead, the wealthy people of Mexico will experience the pangs of hunger and know that the hand of God is against them. Hungry animals will be invited to feast upon their dead bodies, and those who remain will fear God.

Returning to the 16th chapter of the Revelation

Revelation 16:20, And every island fled away, and the mountains were not found.

21 And there fell upon men a great hail out of heaven, every stone about the weight of a talent: (a hundred pounds)

and men blasphemed God because of the plague of the hail; for the plague thereof was exceedingly great.

There is a book the Lord brought to my attention many years ago, the title which is simply "Hiroshima," and it was written by a man named Hershey. You can probably locate one at your public library.

This man Hershey, did travel to the island of Hiroshima, soon after the great catastrophe of the Atomic bomb that was dropped there, and did interview many people who had survived the great blast. He did write down their first hand experiences and their thoughts as well.

It is recorded that sometime after the explosion, I am not sure of how much time, but giant hail stones did fall from the sky on the survivors. I am not a scientist but my understanding is that the great heat of the explosion did rise like a bubble. When this great heat did meet the cold air of the atmosphere it created moisture, and the moisture did freeze and did then fall to the earth, in the form of giant hail stones.

This could well be the explanation of the 21st verse we just read.

In order to increase your knowledge, I must first lay down a foundation to make it easier to understand. Let us turn to the letter that was written to the people at Galatia.

Galatians 3:26, For ye are all the children of God by faith in Christ Jesus.

27 For as many of you as have been baptized into Christ Jesus have put on Christ.

28 There is neither Jew nor Greek, there is neither bond nor free, there is neither male nor female: for ye are all one in Christ Jesus.

29 And if ye be Christ's, then are ye Abraham's seed, and heirs according to the promise.

If we are indeed Abraham's seed, and shall inherit the promises of God, then prophetic scriptures do also belong to us, even though many were fulfilled long ago. Some prophetic scriptures do have a dual meaning, for as Solomon did inform us, history does have a way of repeating itself.

We need to understand there are two different Israels. The one of old that so much has been written about. And because the blood of Abraham does not flow through everyone's veins, we have become the new Israel through the blood of Jesus, which he did shed as the payment for our sins. It is written that In Christ Jesus we have become a new Creation.

Let us listen to the prophet Isaiah as he does say....

Isaiah 10:17, And the light of Israel shall be for a fire, and his Holy One for a flame: and it shall burn and devour his thorns and his briers in one day.

18 And shall consume the glory of his forest, and of his fruitful field, both soul and body: and they shall be as when a standard bearer fainteth.

19 And the rest of the trees of his forest shall be few, that a child may write (count) them.

I realize that many who have written Bible commentary would offer us a symbolic meaning of these verses. Even so, what I want for us to grasp is that all of the forests of America will completely be destroyed in a huge forest fire. The trees that will be left will be so few that even a small child would be able to count them.

Applying the instructions we were given by Isaiah about how we will gain knowledge, for he said "here a little and there, a little."

The prophet Joel did have this to say

Joel 1:18, How do the beasts groan! the herds of cattle are perplexed, because they have no pasture; yea, the flocks of sheep are made desolate.

19 0 Lord, to thee I cry: for the fire hath devoured the pastures of the wilderness, and the flame hath burned all the trees of the field.

20 The beasts of the field cry also unto thee: for the rivers of waters are dried up, and the fire hath devoured the pastures of the wilderness.

Consider the farmers who have much cattle and the dairy farmers with their herds of milk cows. The pastures will be scorched by the fires and the animals will be bawling loudly, for they can find nothing to eat. Eventually, they must all starve.

Joel 2:1 Blow ye the trumpet in Zion, and sound an alarm in my holy mountain: let all the inhabitants of the land tremble: for the day of the Lord cometh, for it is nigh at hand.

2 A day of darkness and of gloominess, a day of clouds and thick darkness, as the morning spread upon the mountains:

I want us to consider what conditions may be like following the day of seven thunders. Because all of the forests will be burning, there will be a great amount of smoke. In addition, where ever oil is stored and even the holding tanks of individual service stations will be burning. An entire nation on fire, even the tires on trucks and automobiles.

Can you remember the thick smoke that covered Kuwait when the oil wells were set on fire. Perhaps in many places, America will be like that and many will perish because of the smoke.

My first little look into my future took place many years ago, and long before I ever read the Bible or surrendered at the cross of our Lord, Jesus Christ. Of course, I did not understand that it was a very brief view of what would happen to me in the latter days, for I considered it to be a very troubling dream and nothing more.

However, it became a dream that was repeated many times, each one being a little different in content but basically the same situation. It was not until I fully understood the meaning of the tenth chapter of the Revelation, that I began to realize that my dreams were more than just dreams, but were a peek through the window of the future. I do not say this about all dreams but only about very special dreams, that I know beyond any doubt come from a divine source.

In my dream, I was in the process of waking from a very deep sleep. Perhaps I had been in a coma, I really could not be sure. My first thoughts seemed to be I must first establish where I am at and evaluate my situation.

I seemed to be laying on the ground and it was cold and damp and my first thought was I must not get my clothes dirty. It was as though laying on the ground and dirty clothes seemed to automatically go together, and I had always had a dislike of wet and muddy clothes.

Since it soon became rather obvious to me that I was indeed lying upon the cold and damp ground, I wondered just how I came to be in this undesirable situation. I thought about this, but my mind seemed to draw a blank, for I could not remember anything about what I had been doing, or where I was, for that matter. I tried again, but my mind seemed to be completely vacant, as to my memory of recent events. It was not like I could not remember anything, for I knew who I was and where I lived and all such important things as that. I just could not remember how I came to be in my immediate situation, for it was as though the events of the past 24 hours or maybe longer, had been completely erased from my memory.

Since the ground was rapidly becoming harder and pressing into my tender flesh, I decided that I must arise if I could and find out whether or not I had any injuries. I stood up and checked and everything seemed to be perfectly normal, except that I was very cold and uncomfortable.

I could not be sure of the time of day, for it was either getting dark or else it was very early in the morning and almost light. The skies seemed to be over cast with low lying clouds and I could feel that the possibility of rain was very near. My next thought was that I must do whatever was necessary to improve my situation, for I was already cold and I did not want to get soaked to the skin in the event the rain would begin to fall.

I looked around in the dim light and tried to determine just where I was and wondered how far I was from home. It did appear that I was near the place where the Slater Road crossed the freeway, and that meant that I was quite a distance from where I lived at Sandy Point.

Almost immediately an idea came into my mind, for I could walk along Slater Road, and cross the freeway, and find a pay phone and call my wife. I knew that Esther would be greatly worried because I had not come home and I needed to inform her that everything was alright. I could just tell her where I was and she would come in her car and get me.

As I thought about my wife, my thoughts of my own situation seemed to diminish and my thoughts of her brought light and hope into my heart. Surely, she should be able to tell me what I could not seem to remember. How I came to be here, laying in a field just off of the Slater Road and without my truck.

Perhaps that was it. Someone had hit me on the head and did take my truck, I thought. However, I did not find any evidence of this, for though I was very uncomfortable and cold, I could not find that I had any lumps or bruises, anywhere.

Since thinking of my wife and how she would soon be talking to me on the phone did bring joy to my heart, I began to walk faster in the direction of the freeway, hoping to find a phone.

As I approached the freeway, I looked across to the little grassy knoll, where the black and white cows could often be seen. Behind it was the unmistakable outline of Mount Baker in all of it's majesty, and between the clouds the sun was announcing that another day was about to begin. As I looked at this familiar sight, a cloud of depression began to settle upon me, for I sensed that something was not right. I stopped on the overpass above the freeway, and then all of a sudden it came to me. There was not a car to be seen in either direction. At this early hour there should have been a great many cars traveling in both directions but there were absolutely none. How could this be, I wondered?

I then looked over in the direction of the Knotty Pine, which was a place I knew quite well, for it was a restaurant and cocktail bar that I frequently patronized. My wife and I enjoyed their steaks and sea foods, and the seating was in little private booths made of knotty pine, for a cozy atmosphere. The service was very friendly and we considered it to be one of our most favorite places to eat and relax in a quiet location.

As I looked in that direction, it was as though the Knotty Pine had completely disappeared. Instead, there was nothing but bent up and twisted scrap metal and rubble that suggested that perhaps a large pole barn or building had once occupied this same space. However, as I looked around at everything along the frontage road, there were no buildings left standing but there was much material that suggested that some kind of buildings had been there before everything had been destroyed.

My mind and my heart was becoming more troubled with each passing moment. Something was terribly wrong but I knew not what. One thing was for sure and that was the fact that I would not find any pay phones here, for everything had been completely destroyed.

This unmistakable truth did cause me to begin to feel panic, for I greatly wanted to talk to my wife and to find out what had happened. Normally, I would have tried to hitch a ride if I saw someone going in my direction, but ever since I first awoke from my strange and deep sleep, I had not seen even so much as one person.

My thoughts returned to what I must do to improve my situation and how very much I wanted to be home with my wife. I could begin walking down the Slater Road toward Sandy Point, but I knew that it would be a good long walk. I thought about this and decided that maybe I should follow the freeway north in the direction of Ferndale, and once I was there I would quickly find out what was going on. It was more than likely that I would find someone I knew and I would be able to bum a ride home.

I decided to walk along the frontage road to the north and past such places that I once knew such as the Winter Garden and the Parachute. These were those drink and dance places that had once been very popular with Canadians, during the age when Sunday laws were in effect in their own country. When the Sunday laws were relaxed, it had a devastating effect on these once popular places, and they were only a memory.

I continued walking to the north, and I was approaching the intersection of the Smith Road. Suddenly, I heard some noise coming from the east and it sounded like the sound of fireworks. I thought about this and I decided that it could also be the sound made by someone firing guns such as at a target range. Maybe the sound was coming from the place where that gun club did hold their skeet contests, I thought to myself. However, it did sound more like it was coming directly from the east and from the area where the old county hospital had once been.

Since this was the first sound of human activity that I heard, I decided to turn in that direction and investigate the source of this sound. I reasoned in my mind that there was a little store on the corner of the Smith Road and Northwest Road, and I could call my wife from there.

As I began to walk along the Smith Road, I thought about the old county hospital and how my mother had been so frustrated and angry with what had once taken place there, many years ago. There had been some elderly people she knew, who had become sick, and when they became unable to pay their medical bills, such people were then taken to the county hospital. There they remained until they died, and then the government sold their property to pay their medical expenses.

My mother had tried very hard to get to this hospital to visit these old folks but it was difficult because the county hospital was a long way from town. She had finally found someone that would give her a ride if she would pay their gas, and that is how she came to understand what took place there.

She found people were sadly neglected, many laying for many hours in their own filth. The people she had sought to visit were badly afflicted with what she said were bed sores, that were for the most part left untreated. Even though I did not go in and observe these things with my own eyes, I never forgot how very much it did bother my mother, for you see, she herself was a caregiver, and she could not stand to see people neglected in this fashion.

I remember that she spent a great amount of time down on her knees, bringing her concerns to her Lord, and eventually the hospital was closed and as I remember, it sat vacant for quite a few years before it was used for other purposes.

As my mind was on the old hospital building, it then moved to the elementary school that had been built in recent years right across the road from the hospital. It seemed as though I could remember that it was called the North Bellingham elementary school, and I found something wrong with that. In fact, there was even a little community here, complete with firehall and it was all called North Bellingham.

What I found wrong with this was that it was actually a long way from Bellingham and I could find no logical reason for calling it by this name. In reality, it was much closer to Ferndale and for the sake of accuracy should have been called East Ferndale. Of course, the view of Mount Baker was so spectacular from this area, that it could just as well have been called Mountain View, or something like that.

Just who is responsible for naming these communities, I wondered to myself, and who or what group of people has the duty of making sure they are doing the will of the people?

When I was young and up until the time I entered high school, I lived in the community that was known as South Bellingham.

Now that was more accurate I thought, for even though it was also know as Fairhaven, due to the protection offered to ships anchoring there, it was really South Bellingham, and therefore, the main city of Bellingham was often called the Northside, by those who lived in the Southside. Surely, if Fairhaven was also known as South Bellingham, then the main part of town was North Bellingham, and this little community just east of Ferndale was an impostor. Just who did these people think they were giving their little community such a misleading name?

Such were my thoughts as I proceeded east on the Smith Road but now the sound of fireworks or gunfire, whichever it was I could not be sure, began to increase and my thoughts of the name of this locality began to fade. Now that I was much closer to the source of this sound, I decided that it must be gunfire.

However, the sound did vary, for there were some that sounded like the sharp crack of a high powered hunting rifle and others more like the pop, pop, of much lower powered twenty-twos or perhaps some that sounded much like the rapid fire of automatic pistols.

It was as though a voice within my mind did speak to me, and said I must be extremely careful, for I was about to come into an area of great danger. I thought about this and decided that it would be best if I were to use my best deer hunting technique and sneak along as quietly as I could, remaining out of sight as much as possible.

It seemed as though the safest way to approach the area where the shooting seemed to be coming from was to get away from the road and find my way through the rubble of the houses and buildings that had all been destroyed. As I left the road, and moved into what had once been someone's back yard, I came across two dead dogs. I looked at them very briefly and it did appear as both of them had been shot. Once again the voice spoke within me, you are now in an area of great danger. You must use extreme caution, for you are in the vicinity of death.

I stopped and I wondered why I had chosen to come this way. After all, my curiosity was hardly worth getting killed for. As I stood there, hiding behind some rubble, I noticed the foot of a child protruding from beneath the rubble. I moved closer for a better look and to help the owner of the foot if it were possible. However, the child was quite dead, and as I looked around I began to see the bodies of other people who were dead.

The shooting was taking place just ahead and so I again moved very cautiously in an attempt to find out just who was shooting at whom. Once I reached my desired vantage point, I remained as still as I could and I began to see some real live people for the first time. It was then that somehow that I really did not understand, the knowledge of what was taking place before me was given to me. It was placed within my mind and I suddenly understood the situation before me.

A time of great trouble had come to our land, and it was also a time of great death. One of the biggest problems was that there was no food to eat, anywhere, and people were starving to death because they did not have any food to eat.

The situation before me was that a few of the local people had discovered some canned foods within the elementary school on Northwest Road. It was most likely some of the food that had been used in the school lunch program, I really could not be sure. However, these local people were trying very hard to hang on to this food, and they were willing to defend their exclusive right to it, even if it meant putting their own lives in jeopardy.

There was another group of people who might have come here from town, I could not be sure, and they were in desperate need of food for their children were starving to death, and their will for survival was very strong. It was for this reason they had taken up their firearms for securing food for their families was a matter of life and death.

I was given to understand that they were so desperate they were even willing to kill, in order to survive. And so it was, both the people who were trying to defend their food supply, and the people who were trying to take it away from them, were from this area and the angel of death was present and death was supreme through out the land.

As I stood there, hiding behind the rubble, watching this real live drama of life and death being played out to it's inevitable conclusion, the hopelessness of their situation overwhelmed me. I did not know what to do or which side to join, for the enemy were my friends and neighbors and ordinary people such as live next door. It did not make any difference which side I should choose for I very clearly could identify with both sides. The reality and permanence of death and the hopelessness of no remedy in sight did penetrate my mind and I began to weep.

I believe that it was the sound of my sobbing and weeping and then I did awake and did realize that it was all a very realistic and very bad dream. Oh how happy I was, to become aware that my dear wife was beside me, and that what had seemed to be so real, had not really happened, but was only a very bad dream.

However, what did begin to trouble me was that I was to have this very same dream with very little variation, again and again. and even to the point I would say to myself, Oh no! not this same dream again. However, it was much later that it was given unto me to know, this was more than a bad dream, for it was actually a supernatural look into what will take place in the near future. Those things I did witness in my dream will become a reality in the days that are ahead.

Chapter 23 Second Look into My Future

I did not receive my next look through the window into the future until after I had become a born again Christian. It was after I had received the understanding of what would take place on the day of seven thunders and what the great tribulation did consist of. Therefore, when I did receive this dream I realized right away that it was from God and that I was seeing things that would become reality in my future.

In my dream I could not actually see myself as I must have looked, but I did see everything else as I would see them, looking through my own eyes. I guess that God did not want me to see myself and I can only think that this was for my own good. There are some things that it is better if our knowledge be limited.

In this dream, I found myself to be in the area just North of Bellingham, but west of Guide Meridian, where the Bellis Fair mall was located. Of course, there was nothing left of the mall but rubble and a big parking lot, but it did seem to be the place where the small group of people I was with did spend much of our time.

I had a rather sturdy stick which I used to steady my trembling legs as I moved about, but I was also using it to turn over small rocks and push aside bits of rubble as we searched for any movement. All of us were looking for bugs and insects to eat for that is all there was left. Even they were in short supply and we were slowly but steadily starving to death.

A great deal of time had passed since our great trouble first came upon us, but I was not sure of the exact amount of time but perhaps it was several years. The earliest days were the ones that were the most dangerous, for so many people did have guns and they did use them to kill one another.

Of course, a great many people died from all sorts of sickness and disease for we did not have any medicine, nor any drug stores to dispense the medicine, nor hospitals to care for anyone. There was so much suffering at that time that it practically goes beyond my ability to describe it.

Then there were the packs of wild dogs and the occasional coyote or cougar. They were so hungry that they did attack and eat humans who were too weak to defend them selves. Of course, these animals were also killed and eaten by those who were able to do this. I suppose that we could think of this time as being the survival of the fittest, or the time when the law of the jungle did prevail.

However, this was not entirely true, for we who loved God with all of our hearts did not seem to be subject to the laws of nature and we did survive because God did help us to survive. Our lives were in his hands and he remained with us, every step of the way.

At first, there had been so much shooting and killing and it was all around us. It was impossible to escape from it, for where ever we did go, there were people with guns shooting and killing and the dead bodies of people and animals were abundant. Indeed, the eagles and the vultures did gather where ever there was a dead body and they could be seen no matter where we looked and the putrid smell of rotting flesh became our permanent companion.

After a while, the sound of the shooting began to subside and it is only natural that it should. I believe that it was because people began to run out of ammunition and we began to find guns that had been left behind, for they were useless without bullets. Eventually, all of the people who used the guns in order to live, died in one way or another, and the birds and animals did feast upon their flesh.

In looking back to those early days of the tribulation, the very first to die were the very old and the very young. Also the very weak and the sick and the crippled. It almost goes without saying, for these were among the first to die.

The very next large group of people to perish were all of the people who had stock piled food and had hidden it, in preparation for this time of trouble. I say they were the next ones to die for there were so many, many people with guns and whatever weapons they could find, that were more than willing to kill the people who had food and were unwilling to share it. Of course, there were some who even killed their own children, to eat them but I do not care to talk about them.

The guns eventually became silent and we could see them laying here and there, amongst the bones and decaying flesh of those who had once used them against others. The animals had all died and then finally the birds did too. However the birds did last quite a bit longer than the animals.

It finally came down that the only people left alive were born again Christians, and there was not many of us left, for many had died and we did our best to give them a Christian funeral service. The same was not so for the heathen and ungodly, for it was not possible for us to bury all of them.

I thought about the great truth contained in the Bible, for mankind was made from the soil of the earth, and we could certainly see the evidence every day that people were returning to the earth from which they were formed. Even still, no matter where we did go, the bones of men and the bones of animals could be found scattered here and there.

Because there was so few of us left, and because we did care for one another with the agape love that cometh only from God, we did band together so that we could help each other any way we could. When we went searching for food, which is what we did every day, we stayed together and kept our eyes on one another should one of us fall down and be too weak to get up.

I did shuffle along on my trembling legs, stopping to turn over those rocks that might have a nice juicy bug hiding under it, but avoiding the ones that were large and heavy for the effort required to move them did drain us of our energy. I knew what I was about for we had been doing this very same thing for what seemed to be almost an eternity.

I slowly became aware that something was out of the ordinary. The man on my left had stopped and seemed to be interested in something other than turning over the rocks. He was staring at something ahead of us, and it had his full attention.

I then looked in the same direction in which he was looking, for there was nothing exciting going on these days and we had nothing to fear except for fear of starving to death. I am sure there must have been times when even that did not seem to be too bad of an idea, for a life of eating bugs was not only monotonous but was depressing as well. Still, as long as there was life there was hope and we all hoped that the government of these United States would come and rescue us from our situation. The will to survive is very enduring.

I looked and I saw the object of interest for it was the woman with the long hair. I cannot recall her name at this moment but it was a very common name and one that we all knew. She was very special to us and we all loved her very dearly.

She had been a music major in college and then later she had become the piano player for one of the many Christian churches that were plentiful in Whatcom county. I was told that her talent for playing the piano was of such quality that she was considered to be a concert pianist. Of course this did not do us much good, for we just lived off bugs and did not have a piano for her to play.

However, during those years when she played the piano in church she must have learned just about every Christian hymn and song that had ever been written. What is more, she had written many songs herself and she was always willing to sing them for us. Her voice was of such a quality that it was always crystal clear and I believe she was naturally a soprano. However, at the same time, she could sing so sweetly, low down and husky, for she had a very wide range in which she could sing. Yes, She was very special to all of us, for singing the old gospel hymns was something we did almost every day and she did lead us in all of our singing.

I do not believe this dear lady could have weighed much more than about sixty pounds, and she had lost so much weight that when she smiled the imprint of her upper teeth could be seen through the thin layer of flesh above her lip. I must confess that she truly did look like the walking dead, for she was little more than skin and bone. However, she was not alone for none of us looked very good, for our ordeal had taken it's toll on all of us.

I forgot to tell you about her hair for it was her private and personal possession and it was quite long and getting longer every day. She had such an abundance of hair that by volume it seemed to be the biggest part of her. Each day, she would find the time to sit, usually off to her self and she would spend a great amount of time combing her hair. We sometimes teased her and said we should cut off her hair but she always gave us such a look that said we must never attempt to do that. Just why the man to my left was busy staring at our song leader I was not sure, so I too, began to stare at her, to see what was so interesting. The look upon her face was one of amazement and she was or seemed to be in a state of shock. She seemed to be trying to say something and though my hearing was very poor, I did hear what seemed to be a moan coming from her mouth.

Suddenly, the moan became a shout and her arm shot up into the air and she began to point at some imaginary object in the sky, to the north. I looked as hard as I could and I noticed that she was pointing in the direction of Lynden, but I knew that just across the border was the Abbortsford airport.

Then the man to my left began to shout and he too, looked as though he had just witnessed something truly amazing. It was obvious something to the north or north east and it was something they could both see. Just then, my ears, though they were impaired, I could hear the droning sound of a multi-engined airplane. I stared as hard as I could and then I too, saw the silver shape in the sky, and it was coming our way.

I looked around, and everyone in our little group of about twenty born again Christians had become aware that there was an airplane coming our direction, and it was the first evidence we had seen in the years that had passed, that anyone else was alive in the whole earth.

As I looked at my companions to observe their re-action to seeing the airplane coming our way, about half of them fell down on their knees before God and began to give thanks that our prayers had finally been answered. The other half, stood with hands raised toward heaven, and began to praise their God, for his tender mercy and for his infinite greatness. The day of our deliverance had come and to God be all the glory and all the praise for he alone is worthy, they cried out.

My first thought, when I was able to see the airplane more clearly, was that it was the United States government come to rescue us, for this is what we had been praying for both day and night. I realized that I should be thankful like my companions but what I felt was a fire beginning to burn and smolder deep within me, for I was angry with the government of these United States.

I continued to watch the airplane and when it had gone a little bit beyond us, we could see many small objects as they began to fall from the airplane. They soon became like little men and then their white parachutes began to open.

It soon became obvious why they did first travel a bit further to the south, for as they came down from the sky, the wind did bring them right to where we were gathered. I say this, for even though the wind was very light, it was sufficient to effect the way they did drift down from the sky.

As I watched the little men begin to grow larger as they floated down from the sky, so did the anger within me grow larger and it grew in both volume and intensity. With the anger came a very large portion of righteous indignation and it came welling up within me and took control of my mind.

Here we were, citizens of these United States, and good, law abiding, tax payers at that. We had worked all of our lives, contributed to many different charities, supported our government in every way we could, and then had been treated like this.

What was bothering me was that I believed the government with the C.I.A. and other agencies could not have been ignorant of our situation. Surely they were aware that the missile attack had destroyed everything in our area, and that we who survived were in great need. Surely they were aware that we needed food and medicine, and I thought about the great multitude who had died because our government had totally neglected them, and my anger waxed very hot.

In my mind, I could imagine that the president and his cabinet had taken a trip to some secret hideaway such as a remote south sea island. There, they lay about in their swim suits, sipping on cocktails while they discussed what they should do about what had happened. Of course, this picture had been painted by my own imagination, but it was a very real possibility to me, and it did fuel my anger and cause it to burn even hotter.

My anger continued to increase as I watched the men float down, and then I noticed that one of them would be landing fairly close to where I stood. I quickly decided to move in his direction to get closer to where he would land in a matter of seconds. Already, I could see the color of his uniform was army khaki and this meant that he was a member of the United States Army Airborne, or so I thought.

This meant that the president of these United States was his commander and chief and that he was here today, because he was following the orders of the president. Now I would have preferred to pour out my anger by launching a verbal attack upon the president, but because that was not possible I would have to settle for the next best thing.

The kettle of my anger was practically boiling over and I fully intended to tell this member of the U.S. Airborne what was on my mind. This was the state of my mind, for I was thinking about all of the things I wanted to say to this young man, just as soon as I gained the opportunity.

The man from the sky did land a short distance, perhaps thirty yards or so, from me, and his back was toward me. I could not help but notice how very clean and neat was his uniform for by comparison, we were all clothed in rags and they were not very clean. His clothes did appear to be starched and neatly pressed, as though he was about to march in a parade.

He began to gather the cords of his parachute and he seemed to be very careful and taking his time, as though his parachute was something of great value.

As I stood watching him and his back was toward me, I could not help but notice what very good physical condition this soldier was, for the muscles of his back and shoulders were bulging within his neat uniform. The thought flashed in my mind that I should pick up a rock and be ready to hit him with it, should the need to defend myself arise.

I looked about to see if I could see one that was just the right size, but then I realized how very ridiculous was my plan, for I could hardly walk without my stick, for I was no different than my companions and we were all nothing but living skeletons. How utterly hopeless was my idea that we should defend ourselves for we moved about with great difficulty and the man before me looked as though he could do a hundred push ups before breakfast and not even work up a sweat.

The man finished whatever it was he had been doing to his parachute and he then removed the harness from his body and then turned toward me. I had slowly been walking toward him, and he must have been aware that I was behind him, for he turned about and looked right at me.

The first thing I noticed was the fact that the man had a rather bushy and thick black mustache, and a very fierce scowl upon his face with dark and piercing eyes that looked upon me with complete and utter contempt.

Suddenly, it hit me. This man was no United States soldier, for he was a foreigner and from another land. I thought for a moment, could he be a Russian soldier, and were they the ones who were responsible for the missile attack?

As I could feel this man's great contempt for me, I realized that he would just as well see me dead, for it was obvious that his hatred for me was very intense. That is when I wished that I had hit him with a rock while his back was turned, for I knew that I would never get another chance. With his face filled with hate, the man began to move toward me, and I felt a great fear for I was afraid that he might decide to kill me. It was then that the knowledge of who this man was came to me, for he was a soldier of Iran. What he was doing here I did not know, but he was coming toward me and I did not have any doubt that he wanted to kill me.

Perhaps I began to struggle, to get away from him and I began to cry out for my companions to help me, but then I did wake and realize that it had all been a dream. Almost immediately I knew that it was a supernatural dream and the things I did witness in my dream would become a part of my future.

However, there was one thing that was very unpleasant and that was I fully believed the soldier from Iran did want to squash me like a bug. I kept seeing the fierce look upon his face as he came toward me, and I thought to myself, this must be the time and place where my life does come to an end and it bothered me greatly.

Chapter 24 Third Look into My Future

꩜

During the weeks and months that followed that supernatural dream, that brief look through the window and into my future, my mind returned many times and I could not forget the look of contempt and desire to commit murder in the eyes of the foreign soldier. I began to prepare myself for the task of delivering unto you this message, but even as I studied the Word of God, sooner or later my mind would return to the end of my very strange dream and I could not seem to prevent this.

The complete irony of it all, I thought to myself. To experience the horror of the missile attack, and then to endure the extreme hardship and the trials of the great tribulation, for what? Why did I experience and endure all of this, only to be killed by a foreign soldier whom I did not even know?

It is true that I did consider hitting him on the head with a rock, but he certainly could not have known that. No, he hated me and wanted to kill me because of who I was, for it was apparent that he hated all Americans and it was as simple as that.

Sometimes I wondered if maybe somehow, I could live my life a little differently and could avoid the situation with the soldier. However, the Word of God did inform me that Jesus was the Alpha and Omega, the first and the last. He certainly did know all about the future and he knew what was ahead in my future as well. It seemed as though other than committing suicide, which I could never do, it was hopeless, for there did not seem to be anything I could do about the soldier I would one day meet face to face.

I thought to myself, how very cruel it must be for those men who have been condemned to die, to live day after day, and even year after year, with the knowledge of which day the death sentence will be carried out. What mental agony and torment must be in their minds and I realized how very good it is, that most people do not know which day nor the hour when the angel of death will come to visit them.

However, I found that my own inability to remove these thoughts from my mind seemed to be hindering me from functioning properly, and making it most difficult to keep my mind on my writing. Perhaps it was because the Lord my God was also aware of my thoughts and my mental state of mind, that I was given one more look into my future. It is because God does love me and is so very kind to me, that he has made it possible for me to finish my autobiography, even before it has come to pass. It is because God does know the future and he is the only one that does, that this is possible. Of all others, I remain very skeptical, for I place my trust in God and in God's Holy Word and not in those who claim to be able to predict the future.

In my final dream and look through the window of my future, I first became aware that I seemed to be in a very dark room. I passed through a doorway and stepped outside into very bright sunlight. My eyes having been tuned to the darkness, now could not immediately make the adjustment necessary for very bright and strong sunlight and I was forced to close them, and I stood there, and waited for my body to catch up with my circumstances. As my eye sight was gradually restored, I looked out and in the distance, I could see several very sharp and jagged mountain peaks and they were covered with snow. Immediately before me and extending to the mountains was a flat sea of dead grass, brown in color and rippling in the wind. It looked as though during part of the year, it might be filled with melting snow water, which later evaporated and became grass during the growing season. It appeared that now both summer and fall had passed and the grass was a rather dark shade of brown, while the evergreens that bordered the sea of grass looked rather scraggly, as though the soil was poor and lacking in nourishment. Here and there among the trees, small patches of snow could be seen, and this seemed to promise that snow would return again, cover this ground.

There was a rather brisk breeze blowing across the sea of grass and it seemed as though it carried the very frigid air from the mountains directly to where I was standing. I say this, for it had a chill and a bite to it that was impossible to ignore, for even though the sun did shine brightly, the temperature was near or below freezing and the effect of the wind was to magnify the cold.

I looked around to survey my surroundings and found myself to be in a village of rather primitive huts and that this village was situated on gently sloping ground at the edge of the sea of dead grass, which did appear to be a dry lake bed.

To describe the architecture of the huts, they were round in shape and made from sticks that resembled alder poles of the Pacific Northwest. The poles were from between three and four inches in diameter, being rather uniform in size, and standing in vertical fashion, one close by the next. Sealing the space between the two was what looked to be ordinary mud, or mud and clay mixed which appeared to have been placed there most likely by hand. Perhaps the mud came from the dry lake bed, for surely there must be a good supply of mud, during the spring and fall of the year.

The roofs of these very primitive huts appeared to be a mixture of a wooden frame work, with little and slender sticks woven in and big chunks of sod added on top. To my way of thinking, these huts looked like they belonged in Africa, but it was rather obvious to me that I was not in Africa, for the wind was far too cold. Instead, I was in a region of snow capped mountains and the air felt rather thin as though perhaps we were at a fairly high elevation.

There were quite a few people walking back and forth, and they hurried as though they might be on their way to work. The first thing I noticed was that they all seemed to be of Asian ancestry, and judging by their facial features I judged them to be some kind of Chinese people, but possibly Mongolians.

Their clothing looked as though we had gone back in time to a much earlier period, and many wore leggings that were similar to burlap bags cut open and into strips, wrapped round and around from the ankle to the knee.

Very heavy and baggy, woolen trousers were worn by most of the men, and funny looking caps that appeared to be made from leather and lambs wool, covered many heads. However, others wore what appeared to be very large and woolen stocking caps and most had heavy scarves about their necks.

For the most part, the color of their clothing was as drab and colorless as the burlap leggings on their legs, for they seemed to just blend in with the sea of dead grass. Their upper garments did seem to vary from one person to the next but many were wearing what appeared to be old army coats, worn and tattered, while others wore something that looked like ponchos made from brown woolen army blankets. To be sure, the fashion designers of Paris had not visited this area.

I could not help but notice that many of these people looked in my direction as they passed and they nodded their heads and smiled at me in polite recognition but did not stop to talk but continued on their way. I continued to stare at them and I could not help but wonder where we were. Were we in Mongolia, or maybe we were in Tibet? Still, China was such a vast country and I knew so very little about it, and I realized that it was possible that I could be within a region of that country that contained snow covered peaks.

As I was thinking these thoughts and continuing to watch as the flow of people had begun to subside, I noticed a small child appear from out of one of the huts. I first seen one and then another and then there was a whole group of children and they seemed to be coming toward me. It soon became apparent they were coming to me because they wanted something from me.

As they came closer and began to gather around me, I could not help but notice how similar were their facial features. Their eyes were like dark almonds and their noses for the most part seemed to be rather flat. Many of them, did wipe their noses on their sleeves as the cold wind did produce many runny noses. How alike, I thought to myself are all the children of the world. These children reminded me of the Eskimo children of western Alaska, and even the terrain surrounding our village reminded me of Alaska.

Many of the boys had thick, bushy hair, cut in the style that we always called "a bowl hair cut," when I was but a lad. I say this for their hair seemed to be in the exact shape of a soup bowl, that is turned upside down and is popular with Eskimo children, that I was familiar with.

Many of the young girls did wear their hair long, combed back and then braided into one long braid. However, some did prefer to wear their hair like the boys and it was hard to tell them apart. Both boys and girls did wear scarves and many did wear stocking hats or other kinds of home made headware.

Now as these children did come to me, they all began to chant something in unison and it seemed to be a request for me to do something. Their language had a certain sound and cadence to it and it sounded very much like Chinese to me. What was so surprising to me, was that I was able to understand what they were saying. Somehow, I had learned this strange sounding language and in fact, I soon heard myself reply to them, speaking in the same language they first spoke to me.

They did address me by my title, and by the prefix of most respected grandfather. My title was storyteller, and that was when I became aware that I was the storyteller for this village. Well, perhaps I should say that I was the story teller for these children, for I do not know beyond that. The fact that I was also quite old, or perhaps I should say, no longer young, for most respected grandfather was a greeting reserved for the elderly.

What they were chanting in unison was something like "Tell us a story, oh most respected grandfather. Tell us a story, for we have been waiting from early this morning for you to arise and to tell us a story. Won't you please tell us a story, for it would make us very happy."

I looked about at all of the smiling and happy little faces and I could not help but think about how very well mannered and polite they all were. It was as though they had been taught to respect the elderly and they did not spend much time in disagreement with each other. Therefore, they were all happy and in good spirits and such a thing can be contagious for they were like a medicine for my heart.

Very well, I answered them, draw close unto me and be still and I shall tell you a story. Shall I tell you the story about Jesus, who loved you so much that he died for your sins? A chorus of groans came to my ears, as many said to me, "No, no grandfather; do not tell us that story. You have told us the story about Jesus so many times that we all know it by heart. We can repeat it back to you word for word, and that is not the story we want to hear this morning. Tell us the story of what it was like to live in that fabulous place, the very beautiful land of America. Yes, tell us all about living in America, the land of plenty, for that is the story that we never grow tired of hearing."

A little boy asked, "Is it really true that most families had at least one television set and some even had two?"

And yet another little boy from the edge of the group asked, "Is it true that most families had at least one automobile and that some even had two?" I heard another boy exclaim, "Do not forget about the tractors. We heard that there were so many tractors that every farmer had his own. They did not even know what it was like to plough with oxen."

As I stood there, I heard others ask about how many bicycles there were in America, while a little girl that was rather timid spoke in a very small voice, asking if all little girls in America had their very own dolls to play with.

I could hardly answer one question before they would ask another and so I pretended to not hear them, for they always asked the same questions and I had answered them on many previous occasions.

I thought to myself, how the message that America did send to the far places of the world, did promote the great love for material goods, and it was firmly imprinted in the minds of these children. I must try harder, I vowed, to wean them from their love of material goods and shift their attention to the Word of God and to the Gospel of our Lord, Jesus Christ. I knew that it would not be easy but I knew that I must do my very best to teach them the way that is right.

I looked around at the group of children that were patiently waiting for me to tell them the story of life in America, for it was by far, their favorite story. They had been taught they must not interrupt when someone else asks a question, but I could detect that some of the children were certainly irritated with those who were asking so many questions.

Sensing their impatience, I said once more, Come close to me, for I do not want to have to raise my voice. And then I began, Once upon a time, Not so very long ago, there were many people, and some were Chinese people, just like you, and they lived in the land of America, the beautiful land that God blessed more than any other. And many of the Chinese people worked very hard and owned very nice restaurants, where they served Chinese food that was so delicious, that people from all over the world came to eat the authentic Chinese food.

The people from all over the world all said, Oh My! this is the best food that we ever did eat. We have never eaten food that tastes so good. I looked around at the faces of the children and it was as though the sound of my voice had completely captured them, and they were under my spell. It was easy to see, that they were before me in body only, but their minds had been transported back in time and over the ocean to that fabulous and wealthy place known as America.

It was the place they loved to visit in fantasy, but in reality, it was gone forever, for there would never be another America, and never is a very long time.

As I looked at my children I realized that quite a strong bond had formed between them and me, and they all loved me very much and I loved each one of them dearly and they were very precious to me.

The peace of God was with me and it flowed through my veins, even as I did tell the many stories to the children. I was aware that there would come a morning when I would not wake from my sleep. I also knew beyond any doubt that the children would be sad and they would weep for me, and then they would give me a funeral that was according to the customs of their people. I knew this, but it did not trouble me, for the peace of God was my security blanket and my robe that I wore every day, and the fact that I must die was something I came to accept a long time ago.

I could truthfully say, The Lord is my shepherd, for he had lead me through the great tribulation. I knew for sure that he maketh me to lie down in green pastures and that he leadeth me beside the still waters.

The scripture does say, Yea, though I walk through the valley of the shadow of death, I will fear no evil, for thou art with me; thy rod and thy staff they comfort me. I could look back in time and know beyond any doubt that all of these verses had become a reality.

I thought about the children God had placed in my care, that I should teach them truth by telling them the stories of the Bible. I thought about how much of my life was left and how I would go on telling them the good news about Jesus until there wasn't any breath left in my body.

The last verses did come to my memory, but not in sequence. He restoreth my soul: he leadeth me in paths of righteousness for his name's sake. Thou preparest a table before me in the presence of my enemies: and I thought about how Jesus had taught us to love even our enemies.

Even so, during the time of tribulation they had died, day after day all around us, and all we could do was love them and comfort them, the best we could.

Thou anointest my head with oil and my cup runneth over. Surely goodness and mercy shall follow me all the days of my life: and I will dwell in the house of the Lord forever.

I think that it was as the Psalms of David were flowing through my brain that I did wake from my sleep and I realized that it had all been a dream.

However, I was also aware that it was not an ordinary dream but was actually a gift from God, for he had allowed me once more, to look through the window into my own future.

I knew that a great burden had been lifted off of my shoulders, for I now knew beyond any doubt that the foreign soldier did not take my life. There could not be any doubt that he hated me for being an American, but this soldier was not here to kill people but to save people. He was here as a part of the New World Order.

I have now shared with you this final look through the window of my future and the time has come for me to bring this part of this message to an end. There are other things we must talk about before this message is complete.

Volume III
Chapter 25 Searching for a Refuge

Salvation

Perhaps you can remember that in Matthew 24, Jesus informed us that the judgment that is to come will be like it was during the time of Noah. Again in Luke 17, Jesus did inform us that it will be like it was when God destroyed Sodom and Gomorrah.

What I believe is important at this time is that in both of these times of God's judgment, God did provide a refuge or a place of safety. Surely we must know that Noah, his wife, and their three sons, and their three wives did enter into that place of safety. Everyone else did perish in the flood.

At the time of the over throw of Sodom, Both Lot and his wife as well as their two daughters did escape across the plain and to the city of Zoar. However, because Lot's wife failed to follow the instructions they were given, and she did look back, she did perish and only three people did survive.

What I want for us to realize is that once more, as God is about to pour out his wrath upon North America, he has provided a refuge, a place of safety, and it is for all who will truly search for it.

Jesus once said, "Seek and ye shall find" and he added "Knock and it will be opened to you." Jesus also said in Luke 17:32 "Remember Lot's wife." We want to be sure that no one make the same mistake she did, for her mistake was simply she could not follow the instructions she did receive, and it cost her, her life.

In the pages ahead, we shall search the Word of God for the one place of refuge that God will provide and we shall also learn about what we must do in order to enter into that refuge.

I want us to keep fresh in our minds the knowledge that was shared with us by our Lord Jesus Christ, concerning the fact that the time of great trouble which is coming will be as it was in Noah's day. Keep this in mind and we shall now listen to another of our Lord's chosen men, the man called Peter.

2nd Peter 3:1-9, This second epistle, beloved, I now write unto you; in both which I stir up your minds by way of remembrance:

2 That ye may be mindful of the words which were spoken before by the holy prophets, and of the commandment of us the apostles of the Lord and Savior:

3 Knowing this first, that there shall come in the last days scoffers, walking after their own lusts,

4 And saying, Where is the promise of his coming? for since the fathers fell asleep, (died) all things continue as they were from the beginning of creation.

5 For this, they willingly are ignorant of, that by the word of God the heavens were of old, and the earth standing out of the water and in the water:

6 Whereby the world that then was, being overflowed with water, perished:

7 But the heavens and the earth, which are now, by the same word are kept in store, reserved unto fire against the day of judgment and perdition of ungodly men.

8 But beloved, be not ignorant of this one thing, that one day is with the Lord as a thousand years, and a thousand years as one day.

9 The Lord is not slack concerning his promise, as some men count slackness; but is longsuffering to us-ward, not willing that any should perish, but that all should come to repentance.

We can be sure that in these last days there will be scoffers and mockers for both Peter and Paul has told us there would be. They will ridicule and scoff at the things I have said and yet, the message I have been commanded to deliver unto you is the same message that is contained in your Bible. Why haven't these people learned to place their trust in God and in God's word? After all, even the inscription on our coins claim that we do. Could it be that they have twisted the true meaning of the scriptures to the point they no longer believe in the promises of God?

In the ninth verse, Peter informed us that the Lord is not slack concerning his promise. He has promised that he would bring judgment against the land and the people if the people refused to keep his commandments. Peter went on to say that the Lord is longsuffering to us-ward. In other words, God has been very patient and the door of salvation has been open for almost two thousand years. He did not want to see any of us perish.

However, once again, as it was in the days of Noah, the patience of God is wearing a little thin. The hour is late, and we can hear the sound of pounding hoofs, as the black horse and it's rider ride through this land. Behold, soon it will be time for the pale horse to appear.

There is one great truth contained in these verses written by Peter that I want for you to cling very tightly to. That is where it said that God does not want anyone to perish. We all need to know that both you and I and our children and all of our loved ones are very precious to God, and he does not want any of us to perish.

There is one thing I do know and that is God has a plan for our salvation and there is only one plan for all people. It was the same plan for the apostle Paul and a man named Peter and it was the same plan for Matthew, Mark, Luke and John, and it is the same plan for you and I. God has a plan and it is a plan that will not fail.

Jesus had something to say to Peter regarding his plan for salvation. We will find it in the 16th chapter of Matthew.

Matthew 16:15-18, He (Jesus) saith unto them, But whom say ye that I am ?

16 And Simon Peter answered and said, Thou art the Christ, the Son of the living God.

17 And Jesus answered and said unto him, Blessed art thou, Simon Barjona: for flesh and blood hath not revealed it unto thee, but my Father which is in heaven.

18 And I say also unto thee, That thou art Peter, and upon this rock I will build my church; and the gates of hell shall not prevail against it.

The rock that Jesus said he would build his church upon was not Peter, as some people believe. The rock that Jesus said he would build his church upon was the very solid rock of his identity, as the Son of the living God. God has a plan and God has a church, and I shall do my very best to reveal unto you God's perfect plan, and the Word of God will identify the church of the tribulation.

Why the church of the tribulation and not some other more glorified church ? Because it is the one that the gates of hell will not prevail against, and it is the only one. In a very short while, the pale horse and it's rider, whose name is Death shall appear upon the scene, and Hell follows along after them. During that time, when hell is here on earth, the churches that are built upon mortal men and teach the commandments of men for doctrine shall fail, but the church that Jesus has built, will endure, even until the end.

Some men a long time ago once asked, What must we do to be saved? This is a question we should all be asking. If we have never asked this question, we are either ignorant or we have an attitude problem. There are many religious people today with an attitude problem, for they claim to know all there is to know, and they can not learn a thing. Let us be as those men in the Bible, who wanted to learn what they were to do, in order to be saved and we shall allow the Word of God to lead us in his plan for our salvation.

Let us begin with these instructions given unto us by Jesus for they do concern our salvation.

Matthew 7:7, Ask, and it shall be given you; seek, and ye shall find; knock, and it shall be opened unto you:

Notice how very positive are these promises, for they are promises that are connected to instructions. We can be very sure that we will be able to claim these promises, if we are persistent in our effort to follow these instructions.

Turning to the gospel of John, we shall learn what John the Baptist has to say about this subject. Notice how troubled the religious establishment was when John the baptist came on the scene.

Perhaps they feared that they would lose some of their religious authority.

John 1:19-23, And this is the record of John, when the Jews sent priests and Levites from Jerusalem to ask him, Who art thou?

20 And he confessed, and denied not; but confessed, I am not the Christ.

21 And they asked him, What then? Art thou Elias? And he saith, I am not. Art thou that prophet? and he answered, No.

22 Then said they unto him, Who art thou? that we may give an answer to them that sent us. What sayest thou of thyself?

23 He said, I am the voice of one crying in the wilderness, Make straight the way of the Lord, as said the prophet Isaiah.

During the very short time of the ministry of John the baptist, and during the time of Jesus, the highly exalted leaders of the religious establishment did all they could to make the way of God very crooked. It was as though they were very proud to be known as God's chosen people, but they were not very willing to share God's ways with the people of the world around them.

In the almost two thousand years that have passed since the birth of Christ, nothing has really changed in this regard. Many of the leaders of the Christian community still claim that their own church is the only true church of God and that all of the rest of the churches have something wrong with them.

Many have tried to make the paths leading to their own churches very straight, but have done all that they could to make the paths leading to the other churches seem as crooked as can be.

Their main concern is not to see souls saved, but is to see their membership roles increased. In this way, they are failing to make the way of the Lord straight, for if we truly do love our neighbors, we will want them to be saved regardless of which church they do choose to attend.

There are some who have gone beyond making the way of the Lord crooked, for they claim that only the members of their church will be allowed to enter into the kingdom of heaven. Some, claim that they are the only ones who will receive salvation while others claim that they are the only ones who have the keys to heaven and hell.

The scripture in John 3:16 say "whosoever," but they are saying "only the members of our church." We think of this as being the exclusive gospel and it was not taught by Jesus. Whenever you hear anyone make such a claim, you can be sure that they are not a part of the church that Jesus is building but do belong to the churches of religious men. The churches of religious men are not built upon the solid rock but are built upon the sinking sand.

The voice of Almighty God has spoken unto me and commanded me to issue a warning to these people. The Lord has said that they must stop teaching this false doctrine of the exclusive gospel and repent, for if they continue in this lie, they will have to appear before God in the judgment and God will hold them personally responsible for all of the souls they have sought to turn away, except they enter in through the narrow doorway of their church.

Therefore, I must say to the leaders of all of these churches which teach that they are the only ones, Make ye straight the way of the Lord while you still can, for the hour is late, and the judgment is close at hand. Repent, for to claim that your church is the only true church is a lie, and the truth is not in you. Repent, while God's grace is still available to you. Humble your self before God and learn to walk in the light of his word, for you are still in darkness.

In order we determine what we must do to be saved, let us start with the instruction we received from our Lord and Savior. Jesus said,"Seek and ye shall find." Let us then begin our search traveling on the path of enlightenment which is the revealed Word of God. We can be sure that God's plan for our salvation is contained within our Bibles, for our salvation is the center piece of the entire Bible. Nothing we may ever do in this life is as important as entering into and receiving God's simple plan for how we may receive the gift of eternal life.

As we begin our journey along the path of enlightenment and even before we reach the first bend in the path, I look up a head and I see a very large stone is blocking our way. I can see from here that there is something written upon the stone and that there is a group of people standing next to it.

As we draw near, I notice a man who does appear to be their leader, and he steps forward to speak to me. "Why are you wasting so much valuable time taking all of your readers on a journey along the path of enlightenment? he asked. "There is no need for you to go any further for we have all the truth you will ever need."

I replied that we are obeying the instructions we were given by Jesus, the only begotten Son of God. He informed us that if we would search for God's plan for our salvation, that we will find it.

Praise God, the man replied. Your prayers have been answered and you do not need to search any further. You have found God's plan for salvation for all you need to do is believe upon the Lord, Jesus Christ and you will be saved. We are all believers here, and you might just as well join with this body and we shall all go to heaven together.

I asked, Are you absolutely sure that all we have to do is believe upon the Lord Jesus Christ? Isn't there something else we must do, such as repent of our sins?

Absolutely not! he said emphatically. That is an old fashioned doctrine that should have been put to sleep long ago. The apostle Paul made it quite clear that we can not be saved by our works. If we believe we must repent then we are saying that we are saved by our works for it takes effort on our part to repent.

You can trust me, he said. I have read the Bible from cover to cover and all that is necessary to receive salvation is to believe. Besides, he added, Jesus did it all and there is no need for anyone to think that they can do anything by their own effort to improve upon what Jesus did. Jesus paid the price for our sins with his blood and all we have to do is believe that he did. That is all there is to it, and we do not want to bother the people with filling their heads full of a bunch of doctrine they do not need. That is the trouble with so many churches today, for all they want to do is fill people with religious doctrine and get them so confused that they do not know what to think.

Deep within me, I hear an alarm bell ringing and I listen as the voice of the Holy Spirit speaks to me, " 1st Thessalonians chapter five and verse twenty-one. Read what it says. **Prove all things; hold fast that which is good.**

How are we to prove all things, you might wonder? By the Word of God. However, it is also helpful if we have more than one witness to prove a point or a doctrine. This simply means that we need more than one scripture to verify a doctrine or to reveal that a doctrine is false. The scriptures do inform us that there is safety in a multitude of counselors and of course, each scripture verse is our counselor for it is the Word of God.

Knowing that there is but a short time left, I am concerned for your safety. I want to be sure that we do locate God's only plan for our salvation, for there is nothing in either your or my entire life that is more important.

However, before we are able to proceed any further along the path of elightenment, we must first remove the very large stone that is blocking our way. Now that we are close to this stone, I am able to see what is written on it, quite clearly. I can make out the words "Easy Believe-ism" and it has prevented many people from receiving the gift of God which is eternal life.

For our first witness that will help us to remove the large stone of easy believe-ism from out of our path, we shall turn to the gospel of John and read a very familiar verse.

John 3:16, For God so loved the world, that he gave his only begotten Son, that whosoever believeth in him should not perish, but have everlasting life.

This is a verse that all Christians should be able to recite from memory. This is also one of those places where we must rely upon the old King James Version for some of the modern versions have changed ever so slightly the way this verse is worded. By doing so, they have greatly altered it's true meaning.

Of course, the first great truth contained in this verse is the fact that God loves each and every one of us, and in fact, he loves us so much, that he formed a plan by which we may receive the gift of eternal life and be with God, forever. However, in order for his plan to be implemented, it was necessary for God to allow his only begotten Son to die a very cruel death upon the cross of Calvary. His death was a sustitution, for he died in our place, so that we may live.

I now want to bring to your attention the second great truth that is contained in this beautiful verse. Notice where it says, "whosoever believeth." This must include all of the people who cling to the doctrine of easy believe-ism, but is not limited to them. Then I want you to notice that it is written that the people who believe should not perish. However it does not say "would not perish." Now if we are completely honest as to the true meaning of this, we would have to conclude that it is possible to believe and still perish.

The third chapter of John does open with a conversation between Jesus and a religious man named Nicodemus. At verse three, Jesus said unto him "Verily, verily, I say unto thee, Except a man be born again, he cannot see the kingdom of God." When we come to John 3:5 Jesus answered, Verily, verily, I say unto thee, Except a man be born of water and of the Spirit, he cannot enter into the kingdom of God.

Just a few verses later, Jesus does inform Nicodemus .....

John 3.15 That whosoever believeth in him should not perish, but have eternal life.

It is important we realize these two scriptures were both in the same conversation between Jesus and Nicodemus. We should be able to understand that what Jesus was saying to him was that it was absolutely necessary that one be born again in order to receive God's one and only plan for salvation. Those who do believe in Jesus should not perish, but they will certainly perish if they are not first, born again. This is a great truth and we will learn all about this in a little while.

In chapter twenty-five of The Acts of the apostles, we learn of how Paul was taken to Caesarea where he was held while those in authority tried to determine what to do with him. The situation had become rather complicated because Paul insisted that he be allowed to plead his case before Caesar in Rome, for he had done the Jews no wrong.

While Paul was being held there, King Agrippa and his wife Bernice, came to Caesarea, to pay their respects to the governor whose name was Festus. When the king learned that Paul was being held prisoner there, he decided to listen to Paul's story as to how he was charged with crimes he did not commit.

Now Paul took hold of this opportunity to share with King Agrippa, how he was once a man who did greatly persecute the Christians and did what ever he could to silence them. He then told King Agrippa of how he met Jesus while traveling to Damascus, and how he then became a born again believer and a servant of Christ.

Let us listen as Paul continues to speak to King Agrippa.

Acts 26:19,Whereupon, 0 king Agrippa, I was not disobedient unto the heavenly vision:

20 But showed first unto them of Damascus, and at Jerusalem,

and throughout all the coasts of Judea, and then to the Gentiles, that they should repent and turn to God, and do works meet for repentance.

21 For these causes the Jews caught me in the temple, and went about to kill me.

22 Having therefore obtained help of God, I continue unto this day, witnessing both to small and great, saying none other things than those which the prophets and Moses did say should come:

23 That Christ should suffer, and that he should be the first that should rise from the dead, and should show light unto the people, and to the Gentiles.

24 And as he thus spake for himself, Festus said with a loud voice, Paul, thou art beside thyself; much learning doth make thee mad.

25 But he said, I am not mad, most noble Festus; but speak forth the words of truth and soberness.

26 For the king knoweth of these things, before whom also I speak freely: for I am persuaded that none of these things are hidden from him; for this thing was not done in a corner.

27 King Agrippa, believest thou the prophets? I know that thou believest.

I want us to notice this question that Paul has asked King Agrippa. There can be no doubt that Paul is speaking of those things that are recorded in the books of the prophets, which things do verify that Jesus is the Christ and the Messiah, whom God would send. Also notice that Paul has stated very clearly that he knew that King

Agrippa did believe what the prophets had to say concerning the identity of Jesus as the Messiah.

We shall now listen to King Agrippa's reply.

28 Then Agrippa said unto Paul, Almost thou persuadest me to be a Christian.

Here was a man who knew very well what the prophets had foretold and who did believe that Jesus was the fulfilling of those prophecies, and yet, even though he did believe, he chose of his own free will to not become a Christian. As it is written in the scriptures, as a believer, he should not have perished, but we can be fairly sure that he did perish. We see then, that it takes more than easy believing, to receive the gift of eternal life.

In my own personal experience, for sure, I believed in Christ as to who he really was and what he did at the cross of Calvary by the time I was twenty-one, but I did not surrender and become a born again Christian until I was forty six years old. If I had died during the time that I believed but before I surrendered, my soul would have perished, for I was still a common and ordinary sinner. It takes more than believing to take away our sins, for even Satan does believe in Christ and he knows very well what Jesus did at the cross.

Chapter 26 Traveling with Paul

In order we come to a better understanding of the truth in this matter of easy believe-ism I think we should read that portion of the Bible where the scriptures are found that these people use to form this doctrine.

In the book of Acts we shall find the apostle Paul and Silas on a missionary journey, as they labor to deliver the gospel message to those people who had not yet heard what Jesus had done for all mankind. As we come to the sixteenth chapter, Paul and Silas are joined by a young man by the name of Timothy.

I want us to come to a complete understanding of all that happened for it will help us understand the situation the way it really was. We shall pick up the story at verse four and five.

Acts 16:4-5, And as they went through the cities, they delivered them the decrees for to keep, that were ordained of the apostles and elders which were at Jerusalem.

5 And so were the churches established in the faith, and increased in number daily.

I have included these scriptures for I want us to realize that the apostle Paul and Silas, and young Timothy were successful in carrying out our Lord's business of establishing new churches and building up the ones that had been previously established.

We shall now take up the story in verse nine and be aware that these men are traveling aboard a ship that is no doubt a cargo laden vessel traveling along a merchant trade route within the Mediterranean sea.

Acts 16:9-13, And a vision appeared to Paul in the night; There stood a man of Macedonia, and prayed him, saying, Come over to Macedonia, and help us.

10 And after he had seen the vision, immediately we endeavoured to go into Macedonia, assuredly gathering that the Lord had called us for to preach the gospel unto them.

11 Therefore loosing from Troas, we came with a straight course to Samothracia, and the next day to Neapolis;

12 And from thence to Philippi, which is the chief city of that part of Macedonia, and a colony: and we were in that city abiding certain days.

13 And on the sabbath we went out of the city by a river side, where prayer was wont to be made; and we sat down and spake unto the women which gathered there.

I would point out that the three evangelists were deep in the country of Gentiles. However, in Philippi, which was the main city in that part of Macedonia, there lived a colony of Jews. These were the people, including the Gentiles who were converted to their religion, who gathered by the river for prayer on the sabbath day. However, the woman named Lydia, that is mentioned in verses 14 and 15 does appear to be a Gentile and we can be sure that she did become a Christian.

Let us keep in mind their location as we take up the story in verse 16.

Acts 16:16-18, And it came to pass, as we went to prayer, a certain damsel possessed with a spirit of divination met us, which brought her masters much gain by soothsaying:

17 The same followed Paul and us, and cried saying, These men are the servants of the most high God, which show us the way of salvation.

18 And this did she many days. But Paul, being grieved, turned and said to the spirit, I command thee in the name of Jesus Christ to come out of her. And he came out the same hour.

I am sure that some are wondering why Paul was grieved with this young women, for it would seem that all she did was follow them and tell people the truth regarding who they were. I do not believe that Paul was grieved with the young woman, herself, but with the demon spirit which was in control of her.

If she had not followed after them, saying what she did, I doubt that Paul would have paid much attention to her. However, her buisness was fortune telling which she did for money. The money was probably not for herself but was for her masters for this young woman was most likely a slave girl. In any event, Paul became grieved with the spirit which possessed the young woman, and in the name of Jesus, cast the demon spirit from her.

Acts 16: 19-24, And when her masters saw that the hope of their gains was gone, they caught Paul and Silas, and drew them into the market place unto the rulers.

20 And brought them to the magistrates, saying, These men being Jews, do exceedingly trouble our city,

21 And teach customs, which are not lawful for us to receive, neither to observe, being Romans.

22 And the multitude rose up together against them: and the magistrates rent off their clothes and commanded to beat them.

23 And when they had laid many stripes upon them, they cast them into prison, charging the jailer to keep them safely:

24 Who, having received such a charge, thrust them into the inner prison, and made their feet fast in the stocks.

I do hope that you have been able to follow this story. Perhaps if Paul had known how much trouble they would get in, he might not have done what he did. However, I am sure that what he did must have seemed to be the right thing to do at the time. I doubt very much that Paul was aware of all that would take place because he cast the demon spirit from the young woman.

Let us pretend that we are there with Timothy, who must be the one who is writing this story, for it does appear that Timothy was not cast into prison with Paul and Silas. First of all, these men are a long way from home, and in the heart of Gentile country which might not be too friendly toward them.

It sounds as though when they provoked these men to anger that a great multitude rose up together against them, and their clothes were torn from their bodies, and they were beaten.

The next verse states that "when they laid many stripes upon them," and let us think about that for a moment. Not only were their clothes ripped from off of their bodies, they were beaten while they were practically naked and many stripes were laid upon them. I want us to consider how we would feel, if such a thing were to happen to us.

To add to their sorry situation, they were brought into the inner prison and their feet were placed in stocks. I believe this was done as a matter of security, but also to guarantee that they would not be able to find a comfortable position to rest their sore and aching bodies. Now that we might have some idea of how serious and how miserable their situation really was, let us go on to learn the rest of this story.

Acts 16:25-30, And at midnight Paul and Silas prayed, and sang praises unto God: and the prisoners heard them.

26 And suddenly there was a great earthquake, so that the foundations of the prison were shaken: and immediately all the doors were opened, and every one's bands were loosed.

27 And the keeper of the prison awaking out of his sleep, and seeing the prison doors open, he drew out his sword and would have killed himself, supposing that the prisoners had been fled.

28 But Paul cried with a loud voice, saying, Do thyself no harm: for we are all here.

Then he (the jailer) called for a light, and sprang in, and came trembling, and fell down before Paul and Silas,

30 And brought them out, and said, Sirs, what must I do to be saved?

I am fairly sure that the jailer had witnessed many times men being beaten with whips and then being placed in the stocks to add to their misery. This is the way it was living under the heavy hand of the Roman Empire.

What I do believe the jailer found strange was that instead of complaining about their miserable situation, Paul and Silas actually began to pray and sing songs of praise and worship to their invisible God. We do not know just how long they did this, but we can be sure that they continued to praise God after they had been held in the stocks for many hours, for the record does show that it was midnight.

While this might have seemed strange to the jailer, what happened next completely caught him by surprise. The invisible God, who Silas and Paul prayed to and worshipped, took hold of the earth and shook it so violently that it caused the prison doors to be opened and the bonds holding the prisoners to be broken. Then to add to his bewilderment, instead of escaping while they could, Paul and Silas remained in the prison as though they had some unfinished business there.

I now want us to focus on what the attitude of the jailer must have been when he asked, "Sirs, what must I do to be saved?" It should not be too hard for us to understand that the jailer wanted very much to serve the God who was so powerful that he could literally shake the earth and set the prisoners free. Therefore, he already did believe by the evidence of things he had seen, and his attitude was one of being willing to do what ever he had to do, to become like Paul and Silas.

I have no doubt that it was his willing attitude that helped Paul and Silas form their answer to his question.

Acts 16: 31, And they said, Believe on the Lord Jesus Christ, and thou shalt be saved, and thy house.

It is upon this one verse that those people who promote the doctrine of easy believe-ism hang their entire doctrine. Some would say they do include John three sixteen, but as we have already learned by examining that verse that it is possible to believe and still perish.

There is nothing wrong with the answer that Paul and Silas gave the jailer except that it is incomplete. In order to better understand it, we must include the next verse, even though a great many religious people have chosen to ignore it completely.

Acts 16:32, And they spake unto him the word of the Lord, and to all that were in his house.

How very important to our understanding is this verse for it tells us the rest of the story. They spoke unto the jailer and all of his house, the word of the Lord. They did not just leave him to believe upon the Lord Jesus Christ without informing him what all that consisted of. It is important that we know not only what to believe but how to believe.

There is more to believing in our Lord, Jesus Christ than with our mind only, for we shall learn that Paul has also instructed us that we must believe with our heart. We must come to understand what this means and we must follow the instructions we were given by our Lord Jesus Christ.

The doctrine of easy believe-ism does sound good but it is incomplete and we must not allow it to prevent us from receiving the gift of eternal life.

Proverbs 16:25, There is a way that seemeth right unto a man, but the end thereof are the ways of death.

I have no doubt that the way of easy believe-ism does seem right to a great many people, but we must ask, is it truly the one and only plan that God has for our salvation? Some people will try to convince you that all you have to do to receive salvation is become a member of their church. Others will offer some other way of salvation, for ever since the tower of Babel, religious men have allowed their imaginations to invent ways of receiving the gift of eternal life, that are not according to God's Holy Word, and therefore, are not God's way.

Remember, God has only one plan for salvation and it is extended to all people of every race. We must make sure that we find that one plan and do not forget that Jesus, our Lord has made us a promise that if we seek we shall find.

Immortal soul?

In regard to God's perfect plan for our salvation, one of the most fundamental things we must come to know is that everyone is in need of salvation. There are a great many people today, who seem to believe that because they have never done anything really bad, they will not perish, nor will they be punished, for when they die they will just go to heaven anyway. They have probably never checked this out according to what is written in the Word of God, but have relied on what someone told them a long time ago.

There are others who believe that when they die, that is the end of life and that God will not be able to reward them for the deeds they have done. They believe they will be placed in the grave and all they have ever done will be forgotten.

They do not believe that God is capable of delivering unto them, the reward they have coming. Both of these beliefs are false.

First of all no one is born with an immortal soul. I realize that many people do believe that we are, but the Bible is very clear about this. To come to a better understanding of these things we must return to the time of creation. I do believe that in the beginning, both Adam and Eve were created with immortality or were at least, provided the opportunity to eat the fruit from the tree of life.

However, when they fell from grace by their willful disobedience, they did lose their immortality, and they were driven from the garden, where the tree of life was located.

Let us return to the garden of Eden and listen as God speaks to Adam regarding his immortality.

Genesis 2:16-17, And the Lord God commanded the man, saying, Of every tree of the garden thou mayest freely eat.

17 But of the tree of the knowledge of good and evil, thou shalt not eat of it: for in the day that thou eatest thereof thou shalt surely die.

This verse quite clearly tells us that God allowed them to eat the fruit from every tree in the garden except the fruit from the tree of knowledge, of good and evil. This obviously means that they were allowed to eat from the tree of life, which did provide them with everlasting life.

Notice that God did inform Adam that in the day that he did eat of the forbidden fruit, he would surely die. However, the record does show that Adam did live many, many years after having eaten of the forbidden fruit. Therefore, we can be certain that on the very day of their disobedience, they became ordinary mortal human beings.

We shall take up the story at chapter three and notice how very subtle the serpent is, as he begins his plan to deceive by asking the woman a question.

Genesis 3:1-4, Now the serpent was more subtil than any beast of the field which the Lord God had made.

And he said unto the woman, Yea, hath God said, Ye shall not eat of every tree of the garden?

2 And the woman said unto the serpent, We may eat of the fruit of the trees of the garden:

3 But of the fruit of the tree which is in the middle of the garden, God hath said, Ye shall not eat of it, neither shall ye touch it, lest ye die.

4 And the serpent said unto the woman, Ye shall not surely die:

Now the serpent did say more than this, in deceiving the woman, but I want us to focus on this first lie. Both the man and the woman were aware by God's Holy Word which did proceed from the mouth of God, that the penalty for eating of the forbidden fruit was death. They knew this for the Word of God did tell them so.

However, the serpent which is Satan did tell them that they would not surely die and they did choose of their own free will to believe Satan instead of believing God which did create them in the first place.

We must ask, did they then die, as they were told? Notice that they did not die right away, for they both lived a long time after they fell from grace and did have quite a few children. However, at the very moment they did eat of the forbidden fruit, they did forfeit their eternal life and the aging process began. From that time on, their natural life was limited.

There are many people today who believe that man is born with an immortal soul and that he will live for all of eternity in either heaven or hell. They believe this way for it is what they have been taught to believe, but in reality, they believe this first lie of Satan.

Let us listen as Paul does have some things to say to Timothy regarding our Lord and Savior, Jesus Christ.

1st Timothy 6:15-16, Which in his times he shall show, who is the blessed and only Potentate, the King of kings, and Lord of lords;

16 Who only hath immortality, dwelling in the light which no man can approach unto, whom no man hath seen, nor can see: to whom be honour and power everlasting. Amen.

It is extremely important, if we are ever to walk in the light and truth of God's word, that we understand that there is only one who has immortality. His name is Jesus, and he is the only begotten Son of Almighty God. That is why we are in need of the gift of eternal life, for not one of us have this gift, except by God's perfect plan we may receive it.

In his first letter to the Christians at Corinth Paul did have this to say, regarding man's immortality.

1st Corinthians 15:51-55, Behold, I show you a mystery; We shall not all sleep, (die) but we shall all be changed,

52 In a moment, in the twinkling of an eye, at the last trump: for the trumpet shall sound, and the dead shall be raised incorruptible, and we shall be changed.

53 For this corruptible must put on incorruption, and this mortal must put on immortality.

54 So when this corruptible shall have put on incorruption, and this mortal shall have put on immortality, then shall be brought to pass the saying that is written, Death is swallowed up in victory.

55 0 death, where is thy sting? 0 grave, where is thy victory?

It certainly does appear that Paul was familiar with the writings of the Greek philosophers as well as the old testament scriptures from the Hebrew Bible. However that may be, these verses certainly do make it clear that Paul did not believe that man is born with an immortal soul, for he made it clear that we must put on immortality at the time when we will be resurrected from the dead. Of course, those born again Christians who are alive at the time of Christ's return will also put on immortality at that time.

It is because this is so, that we can understand that no one is born with an immortal soul. I will go a bit further and say that anyone who does believe they have been born with an immortal soul, believeth a lie.

Let us now turn to the 6th chapter of Paul's letter to the Roman Christians and hear once more, the truth regarding life and death.

Roman 6:23, For the wages of sin is death; but the gift of God is eternal life through Jesus Christ our Lord.

The first part of this verse is the very same thing that God first said unto Adam. If you eat of the tree of knowledge, you will surely die. This does not mean that you will live and suffer forever in hell, as so many people believe, but that your soul will die also.

We know that the scriptures do inform us that all men are appointed to die and then the judgment. This means that our mortal flesh shall die, for we do know that this is so. However, in the book of Revelation it speaks of the second death, and this is speaking of the death of the soul.

However, we must be aware that between the death of this mortal body and the death of the soul, there is a matter of reaping what we have planted during our lifetime. Not even the grave can keep us from reaping what we have planted, for God is able to deliver unto each of us, exactly what we have coming. We can be assured that no murderer, or anyone else will fail to receive what they have coming except they enter into God's perfect plan for our salvation. The second death does not affect those who have received the gift of eternal life.

We know that because of the sin of Adam and Eve, we are all born with the sin nature, for it is our inheritance from them. No one has to teach a child about getting their own way, for they are able to learn selfish habits quite easily without any help. In the same way, they are able to learn to rebel against authority, for they want to be in control even from a very early age. The experts tell us that it is only natural for children to be like this, meaning that it is their nature. No one had to teach them to do what comes naturally.

In regard to sin, Paul has this to say .....

Romans 3:23, For all have sinned, and come short of the glory of God.

In other words, we are all in need of salvation for we have all sinned, and we have incurred a debt that we can not pay. Only Jesus could pay the price for he is the only one who has ever lived his life without sin. He then laid down his sinless life for us, to pay the debt that we owe, for the scriptures have made it quite clear that the wages of sin is death. It is only through the blood of Jesus, which was shed for us, that we are able to receive the gift of eternal life.

I would point out that in God's perfect plan it refers to the gift of eternal life. It is not something that we previously had, or else it would not be a gift. Neither is it something we were able to earn by our own effort, for then it would not be a gift. It is a gift from God and it, is by his grace. We do not deserve it and we certainly can not earn it. We can only humbly accept it, but we can only do so, according to the terms of God's perfect plan.

Let us not forget that Jesus said that if we seek, we shall find, if we knock, it shall be opened unto us, and if we ask, it will be given unto us. Even these instructions should make us aware that there is more to our salvation than easy believe-ism.

Repentance

Earlier, I mentioned that Paul did instruct Timothy that he was to show himself approved unto God, rightfully dividing the word of truth. I believe that it is important, if we are to follow that excellent instruction, that we understand that the story of the cross and our salvation is mainly in the four gospels, Matthew, Mark, Luke and John.

We have already learned that John the Baptist delivered the message, "Make straight the way of the Lord." There is something more that John did teach and I want us to take a hold of this knowledge in our search for God's plan for salvation.

Matthew 3:1-2, In those days came John the Baptist, preaching in the wilderness of Judea, and saying, Repent ye: for the kingdom of heaven is at hand.

There are quite a few religious people today, including those who teach the false doctrine of easy believe-ism, who claim that it is not necessary to repent in order to be saved. I am sure that for many people who are not aware of what the Bible really does say, that this does tickle their ears, for they are not interested in repenting of their sins. This is especially true for those people whose intent is to continue living in their usual sinful way.

In addition to what was said by John the Baptist, we need to hear what Jesus had to say about this very subject.

Matthew 4:17, From that time Jesus began to preach, and to say, Repent: for the kingdom of heaven is at hand.

It should be apparent that when it came to the matter of repentment as it applied to all mankind, Jesus was in complete agreement with his cousin, John the Baptist.

After Jesus had been crucified and was risen from the dead, he did come to that place where his disciples were gathered and assured them that he was not dead but was in fact, very much alive. At that time, he did give them these instructions.

Luke 24:44-47, And he said unto them, These are the words I spake unto you, while I was yet with you, that all things must be fulfilled, which were written in the law of Moses, and in the prophets, and in the psalms, concerning me.

45 Then opened he their understanding, that they might understand the scriptures.

46 And said unto them, Thus it is written, and thus it behoved Christ to suffer, and to rise from the dead the third day:

47 And that repentance and remission of sins should be preached in his name among all nations, beginning at Jerusalem.

We have heard from John the Baptist and from our Lord and Savior, that it is important that repentance be taught. I say that it is important because it is an essential ingredient of God's perfect plan of salvation. There are a great many people today who do believe but have refused to repent of their sinful way of life. John 3:16 informed us that because they do believe, they should not perish, but we can be sure that unless they do repent, they will surely perish.

We shall now hear from Peter, for he has something to say that will add to our knowledge on this subject. The time is the holy day of Pentecost and the disciples and the believers who had tarried in Jerusalem, waiting for the promise of God to be fulfilled, had just received the baptism in the Holy Ghost. Having been anointed by the Holy Spirit, Peter began to preach unto the multitude of Jews that were gathered at Jerusalem. Let us hear what Peter said to them.

Acts 2:36-38, Therefore let all the house of Israel know assuredly, that God hath made that same Jesus, whom ye have crucified, both Lord and Christ.

37 Now when they heard this, they were pricked in their heart, and said unto Peter and to the rest of the apostles, Men and brethern, what shall we do?

38 Then Peter said unto them, Repent, and be baptized every one of you in the name of Jesus Christ for the remission of sins, and ye shall receive the gift of the Holy Ghost.

I want us to focus on the fact that Peter did tell them to repent and I want us to notice that they were to do so, for the remission of sins. Looking once more to what Jesus told his disciples as it is recorded in Luke 24:47

Luke 24:47, And that repentance and remission of sins should be preached in his name among all nations, beginning at Jerusalem.

I want us to notice that repentance and remission of sins seem to go together, for we often find both words in the same sentence. Perhaps we should turn again to Peter's second letter.

2nd Peter 3:9, The Lord is not slack concerning his promise, as some men count slackness; but is longsuffering to us-ward, not willing that any should perish, but that all should come to repentance.

It should be quite clear that according to what is written in this verse, those people who refuse to repent will perish. It is as simple as that. Even those people who do believe in Christ must repent, or else they will perish.

Therefore, I must warn you, beware of those teachers who claim that it is not necessary to repent to receive salvation. The Word of God does show us just the opposite, for without repentance, there can be no salvation.

I realize that it is possible that perhaps some people believe that it means one thing to repent, while other people believe something entirely different. For that reason I shall get out my big old dictionary and share with you, what it states the meanings of the word repent, are.

repent ..... 1 to turn from sin and dedicate oneself to the amendment of one's life. 2 a to feel regret or contrition b to change one's mind.

The first meaning does sound good but it is a little too broad and covers too much time for the person who is seeking God's perfect plan. It is what we are to do, in the long run, for once we have accepted Jesus as our Savior, we must also make him our Lord.

However, there is something we must do first, for we can not forget the instructions we first received from Jesus, the anointed one of God.

The second meaning is not what we are looking for either, for feeling sorry for our sins is good, but it will not remove them. Over the years, when I was deep in alcoholic bondage, I often felt great sorrow and regret when I awakened to find myself very sick from all of the poison I had consumed. Feeling sorrow and regret and suffering from depression are a part of being an alcoholic, but they do not remove the problem.

Neither will feeling regret remove our burden of sin, so we will have to pass the second meaning up and go on to the third meaning given.

The dictionary simply says, "to change ones mind." This is what we are looking for, for this is what must take place before we can receive the gift of eternal life. To better explain what this means I will now share with you one of my favorite scriptures in the entire Bible. We will find it in the book of Isaiah for it contains many very beautiful scriptures foretelling the life and the death of our Lord and Savior.

Isaiah 55:9, For as the heavens are higher than the earth, so are my ways higher than your ways, and my thoughts than your thoughts.

Think about what God is telling us in this verse. For a very long time now, you have been living your life your own way, but your own way is not God's way. God's way is so much higher than our ways, that it is as high as heaven, while our ways are as low as the earth.

It is the same for our thoughts, regardless of our mental capability. Our God's thoughts are so much higher than ours that I am unable to find the words to describe this difference.

Perhaps if we were to visit the hospital and observe the new born babies and realize how each one is different than the rest and how each one is the evidence that our God is the giver of life. As we look upon the new born babies, come to understand that God, with infinite knowledge knew each one of them, while they were in their mother's wombs. Yes, even in the darkness of the mother's womb, God knows each and every detail of the child before they are born.

He even knows all about his children which were not allowed to see the light of day, and he knows what they would have become, had they been given the way of life instead of death.

Perhaps if we would then take our grandchildren on a journey to the sea shore, and help them to examine all that is taking place, day after day, in the tide pools. Even to try and answer all of the questions a young child can ask, proves to be difficult at times. Yet, with God, there are no secrets within the tide pool, for he knows all about each and every creature there, and knows what they do.

Then on a clear night, go out on the deck or porch with a pair of binoculars and spend some time examining the stars and the milky way. Please do be aware that even though there are so many stars that we can not possibly count them all, and yet God knows all about each and everyone of them. He knows where each one is at and when it was first formed.

Then consider that our God is the one who created this universe and when he did so, he hung this world in space. He commanded it to circle the sun in so many days, and it obeyed his command. He then told the earth to spin on it's axis and to make a complete revolution in twenty-four hours or so, and again it obeyed him. He then gave the earth a moon, to reflect the light of the sun by night and he caused the tides to rise and fall, pulled by the gravity of the moon. If we would but consider all of the physical laws of science, we come to realize that each one was designed and put in place by our Creator.

Perhaps if we would consider these things, it would help us to understand when God does inform us that his thoughts are high above our thoughts.

I think we should consider the life we have lived and think about all of the mistakes we have made, because we lived our lives our own way which was not God's way. Think of the sorrow and the heartaches that we have experienced and caused others and come to realize that God's way of life, is much higher than our way of life has been.

This is the change of mind we are searching for, for before we can enter into God's perfect plan for our salvation, we must first admit to ourselves and to others, that God's way of life is much better in every way, than our way of life has ever been, judging by our past performance.

Once more we must examine and know the will of God as it is recorded in the 4th chapter of Deuteronomy.

Deuteronomy 4:2, Ye shall not add unto the word which I command you, neither shall you diminish aught from it, that ye may keep the commandments of the Lord your God which I command you.

We must realize that not even religious men can improve upon what is already perfect in the eyes of God. The scriptures do inform us that the very same God who has created this universe and all that is in it, is also the author and the finisher of our faith. Keep in mind that he is the one who so loved you and me, and everyone else, that he gave his only begotten Son, so that we should not perish but receive the gift of eternal life.

I then want to impress upon you that it was his only begotten Son, our Lord and Savior who said that repentance was to be taught in his name through out the world. Even so, certain religious people do teach that repentance is not necessary and should not be taught. I ask you now, who should we believe? Should we believe Jesus and the Word of God, and such men as John the Baptist, and the apostle Peter, or should we believe those teachers who claim they know more than the Word of God?

It should be very clear that the reason that repentance was to be taught through out the world in the name of-Jesus, is that it is a very important part of God's perfect plan of salvation. Therefore, we must not leave it out.

The kind of repentance we must have when we come to the door of our salvation which is Christ, is a change of heart and a change of attitude. We must become like those men who came in to prison to Paul and Silas and asked, What must we do to be saved or to become like you?

We must be aware that the way we have been living our lives is not good when compared to the way that God wants us to live. We must also be aware that we are unable to change the way we are by our own power.

In this regard we need help from a divine source. I am reminded of all of the people with good intentions that make resolutions each year at the first of the year.

It is as though almost everyone has a desire to improve their lives and I certainly do believe this is good. However, quite often we make promises to ourselves that we fail to keep and this can lead to depression and a sorry state of mind.

When we come to the cross of Jesus, and when we come with a humble and repentant attitude, and we knock, the door of salvation will be opened to us. If we come to the cross, and our attitude is not humble and repentant, we can knock as long as we like but the door of salvation will not be opened to us. It is as simple as that.

We must be sincere in that we are seeking the forgiveness of our sins. We must do more than just believe in our minds as to who Jesus really is and what he has done for us at the cross. We must also believe with our hearts which means that we are willing to change and to allow Jesus to tell us how to live our lives a much better way. In fact, we invite our Lord into our hearts and do allow the Holy Spirit to lead us the rest of the way on our journey to the promised land.

Chapter 27 About Our Faith

Faith

I now want to speak to you about faith and the part it plays in regard to our salvation. I realize that most likely we all have some idea of what faith is, but I believe we should look for a Biblical definition. We shall turn to the 11th chapter of the epistle to the Hebrews and be aware that this is known as the faith chapter of the Bible.

Hebrews 11:1, Now faith is the substance of things hoped for, the evidence of things not seen.

As you are thinking about the true meaning of what faith is, let me explain that our salvation is a matter of faith, for it is something we do hope for but can not see at this present time, but do expect to receive.

Hebrews 11:6, But without faith it is impossible to please him; for he that cometh to God must believe that he is, and that he is a rewarder of them that diligently seek him.

We have just been presented with two very important truths and we must do our best to understand them. We have received a Biblical definition of what faith is, and we have been told that we must have it in order to please God. It should be obvious that we can not enter into God's perfect plan for our salvation without faith. Therfore, our next question should be, what must we do to receive faith? Is it a gift from God?

Paul had this to say about faith and salvation.

Ephesians 2:8-9, For by grace are ye saved through faith; and that not of yourselves: it is the gift of God:

9 Not of works, lest any man should boast.

These verses do make it very clear that we are saved through faith and that our salvation is a gift from God. There is nothing we can do to earn our salvation for even our best works are as filthy rags when compared to the sinless life of Christ. Let us listen as Paul does inform us how we may receive faith.

Romans 10:17, So then faith cometh by hearing, and hearing by the word of God.

You will recall that when the jailer asked Paul and Silas, "What must I do to be saved?" They told him to believe upon the Lord Jesus Christ and he would be saved. However, as we learned in the following verse, they also shared with the jailer and his house, the Word of God. It would have been impossible for the jailer to be saved without hearing the Word of God, for according to our Bibles, the way we do receive faith is by hearing the Word of God. This is why it is so important that I share with you, the truth of God's word and the instructions it does contain regarding our salvation.

I have a few verses in mind that will serve as a faith builder if any seem to be weak in faith. They are verses that truly do demonstrate the fore-knowledge of All Mighty God.

In regard to our faith, I believe that if we combine both prophecy and history that we shall increase the faith of most reasonably intelligent people. That is to say, unless they have hardened their hearts against God's word and refuse to acknowledge what has taken place within the pages of history. I believe that even the most stubborn atheists are aware of what the initials A.D. and B.C. stand for as they both point to a very important place in history, according to our method of measuring time.

I want us to think about the birth of Christ and I suppose you do know that it was foretold in the Hebrew Bible. Have you ever heard about the wise men who came from the East, our Savior they wanted to see. Some people claim these men were wise because they studied the stars and in the story that is told, it is a star that lead them to the town of Bethlehem.

I do not believe they were wise because they studied the stars. I believe the true source of their wisdom was from studying the

Hebrew scriptures. Especially what was written by the prophets concerning the coming of the Messiah, the anointed one of God.

There are many scriptures that did fortell the birth of Jesus and I will share with you a few of them and they will be in two parts. That is first, when the prophecy was given, and second, when the prophecy was fulfilled.

During the time of the prophet Zechariah, that is c.487 B.C., he did foretell....

Zechariah 9:9, Rejoice greatly, 0 daughter of Zion; shout, 0 daughter of Jerusalem: behold, thy King cometh unto thee: he is just, and having salvation; lowly, and riding upon an ass, and upon a colt the foal of an ass.

Matthew, who was a tax collector before he became a disciple of Jesus, did confirm that this prophecy was fulfilled c. A.D. 33 shortly before Jesus was crucified.

Matthew 21:1, And when they drew nigh unto Jerusalem, and were come to Bethphage, and unto the mount of Olives, then sent Jesus two disciples,

2 Saying unto them, Go into the village over against you, and straightway ye shall find an ass tied, and a colt with her: loose them, and bring them unto me.

3 And if any man say aught unto you, ye shall say, The Lord hath need of them, and straightway he will send them.

4 All this was done, that it might be fulfilled which was spoken by the prophet, saying,

5 Tell ye the daughter of Sion, Behold thy King cometh unto thee, meek, and sitting upon an ass, and a colt the foal of an ass.

6 And the disciples went, and did as Jesus commanded them,

7 And brought the ass, and the colt, and put on them their clothes, and they set him thereon.

8 And a very great multitude spread their garments in the way; others cut down branches from the trees, and strewed them in the way.

9 And the multitudes that went before, and that followed, cried saying, Hosanna to the son of David: Blessed is he that cometh in the name of the Lord; Hosanna in the highest.

10 And when he was come into Jerusalem, all the city was moved, saying, Who is this?

11 And the multitude said, This is Jesus the prophet of Nazareth of Galilee.

Even though it is reported that the wise men did follow a star, the prophet Micah did foretell in c.710 B.C. that Jesus would be born in Bethlehem.

Micah 5:2, But thou, Bethlehem Eph'ratah, though thou be little among the thousands of Judah, yet out of thee shall he come forth unto me that is to be ruler in Israel; whose goings forth have been from of old, from everlasting.

Again, Matthew the disciple of our Lord reports

Matthew 2:1, Now when Jesus was born in Bethlehem of Judea in the days of Herod the king, behold, there came wise men from the east to Jerusalem,

2 Saying, Where is he that is born King of the Jews? for we have seen his star in the east, and are come to worship him.

3 When Herod the king had heard these things, he was troubled, and all Jerusalem with him.

4 And when he had gathered all the chief priests and scribes of the people together, he demanded of them where Christ should be born.

5 And they said unto him, In Bethlehem of Judea: for thus it is written by the prophet,

6 And thou Bethlehem, in the land of Juda: for out of thee shall come a Governor, that shall rule my people Israel.

It does appear by what we have read that the people of Israel at that point in time, having read and studied the Hebrew scriptures were well aware that the Messiah would be born in Bethlehem, just as Jesus was born there, over 700 years after it was foretold by Micah, the prophet of God.

These scriptures we have read certainly do reveal that our God does know the future before it even happens. Down through the centuries of time, there have been various different religions that have risen up. Only our God, the very same God who was the God of Abraham, and Isaac, and Moses, does know the future and has told us what would happen before it did happen, time after time. In other words, our God has proven that he is God, by His Holy Word.

Let us listen to these words of God as they speak to us from the mouth of the prophet Isaiah.

Isaiah 46:9, Remember the former things of old: for I am God. and there is none else; I am God, and there is none like me, 10 Declaring the end from the beginning, and from ancient times the things that are not yet done, saying, My counsel shall stand, and I will do my pleasure:

and

Isaiah 45:20 Assemble yourselves and come; draw near together, ye that are escaped of the nations: they have no knowledge that set up the wood of their graven image, and pray unto a God that cannot save.

21 Tell ye, and bring them near; yea, let them take counsel together: who hath declared this from ancient time? who hath told it from that time? have not I the Lord? and there is no God else beside me; a just God and a Savior; there is none beside me.

22 Look unto me, and be ye saved, all the ends of the earth: for I am God, and there is none else.

It is certainly my hope that by hearing and studying the Word of God, as we have done, that none should be lacking in faith.

The book of Proverbs does inform us that the fear of God, is the beginning of wisdom. I have told you of some things which are most fearful. However, it is my greatest hope that the fear that I might have caused you will lead you to that safe place of refuge that our merciful God has provided for us. The time will come when many large missiles will cry out with a very loud roar as they begin their journey to fulfill and bring to completion what they were designed to do. A very short time later, the voices of the seven thunders will reply to announce the news that once more, God has kept his promise, just as it is written in God's Holy Word.

I can not help but think of those fertile places where grains and vegetables and fruit is grown in great abundance. Where cattle now graze on the open range, and where the milk is produced that supplies this nation. The land that once produced an abundance of food will now be given a rest for the nuclear winds shall blow across this land, and nothing shall grow here, any more and it will not be able to support life. In that day, Death and Hell will reign supreme over the land that God once blessed and from sea to shining sea, will become waste and desolate.

Once more, God is about to keep his word, for he has said that he will not always strive with mankind. Once again, he has provided a safe place of refuge, but there will only be a few that will enter into it. It is my very sincere hope that you will be one of the few.

We have learned that in addition to our faith, we must repent. have a change of mind) We must recognize that God's way is the right way, and man's way is the wrong way.

We must admit beyond any doubt, that we are common and ordinary sinners, in need of God's mercy and amazing, saving grace.

We were also made aware that it is necessary for us to forgive those people who have done us wrong, for if we do not forgive them, neither will our heavenly Father forgive us the wrongs that we have done.

We have also learned that we must become as humble small children, for that is the only way we may receive the gift from God, of eternal life. No one who is proud of his religious knowledge need think he will be allowed to enter into the kingdom of heaven, for the Word of God has made it clear that it is reserved for the humble, and the meek, and the poor of spirit. If there be any doubt concerning this I do suggest that you read the beatitudes in the gospel of Matthew.

We have also learned that we must become born again, and that in order for that to happen, the old sinful nature by which we have lived must die. We must be willing to completely let go of the past way of life, in order that we may live in the newness of life in Christ Jesus.

Remember Lot's wife. If we are unwilling to give up our past life, we shall lose our eternal life with Christ.

Lot and his wife and two daughters were made aware of what was about to take place. They had received the instructions that would lead them to the place of safety that God provided for them. Surely they were not too hard to do or too difficult to understand.

I believe that it is the same for you, for you have been warned by God's own word what is about to take place.

It is by hearing the Word of God that we do receive faith. Remember, we must have faith for it is essential to our salvation. Without it, we can not please God.

Let us turn once more to 1st John and we shall receive a very important promise.

1st John 1:9, If we confess our sins, he is faithful and just to forgive us our sins, and to cleanse us from all unrighteousness.

These instructions with a promise are very important to receiving the gift of eternal life. In order for God to forgive our sins, we must first admit to God and to ourselves that we are sinners and in need of cleansing. In this way, we do confess our sins. This is the instruction we are given. The promise we are given in return, is that if we do our part, God is faithful to do his part which is to forgive us our sins and to cleanse us from all unrighteousness. I want to emphasize the word all, for it is important we realize that God will cleanse us from ALL unrighteousness and not just some.

Jesus had some instructions for his disciples regarding how they were to pray.

Mark 11:24-26, Therefore I say unto you, what things so ever ye desire, when ye pray, believe that ye receive them, and ye shall have them. (pray with faith)

25 And when ye stand praying, forgive, if ye have aught against any: that your Father also which is in heaven may forgive you your trespasses.

26 But if ye do not forgive, neither will your Father which is in heaven forgive your trespasses.

Surely, Jesus has made these things very clear and there is nothing I can add to these instructions, for we are to pray with faith and we are to forgive everyone who may have done us wrong. Continuing to harbor hard feelings toward anyone can only hurt us, and to forgive is the first step in becoming like Jesus, for even on the cross he forgave the soldiers who crucified him.

We shall now turn to the 10th chapter of Paul's letter to the Roman Christians and see what Paul has to say about confession.

Romans 10:8-10, But what saith it? The word is nigh thee, even in thy mouth, and in thy heart: that is, the word of faith, which we preach;

9 That if thou shalt confess with thy mouth the Lord Jesus, and shalt believe in thine heart that God hath raised him from the dead, thou shalt be saved.

10 For with the heart man believeth unto righteousness; and with the mouth confession is made unto salvation.

Notice that Paul speaks of believing with the heart and not just the mind. It is only when we believe in Christ with our heart that we become willing to be and do what it is that will please God. To believe with the mind and not the heart is to fail to believe unto righteousness. Let us not forget that righteousness is the act of doing what is right in the eyes of God.

We are to be like the Roman jailer and willing and even eager to do what ever thing God would have us to do. In addition to this, we must be willing to tell our family and our friends and neighbors and even the strangers we meet, that Jesus has become our Lord and Savior and our way of life. We must not be ashamed of this, for if we are ashamed, then Jesus has said he will be ashamed of us, before his Father which art in heaven.

There is one more set of instructions I want us to learn about for it concerns being born again. There are many people who do claim that they have been born again, but perhaps only a few truly do understand what it means to be born again.

There was a very religious and devout Jewish man by the name of Nicodemus who later became a Christian. However, at the time of this conversation, he was very curious and searching for answers, but the way of salvation was not known to him.

John 3:1, There was a man of the Pharisees, named Nicodemus, a ruler of the Jews:

2 The same came to Jesus by night, and said unto him, Rabbi. we know that thou art a teacher come from God: for no man can do these miracles that thou doest, except God be with him.

3 Jesus answered and said unto him, Verily, verily, I say unto thee, Except a man be born again, he cannot see the kingdom of God.

When Jesus said that unless a man be born again, he can not see the kingdom of God, it is like he is saying that unless we become born again, we simply can not understand the kingdom of God, for the natural man is ignorant of spiritual things.

4 Nicodemus saith unto him, How can a man be born when he is old? can he enter the second time into his mother's womb, and be born?

5 Jesus answered, verily, verily, I say unto thee, Except a man be born of water and of the Spirit, he cannot enter the kingdom of God.

Jesus is speaking to this man using very deep language which Nicodemus is having a hard time understanding. However, keep in mind that Nicodemus was a Pharisee and a ruler or religious leader of the Jews. When Jesus said that a man must be born of the water, I believe he is speaking of the water of the Word of God. We must first hear and experience the water of the word as it informs as to what the will of God really is. Jesus then went on to say, born of the Spirit, meaning the Holy Spirit will perform a work in us, to cause us to be born again. Jesus goes on to say

6 That which is born of the flesh is flesh; and that which is born of the Spirit is spirit.

7 Marvel not that I have said unto thee, Ye must be born again.

8 The wind bloweth where it listeth, and thou hearest the sound thereof, but canst not tell whence it cometh, and whither it goeth: so is every one that is born of the Spirit.

It is rather apparent that the things Jesus was saying to Nicodemus were going over his head and he did not understand what Jesus meant. Of course, we must realize that these religious leaders were men of great authority who claimed to know all there was to know about God and God's will.

9 Nicodemus answered and said unto him, How can these things be?

10 Jesus answered and said unto him, Art thou a master of Israel, and knowest not these things?

11 verily, verily I say unto thee, We speak that we do know, and testify that we have seen; and ye receive not our witness.

12 If I have told you earthly things, and ye believe not, how shall ye believe, if I tell you of heavenly things?

13 And no man hath ascended up to heaven, but he that came down from heaven, even the Son of man which is in heaven.

So far, Jesus was speaking things that Nicodemus simply could not understand, for it did not conform to what he had been taught. In this last verse, Jesus actually identified who he was, but this too, was extremely difficult for a religious Jewish man to accept. He then goes on to show that salvation was through him. These were things that Nicodemus could not possibly understand at that point in time, but he would understand them later, after Jesus was crucified and risen from the dead.

14 And as Moses lifted up the serpent in the wilderness, even so must the Son of man be lifted up. (crucified)

15 That whosoever believeth in him should not perish, but have eternal life.

16 For God so loved the world, that he gave his only begotten Son, that whosoever believeth in him should not perish, but have everlasting life.

I would point out that in both of these verses we are informed that believers should not perish but Jesus did not say that they would not perish.

The time has come when we must connect this verse with what Jesus did tell Nicodemus when this conversation first started, for this is something that very few teachers do. Jesus informed Nicodemus that we must be born again, or else we will not be able to see (understand) the kingdom of God. He then informed Nicodemus that we must be born again, or else we will not be able to enter into or become a part of the kingdom of God.

In other words, we must be born again, or else we will not receive the gift of eternal life.

The bottom line is that it is possible to believe in Christ and believe in what Jesus did on the cross of Calvary, but unless we are born again, we will perish. Therefore, we must believe on our Lord, Jesus Christ and we must believe that when he died on the cross, he paid the price for our sins in full. We must also become born again for there is more to our salvation than just believing. We must come to a greater understanding of what it means to be born again.

Jesus told Nicodemus that we must be born again in order to see and understand the kingdom of God. He also told him that we must be born again to enter into the kingdom of God. We need to understand that in order to be born again, we must first die, and I am speaking of the death of the old man of sin.

We must put the old man of our sin nature to death in order that we may live in the newness of life in Christ Jesus.

Let us listen as Jesus has some more to say about this very subject for it is hard for some people to understand.

John 12:24, Verily, verily, I say unto you, Except a corn of wheat fall into the ground and die, it abideth alone: but if it die, it bringeth forth much fruit.

25 He that loveth his life in this world shall lose it: and he that hateth his life in this world shall keep it unto life eternal.

Jesus is saying in the 24th verse that if the old man of sin, which dwelleth within us, dies, then in his place will spring up a new plant which will bear much fruit.

However, if we love our sinful way of life and refuse to allow the man of sin, (our sin nature) to die, we will lose our eternal life with Jesus. But if we despise the sinful life we have lived, and will commit our new life to Christ, we will be with him for all of eternity.

Let us listen as Jesus has more to say to us.

Mark 8:34, And when he had called the people unto him with his disciples also, he said unto them, Whosoever will come after me, let him deny himself, and take up his cross, and follow me.

35 For whosoever will save his life shall lose it; but whosoever shall lose his life for my sake and the gospel's, the same shall save it.

These are very important verses that do show us what we must do to be born again.

It is absolutely necessary that we lose our former sinful way of life, in order we might receive a new way of life in Christ Jesus.

There is only one way that this will happen and that is when we come humbly before the cross of Christ, admitting that we are sinners in need of cleansing. Our attitude must be one of complete surrender. It is important we realize that without our surrender, there can be no salvation. Once we have surrendered, and made a firm commitment to God, that we will live our lives in newness of life, for him, a supernatural miracle takes place, for this is when we become born again. However, we can not become born again unless we are willing for our old sinful nature to die. This is because we must become the dwelling place of the Holy Spirit. The Holy Spirit will not live in the same abode with the man of sin, for there is only room within us for one of them. Therefore, the man of sin must die and we do cause his death when we humbly surrender our will to God.

I realize that some people are so in love with this world and all that it has to offer that they seem to be divided. On the one hand, they certainly do want to receive salvation and the gift of eternal life. On the other hand, they are often filled with vanity and the pride of life and if God should ask them to sell all that they own, in order to follow him, they simply would not be able to do that. Perhaps this is why they prefer the doctrine of "easy believe-ism" for they can claim that they do believe while they continue to live in their usual manner, seeking the pleasure and wealth of this world.

There is another set of scriptures I want you to be aware of, for they deal with this same subject and they contain instructions from our Lord Jesus Christ.

Luke 17:32-33, Remember Lot's wife. Whosoever shall seek to save his life shall lose it: and whosoever shall lose his life shall preserve it.

Why did Jesus tell us to remember Lot's wife? It is because what happened to her is an example for us today and is to serve as a warning. Surely you are aware that Sodom and Gomorrah were exceedingly sinful and because they were, God's wrath was kindled against them and he was about to remove them from the face of the earth. Let us not forget that Jesus has said that in the time of great trouble that lies ahead, it will be as it was in the time of Sodom and Gomorrah.

Genesis 19:15, And when the morning arose, and the angels hastened Lot, saying, Arise, take thy wife, and thy two daughters, which are here; lest thou be consumed in the iniquity of the city.

17 And it came to pass, when they had brought them forth abroad, that he said, Escape for thy life; look not behind thee, neither stay thou in all the plain; escape to the mountains, lest thou be consumed.

18 And Lot said unto them, Oh, not so, my Lord:

19 Behold now, thy servant hath found grace in thy sight, and thou hast magnified thy mercy, which thou hast showed unto me in saving my life; and I cannot escape to the mountains, lest some evil take me, and I die:

20 Behold now, this city is near to flee unto, and it is a little one: Oh, let me escape thither, (is it not a little one?) and my soul shall live.

21 And he (angel) said unto him, See, I have accepted thee concerning this thing also, that I will not over throw this city, for the which thou hast spoken.

22 Haste thee, escape thither; for I cannot do anything till thou be come thither. Therefore, the name of the city was called Zoar.

I believe it is important we be aware that Lot did not want to follow the instructions he had been given. He was only willing to go half way. When we follow the record of Lot's life in our Bibles we can see that he never amounted to very much, after that, even though he did receive mercy from God through his grace.

I believe that it is still this way today, for there are a great many people who have refused to follow the plain and easy instructions we have received in God's Holy Word. They have chosen Man's way instead of God's perfect way.

I often hear people say, "Is it true that all I have to do to be saved is believe?" Perhaps in the same way as Lot, these people never amount to very much as Christians for they are always searching for the way in which they can do the least.

Now to return to the story of the destruction of Sodom and Gomorrah. Mr. and Mrs. Lot and their two daughters did hurry across the plain on their way to the small city of Zoar. It does appear that

Mr. Lot and the two daughter did follow the instructions they were given, but the same was not so for Mrs. Lot. Perhaps she was a little like some children who will almost always do the very thing they are told they must never do.

Imagine if you can, what it was like on the day that fire and burning sulfur rained down upon Sodom. The family of Lot had safely reached the place of their refuge, when Mrs. Lot did the one thing she had been forbidden to do. She looked back to the sinful city from which she had fled.

In a moments time; in the twinkling of an eye, as she beheld the destruction of Sodom and Gomorrah, the moisture content of her body evaporated and all that remained of her was a pillar of salt. All of her hopes and desires and all that she ever was disappeared and she became only a memory in the minds of her loved ones. Of course, the wind and the rain dissolved the pillar of salt and so it provided no lasting memorial. However, her story has been preserved in the Word of God as a lasting warning to all of us, so that none of us should make the same mistake that she did.

Let us listen once more as the voice of Jesus speaks to us from the pages of our Bibles.

Luke 17:32-33, Remember Lot's wife. Whosoever shall seek to save his life shall lose it; and whosoever shall lose his life (present sinful life) shall preserve it. (new life in Christ)

I believe that there are many people today who cling to the false doctrine of easy believe-ism, because they are unwilling to give up their pride of life and their material possessions which they love, should God ask them to give them up. Neither will they give up their lust of the flesh, for they are not interested in living God's way.

On the money they carry in their purse are the words "In God we trust." Of course this is not the truth, for if it was, they would allow Jesus to come into their hearts and sit upon the throne and be the ruler of their lives.

Some of these people attend church each week, and listen to the sermon as though they consider it their duty to God. Some even place a few dollars in the offering plate when it is passed and then sit in the pew, trying to appear as pious as possible When the service is ended, they stand outside the door and shake hands with the people and try to say all of the right words, and then they return home and become their natural selves once more.

For a few hours each week they become actors, acting out the part they believe they are supposed to play. However, if we were to observe them in the work place during the middle of the week, we would have a hard time recognizing them as Christians for we would find them being their natural selves and not acting out the part they play but once a week.

When the old man of sin has truly been put to death and the Holy Spirit has taken up permanent residence within our hearts, then truly, all things have become new and the world around us does recognize that this is so. The Holy Spirit, when he is sitting upon the throne within our heart will help us to over come temptation and together with the Living Word of God, will instruct us in God's way of life. If we should happen to slip and fall they are always there to help lift us up out of the miry clay and place our feet once more on the narrow path that leads us to the promised land and eternal life in Christ.

Ever since the tower of Babel which is mentioned in the book of Genesis, many men have tried to invent a plan or a way to receive eternal life without submitting to God's will. The doctrine of easy believe-ism, even though it is very subtle, is just another plan by religious men, to receive the gift of eternal life without first surrendering to God.

We must not forget that God is the author of our salvation.

John 10:7, Then Jesus said unto them again, Verily, verily, I say unto you, I am the door of the sheep.

9 I am the door: by me if any enter in, he shall be saved, ...
Jesus said that if we would seek, we would also find.

By studying the scriptures we have found that Jesus is the door of salvation. That if we would knock upon the door of God's salvation, that the door would be opened to us. And then he said that if we ask for our sins to be forgiven, they will be forgiven. As a teacher I want for you to notice how God's perfect plan does differ from the plans of religious men.

In looking back at the knowledge we have found as we searched through the scriptures, I do believe that we do possess all of the knowledge we need to know, to allow God's perfect plan to become a reality in our lives. We are now aware that we must do more than just believe with our minds but with our hearts as well.

As I have shared with you, the instructions we have been provided by God's own word, we do know what we have to do to find the safe place of our refuge.

I have shared with you the instructions we were given, not to make the way of salvation more complicated than it need be. But to make you aware of these things lest any of you might seem to come short of God's perfect plan. I do not want anyone to stumble and or be lost, simply because they did not fully understand God's perfect plan.

The prophet of God, Hosea spoke of conditions just prior to the time of God's judgment.

Hosea 4:1, Hear the word of the Lord, ye children of Israel: for the Lord hath a controversy with the inhabitants of the land, because there is no truth, nor mercy, nor knowledge of God in the land.

2 By swearing, and lying, and killing, and stealing, and committing adultery, they break out, and blood toucheth blood.

3 Therefore shall the land mourn, and everyone that dwelleth therein shall languish, with the beasts of the field, and with the fowls of heaven; yea, the fishes of the sea also shall be taken away.

4 Yet let no man strive, nor reprove another: for thy people are as they that strive with the priest. (man of God)

6 My people are destroyed for lack of knowledge: because thou hast rejected knowledge, I will also reject thee, that thou shalt be no priest (or pastor) to me: seeing thou hast forgotten the law of thy God, I will also forget thy children.

Is this the way it is today? Are there religious people today who are critical because I have tried to increase your knowledge concerning God's perfect plan of salvation? Perhaps they would have us believe that their way is a better way, for they have made the way of salvation very easy, or so they claim. In doing so, they have also made the way wide instead of narrow, for this is their purpose.

Let us listen to these words of instruction that we are given by our Lord Jesus.

Matthew 7:13-15, Enter ye in at the strait gate: for wide is the gate, and broad is the way, that leadeth to destruction, and many there be which go in there at.

14 Because strait is the gate, and narrow is the way, which leadeth unto life, and few there be that find it.

15 Beware of false prophets, which come to you in sheep's clothing, but inwardly they are ravening wolves.

I realize that at times it has seemed as though I do not approve of traditional Christianity. It is because I do not approve of people who teach that religious traditions are more valuable than is the truth of God's word. In the time of great trouble that lies just ahead, many will perish because they did not love the truth more than they loved their traditions. In the same way, many will perish because they have chosen the broad way and have rejected the narrow way that is explained in the scriptures.

As we have studied the Word of God together, we have learned that Jesus said that "we must be born again." Jesus said that those who believe "should not perish," but when we put these things together, we come to realize that those who do believe, must still be born again, or else they will perish. There are many today who claim they have received salvation, but not all who claim it will receive it.

The apostle Paul had something to say, in regard to the religious people that will perish and we do need to apply it to the people who are teaching false doctrines today.2nd Thessalonians 2:10, And with all deceivableness of unrighteousness in them that perish; because they received not the love of the truth, that they might be saved.

11 And for this cause God shall send them strong delusion, that they should believe a lie:

12 That they all might be damned who believed not the truth, but had pleasure in unrighteousness.

The unrighteousness that Paul is talking about, is simply those people who have refused to live their lives doing what is right in the eyes of God. Many have insisted they are going to go to heaven but while they are on earth, they will continue to live their lives their own way, which is not God's way. They claim that their salvation is by grace and not by works. Of course, this is true, for we cannot earn our salvation, but because they have refused to surrender to God, they have not been born again. To be born again is also by grace for it is not by works, but is a gift from the Holy Spirit. However, it does require our humble and repentant attitude and our willingness to surrender to God. Without our surrender, there can be no salvation. We can not be born again, if we are unwilling to let the old man of our sinful nature die.

There are two more things we need to know regarding our salvation. First, we must know that the only way we can come to God, seeking the forgiveness of our sins, is by our own free will. God will not force us or abrogate our will in any way for he will not take away from us, our freedom to choose. Therefore, the only way we can come into his divine presence is by our own choice to do so.

The next thing that is required for salvation are these instructions we are given by our Lord Jesus.

Matthew 18:1, At the same time came the disciples unto Jesus saying, Who is the greatest in the kingdom of heaven?

2 And Jesus called a little child unto him, and set him in the midst of them.

3 And said, Verily I say unto you, Except ye be converted, and become as little children, ye shall not enter into the kingdom of heaven.

Jesus repeated these things in Mark 10 and verse 15.

Mark 10:15, Verily I say unto you, Whosoever shall not receive the kingdom of God as a little child, he shall not enter therein.

These instructions are a very important part of being born again. We know they must be important for they are repeated many times through out the scriptures. We must not become proud of our religious knowledge as so many have, but we must become meek and humble like small children in the kingdom of God.

We have traveled along the path of enlightenment and we have now arrived at that place that is known as the valley of decision. I have shared with you the knowledge of the way of truth and the way of life that Jesus first delivered unto his disciples so long ago. The time has come when you must make a decision of your own free will, which way you will go from here. You can decide to remain just as you are, and of course, we do know what your wages will be.

Or you can decide this day, to come humbly before the throne of grace, seeking the cleansing from all unrighteousness that is necessary to enter into life with Jesus Christ. It is my very sincere hope that you have chosen the way of life.

In a little while I am going to ask those of you who have decided of your own free will to come to the cross and accept Jesus into your hearts, to pray with me. However, before I do, I want you to read one more scripture and it is a message that comes directly to you from our Lord, Jesus Christ.

Revelation 3:20, Behold, I stand at the door, and knock; if any man hear my voice, and open the door, I will come unto him, and will eat with him, and he with me.

I believe that at this very moment, Jesus is standing at the doorway of your heart and is knocking. I can not open the door for you because you are the only one that can.

I now want to share with you a glorious promise that Jesus has made to us, it is one we should think about, for it will increase our faith.

Matthew 18:20, For where two or three are gathered in my name, there am I in the midst of them.

I know that your immediate response to this scripture is the question, "How can this apply to me, for I am all alone?" I want you to know that you are not alone, for though I am unable to be with you in body, I am with you in spirit. My spirit is in agreement with your spirit, and we will cry out to the Lord together, and we know that he will hear our prayer, for we cry out in faith.

We also know that praying together is not against the Lord's will, and we know that it is not God's will that any of us should perish. Therefore, we are confident that on this day, your sins will be forgiven.

I ask you now, please be very respectful toward God, for at this moment, the kingdom of God is not far from you. I would ask that we kneel, as humble and obedient children, but if it is not possible, then pray right where you are and believe that you will receive. Let us pray.

Our most gracious, heavenly Father, which art in heaven, holy be thy name. I come before thee this day because I know beyond any doubt, that you really are God who made the heavens and the earth. I know that you are completely righteous and that you cannot tolerate sin in your holy presence.

My heart cries out to you, Oh God, have mercy on me for I am only a sinner. I have sinned against you for as long as I can remember, and my sins are more in number than I am able to count. I ask you now, Lord Jesus, to forgive my sins and to take them from me, for they are a burden that I am tired of bearing. I ask you now, dear Lord Jesus, to come into my heart and take control of my life, so that I might be a new person filled with your love. From this moment on, I shall seek your will for my life, and I will follow you, for as long as I shall live.

I thank you dear Lord Jesus, that you have made it possible by freely laying down your sinless life and shedding your innocent blood for ordinary sinners like me, to become born again and receive the gift of eternal life.

I will testify of what you have done for me, where ever I go, and I shall praise thy holy name as long as I live. I believe in you, Oh Lord, not just with my mind but with my heart. In this way, I shall become a doer of your will, and not just a hearer. I know that according to the promises of your Holy Word, I have been redeemed by your life giving blood, and that you will remain with me, even until the time of the end. May I praise God for evermore! Amen.

If you have prayed this prayer with me, and if you prayed with your heart and meant it, it has reached up into the heavens and has entered into the most holy place. On this day, the angels of heaven are rejoicing for you have been given a new name and it is now written down in glory.

Amen and Amen

Chapter 28 Water Baptism

I now address myself to all who have committed their lives to God and have accepted Jesus Christ as their Savior and have made him their Lord. I want to congratulate you and welcome you into the family of God. We are now very closely related for the blood of Jesus hath cleansed us from all unrighteousness, and has united us into one family. May we never forget to praise God for his mercy which he bestowed upon us while we were still sinners, and the enemy of God.

I want to make you aware that even though we have now entered into life in Christ Jesus, it is not as though we have arrived, for there is quite a distance to travel before we reach our final destination, the promised land.

When you surrendered to God at the cross of Jesus, Satan was forced to give up one of his own. Satan did not give you up willingly, and in the days ahead he will do every thing in his power such as tempt you through your flesh, as well as various other ways, and try to cause you to stumble and fall on the journey we are now on.

However, God has given us a two edged sword which is our Holy Bible, and with the Word of God, and the Spirit of God, which now dwelleth within us, we can overcome Satan, just as our Lord Jesus did, so long ago. Therefore, I do advise you to read and study your Bible daily, until your mind is filled with the promises and instructions we are given in the scriptures. The more we know the Word of God, the more powerful we will be in our ongoing battle with the evil one, providing we become doers and not just hearers.

I want to make you aware that our lives consist of two separate parts so that we can tell where we are at today. The first part is simply from the cradle to the cross. This is the past life we have just left behind. It was a. life of mistakes and errors without the Word of God to guide us along the path of life. If you are old enough in years, then I am certain that there has also been some sorrow and some tears in the life we have lived in darkness. This is only natural for it is the inheritance we have received from Adam and Eve.

The second part of our life is just now beginning and we shall think of it as from the cross to the grave. Remember that the grave could not prevent Jesus from being resurrected from the dead, and it will not be our final destination, either, for the promise we have received is of life eternal.

Jesus said that he has come so that we may have life and have it more abundantly. One of the first things new Christians do experience is how much better their life is, right now, with Jesus and the Word of God, leading the way. Oh what a great feeling it is to wake in the morning and realize that we are now traveling on the high road to glory.

If sorrow and tears were a part of our inheritance in the first life we did live, then the joy of the Lord and the peace that surpasseth all understanding is a part of our new life in Christ Jesus. There are many things I would like to share with you, but I am reminded of the instructions I have received from the Lord.

Therfore, let us turn to the book of Hebrews and we shall examine some things that are said there.

Hebrews 2:2, For if the word spoken by angels was stedfast, and every transgression and disobedience received a just recompense of reward; (God did punish certain angels)

3 How shall we escape, if we neglect so great salvation; which at the first began to be spoken by the Lord, and was confirmed unto us by them that heard him.

God did punish the angels that joined with Lucifer in the rebellion in heaven. As a result, they were cast from heaven down to earth, where they are waiting for God's judgment day.

However, the point I want to make is where we are warned that we must not neglect our very own salvation. There is nothing we have ever owned or been given that is as precious as is our gift from God, of eternal life. The meaning of this scripture does make it very clear that it is possible for us to neglect our precious gift from God. Therefore, we must consider this a warning as well as an instruction and we would be wise to pay attention to it.

Staying in the book of Hebrews, let us turn to the 10th chapter where we shall receive some very important instructions as to how we must not neglect our precious gift from God.

Hebrews 10:21, And having a high priest (Jesus) over the house of God;

22 Let us draw near with a true heart in full assurance of faith, having our hearts sprinkled from an evil conscience, and our bodies washed with pure water. (water of the word of God)

23 Let us hold fast the profession of our faith without wavering; (for he is faithful that promised)

24 And let us consider one another to provoke unto love and to good works:

25 Not forsaking the assembling of ourselves together, as the manner of some is; but exhorting one another: and so much the more, as ye see the day approaching. (day of seven thunders)

I believe that the profession of our faith simply means that we are to continue to witness to others the wonderful work that God is doing in our life. Of course, this also includes our witness of God's perfect plan for salvation, made possible by the death and resurrection of Christ.

However, I want us to focus on the instruction that we are not to forsake the assembling of ourselves together. This simply means that it is part of God's plan and it is his will, that we are to attend church. However, keeping in mind that some of the very first churches did meet in people's houses, for fancy and ornate church buildings of the Christian faith had not yet been built. Keep in mind that church is a group of people and is not a building, made of wood, glass and stone.

I realize that many people, acting by instinct, will claim that they do not want to attend church, for they will just stay at home and study their Bibles alone. Remember the instruction we were given that we must not neglect our gift of salvation. It is very important that we do meet each week with other Christians, who are born again believers, for we do strengthen one another in the faith.

Be sure that you do not make the mistake that so many people have, for it is a very sad mistake to not meet with those people who will be with us, for all of eternity. If we fail to follow the instructions contained in God's own word, then we are guilty of neglecting the very precious gift we have been given.

It is written that one must plant and another must water but it is God who giveth the increase. I am as a man who has planted many seeds and I am well aware that I must soon turn you over to those whom God has called to do the watering. A pastor is one whom God has called to feed and water his flocks from the Word of God.

I am an ordinary man, a fisherman all of my life, saved by the grace of God and called to be a messenger, and a teacher. The message I was given, by our Lord Jesus Christ, was to share with you the knowledge concerning the day of seven thunders and then I was instructed that I was to tell you about Jesus and God's perfect plan for salvation.

In Matthew 24, Jesus informed us that in this time which we are living that many false prophets would arise. He said many for he wanted us to know that many does not mean just a few. These men and women can be found through out the Christian community and many of them are quite popular and their teaching is widely accepted. It is because I know this is so, that I feel that I must do my best to provide you with a solid foundation of truth from God's own word which will help protect you from teachers who are skilled in the art of deception and are very subtle.

We shall learn as we proceed to gain a solid foundation in scripture, that there is a price one must pay, if they choose the way of tradition instead of truth. God's truth will endure forever, but the traditions of men shall all pass away.

It is because so many of the churches today are involved in clinging to their religious traditions, that I want us to search for a people, rather than a church. Just who are these people I want for you to meet, you are probably wondering? We shall allow the Word of God to give us a description of them.

In the 12th chapter of the Revelation and at verse 17 it mentions a dragon as well as a woman.

The dragon is symbolic of Satan and Satan did give his power to greatly persecute Christians to the old Roman Empire. fact, the pages of history do tell us of how they destroyed Christians as a matter of entertainment at the Coliseum in Rome.

The woman in this 17th verse is speaking of the church that Jesus is building, which are a group of people that Satan greatly despises and seeks to destroy. We shall allow this 17th verse to identify these people.

Revelation 12:17, And the dragon was wroth (angry) with the woman (bride of Christ), and went to make war with the remnant of her seed, which keep the commandments of God, and have the testimony of Jesus Christ.

In the previous verse it mentions the earth did help the woman who was being persecuted and we know from history that this is speaking of the reformation. Even though a huge amount of Christians were slaughtered because they refused to submit to the authority of Roman religion, there was always a few who did survive. These few are the remnant or what is left after the reformation brought to an end the terrible persecution and slaughter of the true saints of the most high God.

The 17th verse does provide us with a description of this remnant so that we may identify them. It plainly says they are the ones who keep the commandments of God. This does mean they are doers of the commandments and not just hearers. As we continue down the path of enlightenment, we shall learn of the real reason these people do keep and do the commandments of their God.

By way of contrast, the churches of religious traditions do often claim they are not under the law but are under grace. They say this for they do not want to keep the commandments of God but do prefer to continue in their religious traditions which can be traced back to the Roman Empire, when Constantine was the highly exalted ruler.

There is another reason and that is simply because they have a different idea of what grace truly means.

They seem to believe that they can continue to live their lives their own way, which is not God's way, and because of grace, God will just look the other way. Perhaps it is because the scriptures do make it clear that we can not be saved by obeying the law, that they have decided to reject the law.

However, the apostle Paul did plainly say that we are to establish the law and this is something they refuse to do.

There is a different meaning of God's grace that I will share with you. It is written that "to as many as believed, to them he gave the power to become the sons of God." To word this a little different we could say, "to as many as believed to them he gave the power to over come sin.

The power to over come and rule over sin is by God's divine grace for the believer. Also consider what God did say to Cain, regarding sin. God's divine grace that is extended to us does not give us a license to sin, and according to scripture, sin is the transgression of the law.

Now in addition to keeping (doing) the commandments of God, the Remnant church does also have the testimony of Jesus Christ. Both of these descriptions are important in identifying the remnant church that Jesus continues to build. Keeping the commandments of God is good, but by itself it is not enough. The remnant church must also have the testimony of Jesus Christ.

Turning to the 14th chapter of the Revelation and at the 12th verse we read

12 Here is the patience of the saints: here are they that keep the commandments of God, and the faith of Jesus.

What I believe this means is that these people who were being persecuted even to death, refused to bow to Roman authority, for it meant they would have to give up the commandments of God, and replace them with the commandments of Rome. It was because of their faith, they chose to die rather than surrender to Roman religious authority.

In the last chapter of Revelation and at the 14th verse we read

14 Blessed are they that do his commandments, that they may have right to the tree of life and may enter in through the gates into the (heavenly) city.

I might add that they do not need to ask Peter for permission to do this.

I now want us to examine what is said in Ezekiel 20 and at verse 12

12 Moreover also I gave them my sabbaths to be a sign between me and them, that they might know that I am the Lord that sanctify them. (set apart)

It is when we think about this, we should be able to see that the sabbath day does bear the signature of our heavenly Creator. In six days he made this world and all that is in it, and on the seventh day, he rested from his work for an example for us to follow. In this way, we do recognize it was made by his divine authority, and because he does love us, he wants to bless us with this very special day.

I want for us to now listen to the last words Jesus did speak to his disciple before he ascended up to heaven.

Mark 16:15, And he said unto them, Go ye into all the world, and preach the gospel to every creature.

16 He that believeth and is baptized shall be saved; but he that believeth not shall be damned.

17 And these signs shall follow them that believe; In my name they shall cast out devils; they shall speak with new tongues;

18 They shall take up serpents; and if they drink any deadly thing, it will not hurt them; they shall lay hands on the sick, and they shall recover.

I want us to realize this is also a description of a missionary church, for he told them to go into all the world and preach the gospel. They are a group of born again believers, some of who are able to cast out devils in Jesus name. Also, at least some of them will speak with new tongues and some will lay hands on the sick and they will recover. These are the signs that will be present where ever these people with a mission do go. They do indicate that these people have received divine power from on high, and this power will help them to fulfill their mission.

To sum up what we have learned by these two different Biblical descriptions of born again believers is to determine what kind of people we should want to become. It is my sincere hope that we desire to become like both of them.

Following the instructions we were given by our brother in the faith, the apostle Paul, we shall continue to rightfully divide the word of truth, so that we will not need to be ashamed before God. The most important thing in anyone's life is that they find and receive God's perfect plan for salvation. The next step is the one we have just received and that is the instruction that in obedience to God, we must not neglect the precious gift we have been given. We must not forsake the assembling together with other born again believers, for we are now living in perilous times.

There is one thing I do want to make very clear to you and that is I will not be the one who will choose which church you will attend. This is something that is between you and our Lord Jesus Christ, and if you are lead by the Spirit of God, he will lead you to the one he wants for you to attend. We can be sure that God will not leave you as an orphan to fend for yourself, but he will provide you with a flock and a shepherd that will care for you, and strengthen you, to prepare you for what lies ahead.

The very next step in God's plan is water baptism. I realize that this is the duty of the shepherd that will care for you, but I believe that it is God's will that I increase your understanding of what baptism is and why we need to be baptized.

Let us begin this lesson on water baptism by turning to the gospel of Mark.

Mark 1:1, The beginning of the gospel of Jesus Christ, the Son of God;

2 As it is written in the prophets, Behold, I send my messenger before thy face, which shall prepare thy way before thee.

3 The voice of one crying in the wilderness, Prepare ye the way of the Lord, make his paths straight.

4 John did baptize in the wilderness, and preach the baptism of repentance for the remission of sins.

There are several things I want to make clear to you concerning baptism. First of all, the word baptize comes from the Greek word *bapto*, which means to completely immerse and to get completely wet. It was used when referring to dipping a piece of cloth into a solution of dye, to stain it. It does not refer to sprinkling for I can not imagine that a very good job of dying cloth could be done by sprinkling.

However, even from the days of the early church, there were some who insisted upon improving upon God's way, for God's way is shown very clearly in the scriptures, as we shall see. It was as though religious men, who had become drunk on the authority they held over the people, wanted to replace God's will with their own will. It has continued this way even until this very day.

I believe the second thing we need to know about baptism is that even though John did baptize for repentance and for the remission of sins, the full meaning of water baptism was not revealed until the death and resurrection of Christ.

The people who came to John to be baptized did so, to make a public display that they had repented of their former sinful way of life and had now chosen to live their lives according to God's perfect will. Even though they were dipped under the surface of the water and became completely submerged, the water did not actually wash away their sins. Pay attention to what I am about to tell you. They were baptized because of their commitment to live their lives God's way. However, the act of baptism did not save them. Only the blood of Jesus is able to save. We do not get baptized in order to be saved but we do get baptized because we have come to repentance and have received the forgiveness of our sins, just as we were promised.

Now Jesus was without sin, and therefore, it would not seem as though there could possibly be a reason for Jesus to be baptized. And yet, Jesus came to John and was baptized and we need to learn about why this is so.

Matthew 3:13, Then cometh Jesus from Galilee to Jordan unto John, to be baptized of him.

14 But John forbad him, saying, I have need to be baptized of thee, and cometh thou to me?

15 And Jesus answering said unto him, Suffer it to be so now; for thus it becometh us to fulfil all righteousness, Then he allowed John to baptize him.

16 And Jesus, when he was baptized, went up straightway out of the water; and, lo, the heavens were opened unto him, and he saw the Spirit of God descending like a dove, and lighting upon him:

17 And lo, a voice from heaven saying, This is my Son, in whom I am well pleased.

Jesus, who was without sin, allowed himself to be baptized by his cousin John, in order to fulfil all righteousness. In other words, it was right in the eyes of God, for he set the example for us to follow. If we are to be followers of Christ, then we should be baptized, just as he was baptized, or else we are unwilling to do what is right in the eyes of God.

Notice that the scriptures do inform us that when he was baptized, he went up, straightway out of the water. In other words, in order to be baptized, he first went down into the water and I believe this is speaking of the river Jordan.

Now if Jesus were to allow himself to be baptized by some of the religious men that would come later, none of this would have been necessary. I mean it would not have been necessary for him to go down into the water, for the baptizer could have just had a bucket of water and a sponge and he could have sprinkled a little water on his forehead and mumbled the words, I baptize thee in the name of....

I thank God for the example that Jesus has set before us to follow, so that we too, can be fully submerged under the surface of the water, just as he was. When my wife, Esther and I were baptized, we were baptized in a small stream that flows through a public park and into the Fraser river. The water seemed to be very cold, but it probably wasn't. There was a deep pool and we stood in it, with the water being waist deep. We were both baptized there, under the hand of our pastor, E. L. Saunders, and it was a very blessed day that we will not forget

On the day that we were baptized, there was a large group of Buddhists there at the park, and they were all witnesses to our baptism. They asked many questions of the members of our small church, and the opportunity to share God's word was given unto us.

I do not know of any of those people who witnessed our baptism who were actually converted to Christianity. However, we must welcome the opportunity to share the good news about Christ and salvation and we do not always see the end result of our testimony. This is one of the reasons I favor being baptized in a public place when it is possible, for it often provides an opportunity to witness to others.

John the Baptist did baptize unto repentance, but once Jesus had died on the cross and was resurrected from the dead, three days later, baptism took on a new meaning. It is very important that we do understand this and so we shall listen as the apostle Paul does explain about the meaning of baptism.

Romans 6:3, Know ye not, that so many of us as were baptized into Jesus Christ were baptized into his death?

4 Therefore we are buried with him by baptism into death: that like as Christ was raised up from the dead by the glory of the Father, even so we also should walk in newness of life.

5 For if we have been planted together in the likeness of his death, we shall be also in the likeness of his resurrection.

6 Knowing this, that our old man is crucified with him, that the body of sin might be destroyed, that henceforth we should not serve sin.

7 For he that is dead is freed from sin.

8 Now if we be dead with Christ, we believe that we shall also live with him:

9 Knowing that Christ being raised from the dead dieth no more; death hath no more dominion over him.

10 For in that he died, he died unto sin once: but in that he liveth, he liveth unto God.

11 Likewise reckon ye also yourselves to be dead indeed unto sin, but alive unto God through Jesus Christ our Lord.

We can see that in a symbolic sense, water baptism is closely related to the being born again experience. When we are completely submerged beneath the surface of the water, it is as though the old man of sin we once were, has died and is buried under the water. When we come back up from under the water, it is as though we are being resurrected in newness of life in Christ Jesus. Symbolically, the old man of sin stays beneath the water and a new, born again Christian comes up out of the water.

This in it's self is a miracle, if we but think about it. The original meaning of water baptism is still valid. It is still a public declaration of the fact that we have repented of our former way of life, and have made a firm commitment to live our lives for God and for his glory.

However, as Paul has explained to us, we are also buried with Christ in his death, (speaking of the old man of sin) so that we are also resurrected with him, in newness of life, as true believers who have been born again. It is a beautiful ceremony that has great meaning, for we know deep within us, that it is a confirmation of our obedience to God as his humble children.

I believe that it is important that we realize that we are not baptized into a church. I have heard many people say that they were baptized as a such and such denomination, or baptized into such and such church. This is totally wrong and I do not want you to be lead to believe this way.

Let us listen once more as our brother Paul does explain further about baptism.

Ephesians 4:1, Therefore, the prisoner of the Lord, beseech you that ye walk worthy of the vocation wherewith ye are called.

2 With all lowliness and meekness, with longsuffering, forbearing one another in love;

3 Endeavouring to keep the unity of the Spirit in the bond of peace.

4 There is one body, and one Spirit, even as ye are called in one hope of your calling;

5 One Lord, one faith, one baptism,

6 One God and Father of all, who is above all, and through all, and in you all.

7 But unto every one of us is given grace according to the measure of the gift of Christ.

I believe that it is rather sad that in this country in which we live, there is no longer one baptism, but there are many ways of performing baptism, for we live in the land of great religious confusion. It is for this reason that I do try to explain the truth as revealed in the Word of God, concerning such things as water baptism.

I will now share with you the story of Philip, whom God called to be an evangelist, and the man Philip baptized from Ethiopia.

Acts 8:26, And the angel of the Lord spake unto Philip, saying, Arise, and go toward the south unto the way that goeth down from Jerusalem unto Gaza, which is desert.

27 And he arose and went: and behold, a man of Ethiopia, an eunuch of great authority under Candace queen of the Ethiopians, who had the charge of all her treasure, and had come to Jerusalem for to worship.,

28 Was returning, and sitting in his chariot read Isaiah the prophet.

29 Then the Spirit said unto Philip, Go near, and join thyself to this chariot.

30 And Philip ran thither to him, and heard him read the prophet Isaiah, and said, Understandest thou what thou readest?

31 And he said, How can I, except some man should guide me? And he desired Philip that he would come up and sit with him.

32 The place of the scripture which he read was this, He was led as a sheep to the slaughter; and like a lamb dumb before his shearer, so opened he not his mouth:

33 In his humiliation his judgment was taken away: and who shall declare his generation? for his life is taken from the earth.

34 And the eunuch answered Philip, and said, I pray thee, of whom speaketh the prophet this? of himself, or of some other man?

35 Then Philip opened his mouth, and began at the same scripture, and preached unto him Jesus.

36 And as they went on their way, they came unto a certain water: and the eunuch said, See, here is water; what doth hinder me to be baptized?

37 And Philip said, If thou believest with all thine heart, thou mayest. And he answered and said, I believe that Jesus Christ is the Son of God.

38 And he commanded the chariot to stand still: and they went down both into the water, both Philip and the eunuch; and he baptized him.

39 And when they were come up out of the water, the Spirit of the Lord caught away Philip, that the eunuch saw him no more: and he went on his way rejoicing,

Notice that they both went down into the water and they both came back up out of the water. It does seem to me, that it should be obvious that the method used by Philip was to completely submerge the head of the one being baptized, for how else could it be symbolic of the burial of Christ. Surely these verses does not leave us with the idea that Philip merely sprinkled a little water on this man's head.

Notice also who it was that directed Philip to go there in the first place. Then take notice of what happened to Philip after the baptism had taken place. We should all recognize that these things happened because it was the will of the Lord.

I also believe that it is important that we realize that to be baptized as they were in these scriptures, it is necessary to be fully submerged, for anything less, taketh away from the full meaning of being buried with Christ, in his death. As we begin to understand how very precious our salvation really is, we also begin to understand that the very beautiful ceremony of baptism is by God's grace and a gift from God that will live in our memory forever. Why then, would anyone accept anything less, than complete baptism in the Biblical way?

In order to clear up some of the confusion that exists today, concerning water baptism, let us turn to Matthew 28, where we shall learn about the great commission.

Shortly after his resurrection from the dead, Jesus did appear to his disciples and did have these very important instructions to give to them.

Matthew 28:18, And Jesus came and spake unto them, saying, All power is given unto me in heaven and in earth.

19 Go ye therefore, and teach all nations, baptizing them in the name of the Father, and of the Son, and of the Holy Ghost.

I find it surprising that many religious men who have studied countless hours in Bible colleges do not seem to be able to grasp the full meaning of what Jesus said.

Notice that Jesus said they were to baptize in the name of. The word "name," is singular and not plural. In other words, they were to baptize in only one name. There is one name that is the name of the Father and the same name is the name of the Son and the same name is the name of the Holy Ghost.

The word "Father," is a descriptive title, but it is not a name. Many children do call their father, "Father," but father is not really his name. In the same way, many men do call their sons, "Son," but son is not really his name. In both of these cases, the title "father" or the title "son," are titles that describe who a person is, but their title is not their real name.

We shall turn to the 14th chapter of the gospel of John and try to increase our knowledge concerning this subject which has confused so many educated people. In these verses, Jesus does foretell the coming of the comforter or in other words, the Holy Ghost.

John 14:17, Even the Spirit of truth; whom the world cannot receive, because it seeth him not, neither knoweth him: but ye know him; for he dwelleth with you, and shall be in you.

It should be obvious that Jesus was talking about himself. It was he, that was dwelling with them (present tense) and shall (future tense) be in you. In other words, when they would receive the Holy Ghost at a future time, they would receive Jesus, the same Jesus that was at that time, dwelling with them.

To make sure they did understand what he was telling them, Jesus had something further to say in verse 23.

John 14:23, Jesus answered and said unto him, If a man love me, he will keep my words: and my Father will love him, and we will come unto him, and make our abode with him.

Jesus made it very clear that when they would receive the Holy Ghost at a future time, they would not only receive Jesus, but they would also receive his Father, as well. In other words, both the Father and the Son, would be together in one Spirit, and that Spirit would also be called the Holy Ghost. It should be easy to understand that the Holy Ghost was not really a third divine being, but in reality was only the package that the Father and the Son would come in.

John 14:26, But the comforter, which is the Holy Ghost, whom the Father will send in my name, he shall teach you all things, and bring to your remembrance, whatsoever I have said unto you.

What name did Jesus say the Holy Ghost would be sent in? Did he not say that it would be in his own holy name? This should make it clear why there is only one name by which we may be saved, and why there is only one name in which we are to be baptized, for they are both the same holy name. That is the name of Jesus, and the disciples did understand what Jesus meant, for the scriptures will bear this out.

In the 24th chapter of Luke, the Word of God had this to say about the disciples of Jesus, concerning their understanding and what Jesus did on their behalf.

Luke 24:45, Then opened he their understanding, that they might understand the scriptures.

I want us to realize that this did take place after Jesus was crucified and was raised from the dead after three days.

We then must ask the question, "Did the disciples understand what Jesus was talking about, when he gave unto them the instruction they were to go into all the world and baptize in the name of the Father, and of the Son, and of the Holy Ghost?"

In the 2nd chapter of Acts we shall find Peter, who was there when they first received the great commission from the Lord, as he addresses a very large group of Jews, on the holy day of Pentecost.

Acts 2:36, Therefore let all the house of Israel know assuredly, that God hath made that same Jesus, whom ye have crucified, both Lord and Christ.

37, Now when they heard this, they were pricked in their heart, and said unto Peter and to the rest of the apostles, Men and brethren, what shall we do?

38 Then Peter said unto them, Repent, and be baptized every one of you in the name of Jesus Christ for the remission of sins, and ye shall receive the gift of the Holy Ghost.

There should be no doubt that Peter was there, when the disciples received the great commission from Jesus, who was their Lord. Did he understand in what one name they were to baptize new Christians in? Absolutely, for the scriptures are very clear about this. Let us turn to The Acts the 10th chapter where we shall find Peter some time later.

Acts 10:48, And he (Peter) commanded them to be baptized in the name of the Lord. Then prayed they him to tarry certain days.

We must ask the question, "Is it important what name or names in which we are baptized?" After all, many people have been baptized in the name of the Father and the Son and the Holy Ghost, or at least these are the very words which were said by the person doing the baptizing. However, just to use these very same words, which are titles and are not names, means that the person has not been baptized in any name at all. It is kind of like saying I baptize you in the name of the president and the vice-president and the governor. These are only titles and as such, do not have very much meaning.

To return to the question, is it important how and in what name we are baptized? The scriptures will show us how important it was to the apostle Paul and who can dispute he was a man who lived out his life in obedience to God.

Acts 19:1, And it came to pass, that, while Apollos was at Corinth, Paul having passed through the upper coasts came to Ephesus: and finding certain disciples,

3 And he said unto them, Unto what then were ye baptized? And they said, Unto John's baptism.

4 Then said Paul, John verily baptized with the baptism of repentance, saying unto the people, that they should believe on him which should come after him, that is, on Christ Jesus.

5 When they heard this, they were baptized in the name of the Lord Jesus.

We can see from this Biblical example, that when they learned that there was a more meaningful way to be baptized, they did not hesitate, but were re-baptized right away. So should it be with Christians living in these last days, for there are a great many who should be re-baptized in the holy name of our Lord Jesus Christ.

There are some who will ask, what about our children? Should we have them baptized as well as ourselves? I believe that this is a very important question and one we must consider. I believe there are several different elements which must be present before a person is baptized.

The first one is repentance. No one is to be baptized unless they have first repented of their sins. Now in regard to salvation we learned that to repent could mean that one has changed their mind. They have finally came to realize that God's way is right but their way, which is man's way is wrong. However, repentance as it touches baptism takes on a little more meaning.

The first meaning given in my dictionary does apply now. To turn from sin and dedicate oneself to the amendment of one's life. 2 To feel regret or contrition for the sinful life we once lived. I believe that all three of the meanings given, including having a change of mind, does apply to the one who has repented of their sins, and is waiting to be baptized.

In addition to having repented of our sins, the person to be baptized must confess with their mouth who Jesus is and what Jesus has done for them. Remember that confession is an important part of our salvation.

Another important element that is necessary before one can be baptized is believing. As we have already learned, we must believe with our heart as well as our mind, who Jesus is and what he has done for us.

We also must be willing to forgive others, for this is a condition that precedes being born again. And finally, we must be ready to make a life long commitment to completely forsake the way of sin and live our life in such a way that is pleasing and acceptable unto God.

To be baptized into the death of Christ, and then to live our new life for God is a very serious thing and should not be taken lightly. If a child is too young to understand these things, then they are too young to be baptized.

The practice of baptizing very young children and infants was invented by religious men who sought to have power over their parents. It is a practice that can not be found in the pages of the holy Bible for it is not of God. Young children can be dedicated to the Lord, but in order for their baptism to mean anything, it must wait until the person has reached the age of understanding of what is required and what it is the symbol of. Peter does have something more to say as to the purpose of water baptism

1st Peter 3:21, The like figure whereunto even baptism doth also now save us (not the putting away of the filth of the flesh, but the answer of a good conscience toward God,) by the resurrection of Jesus Christ.

I do hope my dear brothers and sisters, that when the day of seven thunders does come upon us as a thief in the night, and the door of salvation is tightly closed, that your conscience will be completely clear toward our God and that you will have become a born again believer who has experienced the peace of mind that water baptism does provide.

I then offer this advice to all who are to be baptized. If it is possible, it is good to be baptized in a public place, for it is a demonstration to the whole world, that a miracle has taken place within our lives. Also, that from this time on, our life is dedicated to serving God and following in the footsteps of our Lord Jesus Christ, who set an example for us to follow.

I would remind the women that care must be used when selecting the clothing to be baptized in, for some cloth is almost transparent when wet, while other materials might cling as tight to your body as a second skin. I say this not as a judge but as one concerned for your modesty that you do not need to be embarrassed publicly or in any other way.

I do also offer this word of advice to those who will be conducting the baptism service, just as a dear brother once offered it to me. When baptizing in the name of Jesus, it is good to say "I baptize you in the name of our Lord, Jesus Christ." In that way, there need be no confusion as to which Jesus you are speaking of, for in some parts of the world, Jesus is a fairly common name.

I do hope that you will not tarry too long but will seek to be baptized just as soon as you have found that group of Christians that our Lord will provide for you.

Do not be afraid to discuss these things with your pastor, for as a man of God, he should be happy to answer any question you might have, for your cares are his concerns.

One final piece of advice is that you might want to bring a camera and have someone help you record this blessed day for your photo album, for it will become more precious to you, as the days go by.

Chapter 29 Baptism in Holy Ghost

W e will now dwell upon some of the last instructions that were given unto the disciples by Jesus, before he ascended up to heaven to be with his heavenly Father. We must realize that these last instructions were not for the disciples only, but were for all who would come of their own free will, and believe upon our Lord, Jesus Christ with all of their heart.

Our God is a God of order and it is good for us to understand the order in which God has given his instructions to us. First and most important is when we come humbly to the cross to repent of our sins and receive the gift of eternal life. There is nothing, absolutely nothing more important than finding the one and only plan God has for our salvation and then accepting our Lord Jesus Christ as our Savior.

The second instruction we did receive is that we are to be baptized in water, for it is an important part of God's plan for our salvation, and it is for our benefit. It will assure us that we have a clear conscience toward God as to the fact that we have chosen to obey his instructions, following in the footsteps of our Lord Jesus and placing our trust in his word.

We will now return to the great commission our Lord has delivered unto all, who have chosen to be his disciples.

Matthew 28:18, And Jesus came and spake unto them, saying, All power is given unto me in heaven and in earth.

I believe it is important that we realize that Jesus was given ALL power in both heaven and earth for a reason. In this way, he is able to dispense power to whoever he chooses to, to insure that God's will, as it relates to the great commission, is done. This is why Jesus informed us of his power, just before he delivered unto us, the great commission. The next two verses will inform us what God's will is, regarding what we are to do.

Matthew 28:19, Go ye therefore, and teach all nations, baptizing them in the name of the Father, and of the Son, and of the Holy Ghost:

20 Teaching them to observe all things whatsoever I have commanded you: and, lo, I am with you alway, even unto the end of the world. Amen.

During the many years that have passed since Jesus first gave this great commission, there have been many dear men and women of God, who have dedicated their lives to carrying out this instruction. Many left their homes and all of their worldly possessions behind, to travel to a foreign mission field for answering the call of God was their first priority.

Many were met with hostility and did endure all kinds of hardships, while ministering to people who were often so poor they did not have enough to eat. They were often threatened with death from those opposed to their work and many were killed by them. Still others, continued to give their all for the sake of the gospel and lived and died without ever returning to the land of their birth. We can be sure that God has not forgotten any of them and great is their reward that awaits them.

Surely, it should not be too hard to understand that most of us are not naturally equipped with the strength and power it takes to endure such hardships. We can be sure that our Creator is aware of our strengths and our weaknesses and he does want to bestow upon us, the power we shall need to carry out his work. We have already learned of the promise Jesus gave his disciples in the gospel of John, regarding the coming of the Comforter, which is also the Holy Ghost. Therefore, let us listen to these last instructions that were given to the disciples by Jesus, as they are recorded in Luke's gospel.

Luke 24:46, And I said unto them, Thus it is written, and thus it behoved Christ to suffer, and to rise from the dead the third day:

47 And that repentance of sins should be preached in his name among all nations, beginning at Jerusalem.

48 And ye are witnesses of these things.

49 And, behold, I send the promise of my Father upon you: but tarry ye in the city of Jerusalem, until ye be endued with power from on high.

We must remember that this conversation is taking place, after Jesus was crucified and his body was placed in the tomb. His disciples who were so sad and without hope now must be filled with joy, to realize that Jesus really was raised back to life from the dead. Even though Jesus had told them, that he would be raised from the dead, even as Jonah was in the belly of the fish for three days and nights, I doubt very much that they really believed him. Can we even imagine their joy when they finally began to understand that Jesus was not dead but was very much alive.

Even so, we must not forget that Jesus gave them a direct order that they were to wait in Jerusalem until they received power. from on high. As our knowledge is increased concerning the power they were to receive, so will the command that they remain in Jerusalem become more important.

In order we come to better understand how it really was at that time, let us read the remaining verses in this chapter.

Luke 24:50, And he led them out as far as to Bethany, and he lifted up his hands, and blessed them.

51 And it came to pass, while he blessed them, he was parted from them, and carried up into heaven.

52 And they worshipped him, and returned to Jerusalem with great joy:

53 And were continually in the temple, praising and blessing God, Amen.

It is interesting that Luke, who was also a physician and an educated man, we are told was also the one who recorded the things that are written in The Acts of the apostles. I say this, for we must now examine "The Acts" of the apostles, for they contain instructions for all who are followers of Christ.

Acts 1:1, The former treatise have I made, 0 Theophilus, of all that Jesus began both to do and teach,

2 Until the day in which he was taken up, after that he through the Holy Ghost had given commandments unto the apostles whom he had chosen:

3 To whom also he showed himself alive after his passion by many infallible proofs, being seen of them forty days, and speaking of the things pertaining to the kingdom of God:

I would bring to your attention that if Jesus was seen by his disciples for forty days, he was also not seen during the three days and nights that he was in the tomb. This means that the ascension did take place forty-three days after the passover, when Jesus was crucified. I have brought this to your attention for I consider it to be important as it relates to how long before the holy day of Pentecost, was the ascension.

Is this relevant or important to what we are trying to learn? We shall see as we go along.

Acts 1:4, And being assembled together with them, commanded them that they should not depart from Jerusalem, but wait for the promise of the Father, which saith he, ye have heard of me.

5 For John truly baptized with water; but ye shall be baptized with the Holy Ghost not many days hence.

6 When they therefore were come together, they asked of him saying, Lord, wilt thou at this time restore again the kingdom to Israel?

7 And he said unto them, It is not for you to know the times, or the seasons, which the Father hath put in his own power.

8 But ye shall receive power, after that the Holy Ghost is come upon you: and ye shall be witnesses unto me both in Jerusalem, and in all Judea, and in Samaria, and unto the uttermost part of the earth.

9 And when he had spoken these things, while they beheld, he was taken up; and a cloud received him out of their sight.

10 And while they looked stedfastly toward heaven as he went up, behold, two men stood by them in white apparel;

11 Which also said, Ye men of Galilee, why stand ye gazing up into heaven? this same Jesus, which is taken up from you into heaven, shall so come in like manner as ye have seen him go.

This is a very interesting account of what took place at the ascension of Jesus, when he was taken up to heaven. Just where were they at, when the ascension took place?

The very next verse does make it clear that they were in the place known as the Mount of Olives.

Acts 1:12, Then returned they unto Jerusalem from the mount Olivet, which is from Jerusalem a sabbath day's journey.

13 And when they were come in, they went up into an upper room, where abode both Peter, and James, and John, and Andrew, Philip, and Thomas, Bartholomew, and Matthew, James the son of Alphaeus, and Judas the brother of James.

14 These all continued with one accord in prayer and supplication, with the women, and Mary the mother of Jesus, and with his brethren.

The next verse does indicate that all together, there were about a hundred and twenty people who were praying together in one accord. Why were they there we might ask? They were there because Jesus had instructed his disciples to tarry in Jerusalem until they received the power from on high. It should be obvious that about 120 people including Mary, the mother of Jesus, as well as other women who were there, were charter members of the first Christian church, the same which Jesus said he would build.

The very next verse we shall read is the first verse of chapter two. It begins by setting the time as when the day of Pentecost had fully come. It does appear that the disciples and small group of believers, including Mary, the mother of Jesus, did remain there together, praying and worshipping God for at least ten days, during the time between the ascension and the holy day of Pentecost. We must remember that Jesus was seen by many people for forty days and to this we must add the three days he was in the tomb. This means that the ascension must have taken place, forty three days after the passover. I want us all to grasp this truth very tightly, for it shall become more important to us, as our knowledge is increased.

To determine when the day of Pentecost did arrive, we must follow the instructions that are given in the 23rd chapter of Leviticus. They do inform us that we are to begin counting fifty days from the morrow after the sabbath. This will bring us to the day of Pentecost. If we have counted correctly, then we realize that the ascension took place exactly ten days before the holy day of Pentecost.

And now, we shall find out what happened next.

Acts 2:1, And when the day of Pentecost was fully come, they were all with one accord in one place.

2 And suddenly there came a sound from heaven as of a rushing mighty wind, and it filled all the house where they were sitting.

3 And there appeared unto them cloven tongues like as of fire, and it sat upon each of them.

4 And they were all filled with the Holy Ghost, and began to speak with other tongues, as the Spirit gave them utterance.

I want to make it very clear that this was the very first time that anything like this had ever taken place. It marked a very important milestone in mankind's relationship with God. I also want to bring to your attention that these scriptures do say very clearly that they were ALL filled with the Holy Ghost, and began to speak in other tongues. The scriptures do refer to this experience as the "Baptism" of the Holy Ghost.

It is not a little sprinkling on the head, but the whole person is fully submerged in the Holy Spirit. It is not something that would leave people wondering whether or not they had received it, for it is so overwhelming that the person who has experienced this baptism of the Holy Spirit will never forget it as long as they live.

You will recall that the reason they would be given power from on high was to enable them to become very powerful witnesses to preach the gospel message of Christ with the end result being the salvation of lost souls.

Keeping in mind that the time was the holy day the Jews called Pentecost and that on that day, there were many devout Jews which had come to Jerusalem from all over that part of the world, as their custom was. These same men, being very religious did not know what to think when they heard the disciples speaking in tongues and so they accused them of being drunken.

We must remember that Peter had been given the keys to the kingdom and Peter is about to use them. Peter had received the baptism in the Holy Ghost, and the anointing of the Holy Spirit and he was on fire to preach the gospel of Christ.

The very first thing Peter did was assure the crowd of people that the strange phenomenon of speaking in other tongues they did observe was not because anyone had drunk too much wine but was the fulfilling of the prophecy given by the prophet Joel.

Acts 2:16, But this is that which was spoken by the prophet Joel;

17 And it shall come to pass in the last days, saith God, I will pour out my Spirit upon all flesh: and your sons and your daughters shall prophesy, and your young men shall see visions, and your old men shall dream dreams:

18 And on my servants and on my handmaidens I will pour out in those days of my Spirit; and they shall prophesy:

19 And I will show wonders in heaven above, and signs in the earth beneath; blood, and fire, and vapour of smoke:

20 The sun shall be turned into darkness, and the moon into blood, before that great and notable day of the Lord come:

21 And it shall come to pass, that whosoever shall call on the name of the Lord shall be saved.

Peter then went on to preach the Word of God, using the Hebrew scriptures to show who Jesus really was, whom the Jews had crucified. There can be no doubt that because the anointing of the Holy Spirit was upon Peter, he was successful in convincing a great many people of the gospel truths which he preached. This leads us to the question the people then asked Peter.

Acts 2:37, Now when they heard this, they were pricked in their heart, and said unto Peter and to the rest of the apostles, Men and brethern, what shall we do?

38 Then Peter said unto them Repent, and be baptized everyone of you in the name of Jesus Christ for the remission of sins, and ye shall receive the gift of the Holy Ghost.

I want for you to fully understand what did take place there in Jerusalem on the holy day of Pentecost, so long ago. Remember the purpose of why they would receive this power from on high. It was to give them power so that they could do a better job of being witnesses for Christ. The message they were called to deliver was the message of salvation. Peter was sharing with a very large crowd of people the gospel message in order to lead those people to the place they would receive the gift of eternal life, just as we have.

When Peter said they would receive the gift of the Holy Ghost, he was not speaking of the baptism of the Holy Ghost. He was speaking of the very same gift that is promised to all born again believers. The gift of the Holy Ghost and the baptism in the Holy Ghost, are two different things.

I realize that there are many who will disagree with me, but I know that I must share the truth with you, even as I have received it from the Lord. Let us go to the next verse.

Acts 2:39, For the promise is unto you, and to your children, and to all that are afar off, even as many as the Lord shall call.

40 And with many other words did he testify and exhort, saying save yourselves from this untoward generation.

Notice carefully what Peter is saying to the large crowd of mostly Jewish people who were there at Jerusalem. He is not saying anything about receiving the baptism in the Holy Ghost, except what he said about the prophecy given by the prophet Joel. The direction his sermon has taken is leading them toward the cross of Christ and repentance to salvation. Let us now learn the result of Peter's powerful anointed preaching.

Acts 2:41, Then they that gladly received his word were baptized: and the same day there were added unto them about three thousand souls.

42 And they continued stedfastly in the apostle's doctrine and fellowship, and in prayers.

The baptism that is mentioned in the 41st verse is water baptism. I do not believe that it is speaking of being baptized in the Holy Spirit, or else it would be described in some detail.

It is time for us to learn how Peter did use the keys to the kingdom he had been given. It was through his Holy Ghost anointed preaching that this Spirit filled Christian did deliver such a powerful sermon that three thousand souls were converted and did receive the gift of the Holy Ghost, that gift being the gift of eternal life.

If Peter had not first received the baptism in the Holy Ghost, I doubt that he could have convinced even a small handful of people, because it is well known that the Jews are very stubborn when it comes to matters of religion. However, with the super-natural power he had received from on high, three thousand (think about it) three thousand souls were converted to Christianity. It is no wonder that this miraculous day is referred to as the birthday of the church.

We shall read the remaining verses in this chapter and then we shall discuss what took place.

Acts 2:43, And fear came upon every soul: and many wonders and signs were done by the apostles.

I want to point out that many signs and wonders were done by the apostles because they were the one's who had received super-natural power from on high. There is nothing said in these verses that would indicate that any of the three thousand that were converted to Christianity did perform any signs or wonders.

44 And all that believed were together, and had all things common;

45 And sold their possessions and goods, and parted them to all men, as every man had need.

46 And they, continuing daily with one accord in the temple, and breaking bread from house to house, did eat their meat with gladness and singleness of heart,

47 Praising God, and having favour with all people. And the Lord added to the church daily such as should be saved.

We shall now review the things we have learned concerning the promise of God that was given. We shall listen as Jesus does increase his disciple's knowledge concerning the coming of the comforter.

John 14:23, Jesus answered and said unto him, If a man love me, he will keep my words: and my Father will love him, and WE will come unto him, and make our abode with him.

Notice that there is a condition that must be met in order to receive this promise. Also notice, that both the Father and the Son will make their abode or dwelling place, within the person who meets the conditions.

The next verse we are about to read explains how Jesus and his Father will make their abode within us.

John 14:26, But the Comforter, which is the Holy Ghost, whom the Father will send in my name, he shall teach you all things, and bring all things to your remembrance, whatsoever I have said unto you.

It should be easy to understand that Almighty God, who sitteth upon his throne in heaven, has sent to us the Comforter, which is the Holy Ghost, which is invisible because it is Spirit. It is this invisible Spirit, which shall increase our ability to understand things and will teach us the things we need to know, and also help us to remember what is written in our Bibles. It is also important that we realize that this Holy and invisible Spirit has been sent in the Name of Jesus, and in Jesus name we must receive it.

Let us listen once more to the words of Jesus

John 16:7, Never the less I tell you the truth; It is expedient for you that I go away: for if I go not away, the Comforter will not come unto you: but if I depart, I will send him unto you.

There is a great truth contained in this verse and I want us to grasp the full meaning of it. If the Holy Ghost was really a third person, as has been taught down through the centuries, then there should of been no need for Jesus to go away, for they both could have been here on earth at the same time.

However, Jesus has made it clear that it was necessary for him to ascend up to heaven, before he could return to earth, in the form of the Holy Spirit. As long as Jesus remained in the flesh, he was limited by his flesh. In other words, he could only be in one place at a time. But now that he has returned as the Holy Spirit, he is no longer limited but can take up residence in the hearts of all born again believers.

Keep in mind, the scripture has said that his Father would send the Holy Spirit in the name of Jesus.

The next thing we learned was that Jesus, after he was risen from the dead, did instruct his disciples they were to tarry in Jerusalem until they received power from on high.

We then received the promise that Jesus did give his disciples in the first chapter of The Acts.

Acts 1:8, But ye shall receive power, after that the Holy Ghost is come upon you: and ye shall be witnesses unto me both in Jerusalem, and in all Judea, and in Samaria, and unto the uttermost part of the earth.

I then shared with you the knowledge that it does appear that about 120 believers remained in Jerusalem from the time of the ascension ten days until the day of Pentecost had fully arrived. The first four verses of chapter two does inform us that when they received the baptism in the Holy Ghost, they began to speak with other tongues as the Spirit gave them utterance.

Today, there are a great many people who read that they all began to speak with other tongues, and that is as far as they go. The only thing they seem to be interested in is speaking in tongues, for it is as though they are always trying to prove something. I do not want us to be like them, for I want us to grasp what the outcome of this initial out pouring of the Holy Spirit really was.

The scriptures do make it very clear that about three thousand people were converted from traditional Judaism to Christianity, and I consider that to be truly a miracle.

This is what I consider to be important, for there is nothing more important than to lead people to where they might receive the gift of eternal life. This is what I consider to be so very important about receiving the baptism of the Holy Ghost, for it enables us to become very powerful witnesses for the gospel's sake.

Speaking in tongues is one of the gifts of the Spirit and any gift from God is a very precious thing. However, the gifts of the Spirit are like blossoms on a tree, for they contain a promise of the fruit that is to come. If the blossoms do not bear much fruit, then we know there is something wrong.

There are many people today, who seem to be interested mainly in the blossoms, but are not concerned with the fruit the blossoms are supposed to bring. It does appear to me that their priorities are out of order.

I now ask this question. If there is a man who has an orchard, and his business is to grow an abundance of fruit, what will that man do with those trees that produce many blossoms but fail to bear any fruit?

I do not know of any subject within the Christian religion that is more misunderstood than is the baptism of the Holy Ghost. The teachings concerning this supernatural phenomenon vary from one denomination to another and they all seem to teach some degree of error. Of course, the real reason this is so, is because religious men, who claim to know all there is to know, teach their own private interpretation of this subject and do not teach what our Bibles really do say.

We have already learned about what took place at Jerusalem, on the day when the Holy Ghost was first given. The Holy Ghost fell upon about 120 individuals who had tarried there, for ten days and they all began to speak in tongues. However, the end result was that about three thousand people were converted to Christianity, and we must not forget the prophecy that was given by Zechariah, the prophet.

Zechariah 4:6, Then he answered and spake unto me, saying, This is the word of the Lord unto Zerubbabel, saying, Not by might, nor by power, but by my Spirit, saith the Lord of hosts.

We should realize that the conversion of three thousand souls did not take place by the power of man, but by the super natural power of the Holy Spirit.

We now ask the question, "Prior to that day of Pentecost, when the Holy Ghost was given, were there people of God who were filled with the Holy Spirit?" We will look to the Word of God for the answer.

John 7:37, In the last day, that great day of the feast, Jesus stood and cried saying, If any man thirst, let him come unto me and drink.

38 He that believeth on me, as the scripture hath said, out of his belly shall flow rivers of living water.

39 (But this spake he of the Spirit, which they that believe on him should receive: for the Holy Ghost was not yet given; because Jesus was not yet glorified.)

Perhaps you will recall that Jesus did inform his disciples that it was necessary for him to depart, in order for the Comforter to come, whom his Father would send in his name. In this regard we note that the Comforter, the Holy Ghost did not come until ten days after the ascension.

Then some people will ask, what about old testament times? Were not the prophets filled with the Spirit of God for how else could they have foretold the future? There is an important distinction between the way men of God received the Spirit in the old testament, and the way it is received following the day of Pentecost that is recorded in the book of Acts.

First of all, in the old testament, there were only three kinds of people who could receive the Spirit of God. Namely, they were priests, prophets, and kings. These were the only people who could or did receive the Holy Spirit, and they did not receive it in the same way as the 120 in the upper room.

The difference is that the scriptures do show that in old testament times, the Holy Spirit always came upon them. It did not dwell within them or take up residence within them. let us review one more time the beautiful promise we were given by our Lord, Jesus.

John 14:23, Jesus answered and said unto him, If a man love me, he will keep my words: and my Father will love him, and we will come unto him, and make our abode with him.

Notice that the promise is that both Jesus and his Father will make their dwelling place within us if we will love Jesus as he wants for us to love him. This was not the way it was in old testament times and I am reminded of what happened to Elijah, the mighty prophet of God.

Now Elijah had challenged the prophets of the Sun God, Baal, to a contest and after they were defeated, he went on to slay them. What Elijah had done caused the kings wife whose name was Jezebel to become very angry and she sent word to Elijah that she would do to him, as he had done unto the prophets of Baal. Now the affect of her promise to kill Elijah caused him to fear for his life, and so he ran away.

Now Elijah had been fleeing and hiding for more than forty days and we shall take up the story at verse....

1 Kings 19:9, And he came thither unto a cave, and lodged there; and, behold, the word of the Lord came to him, and he said unto him, What doest thou here, Elijah?

10 And he said, I have been very jealous for the Lord of hosts: for the children of Israel have forsaken thy covenant, thrown down thine altars, and slain thy prophets with the sword; and I, even I only, am left; and they seek my life to take it away.

11 And he said, Go forth, and stand upon the mount before the Lord. And behold, the Lord passed by, and a great and strong wind rent the mountains, and brake in pieces the rocks before the Lord; but the Lord was not in the wind: and after the wind an earthquake; but the Lord was not in the earthquake.

12 And after the earthquake a fire; but the Lord was not in the fire: and after the fire a still small voice.

13 And it was so, when Elijah heard it that he wrapped his face in his mantle, and went out, and stood in the entering in of the cave. And, behold, there came a voice unto him, and said, What doest thou here, Elijah?

I have shared this scripture with you so that you might better understand that during old testament times, the Spirit of God did not always remain with the prophets, for there were times when they waited for it to come upon them.

I also want us to remember there was a mighty wind, and then there was an earthquake, and then there was a fire, but the Lord was not in any of them. There was a still small voice. We, who are about to enter into the greatest tribulation known to man, need to learn how to recognize that still small voice. What is more, we need very much to receive the power that comes from on high; that is to say, we need to receive the baptism in the Holy Ghost.

There are a great many religious teachers and preachers who will try to convince us that the baptism in the Holy Ghost was only for the apostles or was only for Biblical times. They say it is not something we need today.

There are others who claim that when we surrendered at the cross of Christ, and became born again, we received all of the Holy Spirit we are ever going to receive. Of course, this is absolutely true for a great many people who are ignorant concerning the baptism in the Holy Ghost. We need to learn what the Word of God will teach us about receiving this super natural power from on high, for there is no need for any of us to remain ignorant of the promises of God.

The truth is, there are many religious leaders who have not received the baptism in the Holy Ghost, and they do not want any of us to receive what they do not have. I thank God that he has not with held either his love nor his promises from us.

Let us turn to the book of Joel and learn first hand what prophecy was given regarding the baptism in the Holy Ghost and keep in mind, that Joel lived in 800 B.C.

Joel 2:28 And it shall come to pass afterward, that I will pour out my Spirit upon all flesh; and your sons and your daughters shall prophesy, your old men shall dream dreams, your young men shall see visions:

29 And also upon the servants and upon the handmaids in those days will I pour out my Spirit.

When the scripture informs us that it shall come to pass afterward, looking back with hindsight, we can see that this is speaking of after the life and crucifixion of Jesus. Yes, we can see that it is speaking of after the resurrection and after the ascension. In fact, it is speaking of what took place on the holy day of Pentecost and is not limited to new testament times in which it was written.

Keeping in mind that during the time of the old testament, the Spirit of God was limited to only three kinds of people, namely the priests, the prophets, and some kings. Knowing this, the prophecy of Joel takes on a new meaning when he said that the Spirit of God would be poured out on all flesh.

He very clearly informs us that the Holy Ghost is not limited to just priests or prophets or pastors or deacons or bishops or religious leaders. It is not limited to the kings of Israel for it is available for all, who are God's children. Notice that he has said it is for old men and for young men. It is for our sons and our daughters, and what is more, it is for servants and for handmaidens as well.

However, there is one way it is limited or perhaps I should say reserved, and by now we all should know what that is. Jesus said that his Father would send the Comforter which is the Holy Ghost, in his name. Therefore, if we have surrendered to God and have become born again, then we have already received the Comforter, as Jesus promised.

I do not want for anyone to become confused, so we must take a moment and discuss what takes place when we surrender by repenting of our sins and make a promise to God that we will allow Jesus to be our Lord. At the very moment we surrender to God, the Holy Spirit does enter into our hearts and mind, and does begin to live on the inside of us. It is from that moment on, that the Holy Spirit begins to prepare us for eternity. We can tell that Jesus is living on the inside of us, for our lives change and begin to go in a different direction. Our choice of words begins to change and perhaps our manner of speech begins to change as well. The apostle Paul once said, Behold, all things have become new, and we both say, for you are now a brand new creation in our Lord Jesus.

At the moment of surrender and as we become born again, we have received a portion of the Holy Spirit, and we have received the gift of eternal life. However, the baptism in the Holy Ghost is something more, for it is additional power from on high to be used for the Glory of God. It is a pouring out of the Spirit in a greater way and I tell you the truth, only a few ever receive it. I shall explain why as we go along.

Let us return to the prophet Joel and to the promise that was given to all of God's children. Now as to how long was this promise valid? The next two verses shall greatly increase our knowledge of that.

Joel 2:30, And I will show wonders in the heavens and in the earth, blood, and fire, and pillars of smoke.

31 The sun shall be turned to darkness, and the moon into blood, before the great and terrible day of the Lord come.

I want us to consider the wonders in the heavens and in the earth. Of course, Joel is speaking of what will take place when the cities of this land are destroyed by nuclear missiles on the day of seven thunders. Even so, there is something more that I want for you to consider.

This verse mentions blood. First, I want you to picture in your mind not just the city of Jerusalem, but the land that surrounds that city and even including the Golan Heights and the Gaza strip and

Palestine. Then I must ask you this question, From the time of Jesus until now, how much blood has been spilled on this ground? Have the children of Abraham, both Jews and Arabs, have they spilled blood upon the land that once belonged to their common ancestor? I want for you to think for a moment about all of the sorrow of the mothers grieving for their children, and think about all of the tears and the drops of blood that have been spilled upon the land of the Bible.

The scripture also mentions fire. Let us think for a moment about fire that falls from the sky. There is a picture that many people have seen. It is of a young girl without any clothes on, and she is running naked through the streets as she is trying to escape from the fire that is falling from the sky. The look of terror and pain on her face assures us that she knows what it feels like to have burning napalm poured out on her naked flesh, and she seems to be asking, "O God, why are they doing this to me?" Remember this dear sweet little lady and ask yourself, are we, in the eyes of God, responsible for the napalm that was poured out on Vietnam and on innocent civilians. Did our tax dollars help to pay for this? Then think about the meaning of the golden rule.

The scripture verse mentions pillars of smoke. The first thought that comes to my mind is a picture I once seen of smoke stacks of factories in Europe. It seemed as though they mainly burned coal, and in turn, the prevailing winds caused the clouds to move toward Norway and Sweden, and the acidic rain was poisoning the lakes and killing fish and destroying their forests. Keeping in mind, there were many smoke stacks in the picture and there were many pillars of smoke. However, the same situation certainly does exist in our part of the world as well.

I do not doubt that these verses in the book of Joel are describing what will take place following the day of seven thunders. There will be much blood shed during the time of great tribulation as we already know. There will also be much fire and much smoke, for our cities will be burnt to the ground. I have mentioned these other situations for I believe that it is easier for us to see and understand things that have already happened than it is for us to understand the future. All of the things we have mentioned have taken place during my life time and I assume yours as well. This means that the baptism in the Holy Ghost is for this time in which we are living.

The next verse is about the future and it should be very easy for us to understand.

31 The sun shall be turned into darkness, and the moon into blood, before the great and the terrible day of the Lord come.

On the day when many missiles do strike and destroy their targets there will first be the distinctive mushroom clouds that accompany a nuclear explosion. Then in the aftermath, there will be a great many fires burning as natural gas lines and oil storage tanks and chemicals ignite and the smoke from the burning will exceed my imagination.

Think if you can, of the oil wells that were set on fire in Kuwait, and think about the thick black smoke those fires produced. Perhaps it will be something like that, only magnified many times for a much greater area will be on fire.

During that time, the light of the sun will be blotted out, just as it has been whenever there has been a major volcanic eruption.

When you consider that not one city will be spared when God's judgment comes against this nation, it is very hard to imagine the amount of smoke that will be produced. It will be a day of darkness and Joel is not the only prophet to foretell of this darkness. Let us hear what the prophet Zephaniah has to say about this very same subject.

Zephaniah 1:14, The great day of the Lord is near, and hasteth greatly, even the voice of the day of the Lord: the mighty man shall cry there bitterly.

15 That day is a day of wrath, a day of trouble and distress, a day of wasteness and desolation, a day of darkness and gloominess, a day of clouds and thick darkness,

16 A day of the trumpet and alarm against the fenced cities, and against the high towers.

17 And I will bring distress upon men, and they shall walk like blind men, because they have sinned against the Lord: and their blood shall be poured out as dust, and their flesh as dung.

18 Neither their silver nor their gold shall be able to deliver them in to day of the Lord's wrath; but the whole land shall be

devoured by the fire of his jealousy: for he shall make even a speedy riddance of all that dwell in the land.

The time of Zephaniah's prophecy was given about 630 BC. but we can see that it is not really any different than Joel's prophecy a couple of hundred years earlier. We must not forget that King Solomon did inform us that history does repeat it self, and this certainly does seem to be so, even when we consider the promises of God which Paul said we shall inherit.

The prophesy by Joel also mentions that the moon will be turned to blood and this too, is fairly easy to understand. I believe there will remain a haze high up in the atmosphere following so much burning, and this haze will cause the moon to appear as red as blood. Perhaps it will remain this way for many days and even after the lower atmosphere has begun to clear from the smoke.

These scriptures do make it very clear that we are now living during the time when God has promised to pour out his Spirit on all flesh. Therefore, we must learn as much as we can, for if we are to survive what lies ahead, and if we are to warn others about what is about to happen, we need to receive the God given power that cometh from on high.

Chapter 30 Peter's Visit to a Gentile

B efore we go on, there is a point I want to make very clear. At the moment when we surrender to God and confess that Jesus has become our Savior and our Lord, the Holy Spirit does enter in and does take up residence within us. As Paul once said, "Know ye not that ye are the temple of the Holy Ghost?"

When we receive the Holy Spirit, we also receive the gift of eternal life. However, if we are not born again, and we have not allowed the Holy Spirit to take up residence within us, then we do not belong to Christ and we do not have the gift of eternal life. In order to have the gift of eternal life we must have the Holy Spirit dwelling within us.

From that time on, we are like pilgrims on a journey through this life, and though we have received the gift of eternal life, we have not yet arrived at our final destination. God has not taken away our freedom to choose and if we decide like the children of Israel once did, that they would rather return to Egypt than travel to the promised land, God will not stop us.

Jesus said for us to remember Lot's wife. She was on her way to safety, but something caused her to look back and she never reached her intended destination. It is the same with us, for we have been given the Holy Spirit and the Word of God, to lead us and to guide us to the place of safety that God has provided. The only one that can prevent us from getting there is ourself, and our own free will. Every morning when we get out of bed, we are given the choice of whom we shall serve. God will not take that freedom of choice away from us and it shall remain ours as long as we live.

We have learned about what happened on the holy day of Pentecost. It is time for us to learn about others, who received the baptism of the Holy Ghost, beside the 120 who were there, when the Holy Ghost was first given. Perhaps we should examine the account that is given in the 8th chapter of the book of Acts.

Acts 8:14, Now when the apostles which were at Jerusalem heard that Samaria had received the word of God, they sent unto them Peter and John.

15 Who, when they were come down, prayed for them, that they might receive the Holy Ghost;

16 (For as yet he was fallen upon none of them: only they were baptized in the name of the Lord Jesus.)

17 Then laid they their hands on them, and they received the Holy Ghost.

It should be obvious that these people of Samaria were already born again Christians. The scripture does make it quite clear that they had been properly baptized in the name of the Lord Jesus. Therefore, it is obvious that they had already received a portion of the Holy Spirit, and had Jesus living on the inside of them. What they did not have was the baptism in the Holy Ghost, which is in greater measure. When the disciples laid their hands on them, they received the Holy Ghost. In other words, they received the additional power from on high, just as the 120 received it on the day of Pentecost.

I want us to take hold of the fact that they were already Christians who had been converted. I do not doubt that they had become born again and had received the gift of eternal life. They still needed to receive the baptism in the Holy Ghost and so do we.

We shall now travel with Peter to Caesarea where we will meet a man called Cornelius.

Acts 10:1 There was a certain man in Caesarea called Cornelius, a centurion of the band called the Italian band, 2 A devout man, and one that feared God with all his house, which gave much alms to the people, and prayed to God alway.

This man was a soldier, a Gentile, but was converted to the Jewish religion. Keep this in mind for this makes this example of the baptism of the Holy Ghost, different from what had previously taken place.

The Jews of that time, were not in the habit of sitting down to the same table to eat with Gentiles. They considered the food of the Gentiles to be unclean, and they felt the same way about the Gentiles themselves. Peter had some trouble understanding what it was that the Lord wanted him to do, but once he did understand, he went to the house of Cornelius. We shall take up the story at verse 34.

Acts 10:34, Then Peter opened his mouth, and said, Of a truth I perceive that God is no respecter of persons:

35 But in every nation he that feareth him, and worketh righteousness, is accepted with him.

36 The word which God sent unto the children of Israel, preaching peace by Jesus Christ: (he is Lord of all)

37 That word, I say, ye know, which was published throughout all Judea, and began from Galilee, after the baptism which John preached;

38 How God anointed Jesus of Nazareth with the Holy Ghost and with power: who went about doing good, and healing all that were oppressed of the devil; for God was with him.

39 And we are witnesses of all things which he did both in the land of the Jews, and in Jerusalem: whom they slew and hanged on a tree.

40 Him God raised up the third day, and showed him openly;

41 Not to all the people, but unto witnesses chosen before of God, even to us, who did eat and drink with him after he rose from the dead.

42 And he commanded us to preach unto the people, and to testify that it is he which was ordained of God to be the judge of quick and dead.

43 To him give all the prophets witness, that through his name whosoever believeth in him shall receive remission of sins.

I believe that what happened next is truly amazing, for Peter has just preached a message revealing who Jesus really is. He has not preached a message of being baptized with the Holy Ghost, but one of remission of sins. Of course, Cornelius and his house were already devout people living God's way. They simply had not yet received the truth of the gospel message until Peter delivered it to them.

44 While Peter yet spake these words, The Holy Ghost fell on all them which heard the word.

45 And they of the circumcision (the Jews) which believed were astonished, as many as came with Peter, because that on the Gentiles also was poured out the gift of the Holy Ghost.

46 For they heard them speak with tongues, and magnify God. Then answered Peter,

47 Can any man forbid water, that these should not be baptized, which have received the Holy Ghost as well as we?

48 And he commanded them to be baptized in the name of the Lord. Then prayed they him to tarry certain days.

In this very special example, these men who were Gentiles, did receive the baptism in the Holy Ghost at the same time they were converted to Christianity. How can we be sure, you might wonder. Because they spoke in tongues and this is one of the super natural gifts of the Spirit. These gifts of the Spirit are only given to those who have received the baptism of the Holy Spirit.

I also would point out that these verses do make it clear that God is not limited in the way he does baptize people in the Holy Spirit. At the upper room, the 120 remained there praying and worshipping God when the Holy Ghost fell, upon them. The Samaritans had the disciples lay hands on them and they were filled with the Holy Ghost. Cornelius and his friends were simply listening to Peter's anointed preaching and the Holy Ghost fell upon them and they began to speak in other tongues. We know by the scripture that Jesus is the baptizer in the Holy Ghost. We can see by the three examples we have been given that Jesus is not limited to baptizing people a certain way, for he does not have to conform to the desires of religious men.

There is just one more example given of people being filled with the Holy Ghost and we need to learn more about it. The preceding examples did involve Peter but this last example is a story of the things that were a part of one of Paul's missionary journeys. There is an account given of Paul's conversion in the 9th chapter of the Acts. At that time, hands were laid upon Paul and he did receive the baptism in the Holy Ghost. However, the account we are about to read did take place quite a few years later.

Acts 19:1, And it came to pass, that, while Apollos was at Corinth, Paul having passed through the upper coasts came to Ephesus: and finding certain disciples,

2 He said unto them, Have ye received the Holy Ghost since ye believed? And they said unto him, We have not so much as heard whether there be any Holy Ghost.

I want to point out that these were disciples, meaning that they were born again Christians that had already been converted. They already had Jesus living on the inside of them for they had surrendered and had repented of their sins, in order to be disciples. However, they had not yet received the baptism in the Holy Ghost for they had not even heard that there was such a thing as the Holy Ghost.

How very different is the teaching of the Bible compared to what is being taught in so many churches today. A great many churches teach that once a person has been converted, there is nothing more they should seek but to live the good life, attend church regularly, and pay their tithes. This is one of the main reasons why there are only a few who ever receive the baptism of the Holy Ghost, is because the failure of the leaders to teach the Word of God.

Let us listen to Paul's reply to these disciples who were ignorant, concerning the Holy Ghost.

Acts 19:3, And he said unto them, Unto what then were ye baptized? And they said, Unto John's baptism.

4 Then said Paul, John verily baptized with the baptism of repentance, saying unto the people, that they should believe on him which should come after him, that is, on Christ Jesus.

5 When they heard this, they were baptized in the name of the Lord Jesus.

6 And when Paul had laid his hands upon them, the Holy Ghost came on them; and they spake with tongues, and prophesied.

7 And all the men were about twelve.

Again, we see that these twelve men had not been baptized into the Lord's death and resurrection. As soon as they learned that there was a more meaningful way to be baptized, they did not hesitate but were immediately baptized in the name of our Lord Jesus.

Then, Paul, who had been filled with the Holy Spirit, did lay his hands on them, and they did receive the baptism of the Holy Ghost and did speak in tongues and prophesied.

I want for us to now pay attention to what happened on each of these examples we have been given. In the first example, on the holy day of Pentecost, there was no laying on of hands, but there was prayer and worship, and when the Holy Ghost fell upon them, they all, or about 120 of them, did begin to speak with other tongues.

In the second example we were given, Peter and John did travel to Samaria, and they first prayed for a group of Christians there, that they would receive the Holy Ghost. After they had prayed, they laid hands upon them and they did receive the baptism in the Holy Ghost. Keeping in mind that they did lay their hands upon them, but the record does not indicate whether or not they did speak in tongues.

In the 9th chapter of the Acts, is the record of what happened to Saul. While traveling on the road to Damascus, the Lord struck Saul with blindness, in order to get his attention. Prior to this, Saul was the enemy of all Christians and did greatly persecute them.

Now the Lord did lead Saul to a certain disciple at Damascus by the name of Ananias, for he had given this man instructions concerning the man named Saul, the enemy of Christ, who would become the apostle Paul, after he was converted.

Acts:9:17, And Ananias went his way, and entered into the house; and putting his hands on him said, Brother Saul, the Lord, even Jesus, that appeared unto thee in the way as thou camest, hath sent me, that thou mightest receive thy sight, and be filled with the Holy Ghost.

18 And immediately there fell from his eyes as it had been scales: and arose and was baptized.

Again we learn that there was a laying on of hands and I have no doubt that Paul received the baptism in the Holy Ghost at the same time he was converted. The scriptures do inform us that Saul was without his sight for three days. We can see that the Lord gave him a little time to think about how his life was going in the wrong direction, before he was converted.

The record does not indicate whether or not Paul spoke in tongues at the time of his baptism in the Holy Ghost. However, it is safe to assume that he did, for later, Paul announced that he was thankful that he spoke more in tongues than anyone.

In the 10th chapter of the Acts, we learn of Peter's journey to the centurions home, a Gentile by the name of Cornelius. In this example, there was no laying on of hands, but the scriptures do inform us that the Holy Ghost fell upon ALL who heard the sermon Peter did preach. The record does show that when this happened, they began to speak with tongues and did magnify God.

And finally we learned of the incident involving our brother Paul, who did re-baptize the small group of Christians at Ephesus, in the name of our Lord Jesus Christ. The record does show that when this had been done, then Paul laid his hands upon them, and they did receive the baptism in the Holy Ghost. The evidence that they had received the Holy Ghost was when they spake with other tongues and did prophesy.

Now that we have examined the Biblical record of how people did receive the baptism in the Holy Ghost, during the time when the Christian church was first being established, I want us to consider what we have learned.

The first and perhaps the most important thing is that the Baptism in the Holy Ghost is an additional experience, where in we receive power from on high to carry out the work that our Lord has called us to do. It is true that in two examples, it does appear that certain people did receive the baptism in the Holy Ghost at the same time they were converted. However, I want to stress that this is not the way it usually happens and in fact, is very rare. In the vast majority of the time, the people who receive the baptism in the Holy Ghost, are people who have been serving the Lord for some time, and who have a great desire to live their lives closer to God.

The next thing, is that in the examples we have been given, the majority of the time, born again Christians, who had been filled with the Holy Spirit, did lay there hands on the born again believers, who had not yet received the baptism in the Holy Ghost. I want us to keep in mind that while this was the way it happened most of the time, it is not the way it happened all the time. In other words, and this is very important, our Lord Jesus Christ is not limited, to baptizing men and women a certain way, for he has received all power in heaven and earth, and does not have to conform to the doctrines of religious men.

The final thing I want us to know and that is in the majority of these examples, the people who did receive the baptism in the Holy Ghost did speak in other tongues. We realize that when Peter and John did lay hands on the Samaritans and they received the baptism in the Holy Ghost, the record does not indicate that they spoke in tongues. By the same token, it does not indicate they did not speak in tongues either.

Is speaking in tongues the evidence that one has received the power from on high, the baptism in the Holy Ghost? It should be obvious that it certainly does seem so, according to the Biblical record we have just examined.

Chapter 31 Instructions from Paul

Gifts
It is interesting to note that even though Peter and John were both there, with the 120 at Jerusalem when the Holy Ghost was first given, it is the man whom God did strike blind on his way to Damascus that shall increase our knowledge of this subject. I am so very thankful that our brother Paul was willing to share his knowledge, concerning the gifts of the Spirit, as well as other truths we need to know.

Let us pay close attention to what Paul wants us to know and be aware that Paul certainly does know what he is talking about. He has a way of describing spiritual things that make it easier for us to understand.

1st Corinthians 12:1, Now concerning spiritual gifts, brethern, I would not have you ignorant.

2 Ye know that ye were Gentiles, carried away unto these dumb idols, even as ye were led.

3 Wherefore I give you to understand, that no man speaking by the Spirit of God calleth Jesus accursed: and that no man can say Jesus is the Lord, but by the Holy Ghost.

4 Now there are diversities of gifts, but the same Spirit.

5 And there are differences of administrations, but the same Lord.

6 And there are diversities of operations, but it is the same God which worketh all in all.

7 But the manifestation of the Spirit is given to every man to profit withal.

I want for you to read verse four through seven again, so that you might concentrate on what Paul is saying. In the next few verses Paul does list the gifts of the Spirit. These gifts are super-natural gifts and are not to be confused with natural ones. There are some gifts that we seem to be born with and then there are other things that seem to develop as we practice and grow older. Some people seem to be naturally gifted with a voice for singing. Of course, there can also be many years of training and practicing to develop to a greater magnitude, the gift they were born with.

I am not going to argue that such a gift is not God given, but this is not what Paul is talking about. He is talking about super-natural gifts we might receive as a result of being baptized in the Holy Ghost. Please keep in mind that there is a very real difference between the natural and the super-natural.

8 For to one is given by the Spirit the word of wisdom; to another the word of knowledge by the same Spirit.

9 To another faith by the same Spirit; to another the gifts of healing by the same Spirit.

10 To another the working of miracles; to another prophecy; to another discerning of spirits; to another divers kinds of tongues; to another the interpretation of tongues:

11 But all these worketh that one and the selfsame Spirit, dividing to every man severally as he will.

If there is anything I want for us to take hold of, is the relationship between these supernatural gifts and the great commission we were given by our Lord. The purpose of these gifts then, is that we might minister unto others and in doing so, carry out whatever task our Lord has called us to do. It is also through these supernatural gifts that the power we receive from on high is made manifest. Keeping in mind, that the real evidence is not the gifts of the Spirit but is in the fruit that is produced.

The apostle Paul said that one is given the word of wisdom. This wisdom is not the wisdom of this world, but is the supernatural wisdom that cometh down from God above. He said to another is given the word of knowledge and it cometh from the Holy Spirit.

This is not speaking of the kind of knowledge one might receive by attending college or the university. It is speaking of the kind of super-natural knowledge that can only come from God, for there is no other way to receive it.

I will remind you that through out the ages, there have been men and women, who dealing in the occult, claim to have supernatural knowledge. In reality, they are mimicking or trying to imitate the knowledge and power of God that came upon his prophets, even in days of old. The priests of Dagon and the priests of Baal and other Pagan religions were such men, for they all claimed to possess supernatural powers.

Following the day when the Holy Ghost was first given, men and women of God, filled with the Spirit have received the super-natural gift of knowledge to be used according to God's purpose.

The apostle Paul went on to say that some Holy Ghost filled people would receive the gift of faith. This faith that Paul is speaking of is not ordinary faith. The gift of faith is speaking of a supernatural amount of faith to be used in a person's ministry, for the glory of God. Remember that Jesus told us that if our faith was as big as a mustard seed, we would be able to move mountains with it. Perhaps then we can understand that to receive faith as a supernatural gift from God, is a very precious and powerful gift.

He then mentions the gift of healing and the gift of the working of miracles. Of course, in each case, God is the miracle worker and he is also the healer, not forgetting the verse that says, "By his stripes we were healed." However, as we are the earthen vessels, then the power of the Holy Ghost does work through us, once we have received it. However, we must not forget that the glory belongs to God and to his Son.

To another the gift of prophecy. I feel that I must explain that prophecy does not always mean telling what the future will be. In fact, usually it is something entirely different. Prophecy could be a word of encouragement to the congregation direct from God. Sometimes it is a warning that an individual or a group need to change the direction in which they are going. The gift of prophecy is delivering a message from God to whoever God is sending it, and it may be to an individual, or to a group of people, or an entire congregation, or a city, or a nation.

I really do not normally interrupt a person's conversation, but I felt that it was necessary for me to expand on what Paul is saying.

Let us now return to the scriptures and listen once more as the apostle Paul does explain to us, the gifts of the Spirit in his own words.

12 For as the body is one, and hath many members, and all the members of that one body, being many, are one body: so also is Christ.

13 For by one Spirit are we all baptized into one body, whether we be Jews or Gentiles, whether we be bond or free; and have been all made to drink into one Spirit.

14 For the body is not one member, but many.

15 If the foot shall say, Because I am not the hand, I am not the body; is it therefore not of the body?

16 And if the ear shall say, Because I am not the eye, I am not of the body; is it therefore not of the body?

17 If the whole body were an eye, where were the hearing? If the whole were hearing, where were the smelling?

18 But now hath God set the members every one of them in the body, as it hath pleased him.

19 And if they were all one member, where were the body?

20 But now are they many members, yet but one body.

21 And the eye cannot say unto the hand, I have no need of thee: nor again the head to the feet, I have no need of you.

22 Nay, much more those members of the body, which seem to be more feeble, are necessary:

23 And those members of the body, which we think to be less honourable, upon these we bestow more abundant honour; and our uncomely parts have more abundant comeliness.

24 For our comely parts have no need: but God hath tempered the body together, having given more abundant honour to that part which lacked:

25 That there should be no schism (division) in the body; but that the members should have the same care one for another.

I would point out that there is a very big division in the body of Christ today, because of a misunderstanding of the meaning of these scriptures. I believe there are errors in church doctrine on both sides of this division. When we have finished reading this 12th chapter, we shall examine the reasons for this division, in the hope that we might avoid becoming involved in this division, through exposing these errors as they are being taught today.

26 And whether one member suffer, all the members suffer with it; or one member be honoured, all the members rejoice with it.

27 Now ye are the body of Christ, and members in particular.

28 And God hath set some in the church, first apostles, secondarily prophets, thirdly teachers, after that miracles, then gifts of healings, helps, governments, diversities of tongues.

29 Are all apostles? are all prophets? are all teachers? are all workers of miracles?

30 Have all the gifts of healing? do all speak with tongues? do all interpret?

We must first understand that Paul is referring to people who have received the baptism in the Holy Ghost. He then asks a series of questions concerning these Spirit filled people. The answer to each of his questions is quite obvious and should be NO! not all will receive All of these gifts. We must cling to this knowledge for it will help us better understand the next verse.

31 But covet earnestly the best gifts: and yet show I unto you a more excellent way.

I want us to take hold of the fact that if there be a more excellent way, then there also has to be a less excellent way. Now Paul has done an excellent job of describing the "more" excellent way in the next chapter. What I want for each of us to do, is take out paper and pen and using the last three verses we have just read and in your own words I want us all to describe the way that is "less" excellent and understand why it is less instead of more. It is my hope that in doing so, that we will choose the way that is more excellent, for a great many do cling to the way that is less.

We must wonder, just what is the best gift? If we are to covet (greatly desire) the best gifts, perhaps we should find out what they are.

As you are thinking about what the best gift might possibly be, I shall supply you with the answer, just as it once was supplied to me by my pastor, a dear man of God, who is also an apostle and a teacher, who has lived more than four score and has served God from the days of his youth. The best gift is the gift that is needed at any one particular time. If the situation that is before us, is one where someone is in great need of healing, then the gift of prophecy or the gift of speaking in tongues is of little help. Therefore, in that situation the super-natural gift of healing is the best gift at that time.

Let us now return to that time when the Holy Ghost was first given at Jerusalem, on the day of Pentecost. What was the gift that was most needed at that particular time?

Remember that there were about 120 individuals, including Mary, the mother of Jesus and other women, who were waiting there for the promise of God to be fulfilled. At the same time, there were many thousands of Jews in Jerusalem to observe the holy day of Pentecost, for it was very important to their religion. Now the Jews considered themselves to be the chosen people of God, and everyone else to be inferior to them. However, the 120 disciples of Jesus, who were gathered together of one accord, in the upper room were certainly for the most part, also Jewish by birth. I do not doubt but what the great majority of religious Jews considered the followers of Christ, to be a small sect of fanatics, following after a man instead of God.

It is when we consider this situation, that we can see that the gift that was needed, was one that would convince the very stubborn Jews that the small religious sect of Christians had indeed, found favor with God.

Let us turn to the 2nd chapter of the book of Acts, so that we might learn exactly how this came about. The first four verses tell us how the 120 disciples of Christ received the power from on high. Verse 4 informs us that "they were ALL filled with the Holy Ghost, and began to speak with other tongues, as the Spirit gave them utterance." This would include Mary, the mother of Jesus, as well as the other women.

Verse 5 does explain how the great crowd of people who were there at Jerusalem did re-act to this.

Acts 2:5, And there were dwelling at Jerusalem Jews, devout men, out of every nation under heaven.

6 Now when this was noised abroad, the multitude came together, and were confounded, because that every man heard them speak in his own language.

7 And they were all amazed and marvelled, saying one to another, Behold, are not all these which speak Galilaeans?

I would assume that the people of Galilee probably did speak a little differently than the majority of the Jews, but I am really not sure. Perhaps they spoke with an accent, that did identify them as being from the area of Galilee.

Let us pretend for a moment that we have been invited to attend a large convention, with people coming from all around the world. The people in charge have decided to seat the people at tables, according to the language they do speak. Now at the table where we will be seated is an Englishman, a member of the merchant marine out of Liverpool, who speaks with a Cockney accent. Next to him, is a man who was born and raised and educated in Boston, and we think of him as being the "Boston man." Then we have a man from Australia, who has spent much time in the outback and who has tended sheep most of his life. Seated next to him is a man who has also tended sheep but he is from the Scottish highlands.

Now in addition to these people we also have a person who was born in Mexico but was raised in Los Angeles. A person from Texas and a native person from Nome Alaska.

All of these people do speak the English language, but they all seem to have trouble understanding one another, and especially the Englishman, for his Cockney accent is almost like a foreign language.

Of course, I have made this situation up from my imagination, but I hope that it will help us to understand the situation the way it might have been at Jerusalem on the holy day of Pentecost. There were Jewish people there from many far away places and I do not doubt but what there must have been a great deal of variation in the languages they spoke and understood.

The scripture we are about to read does indicate that something very strange and in fact, super-natural did take place there.

8 And how hear we every man in our own tongue, wherein we were born?

9 Parthians, and Medes, and Elamites, and the dwellers in Mesopotamia, and in Judea, and Cappadocia, in Pontus, and Asia,

10 Phrygia, and Pamphylia, in Egypt, and in the parts of Libya about Cyrene, and strangers of Rome, Jews and proselytes,

11 Cretes and Arabians, we do hear them speak in our tongues the wonderful works of God.

12 And they were all amazed, and were in doubt, saying one to another, What meaneth this?

I believe the evidence is clear that something very super-natural did take place. Not only did the Holy Ghost take control of their tongues, causing them to speak in a language they had never spoken before, but God also took control of the hearing of the large crowd of people who were listening, and caused each one to hear what was being said in their own individual languages.

We must not forget that the final result of this out pouring of the Holy Spirit, as it was made manifest by the 120 speaking in tongues, was the conversion of about three thousand souls.

Then we must ask the question, "Was speaking in tongues the best gift for this particular situation?" The answer must be a most emphatic yes for it is the gift that was needed to convince the three thousand very religious Jews to listen to Peter in the first place.

This belief that the Jewish people were God's chosen people did not end on the day of Pentecost. We can see that the group of Hebrew Christians that accompanied Peter to Cornelius' house certainly did cling to this belief, as well. Let us review what happened there, one more time.

Acts 10:44, While Peter yet spake these words, the Holy Ghost fell on all them which heard the word.

45 And they of the circumcision (Jews) which believed were astonished, as many as came with Peter, because that on the Gentiles also was poured out the gift of the Holy Ghost.

46 For they heard them speak with tongues, and magnify God.

Was the gift of speaking in tongues the best gift for this particular situation? Of course it was, for it was absolutely necessary to convince the hard headed and spiritually proud Jews that God did bestow the baptism of the Holy Ghost on the Gentiles as well as the Jews. Previous to this, they were totally convinced that God loved them more than any other people and it was very important for them to realize that God's plan for salvation, including the baptism in the Holy Ghost was not limited to the people of the circumcision.

The decision as to which gift is the most needed is not up to religious men, for our Lord Jesus Christ is the baptizer and he is the one that bestows the gifts of the Spirit. I would point out that God always knows what is best, however, quite often religious men seem to think they know more than God.

I say this, for from these four examples we are given of people receiving the baptism of the Holy Ghost, they have formed a doctrine. These religious men claim that God is limited to always filling people with the Holy Ghost as he did in these examples. What they claim, is that a person who has been filled with the Holy Ghost must always speak in tongues at the moment when the Holy Ghost comes upon them. They say that they do know this for sure and unless a person does speak in tongues, they will not accept or believe they have received the Holy Ghost.

We are told in the Word of God that we are to prove all things and that we are to hold fast to that which is good.

The apostle Paul did issue a warning to young Timothy that begins with .....

2nd Timothy 4:3, For the time will come when they will not endure sound doctrine;

This doctrine that everyone must speak with tongues or else they have not received the baptism in the Holy Ghost is not sound doctrine and cannot be proved by scriptures.

Therefore, it is what we call a doctrine of assumption, for it is based on a claim that can not be proven by scripture but does require that we assume something is true. They insist that we must believe that God is limited to baptizing everyone exactly the same way and that everyone who does receive the baptism in the Holy Ghost does speak in tongues at the time of their baptism. I want us all to be aware that this doctrine is contrary to the Word of God and it has hurt many people. I shall explain how they have been hurt as we go along.

The apostle Paul said in 1st Corinthians 12, that....

25 That there should be no schism (division) in the body; but that the members should have the same care one for another.

Today, there is a very great division between the churches, and some have taken things to great extremes. Some even go so far as to claim that unless a person speaks in tongues they have not really received Christ as their Savior. Of course, this is the lie of Satan and we must not accept it.

On the other hand, we have churches that claim that the gifts of the Spirit are not for today, and so they forbid anyone to exercise the gifts of the Spirit within their churches. In this way they have been deceived for this is also a lie of Satan and is contrary to the Word of God.

Is it any wonder then, that nothing ever happens in their churches for they do not believe that God is still capable of filling people with his Holy Spirit, and giving unto them, the super-natural gifts of the Spirit.. They go to church each week, and listen to a sermon that tickles their ears, perhaps take part in a few religious rituals from time to time, shake the pastors hand if they are able, and then go home and watch the ball game.

My dear brothers and sisters, this is not what I have in mind for you, for I know of something that is so much better.

I want us to answer the questions that Paul has asked toward the end of this chapter. Keep in mind that Paul is speaking of born again Christians who have received the baptism in the Holy Ghost. Perhaps if I take the liberty of rephrasing these questions, we might come to a more complete understanding of them.

In verse 29, Paul asks the question, Of those who have been baptized in the Holy Ghost, Are all apostles? The answer is obviously no.

He then asks, Of those who have received the baptism in the Holy Ghost, Are all prophets? Again, the answer is obviously no.

Paul then asks, Of those who have received the baptism of the Holy Ghost, Are they all teachers? Perhaps we all do teach others to some degree but Paul is referring to a ministry. The answer is obviously no.

Paul then asks, Of those who have received the baptism of the Holy Ghost, are they all workers of Miracles. Again the answer is no, for we have not all received the gift of the working of miracles. However, because we have been born again and are no longer what we used to be, but have now become a new creation in Christ Jesus, we are a living, breathing and talking miracle, a child of God.

Paul then asks, Of those who have received the baptism of the Holy Ghost, do all have the gifts of healing? Again, the answer is obviously no.

Pay attention to verse 30. Paul again asks, Of all who have received the baptism of the Holy Ghost, do all speak with tongues? Do all interpret? The answer must remain the same for it is obviously no, not everyone who has been baptized in the Holy Ghost, does speak in tongues or is able to interpret.

The religious men who have formed the doctrine that all who receive the baptism of the Holy Ghost must speak in tongues when they are baptized are aware of these questions that were asked by the apostle Paul and they are equally aware that in each case the answer must be no.

However, they try to slide around this Biblical truth by claiming that there are two different kinds of speaking in tongues. They claim that the kind of speaking in tongues that Paul is referring to in these questions is the gift of speaking in tongues as it relates to the ministry that person has been called to do, by our Lord. This differs they claim, with the speaking of tongues that is required as evidence that one has received the baptism in the Holy Ghost. Even when they are confronted with the Biblical evidence that not everyone who has been baptized in the Holy Ghost will receive the gift of speaking in tongues, they refuse to give up their doctrine of assumption.

Come and let us reason together, concerning the confusion some people are causing. I claim that there are only two ways in which a person does speak in tongues. Either they do so, as the result of having received the ability to do so, as a super-natural gift from God, or else they do so by some other means. Even the people who did speak in tongues as it is recorded in the book of Acts, did so because they had received the ability to speak in tongues as a super-natural gift from God.

Now if anyone does speak in tongues and they have not received the ability to do so as a super-natural gift from God, then they do so because of their own desire to impress others and it is not by the will of God.

How about the claim that we must speak in tongues as evidence that we have received the baptism in the Holy Ghost. I say that there is no evidence needed. There simply is no need to prove to anyone that we have received the baptism in the Holy Spirit. To say that we must produce evidence is to suggest that we are on trial or that it is necessary that we impress some one. While I do consider it to be extremely important that we receive the baptism in the Holy Ghost, I want it to be according to God's Holy Word and for his purpose. Not to prove anything to others for if we be filled with the Holy Ghost, let the fruits of the Spirit be the evidence we are Spirit filled and living our lives for Christ..

We shall now read the last verse of chapter 12 and the first verse of chapter 13 just as though there were no change in chapters. The division into chapters came a long time after Paul first wrote this letter to the Christians at Corinth.

1st Corinthians 12:31, But covet earnestly the best gifts: and yet show I unto you a more excellent way.

13:1 Though I speak with the tongues of men and of angels, and have not charity (agape love) I am become as sounding brass, or a tinkling cymbal.

Let us be sure that we fully understand what Paul is saying to us. In the first place he has said we are to greatly desire the gifts of the Spirit. This includes the gift of speaking in tongues, for it is a very precious gift from God, as are all the gifts of the Holy Spirit. God has not changed any, since these precious gifts were first given, and neither has his super-natural gifts. However, the gift that is needed most can change with each situation.

The charity that Paul is speaking of is probably a good deal different than most of us think about charity. It is not speaking of placing ourselves in the service of others, wherein we hope to be recognized for what we do. Neither is it talking about donating money to the poor, with the main goal being a deduction on our income tax form.

The charity that Paul is speaking of is when we offer our help and our services to others in need, without ever intending to receive anything, not even a pat on the back in return. It is the agape love that cometh only when the Holy Spirit has taken up residence within us. It is loving others, even though they probably will never love us in return. To put it quite simply, it is completely and utterly, unselfish love. It is freely given and nothing in return is expected.

I do not want us to lose track of what Paul is saying to us. He has clearly said that unless the very unselfish agape love is present within us, and made manifest in what we do, the speaking in tongues we might also do does not mean very much. In fact, he compares it to the sound made by two cymbals clanging together. In other words, just a bunch of noise.

What if a pastor or a preacher were to speak in tongues as they delivered their weekly sermon, and then went to the race track to spend the afternoon placing wagers on the ponies or engaged in some other activity that is not pleasing to God. Should we consider his speaking in tongues the evidence that he is filled with the Holy Ghost and living his life for God?

What if there were another person, a woman who does speak in tongues quite regularly when she attends church. Yet, she can hardly wait until she be given the opportunity to share with her friends the latest gossip she has been waiting all week to tell. Should we consider the fact that she speaks in tongues as the evidence that she has been filled with the Holy Ghost, or should we consider that her absolute favorite past time is repeating little stories she has heard about others?

And then there is another woman, who has without any doubt received the gift of speaking in tongues but we must not get on the wrong side of her for she holds a grudge forever and is quick to take offense. I know that it might seem hard to believe but she has a very hard time forgiving people for what she might perceive them to have done.

Does the fact that she does speak in tongues make her any better or more righteous than anyone else? I hardly think so.

And then there is a man, who had been attending church for a long time, and from time to time, this man does speak in tongues. However, he has also developed a sweet tooth and one that does seem to be out of control. Whenever there is a church dinner or a picnic or any occasion when food is served, there is also a dessert table filled with many very tasty treats. Now the problem is that the mothers of small children are teaching them they must not take more than one dessert, for they must be able to control their desire for such things and have good manners.

However, this same man who does speak in tongues, who does seem to be a pillar within the church, can not seem to restrain his appetite for sweets. He has been observed by all as he makes one trip after another to the dessert table, poking them in his mouth, one after another, until he has consumed a great amount of servings. It certainly does seem that the lust of his flesh and his appetite for sweets does rule over the little voice of the Spirit, which speaks to his conscience.

Does the fact that he does speak in tongues mean very much to the mothers who are concerned with the example that is being set before their children? I seriously doubt it.

All of the people I have described are the product of my own imagination and are not meant to portray anyone in particular. The point I want to make here, is that even though there might be many people who speak in tongues, the apostle Paul makes it very clear that if they do not have agape love dwelling within them, and being manifest in the lives they do live, the speaking in tongues they do is merely a loud noise and does not mean very much. Their lives must bear the fruits of the Spirit, for the gifts. without the fruits are not enough.

Even though these are hypothetical situations I have described, I am afraid that similar situations might very well exist through out the land. However, we should seriously consider the example that we are setting before others and whether or not it is pleasing to our Lord Jesus Christ.

So then, let us pay attention to what the apostle Paul has said to us, that we might seriously desire the gifts of the Spirit. Keeping in mind, that unless the fruits of the Spirit are present every day in our lives, the precious gifts we have received from God are not being used as God intended for them to be used, for we must bear the fruits of the Spirit, in order to carry out our great commission.

We must always remember that at all times we must love others as unselfishly as Christ has loved us.

Chapter 32 Shepherds become Judges

Fruits
Across this nation and in many churches, some being small and some rather large, there are religious men who have appointed themselves to be more than just pastors but have become judges. These are the men who promote the doctrine that unless a person speaks in tongues they will not accept that the person has been filled with the Holy Spirit. In this way, they have divided their congregation into two different groups. Namely, those who speak in tongues and those who do not. Those who are Spirit filled and those who are not.

Without any doubt, these people who do promote this division within the body of Christ have done much harm to both individuals and to the church of Christ. We can be very sure that according to God's perfect plan, there must be room in his church for those people who do speak in tongues and those who do not. One is not to be placed on a pedestal over the other, for they are both equal in the kingdom of God.

Through out the years, there have been many new Christians who might have began attending one of these churches. We think of these new converts as being "babes in Christ." However, they soon came to realize that within the church there were two classes of Christians. Those who were recognized as being Spirit filled, and those who were not.

Those who were judged to be Spirit filled were always treated a little better and they were given more respect in all that they did.

Those who were judged to be not Spirit filled were encouraged to speak in tongues at every opportunity.

Now the sad truth of this matter is that the ones who failed to speak in tongues after a reasonable amount of time had passed, were treated as though they were slightly inferior and were lacking. It was ever so subtly suggested or implied that perhaps the reason they did not speak in tongues was that there was still some sin in their lives they had failed to confess or repent of. In this way, they were not only judged by the pastor, but were judged by the entire congregation as well.

Thus we see that the new converts who did speak in tongues were often promoted to hold higher positions within the church, while the ones who did not speak in tongues were treated as though they were still living in sin. After having been treated as a person who is lacking, and who is less in every way, for quite some time, many if not most of these "babes in Christ" decided to leave the assembly which discriminated against them.

Now some moved to the church down the street where they do not believe or teach the baptism in the Holy Ghost, even though the Bible clearly does teach it. Many others, perhaps believed they really were inferior, because the church followed the pastors lead in treating them this way, and so they returned to the world from which they had once escaped. In this Satan rejoices for he is able to re-claim that which he once owned.

Thus we see that many new Christians are faced with three choices. They can remain in the church that discriminates against them, hoping and praying that they will receive the gift of speaking in tongues. (Some do teach them selves to speak in tongues in order to be accepted as equal) Or they can leave that assembly and move to the church down the street, where speaking in tongues is strictly forbidden, which is completely contrary to scripture. Or, they can stop attending church altogether, in which case, the world is waiting to receive them, as the day of judgment draweth nigh.

This makes me very sad, for I want you to know, my dear brothers and sisters, that this is terribly wrong and it is not according to God's plan. We can be sure that every soul is precious to God, for our brother Peter did inform us that God is not willing that any of us should perish but that all should come to repentance.

I now want to share with you the story of a man, chosen by Christ, who earned for himself the nickname of "Doubting Thomas." We shall learn about how he earned this name, toward the end of chapter 20 in then gospel of John. Please be aware that the story we are about to read did take place after Jesus was crucified and had been resurrected from the grave.

John 20:24, But Thomas, one of the twelve, called Didymus, was not with them when Jesus came.

25 The other disciples therefore said unto him, We have seen the Lord. But he said unto them, Except I shall see in his hands the print of the nails, and put my finger into the print of the nails, and thrust my hand into his side, I will not believe.

26 And after eight days again his disciples were within, and Thomas with them: then came Jesus, the doors being shut, and stood in the midst, and said, Peace be unto you.

27 Then saith he to Thomas, reach hither thy finger, and behold my hands; and reach hither thy hand, and thrust it into my side: and be not faithless, but believing.

28 And Thomas answered and said unto him, My Lord and my God.

29 Jesus saith unto him, Thomas, because thou hast seen me, thou hast believed: blessed are they that have not seen, and yet have believed.

I have included this story of how Thomas earned his name, in the hope that those pastors, who because of their own unbelief, are dividing their churches, will see the harm they are doing. They are to use the gifts of the Spirit to win souls to Christ, not drive people away, during these perilous times in which we are living. We are to encourage people to live their lives for Christ, not belittle them because they have not received the gift of speaking in tongues.

Our brother Paul, in his letter to the Galatians, did give us a list of the fruits of the Spirit. I say to you that it is these fruits that are important, for the gifts of the Spirit do not amount to very much unless they do bear these fruits.

Galatians 5:22, But the fruit of the Spirit is love, joy, peace, longsuffering, gentleness, goodness, faith,

23 Meekness, temperance: against such there is no law.

In the gospel of Matthew and at chapter five, Jesus does speak of these very same fruits of the Spirit and we call his explanation, the beatitudes. We all need to read them from time to time, to refresh our memory.

Matthew 5:2, And he opened his mouth, and taught them, saying,

3 Blessed are the poor in spirit: for theirs is the kingdom of heaven.

4 Blessed are they that mourn: for they shall be comforted.

5 Blessed are the meek: for they shall inherit the earth.

6 Blessed are they which do hunger and thirst after righteousness: for they shall be filled.

7 Blessed are the merciful: for they shall obtain mercy.

8 Blessed are the pure in heart: for they shall see God.

9 Blessed are the peacemakers: for they shall be called children of God.

10 Blessed are they which are persecuted for righteousness' sake: for theirs is the kingdom of heaven.

11 Blessed are ye, when men shall revile you, and persecute you, and shall say all manner of evil against you falsely, for my sake.

12 Rejoice, and be exceeding glad: for great is your reward in heaven: for so persecuted they the prophets which were before you.

If we were to examine each one of these in greater depth we would learn that these are a description of a person who is lead by the Spirit, for Jesus lived this way.

Keeping in mind that the very first fruit of the Spirit is the agape love that is unselfish love, let us now examine what is known as the love chapter and is the writing of Paul.

1st Corinthians 13:1, Though I speak with the tongues of men and of angels, and have not charity (agape love), I am become as sounding brass, or a tinkling cymbal.(of no value)

2 And though I have the gift of prophecy, and understand all mysteries, and all knowledge; and though I have all faith, so that I could remove mountains, and have not charity, I am nothing.

3 And though I bestow all my goods to feed the poor, and though I give my body to be burned, and have not charity, it profiteth me nothing.

4 Charity suffereth long, and is kind; charity envieth not; charity vaunteth not itself, is not puffed up,

5 Doth not behave itself unseemly, seeketh not her own, is not easily provoked, thinketh no evil;

6 Rejoiceth not in iniquity, but rejoiceth in the truth;

7 Beareth all things, believeth all things, hopeth all things, endureth all things.

8 Charity never faileth: but whether there be prophecies, they shall fail; whether there be tongues, they shall cease; whether there be knowledge, it shall vanish away.

9 For we know in part, and we prophesy in part.

10 But when that which is perfect is come, then that which is in part shall be done away.(at the second coming of Christ)

11 When I was a child, I spake as a child, I understood as a child, I thought as a child: but when I became a man, I put away childish things.

12 For now we see through a glass, darkly; but then face to face: now I know in part; but then shall I know even as also I am known.

13 And now abideth faith, hope, charity, these three; but the greatest of these is charity.(agape love)

I want to bring to your attention why Paul said so many words regarding the agape love that should be dwelling within us, immediately after he explained to us all about the gifts of the Spirit. It is because not one of the gifts of the Spirit is more valuable to carrying out the great commission we have been given, than is the first fruit of the Spirit which is agape love. Even all of the gifts of the Spirit when put together, do not amount to as much as does the agape love which we should have abiding within us, if we have become born again. If for any reason we do not have this agape love present and within us, being made manifest in all that we do, we will not be able to carry out the work that God has given for us to do.

Paul wanted us to be very much aware of this great truth, before he explained any further about the gifts of the Spirit.

I can not help but wonder how much love did the pastors and the people show toward those new Christians that were driven from their churches, because they did not speak in tongues?

How many people have been turned away, simply because they refused or were not able to speak in tongues in order to impress the church leaders? Where is their love and their concern for these people's salvation?

We shall now return to the instructions we are given by our brother Paul, concerning the gifts of the Spirit and how we are to use these precious gifts.

1st Corinthians 14:1, Follow after charity, and desire spiritual gifts, but rather that ye may prophesy.

2 For he that speaketh in an unknown tongue speaketh not unto men, but unto God: for no man understandeth him; howbeit in the spirit he speaketh mysteries.

3 But he that prophesieth speaketh unto men to edification, and to exhortation, and comfort.

There is something in this last verse we need to examine. Many people have the idea that prophesying is foretelling the future. They probably get this idea from so many fortune tellers who are always predicting the future. Please do be aware that these fortune tellers are not of God in any way, no matter what they may claim.

Paul does make it clear that there are three ways in which a person does prophesy. Number one is to edification. We are to edify or build up and strengthen other Christians.

Number two is we are to exhort. This does not mean that we are to judge others as so many preachers think. It does not mean that we are to judge and be critical, and condemn, but we are to encourage them to do better than they have been doing.

It is a little like the coach at half time, for he wants for his team to go out on the field and play the second half, better than they did the first half. If he goes about this in the wrong way, he will completely destroy their morale and their desire to play the game.

Therefore, we must be very careful when we prophesy unto exhortation, that we produce the desired results and do not hurt the people we are trying to help. If the message delivered is truly from God, we can be sure that it will not destroy a person but give them a desire to do better than they have been doing.

A good example of this can be found in God's message to the seven churches in Revelation chapters two and three. In each case, our Lord had something good to say to them, before he points out their faults. He then gives them encouragement in the form of instructions for how they are to improve. There is probably no better example of exhortation given in the entire Bible.

The third way we are to prophesy is to comfort those who are low in spirit, by bringing them a word of comfort from our Lord, or even to quote to them a very comforting passage of scripture that might apply to their situation. Sometimes, a comforting story will come to our mind, that will bless those who are in need of comforting.

4 He that speaketh in an unknown tongue edifieth himself; but he that prophesieth edifieth the church.

5 I would that ye all spake with tongues, but rather that ye prophesied: for greater is he that prophesieth than he that speaketh with tongues, except he interpret, that the church may receive edifying.

When Paul said, "I would that ye all spake with tongues," it should be very obvious to us, that he was speaking to the Christians at Corinth, and that not all of them did speak in tongues. We must wonder why would Paul say this, if they all did speak in tongues?

I want us to realize that what Paul does say next, includes an exception. He does say, "greater is he that prophesieth, except...." I want us to be very much aware of what this exception is for it is very important. We also need to know why. We shall learn more about this exception when we come to verse 13.

6 Now brethren, if I come unto you speaking with tongues, what shall I profit you, except I shall speak to you either by revelation, or by knowledge, or by prophesying, or by doctrine?

7 And even things without life giving sound, whether pipe or harp, except they give a distinction in the sounds, how shall it be known what is piped or harped?

8 For if the trumpet give an uncertain sound, who shall prepare himself for battle?

9 So likewise ye, except ye utter by the tongue words easy to be understood, how shall it be known what is spoken? for ye shall speak into the air.

10 There are, it may be, so many kinds of voices in the world, and none of them is without signification.

11 Therefore if I know not the meaning of the voice, I shall be unto him that speaketh a barbarian, and he that speaketh shall be a barbarian unto me.

12 Even so ye, forasmuch as ye are zealous of spiritual gifts, seek that ye may excel to the edifying of the church.

13 Wherefore, let him that speaketh in an unknown tongue pray that he may interpret.

This is the exception that was mentioned earlier. If anyone should happen to receive the gift of speaking with other tongues, then they should pray that God would also give them the super-natural gift of interpretation. Why, you might ask? For the purpose being that with the interpretation, cometh the edification of the church.

Otherwise, only God does understand what is said when tongues are spoken and the church is not edified.

14 For if I pray in an unknown tongue, my spirit prayeth, but my understanding is unfruitful.

15 What is it then? I will pray with the spirit, and I will pray with the understanding, also: I will sing with the spirit, and I will sing with the understanding also.

16 Else when thou shalt bless with the spirit, how shall he that occupieth the room of the unlearned say Amen at thy giving of thanks, seeing he understandeth not what thou sayest?

17 For thou verily givest thanks well, but the other is not edified.

18 I thank my God, I speak with tongues more than ye all:

19 Yet in the church I had rather speak five words with my understanding, that by my voice I might teach others also, than ten thousand words in an unknown tongue.

I want us to understand that our brother Paul has said that he is thankful that he speaks in tongues more than anyone in the church at

Corinth. He then goes on to say, Yet in the church, he would rather speak only five words, with his own understanding, that he might teach others.

Today, there are in some churches, those people who do speak many words in tongues, and there is never an interpretation so that the church might be edified.

It is as though the person that is speaking in tongues, does so, because they want the pastor and the congregation to recognize that they have received the baptism in the Holy Ghost. They are always trying to prove something and do take up much of the time that is allotted to the service. I would point out that this is not the way it should be.

20 Brethern, be not children in understanding, howbeit in malice be ye children, but in understanding be men.

21 In the law (old testament) it is written, with men of other tongues and other lips will I speak unto this people; and yet for all that will they not hear me, saith the Lord.

22 Wherefore tongues are for a sign, not to them that believe, but to them that believe not: but prophesying serveth not for them that believe not, but for them that believe.

Now this is quite a statement by our brother Paul. Lest any of us be confused, we need to pay attention to what Paul is about to say, for it is an explanation of what he really means.

23 If therefore the whole church be come together into one place, and all speak with tongues, and there come in those that are unlearned, or unbelievers, will they not say that ye are all mad? (crazy)

24 But if all prophesy, and there come in one that believeth not, or one unlearned, he is convinced of all, he is judged (convicted) of all.

25 And thus are the secrets of his heart made manifest; (word of knowledge) and so falling down on his face, he will worship God, and report that God is in you of a truth.

There are some churches today where everyone is speaking in tongues at the same time. There is no interpretation, and therefore no edification but what there is, is mass confusion. Indeed, if a stranger was to step inside of the door, his first impression would be that they were all possessed or perhaps had run away from the mental institution.

In the second situation that Paul describes, if a stranger should come to a church service where there are many Spirit filled Christians, it is likely if by the word of knowledge, one by one they told this person things about himself that no one could possibly know; the person would be convinced that their knowledge of him was supernatural and they were truly of God.

Beginning at verse 26 Paul does give some excellent instructions for Spirit filled Christians and the church. However, from what I can see, there are few today who pay any attention to Paul's instructions and it is as though they listen only to their pastor and could care less what is written in the Word of God.

26 How is it then, brethern? when ye come together, everyone of you hath a psalm, hath a doctrine, hath a tongue, hath a revelation, hath an interpretation. Let all things be done unto edifying.

27 If any man speak in an unknown tongue, let it be by two, or at the most by three, and that by coarse; and let one interpret.

28 But if there be no interpreter, let him keep silence in the church; and let him speak to himself, and to God.

29 Let the prophets speak two or three, and let the other judge.

30 If any thing be revealed to another that sitteth by, let the first hold his peace.

31 Ye may all prophesy one by one, that all may learn, and all may be comforted.

How very different are these excellent instructions we are given in the Word of God. How greatly they differ from what we actually do witness happening within the Christian churches today.

I want us to pay special attention to these next two verses for they contain a great deal of truth that few seem to understand.

32 And the spirits of the prophets are subject to the prophets.

33 For God is not the author of confusion, but of peace, as in all churches of the saints.

This verse does state very clearly that the people who have received the baptism of the Holy Ghost and have received the supernatural gift of prophecy, are able to control them selves. They do not need to interrupt the order of the service and they are not to begin speaking in tongues in such a way that only causes confusion within the church. If they are truly lead of the Spirit, they will with hold their prophecy until the proper time has come to deliver it. As the scripture does say, God is not the author of confusion.

I am reminded of the word of King Solomon when he said there is a time given for all things. Our God is a God of order and we need to recognize that he is. Therefore, when a person does interrupt the regular worship service and does make a commotion or a disturbance that hinders the order of the service, we should be reminded of this scripture.

33 For God is not the author of confusion, but of peace, as in all churches of the saints.

In these next few verses Paul has decided to upbraid or for lack of a better word, expose some of the religious men at Corinth for their stuffy attitude and for their ignorance. It seems as though they had adopted a religious doctrine from the Jews, and did not seem to realize that God has poured out his Spirit upon all flesh and upon women as well as men.

34 Let your women keep silence in the churches; for it is not permitted unto them to speak; but they are commanded to be under obedience, as also saith the law.

35 And if they will learn any thing, let them ask their husbands at home: for it is a shame for women to speak in the church.

I want to point out that Paul does not really believe what he is saying. He is saying this to expose how very wrong these religious and pious men really are. We must not forget the prophecy given by the prophet Joel regarding the status of women.

Paul is about to blast them for their ignorance.

36 What? came the word of God out from you? or came it unto you only?

37 If any man think himself to be a prophet, or spiritual, let him acknowledge that the things that I write unto you are the commandments of the Lord.

38 If any man be ignorant, let him be ignorant.

This last verse Paul wrote in regard to their very ignorant attitude toward the women of Corinth who were members of their church. Because they had received the baptism in the Holy Ghost as well as men, they also did receive the very same gifts of the Spirit as did the men. In this respect, the women were equal to the men, in the grace of God, and were Spirit filled, even as the men were. Paul said that if any did not agree with this, well just let them remain ignorant. In this respect, there are many religious men who remain ignorant even until this very day, for the scriptures also say that in the kingdom of God, there is neither male nor female.

We shall close this chapter with the last two verses of Paul's letter at chapter 14. Do pay attention to what they say and be aware that our God is a God of order and he does not approve when men conduct his business in a manner that best could be described as without any order.

39 Wherefore, brethern, covet (desire) to prophesy, and forbid not to speak with tongues.

40 Let all things be done decently and in order.

I find it rather strange how many churches have completely ignored Paul's instructions to the churches. We are all to desire that we may prophesy and may we not forget the three ways we are to do so. We are to edify the body of Christ, we are to exhort and encourage ourselves and others to do better, and we are to comfort those who are in need of comforting.

The next instruction given by Paul is that we are not to forbid speaking in tongues within the church. Why are there so many churches today which have absolutely forbidden speaking in tongues? Could it be that they are embarrassed by this manifestation of the presence of the Holy Spirit? Or could it be that they are a completely different denomination than was Paul, and so they ignore his instructions altogether?

I do suggest to you my dear brothers and sisters, when we recognize that we are now living in perilous times, and consider the time of great trouble that is to come, we must hold tightly to the instructions we have been given, in our Bibles.

Chapter 33 How to Receive Divine Power

I am aware that a very large book could be written about the baptism in the Holy Ghost and on the gifts of the Spirit as well as the fruits of the Spirit. However, I am also aware that the Holy Bible is available to all, and it is from this deep well, that I rely upon, more than any other, to supply me with what I need to know. For those who are interested, there are books on this subject available at the public library, but they do not all agree on many things.

There is information concerning the fruits of the Spirit through out the New Testament, if we will only search for it. I do suggest that you obtain a copy of the Beatitudes and place it in a place where it will be visible to you, for as much time as possible, each day. Perhaps in the room where you eat your meals, or some other desirable location, so that you can let your mind dwell upon the meaning of each of them, as you sit idly in thought.

I am aware that in a little while I must allow you to find that place where you shall receive the nourishment you will need, to sustain you, and help you to become strong in the Lord. It is written that one must plant the seeds and another must water the plants as they grow. It is my greatest concern that I provide you with a solid foundation in scripture to prepare you and protect you from the false teachers and false doctrine that abounds through out our land.

The apostle Paul, knew that he had but a short time to live and he had this to say to a small group of Christians whom he loved so very much.

Acts 20:29, For I know this, that after my departing shall grievous wolves enter in among you, not sparing the flock. 30 Also of your own selves shall men arise, speaking perverse things, to draw away disciples after them.

Please pay attention to what Paul has said. He has said that the church of Christ would be lead astray from two different directions. The first way is that religious men, whom Paul likened unto grievous wolves, would enter in. In other words, they came from some place else, but their purpose is to enter in, and once inside to devour the flock.

The second attack against the church would come from within. Paul said "Also of your own selves shall men arise," and the purpose of these religious men would be to divide the church. It should be obvious that this is exactly what happened and it is one of the main reasons why after the reformation, there are so many different denominations today.

I want to make it clear that I do not desire that any should become followers of me, but it is my very sincere hope and expectation that you become a follower of Christ, for he alone is the one who is perfect. Over the years, many have chosen to follow religious men, but eventually became disappointed when they realized that religious men are never perfect, for sooner or later, they stumble over the things Satan has placed before them.

It is for this reason that I want very much for you to receive the baptism in the Holy Ghost, for you will need the extra measure in God's power to help you defeat the power of the enemy. I say that we must learn to be lead by the Spirit which means that we must take control of our flesh and not allow it to rule over us. There is an on going war within us, as the flesh is always at war with our spirit, trying to lead us into temptation and trouble. It is only when we are lead by the Holy Spirit that we have victory, for being lead by the flesh leadeth to the grave, but by the Spirit, to eternal life.

Sooner or later, we must ask the question, "What must I do to receive the baptism in the Holy Ghost?" I am sure that if we were to go around to many different churches today, we would receive many different answers to this question. However, there is the example we were given in the book of Acts, and I believe we should consider this way first.

I do not have any doubt that some where there are chosen men of God, who do lay their hands on those who are seeking the baptism of the Holy Ghost, and those who are seeking are being filled with the Spirit, just as they were during Peter and Paul's day. The problem is, I really do not know where these men are at, and therefore, I cannot direct you to them.

There was a time when I went out to search for them, but I could not seem to find them. What I found was something different entirely, and perhaps I should explain what it was that I did find.

Instead of finding a group of Holy Ghost filled men, laying hands on people in the way that is mentioned on so many different occasions in the Bible, I found something entirely different. I found people that as they were praying for an individual, they did lay their hands usually on the person's forehead. Then at the right moment when the person was not quite sure of what was to happen next, the person praying would give a mighty push and the purpose seemed to be to cause the person they were praying for, to fall down. They call this experience being slain in the Spirit. However, we could all see the real reason the person fell down was because they were pushed by the one doing the praying. I do want you to realize that pushing people down is not a Biblical method of laying on of hands and it can not be found in all of the Bible. Therefore, in my opinion it is a religious ritual invented by religious men.

I would certainly defend those people's right to conduct their services in the way that seemeth right to them. If they want to push people down and then claim they have been slain by the Spirit, it is perfectly alright with me, for God is their judge and not I. However, I cannot recommend it to you, for in the whole time that I observed these things, and on several different occasions, I did not witness a single person receive the baptism in the Holy Ghost, as they once did in the book of Acts.

Therefore, I will share with you from my own experience, and my wife's as well, a different way. I want you to notice that I did not say a better way but a different way. It is also a Biblical way and a good way, and it is a way that God approves, and of this I am very sure.

To better understand this different way, we need to return to the time when the Holy Ghost was first given. Perhaps you will recall that I said according to scripture, they remained in Jerusalem from the time of the ascension of Jesus, until the holy day of Pentecost, waiting for the promise they had received from the Lord to be fulfilled.

Someone might ask, just how do we know that the ascension took place ten days before Pentecost? There are basicaly two ways to determine the amount of days between the ascension and the holy day of Pentecost. The first way is very simple, for all we need to do is look at a calendar that has the important religious days marked. I have just such a calendar in our kitchen, and there are many meaningful scripture verses as well as beautiful pictures of God's creation.

The second way is to learn what the scriptures do say and then count the days for ourselves. A most important clue can be found in the first chapter of the book of Acts.

Acts 1:3, To whom also he showed himself alive after his passion by many infallible proofs, being seen of them forty days, and speaking of the things pertaining to the kingdom of God.

The first day that Jesus was seen was Sunday, and this is also the day after the sabbath, from which we are to count fifty day, to find the day of Pentecost. To determine when the day of Pentecost did occur, it is necessary to use the method that is given in the 23rd chapter of Leviticus. However, I do not have any disagreement with the date of Pentecost as it is shown on most calendars, for the Jewish people use the same method of determining this date they have used for many, many hundreds of years.

It is interesting to note that in the 23rd chapter of Leviticus we are instructed to begin counting from the morrow after the sabbath. This just happens to be the very same day of the week that Mary came to the tomb, very early and before day light.

In the first case we are instructed to count fifty days and according to what is written in the book of Acts, the ascension took place just forty days from the day of discovery. This leaves us with a balance of ten days between the ascension and the day of Pentecost. Having checked with the religious calendar in the kitchen, it does seem to verify the ten days.

There is nothing I know of in the scriptures that would indicate that the disciples were aware of how long they would have to tarry in Jerusalem. Reviewing once more, the instruction by our Lord, as they were given in Luke's gospel.

Luke 24:49, And, behold, I send the promise of my Father upon you: but tarry ye in the city of Jerusalem, until ye be endued with power from on high.

Again, Jesus did give them his final instructions as it is recorded in the first chapter of the book of Acts.

Acts 1:4, And, being assembled together with them, commanded them that they should not depart from Jerusalem, but wait for the promise of the Father, which, saith he, ye have heard of me.

5 For John truly baptized with water; but ye shall be baptized with the Holy Ghost not many days hence.

It does appear that the disciples did not know how many days they would have to remain in Jerusalem, and I doubt that the question was even discussed. You might be wondering why I have made such an issue about how long they had to wait to receive the promise. I must confess, that at times I do wonder myself why I have, and yet I know there is a reason.

Let us pretend, you and I, that we are living during that time when Jesus was crucified, and being followers who follow after his disciples, we have each received an invitation to attend that very special meeting in the upper room. In fact, in this invitation, we have received the same instructions they did receive, for we are to tarry there, until we receive the baptism in the Holy Ghost.

Let us also pretend that we are not the only ones to receive this invitation, for they have been sent to Christians all around the world. We must be aware that even though a great many invitations have been sent out, seating is limited and once the upper room is filled to capacity, no more people will be admitted. Our Lord Jesus is well aware of what he said to his disciples, for he said, "Many are called but few are chosen."

We shall now interview some of the people who have received invitations and find out whether or not they plan on attending this very important and special meeting. Perhaps the first person we ask, might seem a little reserved, and he asks, Just who all is going to be there? I cannot just drop everything I am doing and go off to Jerusalem to a religious meeting without knowing who is going to be there, and what the program consists of.

We can inform him that while we do not know who all will be there, we do know who some of the people are, who will be there and we also know a little about the program. Looking to the list we have been given in the first chapter of the book of Acts, we are able to identify some of the participants.

We see that Andrew, who once introduced his brother Peter to Jesus, will be there, as well as Peter. They are both fishermen. James and John, who are also brothers, and fishermen will be there as well. Perhaps I should tell you that James will be the first of the apostles whose life will be taken from him, because of his love for Jesus and for the gospel message he will preach.

Philip, the evangelist, who baptized the man from Ethiopia, and Thomas, who became known as "Doubting Thomas," will be there as well. Bartholomew, one of the twelve chosen by Christ, and Matthew, also chosen, a tax collector who later became the author of the gospel of Matthew will be there. James, the son of Alphaeus, and Simon Zelotes, and Judas, the brother of James will all be there, of this we can be sure. And so will Matthias. who was chosen to replace the betrayer.

Now in addition to this, I believe we can expect Joseph of Arimathaea to be there with his friend, Nicodemus, who helped him place Jesus' body in the tomb.

As far as we know the program will consist of early morning prayer meetings, a time for fellowship, a time for testimonies, with an afternoon worship service, as well as the main service in the evening, which will be followed with prayer. We can expect the men we have just mentioned to be the speakers at these meetings, with a different speaker at every meeting. Of course, we can expect to hear from each of these men, their personal testimony as to how they came to be followers of Christ, and share with us from their many experiences, as they walked with Jesus along the shores of Galilee, and traveled from town to town.

Now in addition to this, we expect Mary Magdalene to be there, as well as Mary, the mother of James and Salome. Perhaps Martha and her sister, who have a brother named Lazarus, who were from the town of Bethany, will be there also.

These women each have a message for us, and we can expect them to speak to us at the afternoon meetings. I do expect that their messages will be drawn from their own personal experiences and should be very interesting.

I must tell you that Mary, the mother of Jesus will be there, but I do not know whether or not she will choose to speak before the whole assembly. The one thing we can be very sure of is that everyone who will come to this very special gathering is looking forward to meeting the woman who has been blessed above all women, for we do want to show her our most sincere respect, knowing the great sorrow she has experienced.

Now the highlight of this very important special meeting in the upper room, will be when Jesus does come into our midst, Coming not in the flesh but in the form of the Holy Spirit, and does fill us to overflowing with his divine presence. This will be the very first time that this has ever happened in the entire history of mankind. We have been invited to be the first of all mankind to receive this blessing from heaven.

The man I am speaking to does choose this moment to ask this question. Just when do you expect Jesus to arrive? If I knew when he was going to arrive, I could make plans to be there for that day. However, in looking at the program as you have described it, it does appear to last longer and will take more time than I can spare. You see, I am a very busy man, and I have to use my time wisely and to my best advantage. You just tell me when Jesus will arrive and I will try to be there.

I politely informed him that I was unable to do that, and thanked him for his time and his trouble. The next person we will come to is an attractive young lady who has just received the same invitation that we did. I ask her the same question and provide her with the same information we just gave to the first man we talked to.

The effect that this information, plus the question we asked, as to whether or not she planned to attend the meeting in the upper room, caused a worried expression to form on her face. Oh dear me, she replied. Normally, I would just ask my parents for a little loan to pay for my trip and I would be on the first plane for Jerusalem. Perhaps I would even be able to visit Rome and Paris on my way home, and do a little shopping.

However, I am engaged to be married and the wedding will be late in the spring, and then there is the honeymoon. There is so very much that has to be done and so little time to make all of the arrangements and plans that are necessary for my wedding to be a success. If Jesus had scheduled his visit in the fall or winter, I would have been more than glad to have attended but the way things are, there is just no way I can make it. She said this with a little shrug of her shoulders, gave us a big smile and departed.

I then approached a young to middle aged man, whose hair was beginning to turn gray at his temples, and asked him the very same question and provided him with the same information as the other two.

His manner was very kind and he was soft spoken. He informed me that normally he would not even have thought twice about it, for he would love to be there in the upper room, except that something had come up. His elderly father was retiring from the family business and because he was the eldest son, he must now take over as the one in charge of the business. His obligation to do so, was to all of the family members, for they were depending upon him to safe guard the family fortune in these perilous times of corporate raiders. Therefore, it was absolutely impossible for him to take a trip at this particular time.

We thanked him for his time and we proceeded on, until we noticed a young man who was a rather famous athlete. We noticed that he must be a Christian for he too, had an invitation in his hand to attend the meeting in the upper room at Jerusalem.

Again, we asked the same question and provided the same information. The young athlete smiled at us, and then said, as you probably know, I am being paid a rather large salary. Now the amount of this salary is based upon my performance as a ball player. First, there is spring training, and to miss any of it would be to place my salary in jeopardy. I am afraid that my manager just would not approve of me taking a trip to Jerusalem at this time of year.

We thanked him for his time and his thoughts and we departed. Again, the words of Jesus return to me and I can not help but think, Yes, many are called, but only a few ever do answer the call. Thus, many are called but few are chosen.

However, I happen to know that across this land and around the world, there are many, who if they knew ahead of time, would sell their homes and all that they own, in order to be there with the disciples and with Mary, the mother of Jesus, and with the one hundred and twenty in the upper room. Without any doubt they would be there, to receive the promise of the Father, to receive the power from on high. I say that they would be there, for you see, I am one of them.

There is no material thing I own, that is more precious than to accept a personal invitation to receive the blessing of being baptized in the Holy Ghost. There is nothing in this entire world that can equal the experience of being completely and totally submerged in the Holy Spirit and to be filled to over flowing with the divine presence of our Lord, Jesus Christ.

I am now going to ask you, who I care about, if you are allowed to choose the time, are you willing to remain in a symbolic upper room, for however long it takes to receive the baptism in the Holy Ghost? I want for you to consider the time in which we are living and I want for you to consider what shortly must come to pass. The promise of the Father, of receiving the power from on high is extended to you. Our Lord Jesus Christ has his hand stretched out to you, and he asks, "Won't you please come?"

When Jesus instructed his disciples that they should remain in Jerusalem until they received the power from on high, he knew that the amount of people the upper room could contain was limited. However, he has not limited us, as to who may receive this power, for the promise is given that it shall come to pass in the last days, that he will pour out his Spirit upon all flesh. This promise does extend to you and me.

However as that may be, not all flesh will seek the baptism in the Holy Ghost, for many are afraid of it and many do not want it. We can be assured that God will not force anyone to receive the baptism in the Holy Spirit, if they do not want to receive it. However, when we become aware of the real reason the promise was given, so that we might receive the divine power to carry out our great commission, we would be foolish to not seek it. To receive divine super-natural power is a precious thing and we should be extremely thankful that our loving and merciful Creator, has chosen to bestow such a precious gift upon us, who are his children.

A scripture verse in Hebrews comes to my mind.

Hebrews 11:6, But without faith it is impossible to please him; for he that cometh to God must believe that he is, and that he is a rewarder of them that diligently seek him.

The thought I want for us to grasp is that not only must we have faith, but we must believe that God will reward us if we seek him diligently.

Is this not what the one hundred and twenty people in the upper room did? Did they not seek our Lord's presence night and day, in prayer and supplications, worshipping God, while patiently waiting with faith for the promise of the Father to be fulfilled? I would point out that they did not just seek God, but they did seek him diligently. They completely set their worldly concerns aside, and focused their attention on heavenly things, for they were seeking a heavenly reward.

At the time that Jesus did instruct his disciples they were to remain in Jerusalem, this city was considered the most holy city on earth by all of Israel, because the temple of God was located there. In other words, it was a holy place, and there is a symbolic meaning we need to understand. If we are going to follow the instructions that were given to the disciples in a symbolic way, then we must be willing to tarry in a holy place, until we have received the power from on high.

The holy place I have in mind is in the Holy Bible, for it is there that both my wife and I tarried, until we were both filled with the Holy Ghost. However, there is a great deal more to this, than what you might think at first. What I am suggesting is not a small thing, but is similar to the tarrying that was done by the one hundred and twenty, so long ago.

I realize that a great many people are either not able or are unwilling to tarry in the Holy Bible until they receive the power from on high. Perhaps they think they can just read a chapter now and then, as they find time.

While this would be acceptable at any other time, it will not fulfill the instructions we have been given. We are to tarry in a holy place until we receive, and this means that God wants our undivided attention during this time.

Of course, they can always seek for those places where holy men of God continue to lay hands upon God's children and may receive the baptism in the Holy Ghost in this manner. This is a Biblical way, and I do not find any fault with it, but there is a little more we must know.

I must point out that of the many people who do come this way, seeking to be filled with the Holy Ghost, only a few do actually receive it. I am sure that you are probably wondering why this is so? I believe that God is certainly willing and does want to fill people with the Holy Ghost. However, I believe the reason can be found in the scripture we just read. God is a rewarder of those who diligently seek him. Could it be, that the Christians of our day have become spiritually lazy, and are no longer diligently seeking God and therefore are not receiving God's reward?

Of course, many are ignorant concerning the baptism in the Holy Ghost, for they have depended upon religious teachers instead of the Word of God. It is as though everyone is seeking the easy way, and no one is willing to make an effort to draw closer to God. For many, it is a matter of time.

Perhaps I should explain myself further on this subject.

We are living in a time when many people are very busy and they are running to and fro.

From morning till night they go about their business of earning money and raising children, always seeking to better their position, and they just do not have any time left over to devote to God, or to seek diligently, for his will, in their lives.

Jesus said that if we seek first, the kingdom of God, then the very same things that people are running to and fro and trying to obtain, (the necessities of life) will be added unto us. However, most people today are more interested in doing it their way and are not seeking God's way.

God is looking for a people who will put him first in their lives. He is looking for a people who will diligently seek him and when they show God that they are aware of his promise, and will put the matters of this world, temporarily aside, to turn to him, he will reward them by fulfilling his promise. Is this not what he did for those 120 faithful who remained in Jerusalem until the promise of God was fulfilled?

I am aware that there are many who preach the Word of God who will insist that the laying on of hands is the Biblical way. However, the way that I do suggest is also Biblical and I am absolutely sure that many people will receive the baptism in the Holy Ghost, if they do follow the instructions I am about to share with you. I can say this for the Lord has assured me that it is so.

I am well aware that each of us, our lives are very different. The situations that exist in one persons life may be altogether different than in another persons life.

I would point out that God is well aware of these differences for it is written that he even knows the number of the hairs upon a persons head. How much more is he aware of each of us and our individual struggles to live our lives the best way we know how.

I have said this for I am also aware that at the time you read this, you might not be able to follow these instructions due to your own individual situation. Even so, I do suggest that you begin to make plans for the future that will enable you to diligently seek the Lord in the manner I am about to describe.

The first thing we must do, is arrange to take some time off from work. Perhaps we might have some vacation time coming and we can take advantage of this, to use that time for this very special purpose. After all, is this not the example that the 120, including the twelve disciples and Mary, the mother of Jesus set before us, that we might follow? We can be sure that they all took time off from their regular activities, to accept the invitation to attend the special meeting in the upper room. To become charter members of the first Christian church and the first to be filled to overflowing with the Holy Spirit. I again want to point out that it was absolutely necessary for each and everyone of the 120 to completely set aside the routine of their normal lives, in order to receive the promise from God.

Whenever we mention anything as serious as taking time off from work, therefore having an affect on a person's money, we divide the group, for many are not willing to give up the money they would earn. Of course, there are many who simply cannot afford to take time off from work, and for those I have a few suggestions I will make later on. We can see that the method I am explaining to you is limited, for it is limited to those people who want the reward that is promised and that are willing to give up even the money they would earn, in order to receive it.

Now that the size of our group is much smaller, we shall continue on. The next thing we shall discuss is the location of where your personal upper room may be. If your home is quiet and a place where you can be alone with your Bible and can devote many hours to reading your Bible and to prayer each day, then your home is the place where you can seek God while you wait for the promise to be fulfilled.

However, I am aware that for many people their homes resemble Grand central station. The phone never stops ringing, and people are constantly dropping by and you do not have hardly any privacy, of the type that is necessary. If this is the case, then you must try to find a better and more private place to become your upper room.

I say this is very important, for the 120 in the upper room were of one accord, and if we are going to achieve this same kind of atmosphere, I know of no other way than to be alone with God.

Every time the telephone rings it will rob you of your focus on heavenly things and spiritual high places. If your friends or family just drop by to chat for a while, even when you least expect them, it will completely remove you from your symbolic upper room, and it will become very difficult to keep your mind focused on what you are reading. These interruptions will also rob you of the spiritual closeness to God that we must achieve.

It is for this reason I am going to suggest that we find a more suitable location to be our upper room. I am sure that we are all familiar with the cartoonist's concept that certain very religious men do climb to the top of very tall mountains, seeking the privacy they need to meditate and be alone with God. While I am sure that such privacy is not limited to a mountain top location, I certainly do agree that there are times when we all need to seek the time and place where we can be alone with God. The time to gather our thoughts and focus on the complete righteousness of God and to consider the life we are living, and the direction we are headed.

From my living room, I often look out the window and observe the small ferry as it tirelessly labors to deliver it's passengers back and forth from the mainland, to beautiful, and scenic Lummi Island. It is a place where those who are skilled in painting pictures do linger, and it is also a home for some who write poetry, while others write books. It is a place that is removed from the hustle and bustle, of living close to the cities and freeways.

There is only a small body of water that separates us from Lummi Island, and I have sailed through it many times and it is known as Hale's Pass.

If I look beyond Lummi Island, I can see the mountain on Orcas piercing the clouds, and I am reminded of the narrow road I once traveled to the top of that mountain. The view from the top of the mountain is breath taking, for on a clear day, one can see more than one hundred miles in any direction.

There are places, where young lovers walk with hand in hand, along lonely beaches, leaving their foot prints in the sand, as evidence of their passing.

There are also places where children play in the tide pools among the rocks and admire the beauty of God's creation, while their parents lay, soaking up the sun. Where eagles soar, riding high on currents of air, and seals lay, baking on the rocks, while killer whales, looking for salmon to feast upon, cruise close to the shore. Where sea gulls argue over whose right it is, to claim the spoil and clam diggers hurry, to fill their quota, before the tide rushes in.

I think that it is good that we are able to travel to the mountains and to the sea shore, but in seeking a location for our personal upper room, I do not believe that it is necessary that we find such an attractive setting. What I do consider important is that we do not exceed our financial limitations, for if we spend as much as ten days, as they once did in the upper room, in a motel or hotel, it can be rather expensive.

What I am going to suggest is that we obtain a list of motels and their cost, in that part of the country where you now live, or might like to visit. I recall, that when I traveled some a few years ago, there were some areas where the cost of lodging and motels was a great deal less than in others. As I recall, the cost in or near large cities was much higher than it was in small towns in a rural location.

I also remember that certain areas that were strategically located between major population centers, where the motel business is a major source of the economy, are also more expensive, except some do have winter or off season rates. This is why we need to do some research and find a place where the prices are very reasonable and in line with our resources. I say this for the price of motels does in some degree, reflect the price of restaurants and therefore the cost of living for it is all relative. I think it is possible we will find the economy we are searching for some where off of the beaten path.

Once we have determined the right city or town, I suppose that it is reasonable for us to take all of the normal precautions when searching for the right motel and for the right room. First, we hope that it is in a location that is reasonably quiet, for an abnormal amount of noise will make it hard for us to concentrate on our reading. Therefore, we must notice the surrounding area and the type of businesses that are nearby. I once lived in Seattle and very near Boeing Field and the place where they tested jet engines each morning. The noise was sufficient to rattle the windows in our small apartment, and our neighbors did wear ear plugs.

Our apartment was also located along a very busy truck route, very near a curve and the train tracks were just across the road that is known as Airport Way. Believe me when I suggest that you do not want to get a motel in such a noisy situation.

The next thing I believe we should notice, is that it be located near what I think of as family restaurants. Fast food is acceptable part of the time, but I do not recommend it for prolonged periods of time. Because we have now become the temple of God, we should give some thought as to what we eat, for we have a responsibility to God that we eat what is good for us. We must not forget, the life we now live was purchased by Jesus' blood on Calvary.

Ideally, the places where we will be eating will be within walking distance of the motel. Because we will be spending many hours reading our Bibles, it is good for us to be able to walk back and forth from the restaurants. If we find that we must drive, then we still need to do some walking, for it is not healthy to get no exercise whatsoever. Of course, some of us will bring a small amount of exercise equipment with us, for we are able to get some exercise within the privacy of our room.

I also recommend that we take along suitable clothing and enough of them, for the time of year and location where we will be going. In addition to this, I believe it is good that we bring the kind of clothes we will be comfortable in, as we are confined to our rooms and our reading. We should have our "in room," reading clothes, and then have our "going out to dinner" clothes as well.

Besides our clothing, It might be helpful to bring a reading lamp from home, for the ones that are often furnished in the rooms leave a little bit to be desired. The same goes for pillows, for I like my own the best, and I do often bring it with me when I travel and stay in motels. I also bring an electric hot pot, for heating water just in case one is not supplied.

I do suggest that you bring along your own music machine and music, which you find to be spiritually uplifting. This could be what we think of as a boom box with a cassette deck, or it might be a portable disc player as I understand these are also very convenient. Choose the music that seems to speak to your heart and that glorify God. The ones that you feel deep down in your soul, for they shall prepare us, and help us come closer to God and to our goal of receiving the promise of God.

I must confess that I am rather old fashioned, and I am partial to the kind of music I listened to as a boy. The old gospel hymns of yesteryear is what I love best, and especially as they were recorded by some of the very dear people who have now passed on.

From time to time, I search through certain second hand stores in search of old record albums containing the kind of religious music I prefer. Some of them are by well known artists and some are by little singing groups you probably never heard of before. I then transfer them to cassettes so that I am able to listen to them in our car as we are traveling.

What a joy it is to select one of my old favorites, crank up the volume just a bit, and listen to those dear souls whom God gave so much talent. Often, I sing along with them, and it is almost as if they were with me, even now.

The single most important item we must choose is the Bible we intend to read, as we tarry in our upper room. If you have trouble understanding the King James Version, I do recommend that you choose one of the easy to read and understand, modern versions. Be sure and acquire one with large print, for there is no need to place undue strain on your eyes by trying to focus on very small print.

Of course, It might not hurt to have another Bible with you, for I find it interesting to compare one translation with another if I do not completely understand a verse. It is also good to have a dictionary handy, lest we do not receive the fullness of what the author is saying, or if the translators have used words that are diffi-cult to understand.

So far, I have not said much about how very serious is this thing I am suggesting to you. This is not to be thought of as just another vacation, but as probably the most unforgettable experience you will ever have.

What we are about to undertake is to completely read our Bibles from cover to cover. It is this tarrying in a holy place, in the pages and verses of our holy Bibles that will bring the promise of God upon us and we need to approach what lays before us with a very serious and a most respectful attitude. We should also be extremely thankful, that our Loving heavenly Father is willing to make a way to bestow such a precious gift upon us.

It is only natural for those who are married to take their vaca-tions at the same time, so they can be together. It certainly would not be much fun to travel to a town where you do not know anyone, and then spend a great deal of time alone in your room, while reading your Bible. Perhaps I should remind you that the purpose of our undertaking is not for fun.

Even so, I do expect married couples, if they have both accepted the Lord, to both tarry in this symbolic upper room until they are both filled with the Holy Ghost. However, if you are not both Christians, and have not both, been born again, then I suggest that the born again person do seek the baptism in the Holy Ghost without being in the presence of an unbelieving spouse. As hard as it might seem, I do advise you to choose your own personal upper room, where you might be alone with God, and where you are able to read your entire Bible, from cover to cover. Of course, I am only speaking of the time that we are to tarry in a holy place and I am not speaking of after you have received the baptism in the Holy Ghost.

The purpose of tarrying in a holy place is so that we might draw nearer to God than we have ever been before. I realize that when you surrendered to God and repented of your past sinful life, that you did feel the divine presence of our Lord, as he came into your heart and mind and did take up residence within you.

However, just as it was for the twelve disciples and for Mary, the mother of Jesus, to receive the baptism in the Holy Ghost we must come closer to God than we ever have before, and I am reminded of why Moses did hide in a cleft in the rock. It was a very unique and unforgettable experience for them, and it shall be for us as well. We are to be serious and most respectful but not afraid.

I know there are some, who did receive the baptism in the Holy Ghost quite some time ago, but in these latter years you do not seem to be as close to God as you once were. If this is how you feel, then I believe it would be good for you to come along with us, and enter into your own upper room. Receiving the baptism in the Holy Ghost is a little like taking a drink from a very sweet tasting well. From time to time, we need to return, to drink again and be refreshed in the Spirit.

I now want to share with you some instructions that were given to a people who were about to come closer to the very same God we know, than they had ever been before.

Please listen and do pay attention to these instructions, for our God is still the same today, as he was when these instructions were first given.

Exodus 19:10, And the Lord said unto Moses, Go unto the people, and sanctify them today and tomorrow, and let them wash their clothes.

11 And be ready against the third day: for the third day the Lord will come down in the sight of all the people upon mount Sinai.

12 And thou shalt set bounds unto the people round about, saying, Take heed to yourselves, that ye go not up into the mount, or touch the border of it: whosoever toucheth the mount shall surely be put to death:

13 There shall not an hand touch it, but he shall surely be stoned, or shot through; whether it be beast or man, it shall not live: when the trumpet soundeth long, they shall come up to the mount.

I want to bring to your attention how very serious it is when we draw close unto a holy and completely righteous God. How very thankful we should be that these instructions were given at Mount Sinai, and not at the upper room.

Yet, when we take time out from our work and our regular activities, and devote our minds and our thoughts to God by reading His Holy Word, as we are about to, it is as though we have climbed clear to the top of Mount Sinai, and are holding God's outstretched hand.

When Moses does sanctify the people and they do wash their clothes, it is symbolic of the sanctification that would take place in our lives, many years later. When we surrendered at the cross and our sins were washed away by the blood of Jesus, we were sanctified and set apart from all people for God's purpose.

There is a certain scripture I want for us to be aware of and in it, the apostle Paul is speaking of Jesus and his church.

Ephesians 5:26, That he might sanctify and cleanse it with the washing of water by the word.

27 That he might present it to himself a glorious church, not having spot, or wrinkle, or any such thing; but that it should be holy and without blemish.

I would point out that the people were responsible for allowing the washing by the Word of God to take place, as it is stated in Paul's letter. It could not be done or would not happen without some effort on their part, for they must read and hear the Word of God, even as we are about to.

When the people did wash their clothes, just prior to God's visit to Mount Sinai, it was a type of the effort we must make, to keep ourselves clean from the pollution of this world, when we come into the presence of Almighty God. We are not to defile ourselves by filling our minds with unclean thoughts, and violence, and pornography, via the means that are available today.

14 And Moses went down from the mount unto the people, and sanctified the people; and they washed their clothes.

15 And he said unto the people, Be ready against the third day: come not at your wives.

This verse is extremely important to all who seek the baptism of the Holy Ghost. What Moses has commanded them, is that for three days preceding the time when they would come into the presence of God, they were to completely abstain from having sexual relations with their wives. It is the same for us today, for if we truly are serious about coming into the presence of God, then we are to completely abstain from having any sexual relations, whatsoever, during the time when we shall tarry in our upper room.

Before you even begin to protest, I want for you to think about how it was in the upper room, during the time between the ascension and the holy day of Pentecost. We can be absolutely sure that not one of the one hundred and twenty children of God, had their minds on sex. Period!

And they, my dear brothers and sisters, have set the example before us that we must follow.

Now if anyone does not think they can abstain from all sexual relations for ten days or so, I do advise them to wait until which time they can control their appetite for sex. As I have said before, the flesh does always war against the spirit and if we are ever to rise up above this plain where we are at, we must take control of our flesh. I realize that I do speak to you as though you were children, but only because I do care for you.

Please believe me when I say that I am not interested in invading the privacy of your bedroom. I am well aware that we are more than able to avoid sex for a few days or even weeks, in the pursuit of our goal. I can not help but think about how it has been through out history for countless men and women, who were separated during the time of war. Are not we also involved in a war?

As one who has been called by our Lord, to deliver a message, and also to be a teacher, I know that I am responsible before God for those things which I teach. If I did not share with you, the meaning of these verses, I would be ashamed for failing to instruct you, according to the Word of God. And then, if you did not receive the baptism in the Holy Ghost, the fault would be mine. It is much better that you receive this warning, and in this way you will be better prepared to come into the presence of Almighty God.

I do hope that you will be able to remain at home and that your own personal upper room will be there. It is so much more convenient and less costly than traveling and staying in a motel for a week or more. At the same time, I realize for many, getting away from home for a little while, and to seek a retreat from the cares of this world might be the best medicine the doctor could prescribe.

Let us pretend that you have chosen the location of your upper room and retreat, and it is located about five hundred miles from where you live, in a neighboring state. It is a day's drive by automobile. The town you have chosen is neither large nor small but is what we would think of as being a middle sized town. It is big enough to have a shopping mall and good sized super markets, but is small enough to not have any major traffic problems.

Now in addition to this, on the edge of this fair sized community, there are several new and modern motels and quite a few restaurants that cater to people from all walks of life. In addition to these restaurants, there are the usual amount of fast food places, offering a variety of fast foods.

I hope that the room you have chosen is in a convenient location but with some privacy, and that there are enough windows to let in an abundance of light during the day. Also, that there is a small table with comfortable chairs, where you will spend many hours reading your Bible. To put it another way, I hope that it is a room that you feel good about, and one that you do not mind living in.

As I have said before, what we are here for, is very serious. This is not just another vacation, with much time spent at the swimming pool. We are here for a specific purpose, and it is to follow in the example that has been set before us, by the twelve disciples and by Mary, the mother of our Lord Jesus. We are here to tarry in a holy place, to draw closer to God, and to receive what we have been promised in the Word of God.

The next thing I am going to suggest to you might seem strange, but there is a reason. I want for us to forget about being here to receive the baptism in the Holy Ghost, except when we pray. I want us to concentrate and devote our time to doing our part, and we can be sure that God will do his part. He always has and he always will, and therefore, there is no reason to doubt that he will do his part, now, just as he promised his disciples, so long ago.

The thing we must focus on, is that we do our part. What we are to do, is read our entire Bible from cover to cover, and then retain as much knowledge as possible. I know that this must seem like a very difficult thing to do, but I can assure you that it will not be more than we are able, for God will help us in our effort to get to know him better, through reading His Holy Word. Also, I will make suggestions that are meant to help us to take one step at a time, making it easier to reach our goal.

The first thing I want, is for us to think or pretend, that we are being paid to read our Bibles, and that we have just been hired by a very wealthy employer to do so. A scripture verse does come to my mind and it is one we are all familiar with.

2nd Timothy 2:15, Study to show thyself approved unto God,

a workman that needeth not be ashamed, rightfully dividing the word of truth.

This should be our goal at this particular time, for we are seeking God's approval. Let us pretend that when we have finished reading, we shall receive a test on how much of the history of God's relationship to mankind, that is recorded in the Bible, we have retained. This test will also include questions concerning general knowledge and time and events, and will not be at all complicated. It is for us to gain the story of the people in the Bible and we are not overly concerned with deep spiritual truths at this time. The wages we will be paid shall be determined by how well we do our job, and by the test about people and events, and the history they helped form.

It is because we are new on the job, and want to make a favorable impression on our employers, that we know that we must not be late for work, or slack in any way. It is for this reason, that we must form a plan and a daily routine, to insure that we use the time we have been given, to the very best of our ability.

We shall begin forming our daily routine with the start of our day. I realize that we do not all get out of bed at the same time, so let us listen as our brother Paul has this to say to us.

1st Thessalonians 5:5, Ye are all the children of light, and the children of the day: we are not of the night, nor of darkness. 6 Therefore let us not sleep, as do others; but let us watch and be sober.

We must not forget that we have been given a great commission to fulfill, and Jesus has not called us to be people who love to sleep and never accomplish anything. We have taken time off from our jobs, for we are very serious about why we are here. We have all been hired to read our Bibles and learn what is written in the Word of God. Therefore, we must arise from our beds early as workers worthy of our hire.

I believe many people rise at six and many at seven and perhaps some as late as eight. Of course, this is an individual decision, and so we shall compromise and for an example, we shall choose to rise at seven, even though six would be better.

I might add that studies have been made wherein it has been determined that the people who go to bed early, and then get up early, do live longer than people who sleep later during the day, and stay up later at night. It is because I know that our loving heavenly Father wants the very best for us, that I believe that it is his will that we arise at a time, when we will be most productive for our own good. After all, is this not why day-light saving time was even invented?

It is because of the promise of a new day with my Lord Jesus is greater than is my desire to satisfy my flesh by remaining in bed, that causes me to roll out of bed while I am still quite sleepy. I shuffle around and I usually follow a certain routine that I am able to perform, even though I am not yet fully awake.

At home, I begin with feeding my fish, and then my dog and also my cat. Once my animals have been taken care of, I take my prescriptions just as the doctor has ordered. This is followed with heating the water for whatever beverage it is that we normally drink in the morning. While the water is heating, I put on my coat and make a trip to the mailbox on the far side of the road, for the morning newspaper. The large German Shepherd insists that she be allowed to walk with me, for she is afraid that I might go someplace without her.

I am aware that many of the men whom God has chosen to be the shepherds of his flocks would seize upon this opportunity to speak to you about the dangers of drinking coffee and partaking of addictive substances, such as caffeine. However, I am certainly not going to look over anyone's shoulder to see what kind of beverage they are drinking for I consider that to be their private business. However, I do suggest moderation in all things and it is good that we should limit ourselves to not more than two cups.

This is also the time when many people begin their day with a muffin or some other treat from the grocery store, however our habits do vary and I do advise that we limit ourselves to treats that are nutritionally sound and good for us.

I usually switch on the radio and listen to the morning news during this first part of my day, but I believe that we need to strictly limit what we do during this special time. What we allow to enter into our minds during the time when we are seeking to be closer to God than we have ever been, could have an adverse effect and make it more difficult to obtain our goal. Therefore, it might be a better idea that we do examine the morning newspaper, and forget the television, but we must make this decision for ourselves.

By eight o clock or maybe a quarter after, I have turned the radio off and I am now fully awake. I now begin the remainder of the day with prayer, and I do want to explain a little more about this. The reason I do not pray when I first get out of bed, is because I want to be mentally alert, for I consider talking to God to be a very serious thing. This is why I usually wait until I am fully awake, so that I might speak to God as an adult and not as a sleepy child, making childish requests.

This is the time, at the beginning of a new day that we need to bring our burdens to the Lord and lay them down before him. In this way, they will be in his hands and we do not have to carry them around all day. This is the time when we need to pray for our loved ones and those whom we know are in need of our prayers. We pray for their health and for their welfare and we pray that their marriages will last, and that their children will not have to suffer because of a divided home. We also pray for their salvation without ceasing.

Once that is done, we then begin to pray for the new day that is before us, and for what we must do. We must pray that God will help us to use our time wisely, and that within our lives, that God's will, will be done. In light of our present situation, in our own upper room, we ask God to help us as we tarry in that holy place, God's own Holy Word. We ask that God will open up our understanding, just as he once opened up the minds of the twelve apostles, so that they did understand the scriptures.

Finally, we ask God to take control of our minds and allow us to come into his presence, to fill us with his Holy Spirit, and equip us for the job that he has for us to do. We then bring our conversation to an end by thanking him for all that he has done, and also for what he is about to do, in our lives, as we search for him diligently.

Our brother Paul does have this to say to us.

Philippians 4:4, Rejoice in the Lord alway: and again I say, rejoice.

5 Let your moderation be known unto all men. The Lord is at hand.

6 Be careful (do not worry) for nothing; but in every thing by prayer and supplication with thanksgiving let your requests be made known unto God.

7 And the peace of God, which passeth all understanding, shall keep your hearts and minds through Christ Jesus.

Let us not forget the scripture in the book of Hebrews that informed us that we are to believe that God is a rewarder of those who diligently seek him. I believe that it is very important that we begin our day with prayer, for it is one of the ways that we do diligently seek for God, so that we might know his will for our lives.

I once met a woman who believed that God was like a huge computer with many buttons. She believed that if she could only learn where the buttons were and what they represented, she could then push the right buttons, and in doing so, receive whatever it was that her heart desired. Of course, it is obvious that it was her intention to manipulate God. How terribly wrong she was, for our God is not like that and he cannot be manipulated by clever men and women.

He does know all things, and knows at all times, the intent of our thoughts and the contents of our hearts. We must never think that we can twist God's arm, through our prayers, for he will give us the things we ask for, if our requests are according to God's word, and for a good purpose.

I say again, our prayer in the morning is a start of day prayer, and it should reflect our concern for the day and what we may do, as it lays before us. We make our needs and requests known and then we close our prayer with a thankful attitude, always remembering to mention we ask in Jesus name..

By eight-thirty, we are ready to begin reading our Bibles, starting in the book of Genesis.

Perhaps someone will ask, What about breakfast? I do believe that during this very special time we should limit our eating to two meals a day. We will not be engaging in any strenuous activity and I am sure that we can survive, very well on just two meals each day.

Someone will ask, if less is better, wouldn't it be better for us to fast during this time, that we are seeking the Lord? I am reminded of the wisdom of Solomon who said there is a time given for all things. I do not believe that this would be a good time for fasting. Perhaps later, after you have received the baptism in the Holy Ghost, you will want to learn about fasting, and I am aware of what Jesus did say. He said when you fast, not if you fast, so I do not have any doubt but what you will fast later, but not now.

If you have never fasted before, let me just explain to you what will likely happen. On the very first day when you begin fasting, your flesh and namely your stomach will begin to scream in a very loud voice, "Please give me something to eat, for I am starving and I need food." The voice of the flesh will become increasing louder and more demanding as the day wears on, and the overall effect the voice of the flesh will have on you, is that it will become extremely hard to retain the knowledge of what you are reading. The voice of the flesh will give you no peace until you give in and meet the demands of the flesh.

It has been my experience, that on the second day of fasting, that the voice and demands of the flesh are much louder. It will scream at you with all of it's might for quite a long while, and then it will try another way. It will seek your sympathy and cry unto you in a pitiful small voice and beg for someone to please just give it a tiny morsel of food to sustain it, for it will try to convince you that you are weak and even dizzy, from lack of food. Of course, This is not really true, but the voice of the flesh is very persistent and will not allow you to have any peace. It is not until the third day, that the voice of the flesh becomes much quieter, and it is then that you begin to realize that you have taken control and that the flesh must obey you, from this point on. I do not recommend that any should fast at this time, for it would hinder us more than it would help.

I do recommend that we begin reading as though we mean business, having had an early morning snack, we should devote at least two solid hours to reading in the book of Genesis. I do think it would be wise and a good idea to have before us on the table, a tablet and pen for taking notes, a highlight marker, for marking scriptures we feel are important. And I think it would be good to include a dictionary, for very few people have such a good command of the English language that they truly do understand every word in the bible.

I suggest that we begin reading, while keeping notes in the tablet so that we might note what the main subject of each chapter is about. I would suggest that we do it in such a way that we could form an outline of each book of the Bible by studying our notes.

However, I do not want you to become so involved in taking notes that it slows down your reading a great deal. I realize that somewhere in between there is a middle of the road approach, so that our notes pick up the theme and important events, but do not reflect every little detail.

In the same way, I believe certain scriptures will leap out and grab your attention, in which case you should underline them with your special highlighting marker. In this way, they are easy to find when you want to return to them, at a later time. My Bible is marked in such a way from one end to the other and I know many people whose Bibles are marked the same way. I do consider this marking of important scriptures to be very important for the child of God who is a student of the Bible. Are we not all students?

I want you to pay attention to what happens, so that you will follow the story right from Adam and Eve, to Abraham and Isaac, and on to Jacob and Esau, and right on down to Moses. These are beautiful stories and they are even a bit complicated with many small details that are also important. However, altogether they form the history of the Patriarch's and it is one that we all need to know.

There are educated men, with many degrees after their names, but if they have never read the entire Bible from cover to cover, I consider them to be totally ignorant of what is most important. When we consider the long history of Almighty God, Creator of the universe and the record of his ongoing communication with mankind, it is hard to understand how anyone with any intelligence whatsoever would refuse to read it.

Long before we come to the story of Moses, your stomach will inform you that it is time to eat. Let us then put down our reading, and then go out to eat. The time should be in between breakfast and lunch. However, this is to our advantage for in most restaurants we are offered the choice of eating either breakfast or lunch, whichever we may prefer.

I do advise you to eat well and eat healthy, but do not eat too much. I also do suggest that we think of our food as being something light and not too heavy on our stomach. I suggest that before you feel completely full, that you stop eating. There is an important reason why I do suggest this. When we eat too much, we become lethargic, and even sleepy. This is because it takes a great deal of blood and energy to digest all of the food we have just eaten. I believe this is why in many countries there is the custom of taking a short siesta, or nap, after the noon time meal.

We must keep in mind that we have a very important job to do, and only so much time to do it. We are children of the light, and therefore, we do not take afternoon naps during this time, when we are reading the Bible. Maybe I should say that I do not recommend it, for we must take our work seriously. There is a great deal of land within the Bible that needs to be possessed and we must do our best to claim as much of it as possible, while we are in our upper room.

Therefore, it is good that we walk briskly to and from the restaurant, for it gets our hearts pumping and the blood flowing, and some will flow to our brains and will help us to be mentally alert. We must not forget that this is our very first day on this job and we do not want our new employer to think that we are lazy, and not capable of reading and understanding what we read, nor are we the type of people who get very little accomplished after we eat.

We return to the task at hand, and we begin to read and we become so involved in the story, that we are not even aware of how fast time is flying by. After we have been reading steadily for several hours, I suggest that we stop and take time out for afternoon prayer. Perhaps about two-thirty or three o'clock.

Our morning prayer was a start of day prayer, but our afternoon prayer shall be a little different. We must make a sacrifice of praise, and praise God for what he has done. We need to thank him and praise his holy name. We must thank him for His Holy Word, and thank him for the knowledge we are being given. We thank him for what he did at Calvary, and we thank him for Pentecost. We thank him for the promises of His Holy Word, and we thank him for loving us, and revealing himself unto us. We need to lift up our hands toward heaven and praise him, for he is worthy of being praised.

I now offer you these selected verses from the writing of King David, who knew about the value of worshipping God and offering up to him who is holy, a sacrifice of praise.

Psalms 146:1, Praise ye the Lord. Praise the Lord, 0 my soul.

2 While I live will I praise the Lord: I will sing praises unto my God, while I have my being.

Psalm 149:1, Praise ye the Lord, Sing unto the Lord a new song, and his praise in the congregation of his saints.

2 Let Israel rejoice in him that made him: Let the children of Zion be joyful in their King.

3 Let them praise his name in the dance: let them sing praises unto him with the timbrel and harp.

4 For the Lord taketh pleasure in his people: he will beautify the meek with salvation.

5 Let the saints be joyful in glory: let them sing aloud upon their beds.

6 Let the high praises of God be in their mouth, and a two edged sword (Bible) in their hand;

I now suggest again, that we raise up our hands toward heaven and toward his throne of grace, and praise our Lord, for he is worthy of being praised.

When we have finished praising God with our voice, and a brief rest from the work we are doing, we then return to our reading and read and take notes until dinner time. However, I do hope that you have been able to read and study until at least five PM. and that you have chosen a place to stop reading that is at the end of a chapter. We must do our best to keep at it, for there are many pages to read and notes to take.

Of course, it is good to take a shower and freshen up before dinner, and change clothes. Again it is good to eat a good and healthy meal, even if it is a bit later than usual, and if it is possible, get in some walking to stretch the legs and help our digestion as well.

Perhaps a walk through the mall might be good, but I do not advise doing any shopping at this time, for I want our attention to be on what we have been reading. I want us to indeed tarry in a holy place, and I do not want us to allow our minds to wander off into those areas that are pleasing to the flesh but are not of the spirit.

When you return to the room, I suggest that you forsake watching television, and do listen to Christian music instead. It is possible that some of the things we might see on television, including many commercials is of a type and quality that pollutes the temple of

God, that temple being within our minds. Remember that the people in Moses's day had to wash their clothes, and we must not allow anything to invade our minds, during this time of coming into the presence of God, that does not belong there.

The Word of God, as we read all day, does wash our minds, but we must do our part to keep our minds clean, in the evening, before we go to bed.

As we are resting after dinner, listening to inspiring Christian music, we might want to review our notes. In this way we can think about how much we have learned.

I am sure that because our dinner tasted very good, and because we ate a little too much, we soon become sleepy, and we turn back the covers and call it a day, even as we are listening to the very spiritual and uplifting music.

It is only right that even as we began our day in prayer and communication with our heavenly Father who does love and care for us, so must we conclude our day in prayer. We kneel down beside the bed and begin to tell our heavenly Father how very thankful we are, that he has made it possible for us to enter into our own personal upper room. We thank him, for we can feel him drawing us ever closer to him, as we study His Holy Word. We thank him for all that he has done, and we thank him for the promise of the power we will be given, from on high. At this time, we can be very sure, that we shall receive it, not many days from now.

Our brother Paul does have a very short word of advice for us, concerning prayer.

1st Thessalonians 5:16, Rejoice evermore.

17 Pray without ceasing.

18 In everything give thanks: for this is the will of God in Christ Jesus concerning you.

To pray without ceasing means that we are to develop a regular routine of praying and communicating with our God, who is our Father, and do it every single day. If we are ever to complete our great commission, we must not forsake these times of prayer, for it is our very lifeline between us and God. It is also very important to keep this prayer line to God in working order during the time we are in our own upper room, for it was the example that was set before us, not only by the twelve apostles, but set before us by Mary, the mother of our Lord Jesus as well.

Looking back in review, we began with the start of day prayer, when we laid our burdens down and prayed for the welfare of others. We also prayed for the day before us, that all may go well, and that we will accomplish what needs to be done.

Then there was the mid-afternoon prayer, and it was a sacrifice of praise. There is a great deal that we need to praise God for, he is the only one who has always known what the future will be, even from the beginning. He is the one who has created all things, and then because he loves us so much, kept an appointment with death, so that we might live. He is truly worthy of our praise.

We then returned to business at hand of reading and learning the story of the Bible.

Now, as the day has come to an end, as we have been listening to some very inspiring and uplifting music, we finish our day by giving thanks unto God for all that he has done and all that he will do for us and others. It is appropriate that at the close of the day, we tell our loving heavenly Father how much we do love him and how very thankful we are that he has chosen us, to be his children.

In the night time, and as our head is upon the pillow, we begin to dream about the places and situations we read about in the pages of scripture. Even though we might not be fully aware of it, even now, as we sleep, our heavenly Father is watching over us and the Holy Spirit is within our minds in a greater volume than ever before. We have spent many hours reading about the people of the Bible and the word we have received into our minds is the Living Word, and it is Spirit.

Chapter 34 Remaining in Upper Room

꧁

Day Two
We now begin day two of our tarrying in a holy place. The main difference between day two and the first day, is we now recognize little things that we need to improve. Perhaps we need to move the table to a different location, closer to the window, or maybe today we will choose clothes that are more comfortable. It is on day two that we are able to make some little improvements and therefore, day two should be even more productive than was day one.

We again follow the same routine we established the first day, and because we are not lazy but are workers worthy of our hire, we roll right out of bed with a joy in our heart. We are absolutely sure that what we are doing is clearly the will of God. As we go about our early morning routine we might find that within our heart is a melody, and it is a melody of love for our Lord Jesus.

We are somewhat surprised, because we are not our usual and grumbling self, but actually feel good about getting up early and getting started. In this way, we begin to hum the melody as we take our start of day shower, and choose our clothes for the day.

We again begin with prayer, and perhaps we are a little surprised because on day two, we find more things to pray about than we did on day one. This is only natural, for on day two, we are ever so little changed from the person we were on day one. It is because the Word of God which we are consuming, is ever so slightly changing us, even though we are not really aware of it.

Today, we are a little better prepared for the idea of eating only two meals a day, and so we have been to the lobby this morning, where they were serving a variety of early morning beverages and several different breakfast rolls and cookies.

Having now returned to the room, we are now ready to begin the job we have been hired to do, and so we begin reading and taking notes, doing our very best to learn the history of the people whom God called to be separate from all nations on earth. I have no doubt that for some, such reading and studying will remind them of when they were in college, and had to prepare for exams. For others, it is a new experience, but as the story of Israel begins to unfold, they may find that it is better than any movie they ever did see. Of course, it is only natural that as we are reading, scenes from such movies as "The Ten Commandments" will come to mind, for we are now reading the scriptures upon which the movies were based.

There is one thing I want to make very clear to you. The routine I have described to you, is meant to help you, with the goal being, to read and understand book after book. However, I am sure that many people might not want to follow the same exact routine that I have described. That is perfectly alright, for we are not all the same and neither do we think exactly alike.

For example, some people might find it very hard to read and study in the afternoon without first taking a small nap. For some, it is likely their eyes will need a rest from so much reading and they may need to close them for a little while.

Again I say, we are not all the same and I do understand this. I see nothing wrong with taking a little nap, or a rest from your reading, providing you do not turn away from what we are doing, in order to replace it with something else. When it comes to spiritual matters, there is something I want for you to think about.

If you should happen to find reading the Bible to be boring, and you want to do something else. Should you happen to want to switch on the television to watch one of your favorite daytime shows, or perhaps put on your bathing suit and linger by the pool, there is a price you must pay. To do any of these things means that you have failed to follow in the example we have been given, and will not receive the reward for tarrying in a holy place.

Think for a moment about that day on the mount of Olives, when Jesus gave his disciples his last instructions, and was then taken up to heaven, even while they were watching. Those men who were there, did not dilly dally along the way, but proceeded to go directly to the upper room, because they had business that needed to be taken care of.

However, the record will show that they remained there and that they were all of one accord. It is interesting that the record also shows that they were not alone for there were about one hundred and twenty who remained there with them, including women and specifically, Mary, who was the mother of Jesus.

I certainly do believe that all of these people were well aware that this meeting was not an ordinary meeting, but was an extra-ordinary meeting. It was a very special meeting, and I do not believe that any of them, during the entire ten days they were there, ever got bored, or decided to go for a swim down at the pool, or went shopping for new clothes.

If it be possible that you do not want to follow in the example of such men as Simon Peter, and James, and John, and the rest of the twelve men chosen by our Lord Jesus Christ, then consider this.

Do you think that it is right that you should follow in the example that has been set before you by the woman who was a virgin, when she became a mother? The woman who is the mother of our Lord. I then say unto you, that Mary, the mother of Jesus has set the example that all women should follow. She tarried in the upper room for ten days and then she received the baptism in the Holy Ghost and did speak in tongues, for it is written in the pages of scripture that she did.

Let us then continue on, and be aware that on the second day, we are closer to receiving the promise than we were on the first day. We continue on and we are getting deeper and deeper into the scripture and are learning of how God continued to communicate with Israel, even though they did stumble along the way.

Eventually, we find ourselves on top of mount Nebo with Moses as he looks upon the promised land that he will not be allowed to enter.

As we think about why, we realize that even in this story, there is a warning for us. In some ways, we are similar to those people for we have come out of Egypt (sin), and we are on our way to the promised land but we have not yet arrived. There are still many dangers and pitfalls, before us, and the war our spirit is having with our flesh continues. It is true that we are often tempted, but we are sure that we will have victory, for we are here in our upper room, tarrying in a holy place, until we receive the power from on high.

We are standing on the promises of God, and we are studying the Word of God, so that we might learn just what those promises are. We are learning that with the promises of God are the conditions of God, for unless the conditions are met, we can not claim the promises.

There is a little song that is often sang in church, which states, "Every promise in the book is mine... Every chapter, every verse, every line." Of course, this is not true unless we meet the conditions, and few there be that understand what they are. In this way, they sing the song, but if we were to ask them about the conditions, they would not know what we are talking about.

By day three, we realize that something is beginning to happen to us, and we are not sure of just what it is. The presence of the Lord is very strong, upon us, and it remains with us, even when we leave our room to eat. Do not be afraid, for it must have been the same way for those who there on that day of Pentecost, so long ago.

We must continue on, reading and studying, and learning as much as we can. We now spend more time in prayer, down on our knees, and we are so very thankful that God is now revealing himself to us in such a powerful way. I must advise you that as wonderful as this is, this closeness to God, it is still not the baptism in the Holy Ghost for that is yet to come.

It is as though we have come to the mountain of God, and we have spent three days washing our minds with the water of the word. We are now clean enough to approach even closer to a completely righteous and holy God, and he has reached down to us from the mountain, and he is drawing us ever closer to him. The experience has left us speechless, for we are unable to find the words to describe how we feel. And yet, there is more to come.

We must not stop now and we must not turn back, for we are as soft clay in our Master's hands. We pray each day, thanking him for this opportunity to come into his presence. We are very thankful for we know that the promise, even as it was first given by the prophet Joel, is very close to being fulfilled.

Each afternoon, we kneel down and we lift our hands in praise, praising God for his mighty works and for his excellent greatness. We praise him, for having created us in his own image, and we praise him for laying down his holy life, that ordinary sinners could be born again.

We praise him for Pentecost, and for what took place on the day when three thousand souls were converted to Christ. We praise him for sharing with us, his magnificent power, for it will help us to fulfill our great commission. We praise him, for he first loved us, even before we loved him. We praise him because he is worthy to be praised, and because, we who are the children of God, have been given the honor of praising him.

We continue on through day four and day five and day six. Oh how great is our knowledge becoming, for we now know things we never knew before. What a very humbling experience it is, to really begin to understand the story of the Bible and begin to understand that even from the beginning, God had a plan.

I will now share with you a plan for reading and learning the Bible. Of course, our first goal was to read the first five books of the Bible, for they are called the books of Moses. In them, the character and personality of God is rather well defined. We should soon become aware as we read this portion, that God is both holy and completely righteous and he always was and always will be.

We then proceed to read Joshua and Judges and when we are through, we read the short book of Ruth which might not seem important to us now, but will become important later.

Next, we read from first Samuel, straight through to and including second Chronicles. Of course, this will take quite a while. I do advise you to pay attention to the life of King David, for at first you might very well not like him, but in the end we come to know that not only has he been chosen by God, he is also a prophet of God.

By the time we have finished reading second Chronicles, we should see how God did keep his promises to Israel. How true is that scripture that does say, "The wages of sin is death." Yes, Israel certainly did receive the wages that was due her, just as another nation is close to receiving her wages.

I then want us to read the books of Ezra and Nehemiah, and we realize that our God is a God of new beginnings. How very heart breaking it must have been, to send away the sons and daughters and foreign wives, they were not allowed to bring with them. Not much is said about this, but I can understand how very hard it must have been. Still, there can be no question but what it was the will of God, and we cannot dispute that it was.

When you have finished reading the book of Nehemiah, then I am going to suggest something very different. The story line that we have been following does come to an end here, and we must take it up in the New Testament. Now if it were just a matter of history, I would suggest that you obtain the books of the Macabees, that is contained in my Jerusalem Bible, but perhaps another time. We shall not concern ourselves with that at this particular time.

There is about a five hundred year gap in time, between Nehemiah and the gospel of Matthew, but let us not forget, what we are doing is for a reason. Therefore, I do suggest that you read one at a time, the four gospels. Take your time, read slowly, and try to understand as much as you can, the words and teachings of our Lord, Jesus Christ.

When you have finished reading the four gospels, then continue on, reading first the Acts of the apostles, and then the epistles, one after another, and the book of Revelation as well. I am well aware that before you ever reach the book of Revelation, the Holy Ghost will have come upon you, and you will be filled with the power from on high.

Even so, I will continue with this plan for reading the Bible for to continue reading is to remain in a holy place. When you have finished reading the book of Revelation, then we must return to the prophet Isaiah, and begin to read the many different books of the prophets. Please do take the time to notice when and where each of these prophets did live, and try to keep them in chronological order within your mind. In this way, we become aware of when the prophecy was first given and in many cases we should be aware of when they were fulfilled. We continue to read and keep notes, right on through the book of Malachi.

When the books of the prophets have been read, I have no doubt that the time of your vacation will have come to an end. Even so, I do suggest that you next read the book of Job, which is a very deep and complicated book, and a very interesting one, I might add. Of course, Job lived during the time of the Patriarchs and before the Exodus. This means that Job is one of the oldest books in the Bible.

I then suggest reading both Ecclesiastes and Proverbs, and be sure to have your marking pen handy, for you will find many scriptures that do speak to you.

In this way, we have saved the Psalms of David for last. Do read them, and try to remember the troubled life that David did live. The problems he had within his own family and his love for his friend, the son of the man who sought to destroy him. The many enemies who were constantly seeking to kill him, and the mental torment he must have endured.

In a way, the Psalms are very much different than any other scriptures in the entire Bible. Even in the face of great adversity, David found the time to lift up his hands to heaven and praised God with all of his heart. He also found the time to record his thoughts, so that we might learn of them, also, and be blessed.

Much of the Bible is God speaking to mankind, but the Psalms are more like mankind, worshipping and praising and speaking to God.

Some observant person will notice that I have left out the books of Esther and the Song of Solomon. I do suggest that you do read these books later and at your own convenience. Due to the subject matter contained in these two books, I did not consider them to be as important to what we are trying to learn at this time, as I did the rest of the books.

I do hope that this plan for reading the Bible will be helpful to you.

Of course, you could just begin at the beginning and read it straight through, even as I did, the first time I read the Bible from cover to cover.

However, I now find it easier to divide the Word of God into sections, and in that way, it does seem to make my goal of reading each section easier to obtain. In this way, I do not look clear to the top of the mountain, but only to the part I intend to climb today. When tomorrow comes, I shall again look up to the second level and that portion I will climb on the second day. It is when I complete each step, one at a time, that the overall task of climbing the mountain does not seem to be nearly as difficult. By and by, I shall come to the summit, and that is when I discover that climbing this mountain was not nearly as difficult as I once thought it was, for it was conquered one stage at a time.

I believe this method does apply to all of our goals in life, for we must begin in the right direction, and continue to take one step at a time, and by faith, we are confident we will reach our destination, as long as we keep on putting one foot in front of the other. We must not stop and we are not to look back, for that is what Lot's wife did, and she failed to reach her destination.

Therefore, it is good to have a plan, and I have shared with you, my plan for reading the entire Bible, from cover to cover.

We now return to our daily routine of reading and remaining in a holy place. We have now completed day four, day five, and day six, and day seven is about to begin.

We have now climbed very high up on the mountain, and we are sure that our goal of reading the Bible from cover to cover, is well within our grasp.

We are now experiencing the very closeness of God, and it is as though his great love has descended upon us and has surrounded us like the water of the sea. Even though we have been in our upper room for almost a full week, the love of God gives us joy in our hearts and our joy gives us the strength to continue, and we are eager to do our part.

Our part is to read and learn what is written in our Bibles, so that we should no longer remain ignorant, concerning the truth of God's Holy Word. We have been washing our minds in the water of the

Word of God for many days, and in return, God has revealed himself to us in a mighty way, and none of us, will ever be the same again, for we are changed forever. In ways we cannot see, we have been formed into the likeness of our Lord Jesus.

We now realize more than at any time in our entire life, that our mighty God, is also a God of tender mercy and love without measure, and we are completely submerged in his love, and it flows through us like a river. We are in the privacy of our own upper room, and we are completely alone with God, and it is as though God has given us his undivided attention.

As we continue to feed upon the Word of God, it is as though we are walking on air, and our feet do not hardly touch the ground.

Some will no doubt think that they have now received the baptism in the Holy Ghost, but I do advise you there is more that is yet to come. Our God is an all knowing, and all powerful, omnipotent God, and I can not tell you just when you will receive the baptism in it's fullness. I can assure you that you will know, for it is an experience that you will never forget, as long as you live.

The Holy Spirit of God will sweep over you and cover you completely, and will then enter into your innermost being and shall flow through you, and through every vein and blood vessel in your entire body, and you will know then, that the very life and presence of God is in your blood.. There is no experience known to man that can duplicate it or even come close to what I am trying to describe, for it surpasseth my ability and my limited vocabulary to do so. This divine experience is so glorious and so magnificent, that you will want it to last forever for you are completely overwhelmed and speechless.

Even after you have received the fullness of the baptism in the Holy Ghost, you will want to continue in the Word of God to complete what you originally set out to do. There is a great reward for those who have read their Bibles from cover to cover, and that reward is now and forever. There is not a day that goes by that I am not thankful for the Word of God and what it has done for me. It is truly the treasure of free men.

Chapter 35 The Jealousy of Esther

Words of Advice
When you have finished your stay in your upper room, and have returned home to family and friends, you may be in for a surprise. Some of the people who know you will soon discover that there is something very different about you. In fact, do not be surprised if some are even a little afraid of you, for the Spirit of God within you, does seem to intimidate some people.

I am reminded of Moses, when he returned from the mountain the second time, for he had to wear a veil, for his countenance was changed. I am quite sure that none of us will need to wear a veil, but do be aware that when we tarry in the presence of God as we have, you will never be quite the same as you were,

for you will be changed forever. This change will make some people feel quite uncomfortable and they will avoid you. Do not let this bother you but instead, be glad.

I firmly believe that the baptism in the Holy Ghost that was experienced by the one hundred and twenty who tarried in Jerusalem, until they received the power from on high, was in greater measure than was those who did receive it by the laying on of hands. Of course, I am aware that the apostle Paul did receive it by the laying on of hands, but who is to say that Paul did not tarry in his own upper room, at a later time and place?

Please do understand me, for I do not find any fault with those who have received it by the laying on of hands, but I am aware that our God is a rewarder of those who diligently seek him.

Our God does not need to ask the permission of religious men, for he is able to bestow his rewards upon us, as he chooses to. It is the same for the gifts of the Spirit, for God is able to give us, the gifts we will most need in the ministry we are called to do.

This brings us to the question, will we then, speak in tongues? I believe that some, and perhaps many will speak in tongues, but certainly not all. However, I do not believe you will speak in tongues during the time when you are receiving the fullness of the baptism. It was during that time, and the same for my wife, that we found ourselves to be completely powerless and without speech. We were both aware that the Holy Spirit had filled us to over flowing and we were unable to even move or do anything, for we were completely under the control of the Spirit which did totally possess us. This experience was not of short duration but did last for many hours and through out the night.

I do believe that it is possible that afterward, and maybe at the time of the afternoon prayer, you will feel a great desire to praise God, even as we have been doing, every afternoon. However, this time might seem to be a little different and it is as though you do not have the normal control over your speech you usually do have. You might even experience some trembling and it is causing you to stutter and you cannot seem to gain control of it. If this should happen to you, remember, you are still in your upper room, and there is no one there but you and God.

God does understand, exactly how you do feel, so just open up your mouth, and let the words come out. Do not worry about what they sound like, for God is able to understand them. Just continue to praise God as you have been doing, and rejoice, for God has smiled upon you.

I do advise you, that after you return home, you take a little time each day to be alone with God and tell him about how you feel about him. We are to praise our God continually, for he is worthy of being praised and because this great honour has been given unto us. I would advise you that you do not suppress the strange sounding words that come out of your mouth, but offer them up to God, as a sacrifice of praise.

Then I would remind you of the instructions we were given by our brother Paul. He said that if we have received the gift of speaking in tongues, then we should pray and ask God to give us also, the gift of interpretation, so that we may edify the body of Christ.

If you do not receive the gift of speaking in tongues, and in fact, do not seem to be aware of any of the gifts of the Spirit, do not be overly concerned. If you have tarried in the holy place, and have indeed, felt the fullness of the Spirit, as he has made himself known to you, you are still in God's hands.

You can be sure that as long as you do walk close to our Lord, that he is preparing you for your ministry. There are a great many ways that we are called to minister unto others, and we are not all called to perform the exact same service.

We are not all apostles and we are not all evangelists. We are not all pastors and prophets. However, we have all been called to be humble servants and there are many ways we can serve our God and our fellow man. We must learn to be lead by the Spirit and we must learn to recognize that still, small voice. We must learn to trust God and we must learn to be obedient in all things. Do not be worried, for in due time, God will make it known to you, what he has for you to do. In the meantime, we must follow the instructions we have been given in the Word of God.

We must not neglect our salvation, and we must not forsake the assembling of ourselves together in these last days. Let us not forget that our heavenly Father is equipping us with what we will need to be of service and is preparing us for eternity. We must pray without ceasing and remember the promise of our Lord and Savior that he will not leave us or forsake us.

I now have a few instructions for those who are unable to take time off from work, and who can not afford the cost of traveling to another city, much less the cost of a motel room for a week or more. It was shortly after the Lord had made it known to me, that he was calling me to be a servant, that I knew that I must read and study the Bible, for it was what the Lord wanted me to do. There was a great desire in my heart to read every word and to learn as much as I possibly could. I might add, there are no shortcuts, for the only way to know the Word of God, is to read and study the Word of God.

I began to do this, late in the fall, when the fishing season had just ended, and I was able to tie my boat up, and spend some time at home. We also lived quite a distance from town, and since I had become a Christian, I no longer had the visitors I once had. Our home was very quiet, and so I was able to spend many hours each day, reading and studying the Bible.

At this time, my wife, who had also become a Christian at almost the same time, was working and she continued to work, just as she has done through out her life. Each morning, she would arise early and go off to work, and I would stay home and read chapter after chapter in my Bible.

When the day was over, she would come home and together, we would eat the dinner that I prepared. After dinner, I would again take up my Bible and resume my reading and studying. Now the effect of all my studying was that I was completely ignoring my wife, even though I really did not mean to.

Her attitude suggested that perhaps she was a little hurt by the absence of my normal attention she had always received. It was a little like I had taken up some strange new hobby and I no longer had any time for her, for I found my new hobby to be much more interesting.

In fact, on more than one occasion she said something to me that suggested that her feelings were a little hurt. After all, it did not seem fair for her to go off to work all day, and then return home to a husband who hardly had anything to say to her.

As soon as dinner was finished, I would return to my Bible and would completely forget about everything else, for nothing was more important to me, than preparing myself to be ready to serve my God, for I had been called.

I assured her that I loved her very much and I explained to her how very important it was for me to read and understand the entire Bible. I am quite sure that she did understand to some degree, but even so, her feelings of being abandoned for a book did remain.

She then decided to fight fire with fire, and she went to the book store and she purchased for herself, a copy of the very same Bible I was reading. It is called, "Good News" and some are called good news for modern man. Her's was a soft cover edition and mine is a deluxe hard cover edition I received from my younger brother.

I think that it is possible, that even as I spent many hours each day, completely immersed in God's word, so did the Word of God begin to change me, and my wife was able to notice this change. It is possible that she became ever so slightly jealous, for it was obvious to her that I was receiving something she did not have.

It is for this reason, that just as soon as she arrived home each day, she would bury her nose within her copy of the "Good News" Bible and it remained there until it was time for her to go to bed.

I often stayed up much later, reading and studying, and then I would come to bed after she had been sleeping for several hours. In this way, we hardly even seen each other, even though we were both living in the same house.

There is one thing I want to make clear to you. During this time, after my wife began studying her own Bible, she no longer watched television, for the focus of all of her attention, was to be just as knowledgeable and as well read in scripture as I was. She knew beyond any doubt that something was happening to me, and she wanted to have whatever it was, that I was receiving.

When the power of God came upon me, I was aware of it and there was no denying it. At the same time, I realized that my wife was covetous of what I was receiving, and I did not want to make her jealous, and I hardly knew what to do. Therefore, I continued to read and study, and so did she, and about the only time we did see each other or communicate was at the dinner table.

I do not know if it was because I did not want to hurt my wife by causing her to know I had received something from the Lord that she had not, I really do not know. However, when I did receive the fullness of the baptism in the Holy Ghost, it seemed as though it was something very personal and just between me and God. It did not include anyone else, for no one else was involved.

As I have already described to you, the closeness to God did last for several days, and then when the fullness of the complete baptism in the Holy Ghost did come upon me, it lasted for many hours and through out the night.

I did not want to hurt my wife or make her jealous in any way. I was afraid that she would not understand me should I try to explain it all to her. I could not very well explain it to her, for you see, I was not really sure myself, of what was happening to me. I was not aware of the promise, nor was I aware that I had been tarrying in a holy place. What had happened to me came as a complete surprise and having never read the scriptures before, I must confess that I was ignorant of such things. It was for this reason that I never told even a soul, for I regarded what happened to me as my very own private business. I realized that God had filled me with his presence, and that I had been blessed beyond measure.

I knew beyond any doubt that I was not worthy in any way of such a tremendous blessing. I did not know why God had chosen to bestow such a precious gift on me.

I finished reading my "Good News" Bible and eventually my wife finished reading hers. The main difference was that it did take her a good deal longer, as she went to work each day and could not read until evening.

Even though the powerful presence of the Lord did remain with me for quite some time, eventually my life began to return to it's normal patterns and so did my wife Esther's. Once more we began to do all of the normal things we did together, and if anything, we were closer that we had ever been. Our lives were very rich, for we were now aware of the promises of God, and we were beginning to experience the joy of more abundant living with Jesus, our Lord in control.

It was not until several years later that I did explain to her, how I did receive the baptism in the Holy Ghost, even as I was spending so many hours each day reading and studying God's word. I described in detail to her, how the Holy Ghost had come upon me, and how I had been speechless in my bed.

She listened to every word I said, and her dark eyes opened wide, as though she was surprised by what I was telling her. She then informed me that she had experienced the very same thing, and that even though she did try to speak, the power of God upon her was so great that she was unable to speak. She went on to describe in every detail, the very same experience that I had, and then I knew, God did not favor one of us more than the other.

Even though my wife had to work each day at her regular job, she received the very same baptism in the Holy Ghost as I did, for God was aware that she was covetous of what I was receiving. What is more, she did her very best to remain in a holy place, as she did read her Bible from cover to cover, even though it did take her quite a bit longer.

I would remind you that Esther did not watch television nor did she go shopping for I did all of the grocery shopping that needed to be done. When she was not at work, she was in her own upper room, except for when she was sleeping. She even told me that when she dreamed dreams, they were dreams about the scriptures she had been reading, even as mine were.

I have told you about Esther's experience and how she did receive the baptism in the Holy Ghost, so that you will have hope and so that you may seek the baptism in the same manner as Esther did, even though you cannot afford to take time off from work. God is able to bless those who have to work to earn a living, and if they are willing to forsake all else, and do remain in the holy place until they have received power from on high, they will be blessed beyond measure.

The promise that was given, both by the prophet Joel and by our Lord to his disciples and the one hundred and twenty faithful souls who did remain in Jerusalem until the holy day of Pentecost, does extend to us as well.

The promise can be yours if you are willing to do your part and are willing to tarry in the pages of your holy Bible, until you receive the power from on high. The way has been made known to you and now the rest is up to you. There simply is no question but what God will do his part if you do yours for God has always kept all of his promises and this is why I have been called to share this knowledge with you.

May God bless you in the same mighty way that he has blessed my wife and I. May we never forget to praise his holy name.

Chapter 36 The Engrafted Word

Ark

The Bible does tell us the story of two different arks, the first one being Noah's ark, and the second ark being the ark of the covenant, or sometimes described as the ark of the testimony. The first ark was a place of safety and a refuge for the animals and for the family of Noah, when God destroyed the life he had created by the waters of the great flood.

Only a few people realize it but the second ark and what it contains is also a safe place and a refuge for all who have turned to the Lord in these latter days. When the day of God's great wrath does arrive, and the missiles of great destruction begin the job they were intended to do, we need to have the contents of the second ark firmly planted in our hearts.

Even now, in this year of 1998, I can hear the drums of war announcing the news that two more nations have been added to the list of those capable of engaging in nuclear warfare. In a little while, the nuclear winds shall blow across this land and the food supply for both man and beast shall be cut off.

In America there are many guns and those guns will now be used by the citizens to both protect themselves and to murder others in order to gain their food supply. In that day, from sea to shining sea, death shall reign supreme. Many then will understand the words of Jesus when he informed his disciples that where ever there were dead bodies, there the vultures will be gathered.

How many, O Lord I pray, will have the blood of the lamb over the door frame of their hearts, and how many will know enough to seek that place of refuge within the ark of God?

Let us consider for a moment, that the second ark was made from the wood of the Acacia tree. This wood speaks of an earthly origin and it is a type of Jesus. Jesus was born in the flesh of the virgin, Mary, and the Bible does tell us of her ancestry. In the beginning, God made mankind from the dust of the earth, and the Acacia tree does send it's roots down into the soil of this earth. Therefore, the wooden box of the ark was designed by God but made by man. Is it not the same with Jesus? for he too was designed by God, but came forth from the womb of a woman, just as we all have.

The second thing we notice is that the wooden box of the covenant, was lined with pure gold, and gold is a symbol of the pureness of God. This lining of gold is symbolic of the Holy Spirit, for Jesus was filled with the Spirit of his Father without measure.

Matthew 3:16, And Jesus, when he was baptized, went up straightway out of the water: and, lo, the heavens were opened unto him, and he saw the Spirit of God descending like a dove, and lighting upon him:

17 And lo a voice from heaven, saying, This is my beloved Son, in whom I am well pleased.

Now the covenant box was not only lined with pure gold, but was also covered with pure gold on the outside. Of course, this speaks of living a Godly life, with the Holy Spirit in control. This is also a description of how Jesus lived his life, for the gold on the outside speaks of how Jesus did appear to others, who knew him. The scriptures do inform us that Jesus lived his life without sin, and the gold covering is symbolic of the pureness of God, being made manifest through the life of our Lord, Jesus Christ.

We shall now look briefly at those items that were kept inside of the ark, and let us not forget that the ark of the covenant did occupy the central place within the inner chamber of the tabernacle, that was known as the Holy of Holies. This very clearly means that while there are some things which are holy, and then there are some things which are more holy. The Bible does describe the area that was behind the veil as being the "Holy of Holies, or in other words, the holiest of all. This means that within all of heaven and earth, there simply was nothing to be found which was more holy.

The first thing we will examine is the golden pot of manna. I believe that the manna represents spiritual food that came down from heaven to nourish God's people. I believe it is symbolic of the pure Word of God that can be found in the Hebrew Bible, our old testament, if you will. It is not that portion of God's word that contains a record of man's sins, but is that portion which is food for our soul.

Jesus had this to say about the manna.

John 6:32, Then Jesus said unto them, Verily, verily I say unto you, Moses gave you not that bread from heaven; but my Father giveth you the true bread from heaven.

33 For the bread of God is he which cometh down from heaven, and giveth life unto the world.

Of course, we should all be able to see that Jesus is talking about himself, and this does indicate to us that Jesus was that Word of God that did feed God's people during old testament times.

We then must consider that the main item within the ark was the two tablets of stone containing the ten commandments. There is so much symbolism here that an entire book could be written about them. However, I do not want to get into this subject so deep that no one can understand for I have no desire to confuse anyone.

Even so, there are two tablets of stone and I believe this is symbolic that they do contain the will of God the Father, as well as the will of his only begotten Son, our Lord, Jesus Christ.

They have the commandments written on them on both sides, and I believe this is symbolic that they are the will of God both in old testament times, and in new testament times, as well. Of course, I believe they are just as important to God this very day as when he first wrote them on tablets of stone.

There were two different sets of tablets for Moses cast the first set down and did break them in his wrath, because he found the children of Israel fully involved in sin, when he returned from the mount. Even though the tablets of stone were broken into many pieces, Moses in his wrath did not destroy the Word of God, which was written on those stone tablets.

I say this for later God did command Moses to hew out two more tablets of stone and to carry them up the mountain and to present them to God. When Moses did as he was commanded, God then wrote his commandments on stone for the second time. This should indicate how very permanent they are for the Bible does inform us that the Word of God shall endure forever.

When God wrote them again on the second set of tablets, I believe this is symbolic of where he promised to write them during the time of the new covenant. You see, God's will is just the same and the main difference is that he has promised to write his law on the tables of our hearts, instead of on tablets of stone.

Let us then be aware that they do contain God's perfect will for all mankind. If everyone in the world lived their lives by God's perfect law, there would be no more wars and there would truly be peace on earth. This is what we pray for when we recite the Lord's prayer, for in reality, we are praying for God's will, the ten commandments to be done on earth as it is in heaven. Let us not forget that this is what Jesus did pray.

The thing I want most for us to grasp is that the ten commandments are an exact description of the life of Christ. They are a road map for our feet, for they do show us exactly how we are to live, if we are to be the faithful followers of Christ. However, let us keep in mind that unless we have truly surrendered to God and have invited our Lord Jesus Christ into our heart, we will find it difficult to allow the commandments to become our way of life. It is only when we are lead by the Spirit to follow in the footsteps of Jesus, that we begin to experience the more abundant life that Jesus promised us.

The 119th Psalm written by David certainly does inform us of how very important they are and may we never forget that God, himself described David as being a man after his own heart.

Let us listen once more to these instructions that were given in regard to the ten commandments.

Deuteronomy 4:2, Ye shall not add unto the word which I command you, neither shall ye diminish aught from it, that ye may keep the commandments of the Lord your God which I command you.

We know that the ten commandments are the life of Christ, for the record does show that Jesus lived his life without sin. This could only be possible by allowing all ten of the commandments to be his way of life, for it is the only way he could remain obedient to his heavenly Father's will at all times.

Let us not forget that Jesus once said to his disciples and to you and me, "Come and follow me, and live your life as I have lived mine."

Those Christians who have insisted upon rejecting one or more of the commandments, having come to the throne of grace seeking forgiveness for their sins, then took out their butcher knives and did cut off one of the fingers from his nail scarred hands. This is what they have done, when they reject the commandments of God, for they have rejected the life of Christ.

Then we come to the third item which was placed within the ark of the covenant and that is Aaron's rod that budded. It is very easy to see that this rod is symbolic of the royal and divine priesthood. It is symbolic of Jesus, who has become our high priest and our mediator.

However, the fact that Aaron's rod not only budded, it also blossomed and did bear fruit. This then is symbolic of the gospel of Jesus Christ, and to be more specific, it is speaking of the red letters in most new testaments. It is symbolic of the words spoken by Jesus, for they too, have budded and blossomed and will bear much fruit.

Of course, I am speaking of those who were once dead in their sins and trespasses but are now alive in Christ Jesus. Yes, Aaron's rod that budded does speak of you and I, for as Jesus has become our high priest, we are that fruit which he will offer up to his heavenly Father.

When we consider the wood of the Acacia tree we can see that it is also symbolic of you and I for we are formed from the material of this earth. We can see that the ark and all that it contains is filled with symbolism pertaining to Jesus. We also know that Jesus will take up residence within our heart when we do invite him with the proper attitude.

The apostle Paul did ask the question, "Know ye not that ye have become the temple of the Holy Spirit?" The inner lining of pure gold does speak of the presence of the Holy Spirit, and of course we do receive the Holy Spirit when Jesus comes into our heart.

The outer covering of pure gold speaks of how we are to appear to others, for it speaks of living a Godly life which we will live if we allow the Holy Spirit to have control.

I would ask you to consider the hundreds and hundreds of missionaries who left their worldly possessions behind and then traveled to some far off place in order to share the gospel of Christ with those people who had no knowledge of salvation. It is from where we now stand that I hope that you can see the outer covering of pure gold that is made manifest in the lives they have lived and have dedicated to God's service.

The golden pot of manna speaks of the pure Word of God in the Hebrew Bible, our old testament, and we know that God wants us to receive it, for it is how we are to come to know him better, and it is how we learn of his promises and his will for our lives. Let us keep in mind that there first had to be an old testament before there could be a new one. It is the foundation upon which the new one is placed.

Aaron's rod that budded, is symbolic of the royal priesthood, and we are now aware that Jesus has become our high priest and mediator between us and God. Being fully aware of this we also know that it is symbolic of every word that Jesus did speak and we are able to read and study them until they are permanently planted in our hearts and our minds.

I want for you to try to trade places with David, following what happened to Uzzah and during the three months that the ark of God remained at the home of Obed-edom. Think about how very precious it is in the eyes of God, that he would even strike a man dead, for being careless about following the instructions regarding the ark. Then also understand that the man was a Levite, which is a type of the men today who have been chosen to deliver the Word of God unto the congregation of the people. God will hold them accountable for the way they have handled and treated his most Holy Word.

Then I want you to understand that the ark of God and all that it contains, and all that it represents, which are the most holy in all of heaven and earth. They are precious and very dear to God, and he wants for you to have all of them as your permanent possession for all of eternity.

Let us learn of this in the scriptures, for it is very clearly the will of God. Perhaps, we should remember that God described a young shepherd boy as being "a man after mine own heart." Later, King David came to realize that within the ark of God was also the love of God for his Creation.

Let us now listen to this promise of God, which promise has now become ours to keep through the blood of Jesus.

Jeremiah 31:33, But this shall be the covenant that I will make with the house of Israel; After those days saith the Lord, I will put my law in their inward parts, and write it in their hearts; and they shall be my people.

After reading and carefully studying this verse, the question we all should be asking, is when will God write his law in our hearts? Did he not say, After those days?

Let us look to the first line of this verse. Notice that God, speaking through his prophet does inform us that he will make a new covenant with the house of Israel. Just who are they? you might wonder. Galatians 3 and verse 29 does inform us that if we belong to Christ, then we have become Israel and shall inherit the promises that God made unto Abraham.

Perhaps you are wondering, after which days? This is fairly simple for he is speaking of after the first covenant had expired. When did it expire? It came to an end when Jesus cried out from the cross "It is finished."

From that time on, God would seek to write his most holy law in the hearts of all born again believers. However, not all Christians would allow him to, for many have rejected his most Holy Word, and have refused to allow the commandments of God to become their way of life. Most of these people are very quick to inform us that they are not under the law but are under grace.

Perhaps they are not aware that soon and very soon, God will keep his promise, for he said that he will not always strive with mankind. Once again, God's saving grace will be withdrawn and the door of salvation will be closed. In that day, a great many people will come to realize how very serious their mistake is, for they did not choose to love God in the three ways that is described in the scripture.

Please do not misunderstand me, for I am not threatening those people. Everyone has the right to decide for themselves for we were created in the image of God, and we are not mindless robots. However, the scriptures do clearly reveal that the reward they will receive will be according to their works, or in other words, according to the lives they have lived.

They have the right to reject God's love if they do choose to. I say this for the commandments of God do show how very much God does care for us, and wants for us to have the very best life that is possible to live. That is the life that Jesus did live as an example for us to follow.

James

I do want us to listen to some very important instructions that were given to the twelve tribes of Israel that were scattered abroad by James, our Lord's brother. However, before we listen to James, perhaps we should listen to Jesus as his words will give us a greater understanding as to what it means to truly love God in the same manner as Jesus. Let us take up the story at verse one.

Matthew 4:1, Then was Jesus led up of the Spirit into the wilderness to be tempted of the devil.

2 And when he had fasted forty days and forty nights, he was afterward an hungered.

3 And when the tempter came to him, he said, If thou be the Son of God, command that these stones be made bread.

4 But he answered and said, It is written (Deut.8:3), Man shall not live by bread alone, but by every word that proceedeth out of the mouth of God.

The first thing I want for us to notice is that Jesus has used his ability to remember and quote old testament scripture as one of his most powerful weapons in this spiritual warfare. However today, we have a new testament and the Bible has become our two edged sword. May we all learn to use it in the same manner as did our Lord Jesus, for it is truly, a mighty weapon.

The next thing we are to take a hold of, is the fact that we do not live by the food which we put in our belly alone. We also need to have spiritual food to sustain our soul. We are more than flesh and blood for we are created in the image of God.

What is this spiritual food that is needed for mankind to live? Jesus very clearly quoted Deuteronomy 8 and verse three, and he said that we are to live by EVERY word which proceedeth out of the mouth of God. There can be no doubt that Jesus is speaking of the Testimony of God, for it is this word which did proceed from the mouth of God. When Jesus stressed the word "EVERY" word, he simply meant that we are not to leave any of the commandments out, for it was this word, which was first spoken by God, before it was written by God, on tablets of stone, twice. I say twice, for it is to remind us that God's perfect will for mankind is just as valid in the new testament as it was in the days of Moses.

Let us now turn to the book of Hebrews and the 8th chapter where we shall hear the words of Jeremiah the prophet repeated.

Hebrews 8:10, For this is the covenant that I will make with the house of Israel after those days, saith the Lord; I will put my laws into their minds, and write them in their hearts: and I will be to them a God, and they shall be to me a people;

I have included this scripture from the letter to the Hebrews to make sure that you realize that this is a promise made to Christians who have come to know our Lord Jesus Christ as their Savior.

Please do be aware that Jesus said we are to live by every word and not just some. A great many Christians today, of their own free will have decided to live by some of the commandments, while others they completely ignore.

John, the disciple of Jesus, had this to say about Christians who did not choose to follow Christ, in keeping all of God's commandments.

1st John 2:3, And hereby we know that we know him, if we keep his commandments.

4 He that saith, I know him, and keepeth not his commandments, is a liar, and the truth is not in him.

I realize that some people today believe that there is a great deal of difference between the commandments of Jesus and the law of

God, the ten commandments. As we go along, the scriptures shall reveal unto us that they are exactly the same, for there is no disagreement between the Father and the Son.

I want for us to listen to James, the Lord's brother as he does inform us of something that few Christians today seem to understand. First of all, I want us to be aware of who his letter is addressed to.

James 1:1, James a servant of God and of the Lord Jesus Christ, to the twelve tribes which are scattered abroad, greeting.

James does say some things which were easy for the children of Israel to understand, for they had a good foundation in the scriptures of the Hebrew Bible. The same was not so for the Gentiles, many of whom claimed to be of Christ, while clinging to their Pagan customs and times of celebration. The true meaning of what James has said remains hidden to many, today.

James 1:21, Wherefore lay apart all filthiness and superfluity of naughtiness, and receive with meekness the engrafted word, which is able to save your souls.

I am sure that most of the Hebrew children would recognize that James was speaking of the ten commandments, and specifically the ten commandments. However, most Christians do not want to believe this, for they would prefer to give this a very broad meaning. To them, the engrafted word could mean any scriptures in the entire Bible, and they do not want it to mean the ten commandments. It is possible that in their hearts, they are still a little rebellious, and do not like being told what to do. Perhaps they have already forgotten the promise they made to God at the cross of Jesus.

I am sure that you are probably wondering how I am so sure that James was speaking of the ten commandments and not some other Word of God? It is because we who have studied the scriptures, as did the people James was writing to, do recognize that James has been influenced by the Psalms of David. Let us now compare the words of David with what James has said.

Psalm 19:7, The law of the Lord is perfect, converting the soul.

James described this same word as "the engrafted word, which is able to save your souls. It should not be too hard to understand that both men are speaking of the same very precious, and most Holy Word of God, which according to the promise, is to be written in the hearts of God's children today.

We then must ask, just how is the ten commandments able to convert us or save our souls? Surely we all know that salvation did not come by the law, but by God's grace and through the blood of his only begotten Son. The scriptures do speak to us very loudly that no one can be made right with God through obeying the law, for it would mean that we are able to earn our salvation.

In order that we better understand both James and King David, who were separated by at least one thousand years, we must look to the first and primary reason the law was given. The first reason is that the ten commandments do reveal to us God's right way of living. They do make very clear how God wants for us to live, for he does not want us to hurt and kill one another, even as Cain did hurt and did slay his brother Abel.

If we would but examine them a little deeper, then we would understand they are actually God's eternal instructions for how we are to love. The first four do instruct us how we are to love our God and the six remaining commandments do instruct us how we are to respect the rights of other people who are also made in the image of God.

The second purpose of the perfect law of God, or the life of Christ, for there is no difference, is to reveal unto us what sin really is. Sin is quite simply rebellion against God and rebellion against his spoken word, which did first occur in the garden of Eden.

We again ask the question, "Just how are the commandments of God able to convert or save our souls?" Surely we have not already forgotten the first step that was necessary for our salvation. We must first become aware that we are all guilty of sin and that we are sinners who are not able to wash away our own sins, and come into the presence of God. It is only when we humble ourselves before the cross of Christ, freely admitting that we are sinners in need of God's saving grace that we do enter into God's one and only plan of salvation.

Therefore, let us not forget that it is by the law of God that we first became aware that we were sinners in need of Christ's life giving blood. It is in this way that the law, the engrafted Word of God has participated in leading us to the cross of Christ.

However, let us listen as James does have more to say about this engrafted word.

James 1:22, But be ye doers of the word, and not hearers only, deceiving your own selves.

23 For if any be a hearer of the word, and not a doer, he is like unto a man beholding his natural face in a glass:

24 For he beholdeth himself, and goeth his way, and straightway forgetteth what manner of man he was.

Because he is not a doer of the commandments, he soon forgets that he is supposed to be a follower of Christ who lived the commandments of God, everyday of his life.

25 But whoso looketh into the perfect law of liberty, and continueth therein, he being not a forgetful hearer, but a doer of the work, this man shall be blessed in his deed.

In what way are the commandments of God the "perfect law of liberty?" Deuteronomy chapter four and verse two have already informed us of how they are perfect in the eyes of God. We have received the commandment that we are not to add anything to them, nor are we to subtract or take anything away from them. In other words, not so much as the dot of an eye, nor the cross of a t is to be taken away from what is perfect in the eyes of God. The ten commandments are absolutely perfect.

We then ask, how are the ten commandments the perfect law of liberty? I believe that it was the apostle Paul in his letter to the Romans that did inform us that "by the law is the knowledge of sin." It is important that we become aware of what sin is for two reasons.

First, is so that we can come before the throne of grace and seek forgiveness for our sins. We all know the promise of God's Holy Word which does say that when we confess our sins, God is faithful to forgive our sins and cleanse us from all unrighteousness. Once our sins have been forgiven, we are free of their burden and do receive liberty. Again we can see that our liberty is by the grace of God and the shed blood of Christ, but it is the perfect law of God that first made us aware that we were in need of it.

It has been said that ignorance is bliss, but to be ignorant of our sinful condition, which we once were, is to remain in bondage to sin, which is death. On the. other hand, to become aware that we are sinners in need of Christ's cleansing blood, is the first step on the path to the cross where Jesus will meet us and take away our burden of sin and guilt and bestow upon us the gift of eternal life.. We should never forget the part that the commandments play in leading us to the place where we do receive our liberty in Christ.

Let us now turn again to the first letter of John who does make a rather plain and easy to understand statement regarding sin.

1st John 3:4, Whosoever committeth sin transgresseth also the law: for sin is the transgression of the law.

We must take hold of this truth for it is a Biblical definition of what sin really is. It is rebellion against God's perfect will, which is revealed unto us through his ten commandments, which were first spoken by God.

Chapter 37 Loving God How?

Receiving James did advise us to receive the engrafted word with meekness, but he did not give specific instructions for how we are to have this thing happen, other than with meekness. This is because he was talking to the Hebrew children and they were very much aware of what he was speaking of and how they were to receive it.

Therefore, we must receive our instructions from our Lord Jesus Christ, and we can be sure that it is his will that we do receive this engrafted word, for he wants us to follow in his footsteps. Let us listen as this question was asked Jesus regarding the commandments of God.

Mark 12:28, And one of the scribes came, and having heard them reasoning together, and perceiving that he has answered them well, asked him, Which is the first commandment of all?

29 And Jesus answered him, The first of all the commandments is, Hear, 0 Israel; The Lord our God is one Lord:

30 And thou shalt love thy God with all thy heart, and with all thy soul, and with all thy mind, and with all thy strength: this is the first commandment.

31 And the second is like, namely this, Thou shalt love thy neighbor as thyself. There is none other commandment greater than these.

I want us to notice that Jesus did inform the man that he was to love God in more ways than one.

I am afraid that if we were to ask most Christians today, what those ways are and to explain them, they would not even know what we are talking about. We might find that there are a great many who do profess to love God with their mouths, but fail to love him in any other way.

Let us now return to the 6th chapter of Deuteronomy, for it will provide us with the rest of the story. Please do be aware that when Jesus answered the man's question he was quoting from this scripture in Deuteronomy and it was one that most Hebrew children were familiar with and knew by heart.

Deuteronomy 6:4, Hear, 0 Israel: The Lord our God is one Lord: 5 And thou shalt love the Lord thy God with all thine heart, and with all thy soul, and with all thy might.

I feel that I should explain a little further what is meant here. To love God with all of our heart, is to love him with our deepest emotion. We are to love him so much that we want to please him with all that we do. Pleasing God should be the utmost desire of our heart and it is through our obedience to his commands, that we do show our love.

To love God with all of our mind and soul, is to love God with all that we are and even to the innermost depths of our being. It is to love God so much, that we even yield our thoughts to his righteousness. We are to continuously try to think and see as Jesus does, and by doing so, become aware of what we are supposed to do.

Finally, to love God with all of our might or our strength is that we are to show our love for God by what we do. We are even to love him with the strength of our actions. Even by the sweat on our brow as we labor to help those who are in need, for charity is certainly the will of God.

There are a great many dear souls who loved Jesus so much that they gave their lives for the sake of the gospel of Christ. Many have died on the foreign mission fields where they lived out their lives in the service to which they were called. A great many others were put to death in every imaginable way. Some were beaten to death while a great many were chained to the stake and burned to death, even while they offered up to God a sacrifice of praise. May our love for our Lord be as strong as their's, if we are ever faced with that decision.

The promise we were given in Deuteronomy is that if we love God in the ways that he has made known that he desires to be loved, he will then write his most precious word in our hearts and it will become our way of life.

6 And these words, which I command thee this day, shall be in thine heart:

Of course, this is speaking of the ten commandments that were given unto the children of Israel on that very day just as it is recorded in Deuteronomy chapter five. This is how we are to receive the engrafted word and it is the same way that so many people of the Bible did receive it.

We must learn to love God in the three ways that he does desire for us to love him, and he will write his most precious and perfect law upon the fleshly tables of our hearts, and it shall remain with us, for all of eternity.

There is an important point I feel we need to make. It is impossible to obey the two great commandments given by Jesus, which is also known as the Royal Law, without receiving the promise of God. If we love God in the ways that Jesus commanded, then the promise of God will be fulfilled in us.

To have the most precious Word of God which did occupy the space between the two cherubims, (which are symbolic of guardian angels), with outstretched wings, within the Holy of Holies; to have that precious Word of God written upon the fleshly tables of our hearts, is a most glorious thing.

We must remember that not only is our loving heavenly Father preparing us for the great and most terrible tribulation known to man, he is also preparing us for what we shall be, for all of eternity.

How true were the words of Isaiah for he informed us that we would not receive all of the knowledge we are searching for in one place within our Bible but that we would find a little here and a little there, and precept must be upon precept and line upon line.

James, the Lord's brother did instruct us to receive with meekness, the engrafted word which is able to save our souls, while it was Moses who did inform us that if we loved God in the three ways he desires to be loved, then God would write his most precious and most Holy Words in our heart. It is important that we realize that once they have been written there, they will have become our way of life.

Even as God has only one plan of salvation and there is only one name by which mankind can be saved, and there is only one name in which we are supposed to be baptized, so is there only one way in which we can receive the engrafted word.

We shall listen once more to the beautiful words that were written by King David.

Psalms 19

7 The law of the Lord is perfect, converting the soul: the testimony of the Lord is sure, making wise the simple.

8 The statutes of the Lord are right, rejoicing the heart: the commandment of the Lord is pure, enlightening the eyes.

9 The fear of the Lord is clean, enduring for ever: the judgments of the Lord are true and righteous altogether.

10 More to be desired are they than gold, yea, than much fine gold: sweeter also than honey and the honeycomb.

11 Moreover by them is thy servant warned: and in keeping of them there is great reward.

I want us to notice that in verse seven, David does say that the law of the Lord is perfect, converting the soul. In verse eleven he does tell us how. It is by the commandments of God that we receive the knowledge of sin, which does convict us and will lead us to repentance, if we allow it to.

Now the same is not so for all ungodly sinners for most are somewhat ignorant of the law, and there are many who are not even aware of what sin is. Of course, Satan rejoices because of this because many will perish because they just do not know. God, speaking through the prophet Hosea did have this to say

Hosea 4:6, My people are destroyed for lack of knowledge: because thou hast rejected knowledge, I will also reject thee, that thou shalt be no priest (pastor) to me: seeing thou hast forgotten the law of thy God, I will also forget thy children.

This very stern warning applies just as much to those who teach and preach the Word of God today, as it once did to the old testament priests of Levi.

So then we can see that the way that the law does convert the soul, is by making us aware that we are guilty of sin, just as the apostle Paul was. Isn't this the very thing that Paul did say? for he was not aware of what sin really was, until the law informed him of it, and he became aware of his own sin.

Once we are aware that we are guilty before God and in need of cleansing, we do know what we are supposed to do, for we have received the instructions that we must confess our sins to our Lord, Jesus Christ, who is our mediator, between us and a completely holy and righteous God and that we must repent.

My object here is not to repeat again the basic instructions for our salvation, but is to expand and increase our knowledge of the second ark and the engrafted word, for we must prepare for what lies ahead.

Jesus did say in Matthew 24 and again in Luke 17 that in these last days, many false prophets shall arise and teach things that are not true. The Lord has brought to my attention that some are twisting the words of the apostle Paul and causing them to say things that Paul did not really say. Their purpose is to bring harm to you, and to rob you of the engrafted word which is your heritage in Christ Jesus. I am sure that it is the Lord's will that I do my best to remove the stumbling stones which they have placed before us.

The apostle Paul, in his letter to the Romans had many things to say regarding the law. In the opening portion of his letter Paul does make a comparison between the Jews who were very familiar with the law of God, and the Gentile converts who were rather ignorant of it.

Let us not forget that Peter has informed us in his second letter that Paul did write some things that are rather hard to be understood.

I believe that this is the case in these scriptures we are about to examine, for many only hear what they want to hear, and are deaf to everything they do not want to hear.

We shall take up the story in chapter three where Paul is continuing with his comparison of Jews versus Gentiles.

Romans 3:9, What then? are we better than they? No, in no wise: for we have before proved both Jews and Gentiles, that they are all under sin;

10 As it is written, There is none righteous, no, not one:

It should be very clear by what Paul has said, that both the Jews and the Gentiles are unclean in the eyes of God. Because our God is completely righteous and completely holy, he cannot stand to be in the presence of either of them because of their sin.

I do ask that you put aside any preconceived ideas and try very hard to understand what Paul is saying. We shall now take up the story at verse .....

19 Now we know that what things soever the law saith, it saith to them who are under the law: that every mouth may be stopped, and all the world may become guilty before God.

20 Therefore by the deeds of the law there shall no flesh be justified in his sight: for by the law is the knowledge of sin.

If it were possible that any could be justified by keeping the commandments of God and obeying the laws of Moses, then there would be no need for Jesus to shed his innocent blood for the sins of this world. If we were made just and were justified through our own effort to obey the law of God, then it would mean that we are capable of earning our own salvation and there was no need for Jesus to die such a cruel death upon the cross of Calvary.

Keep in mind that Paul has informed us that by the law is the knowledge of sin, and we must first realize what sin is, else how would we be able to repent of our sins?

21 But now the righteousness of God without the law is manifested, being witnessed by the law and the prophets; (Hebrew Bible)

22 Even the righteousness of God which is by faith of Jesus Christ unto all and upon all them that believe: for there is no difference:

23 For all have sinned, and come short of the glory of God;

24 Being justified freely by his grace through the redemption that is in Christ Jesus.

25 Whom God hath set forth to be a propitiation through faith in his blood, to declare his righteousness for the remission of sins that are past, through the forbearance of God;

26 To declare, I say at this time his righteousness: that he might be just, and the justifier of him which believeth in Jesus.

Through out the ages, there were many religious Jews who believed that through their obedience to the law of God, as well as their observance of the feast days which always included the sacrifices of animals, that they were righteous before God. Of course, God did forgive their sins, for it was for this reason the sacrificial system was instituted in the first place. However, the letter to the Hebrews does clearly show that the record of their sins was not blotted out, for only the blood of Jesus could accomplish that.

We must not forget that our brother Paul did say quite clearly "that all have sinned, and come short of the glory of God." To be sure, we are not made just by our own righteousness but only by the righteousness of Christ and through his shed blood.

27 Where is boasting then? It is excluded. By what law? of works? Nay: but by the law of faith.

28 Therefore we conclude that a man is justified by faith without the deeds of the law.

I want to make sure that we do not miss the meaning of what Paul is saying to us. Notice that this is the conclusion of all that Paul has just said regarding the law and the lives we might live in obedience to the law. He has said that righteous living in obedience to the law is not enough to make the religious Jews, nor any of us, just and right before God.

Some might wonder what it means to be justified? A very simple explanation is, to be justified is to be just, as if we had never sinned in the first place.

In other words, the record of our sins has been blotted out by the blood of Jesus when we become justified by our faith in what Jesus has done for us.

There are a great many people who stop right here, for this is the end of the matter as far as they are concerned. Because they only hear what they want to hear, they believe that there isn't any reason to obey the law of God, because Paul did make it quite clear that our obedience does not make any of us, just before God. If their justification is through and by their faith and not in deeds according to the law, then they do choose to ignore the law of God, and do choose the way of their flesh.

However, Paul did have some more to say, for he was not through talking about this subject.

29 Is he the God of the Jews only? is he not also of the Gentiles? Yes, of the Gentiles also:

30 Seeing it is one God, which shall justify the circumcision by faith, and uncircumcision through (the same) faith.

31 Do we then make void the law through faith? God forbid: Yes, we establish the law.

We might think of this as the bottom line. There are two important truths that we must cling very tightly to. The first one was the conclusion of the matter. That is to say that no one can be made just and right with God through their obedience to the law of God. Obeying the commandments of God is certainly the right way to live, but it is not enough to redeem us or pay the price for the sins we have committed. Therefore we must have faith in what Christ has done for us.

Remember the verse in Hebrews that informed us that it is impossible to please God without faith. Our faith must extend beyond the existence of God, and must include his one and only plan of salvation.

We need to notice that in the verses we have just read, that both Jews and Gentiles alike must enter into a relationship with God, through the sacrifice of Christ. If there be any Hebrew blood which flows through our veins, be aware that it cannot save us. The only blood that can save us was poured out at Calvary and it is the blood of our Lord, Jesus Christ, our passover lamb.

Now that we are aware that we cannot be justified by our own righteousness, which is the life we live, then we must consider the bottom line. Paul then asked the question

"Do we then make void the law through faith?"

He then went on to give us the answer to his question. He quite clearly said that God does forbid that we should make void his holy law. I believe this verse is so important that we all need to underline it in our Bibles.

I want us to be aware that today, there are many churches where they teach the very thing that Paul said that God forbids. They do teach that the law is now void, having been taken out of the way and that it was nailed to the cross. These people make no difference between the law of God, which is eternal and the laws of Moses that pertained to sin and animal sacrifices, which were temporary.

Let us be aware that what they teach is totally false, for Paul does make it very clear that "we are to establish the law," and he is speaking of the law of God.

The next question should be, Just how do we go about establishing the law? Should we form many religious laws, including some that deal with what kind of businesses will be allowed to remain open on Sunday, and what kind of businesses must close? Should we then employ the civil authorities to help us enforce these religious laws?

I think not, for the way we are to establish the law is the same way that Jesus did. It is by following in his foot steps and through the life we live, setting a good example for others that we do encourage others to question what the motivating force is, that causes us to live this way.

Of course, this will lead us to the first of the great commandments that were given by Jesus. That is that we are to love our Father, which art in heaven, with all of our heart, and with all of our mind and soul, and with all of our strength. If we truly do love God in these ways, then the life we live will manifest our Love for God.

That is to say, that God does want for us to love him with all that we are. From the bottom of our hearts and with our deepest and innermost desire. We are to love him even more than we love our very own life, for this was the example that was set before us, first by John the Baptist and then by Jesus and then by the apostles. It is because we do love God with all of our heart that we do want to obey him and to please him.

We do not obey him in order to be justified but because we want to please him and we place our trust in him, because we know that his ways are high above man's ways, just as it was written by the prophet Isaiah.

Then we are to love him with all of our minds and our soul. We must do our very best to surrender even our thoughts to Christ Jesus for we have become the dwelling place of the Holy Spirit. This means that we must do our very best to keep a clean house (mind). We must try to see things and circumstances through the eyes of Jesus, and from time to time we must ask ourselves, "What would Jesus do, if he were faced with this same decision?"

Sometimes, almost immediately we receive the answer from the Holy Spirit, while there are other times that we must pray and have patience as we wait for an answer from the Lord.

Thirdly, we must show our love for God by what we do and the life we live. This is our most powerful witness of all, for the whole world does judge us, not by what we say but by what we do. If we say we love our neighbors and yet do not show our love by acts of kindness when we come across those in need, then the whole world realizes that the love we profess is just lip service and does not mean very much.

In the same way, if we claim that we do love God, and yet we refuse to keep his commandments, the whole world will know that we are liars. Perhaps this is why John, the beloved disciple of Jesus had this to say....

1st John 2:3, And hereby we do know that we know him, if we keep his commandments.

4 He that saith, I know him, and keepeth not his commandments, is a liar, and the truth is not in him.

5 But whoso keepeth his word, in him is the love of God perfected: hereby know we that we are in him.

6 He that saith he abideth in him ought himself also so to walk, even as he walked.

And so we can see that those religious leaders who teach that the commandments of God are no longer valid or important, are liars and they really do not even know God, or else they would not teach doctrines that are contrary to the Word of God.

Sin is still sin, and by the law is the knowledge of sin. We can be sure that God does not want us to remain ignorant of sin. How do we know this ? It is because the ten commandments are written not once but twice in the Word of God and we know that it is truly the will of God for all mankind.

The 5th verse states that "whoso keepeth his word," which means to keep in our heart and to allow the law of God to become our way of life, in such is the love of God, truly perfected. Let us be aware that the commandments of God are an expression of our heavenly Father's deep and caring love for us, for he wants for us to have the very best life that is possible for us to live.

The next verse states that "Hereby know we that we are in him."

When we allow God's ways to become our ways, then we can be sure that we do belong to God, and not the evil one.

The law of God is also the "Living Word," written upon our inward parts, which does speak to us and does warn us when we might find ourselves being tempted through the desire of our flesh. If we then obey the voice that does warn us of sin knocking at our door, we are very sure that we are God's very own private property, whom he loves very much.

Verse 6 simply informs us of how we are to establish the law of God in our lives. It is simply by following in the example that Jesus set before us. We can be very sure that never once in the 33 and one half years that Jesus lived, did he disobey his heavenly Father, for the Word of God does show that he lived his life in perfect obedience to his Father's will, even unto his death upon the cross.

Our brother John did also reveal unto us that...

1st John 3:4, Whosoever committeth sin transgresseth also the law: for sin is the transgression of the law.

Therefore, we can be sure that to follow Jesus in the way that he wants for us to follow him must include the keeping of all ten of the commandments, for to ignore even one is rebellion against God.

If we were to carefully study the two great commandments given by our Lord and Savior, known also as the Royal Law, we would find that in reality they are the same as God's holy law, the ten commandments. All ten of the ten commandments do hang upon the two great commandments given by our Lord Jesus.

The first four commandments deal with how we are to love God and the remaining six commandments deal with how we are to treat our neighbors. They explain in greater detail the same truth contained in the two great commandments.

In the next few verses we shall examine it should be apparent that James, our Lord's brother was well aware that the Royal Law, and the ten commandments are exactly the same.

James 2:8, If ye fulfil the royal law according to the scripture, Thou shalt love thy neighbor as thyself, ye do well: 9 But if ye have respect to persons, ye commit sin, and are convinced of the law as transgressors.

This simply means that we are not to be respecters of persons, but we are to treat all people fairly and respect their dignity as human beings that are made in the image of God. We should not highly exalt some while we show our contempt for others for it is very clearly not the will of God. I do believe that James is saying quite clearly that we are all equal in the eyes of God, and I also believe that our bill of rights of these United States does reflect that belief.

James then does explain that we can not obey some of the commandments and choose to ignore others, without suffering the consequences.

10 For whosoever shall keep the whole law, and yet offend in one point, he is guilty of all.

11 For he that said, Do not commit adultery, said also, Do not kill. Now if thou commit no adultery, yet if thou kill,
thou art become a transgressor of the law.

We can clearly see by what James has said, that he fully realizes that there is no difference between the royal law and the ten commandments that were given at Mount Sinai. He then goes on to inform us that we can not keep some or even most of them, while choosing to ignore even one, for it is rebellion against God to do so.

In the interest of making this abundantly clear, let us use a different commandment to reach the same conclusion.

For he that said do not commit murder, also said "Thou shalt not take the name of the Lord thy God in vain; for the Lord will not hold him guiltless that taketh his name in vain."

I want to make sure that we do understand that the person who does use the holy name of our Lord Jesus Christ in a careless or in a vain and profane way, is the same as a person who has committed murder, in the eyes of almighty God.

There is no difference between the two, for if one does break or does choose to ignore one of the commandments of God, he is guilty of breaking them all.

Let us allow James to continue what he is saying to a people who were well aware of the most holy law of God, namely, the twelve tribes of Israel that were scattered through out the whole earth.

12 So speak ye, and so do, as they that shall be judged by the law of liberty.(also perfect in verse 25)

13 For he shall have judgment without mercy, that hath showed no mercy; and mercy rejoiceth against judgment.

We now bring this chapter to an end with this very meaningful verse about judgment and mercy. The law of God will judge the people while we have obtained mercy through the blood of Jesus that is applied to the mercy seat. I have warned you that the judgment of God is close at hand. I say unto you my dear brothers and sisters, as we see the day approaching, let us be merciful unto others now, in the hope that our mercy will be returned unto us, in the days of God's great wrath.

Chapter 38 Final Instructions

B ecause there is such a great burden on my heart for the great many people who have always been taught that Sunday is the Lord's day, I want all of us to pray for them. And not just for them, but for all of the people who were included in the two false doctrines mentioned in Isaiah 56. To be more specific, I am speaking of the sleepy shepherds (pastors) as well as the priests who are fetching the wine, whose own rulers have turned against them and have condemned them to death.

Our heavenly Father, which art in heaven, hallow be thy name. We do come before thee O God, praying for the vast multitude of people, as well as the priests and sleepy shepherds. We do pray may they become aware of their errors and their sin of rebelling against your most Holy Word. We pray the mighty Spirit of conviction will come upon them and they will truly realize they are guilty before God.

It is our hope that they will then humble themselves before thee O Lord, get down on their knees and repent of their rebellion. I do believe it is so very important that they seek your forgiveness while it is yet available, and before that great and terrible day of your wrath is poured out on this land.

We do especially pray for those men and women you have called to be evangelists, and pastors and teachers for I do hope they will awake at this late hour and will begin to sound the alarm that your judgment day is close at hand. We do pray O heavenly Father, may revival break out and quickly spread across the land from sea to sea, and to the saving of a great multitude of souls.

We know Lord, according to what was written by Peter, it is not thy will that any should perish, but that all should come to repentance in thy holy name.

I now add to this prayer the request that may a great many dear souls heed and pay attention to the last instructions they are about to receive in this message. I do consider them to be so very important and I am afraid that a great many people are so in love with their great possessions, and the life they are now living they may hear them and still not do them.

We also do pray for all of the unsaved loved ones, Lord, as children are praying for their parents and parents are praying for their children and many more. We do hold all of them up to you in prayer, that many will come to the knowledge of salvation and your saving grace.

We do pray all of these things in the precious and holy name of our Savior, our Lord Jesus Christ. Amen!

The time has come when I must give to you these final instructions. Let us turn to the 18th chapter of the Revelation, which does inform us of the destruction of Great Babylon. The very wealthy and beautiful land that is filled with religious confusion, and we now realize is speaking of North America.

Let us go directly to verse four and listen to the voice of our Lord and Savior.

Revelation 18:4 And I heard another voice from heaven, saying, Come out of her my people, that ye be not partakers of her sins, and that ye receive not of her plagues.

5 For her sins have reached unto heaven, and God hath remembered her iniquities.

The first thing to notice is that Jesus is speaking to His people. This simply means that if you do not belong to Jesus and have not been born again, these instructions are not for you. They are specifically for those people who have surrendered their will to God's divine will (repentance) and are now walking along the high road to glory.

If you do not know Jesus as your Savior and have refused to repent of your sinful way of life, it does not make any difference what you do, or where you will go, for you will soon be paid the wages you have coming for the life you have lived.

Then there is a great multitude of people who do know Christ, but have insisted that Sunday is a better day to worship God, than is the day God created holy, to be set aside as a day of rest and worship. In this way, these people have rebelled against God's most Holy Word, and are trampling on the life of Jesus Christ.

I do advise these people that they should repent of their rebellion while there is still time, for on the day that will soon come as a thief in the night, the grace of God will be withdrawn and the door of salvation will be closed, just as it was in the days of Noah.

To those dear people who have followed the instructions you have been given, and have found the one and only plan God has for salvation. Listen to the voice of the Lord as he is calling you to come out of North America, and come out quickly.

Do not make the mistake of lingering here because of your wealth or your great possessions. You must begin making preparation this very day, so that you will leave as soon as possible. Find out this very day what you must do to receive a passport and get it in order.

Jesus said in Luke 17 and verse 32, **"Remember Lot's wife."** Do not worry about worldly belongings you have to leave behind, for I want for you to consider what it is that you own that is worth more than your new life in Christ Jesus.

Of course, I want for you to take your family with you and it is with a great urgency you must pack your things and theirs as quickly as possible. Be sure and do not take too much as it is wise to take only the bare necessities, for everything else will be available when you arrive at your destination.

When we hear the voice of Jesus saying "Come out of her my people," we must add something else Jesus did say.

Matthew 28:18, And Jesus came and spake unto them (and we who are his people) saying, All power is given unto me in heaven and earth.

19 Go ye therefore, and teach all nations, baptizing them in the (one) name of the Father, and of the Son, and of the Holy Ghost.

20 Teaching them to observe all things whatsoever I have commanded you: and lo, I am with you alway, even unto the end of the world.

It is for this reason that I do hope you have done your part and did receive the power from on high, just as God has promised us, if we have tarried in a holy place, just as the 120 did in the upper room.

I realize that you might not know where to go, and all of this seems to be so sudden, and you are not really ready. Think of Lot's wife and how much time she and her family had, when they were told they must leave their home in Sodom behind. Surely you are aware they were given very short notice, and they had to flee quickly in order to save their lives.

It is the same for us, for you must leave this place that has been given the symbolic name of Sodom, as well as Babylon.

Do not be afraid for the Lord will be with you and will guide you as you go. Across this world and in just about every nation on earth there are people who know and love Jesus. These people will help you and the Holy Spirit will lead you to the place that God has prepared for you. You must learn to walk by faith and continue to pray without ceasing, just as others do, who have taken a missionary journey.

I have shared with you a view of what life here will soon be like after the day of seven thunders. In case I have not used the words to properly describe this to you, I do advise you to obtain the little book by William Hershey, the title which is simply "Hiroshima."

Perhaps the personal testimony of those who survived the great massacre at Hiroshima will be able to convince you that you must leave America as soon as possible. Believe me when I tell you that I do not want you to be here in the land of Death, when you can be helping others to understand the Good News of our Lord Jesus Christ.

After all, have we not all received the great commission. to go into all the world, and share the good news that God has a plan, and only one plan for everyone's salvation. We must then teach them what is right so that they do not make the same serious error as so many people of America have.

It is now time that we should learn a little more about the New World Order. First and foremost, it will be a religious order that will rule over everyone on planet earth, if that be possible. At this present time there is one thing that is preventing this new world order from rising to power and that is these United States.

Once the United States is removed from off of the face of this earth, and the vast population has been exterminated, the new world order will rise very quickly into power. I say this for the people who have made the plans for this new world order, according to Malachi Martin, have been working out every detail for many of years. We can be sure, they know just what they shall do.

However, let us listen to the Word of God, as he will describe this new world order from his heavenly perspective.

Revelation 13:11, And I beheld another beast coming up out of the earth; and it had two horns like a lamb, and he spake as a dragon.

12 And he exerciseth all the power of the first beast before him, and causeth the earth and then that dwell therein to worship the first beast, whose deadly wound was healed.

13 And he doeth great wonders, so that he maketh fire come down from heaven on the earth in the sight of men.

14 And deceiveth than that dwell on the earth by the means of those miracles which he had power to do in the sight of the beast; saying to them that dwell upon the earth, that they should make an image to the beast, which had the wound by a sword, and did live.

15 And he had power to give life unto the image of the beast, that the image of the beast should both speak, and cause that as many as would not worship the image of the beast should be killed.

16 And he causeth all, both small and great, rich and poor, free and bond, to receive a mark in their right hand, or in their foreheads:

17 And that no man might buy or sell, save he that had the mark, or the name of the beast, or the number of his name.

18 Here is wisdom. Let him that hath understanding count the number of the beast: for it is the number of a man; and his number is Six hundred three score and six.

It should not be too hard to understand, following the complete destruction of North America, as well as the death of close to 300 million people in the United states alone, that a great fear will cover the earth.

I believe that all nations will agree that something must be done to insure that what has happened must never be allowed to happen again. Therefore, they are looking for anyone with a plan that will guarantee world peace forever.

It just so happens that the rulers of Roman religion will have such a plan, and are ready to implement their plan as soon as possible. This will bring up the new two horned beast that will be like a lamb at first.

I believe that even though a great deal of what has happened was done in secret, I believe it might be necessary for the scarlet coloured beast to disappear. Once more it is possible that in some people's eyes it has again struck without any warning, a deadly blow by the use of the ten horns which do belong to the beast. It is for this reason, being mainly it's bad reputation, as well as the fear many people will have, the scarlet coloured beast does now exit the scene, temporarily.

It is my opinion that the two horns on the lamb are the symbol that the new lamb like beast will represent both Catholics as well as Protestants. Together, they will form a union whereby they will seek to rule over the whole earth. I believe that the beast will appear as a lamb, as it is the impression that it's designers want to create.

It will be as harmless as a lamb, or so many will think, but our Bibles have informed us that it will speak as a dragon.

In other words, it has received the power and the voice of Satan and within a few years it will begin to exalt the beast that was. In time it will attempt to force everyone on planet earth to bow down and worship the beast that was or else be killed.

Of course, all of these things are of no concern for the millions upon millions who are about to perish in the total destruction of North America. They will be gone and none of these warnings will help them, for they did not seek God nor did they believe what is written in their Bibles.

However, my dear brothers and sisters, and I am speaking to those who have become born again, to those who have received the divine power from on high, and especially to all who have received with meekness, the engrafted word. To all who are about to obey the voice of our Lord and Savior as he calls out, "Come out of her, my people." It is to you who are about to travel to foreign lands and who will be Ambassadors for Christ, the bible does now speak to you,

Revelation 14:8, And there followed another angel, saying, Babylon is fallen, is fallen, that great city, because she made all nations drink of the wine of the wrath of her fornication.

I want to bring to our attention that this 8th verse does set the time for these next verses to apply which is soon after the destruction of America is complete.

9 And the third angel followed them, saying with a loud voice, If any man (or woman) worship the beast and his image, and receive his mark in his forehead, (what you believe) or in his hand, (what you do)

10 The same shall drink of the wine of the wrath of God, which is poured out without mixture into the cup of his indignation; and he shall be tormented with fire and brimstone in the presence of the holy angels, and in the presence of the Lamb.(Jesus)

11 And the smoke of their torment ascendeth up for ever and ever: and they have no rest day nor night, who worship the beast and his image, and whosoever receiveth the mark of his name.

I do want to impress you with the fact that these verses are as immutable as any warning given in the entire Bible. There is no half way and there is no in between. This is why I have tried to tell you how very important it is that you come to understand the way in which we do receive the engrafted word with meekness. It is so very important that all of us have received this great blessing by loving God in the three ways the Word of God has made known to us.

12 Here is the patience of the saints: here are they that keep the commandments of God, and the faith of Jesus.

In reading this verse there is a word which comes to my mind. That word is endurance. Let us remember that patience is one of the fruits of the Spirit but our faith must be strong enough to insure that we will endure until the end. This is what this verse is speaking of for the faith that Jesus had remained strong and he endured to the end on the cross of Calvary.

Let me bring to your attention the people of this world did not approve of or love Jesus. Instead, they demanded that he die on a cruel cross, even though he had done them no wrong. Because of this, do not be surprised when you learn that the people of the new world order will despise you and hate you, for teaching people the truth about our Lord Jesus Christ.

I have no doubt in the years that are ahead, as you who are the faithful children of God do carry out the work that God has called you to do, that trouble shall come looking for you. The people who are the servants of the beast will first command you to stop keeping the sabbath day holy. They will then insist that you rest on Sunday and that you worship the beast.

The reason is simply that the changing of the sabbath to Sunday, is the sign of the authority of the beast. It was this way even during the 1260 year reign of terror and many refused to obey the commandments of religious men and did cling tightly to the commandments of God. It was for this reason they were put to death in many different ways.

Another sign of their authority is when the priests mumble the words in Latin over the goblet of wine, saying "hocus pocus," the wine has now been changed into the blood of Christ.

It is when you shall teach others the truth, regarding this lie, and because you do choose to worship our holy and righteous God on the very day he created for rest and worship, they will greatly hate you and will condemn you, just as they did so many of God's dear children.

Do listen carefully to this next verse for it does contain the promise of our heavenly Father.

13 And I heard a voice from heaven saying unto me, Write, Blessed are the dead which die in the Lord from henceforth: Yea saith the Spirit, that they may rest from their labours; and their works do follow them.

The time has come when I must send this message to the publishers so that it can continue on it's way to be delivered to as many as can receive it. I cannot find the words to express to you how very much I do care for you and I will continue to pray for all of you without ceasing. You will be in my heart always.

I ask you please, do not neglect anything as precious as your salvation and we must not forsake the gathering together with other born again Christians for prayer and for worship.

Do not forget our great commission to go into all the world, for this is the will of our Savior. You must teach them about God's one and only plan for our salvation and if it be possible you should share with them how they can tarry in a holy place until they receive the power from on high.

James did tell us to receive the engrafted word with meekness. Meekness does mean we have power but our power is under the control of the Holy Spirit. I believe it is easier to receive the engrafted word if we first tarry in a holy place.

If we cling tightly to the engrafted word and refuse to let go of it, even in the face of adversity, while living in perilous times, it will lead us home and our journey will be finished.

If at this point in time, we were to claim that we now know the rest of the story, it would not quite be true. Even though I am sure that we now know more than we did when we first started, the last chapter has not yet been written, nor can it be, as it applies to each of us as individuals.

I have no doubt that many of you will eventually come to that place, where you must decide either to live a little longer with the beast, or else die in Christ Jesus, and live with him, forever. When that time comes I want you to remember that Jesus laid down his life for us, while we were yet sinners, who were not worthy of his blood.

Therefore, if we are given the opportunity to lay down our lives for the sake of the gospel, we should consider it a great honor. It will mean that once more, God has smiled upon us and wants us to receive a heavenly reward.

Because this is so, there is a great multitude who have traveled down this same path we are on, and they shall be there to welcome us, when we arrive at the heavenly city of God.

The time has come, to bring this message to a close. It is because I am only a messenger and because this message is now complete I shall now call upon one who is worthy of having the final word. I am speaking of the man from Tarsus that our Lord Jesus Christ called to be an apostle, who laid down his life for the sake of the gospel. Let us listen to these words of our brother Paul.

Romans 8:35, Who shall separate us from the love of Christ? Shall tribulation, or distress, or persecution, or famine, or nakedness, or peril, or sword ?

36 As it is written, For thy sake we are killed all the day long; we are accounted as sheep for the slaughter.

37 Nay, in all these things we are more than conquerors through him that loved us.

38 For I am persuaded, that neither death, nor life, nor angels, nor principalities, nor powers, nor things present, nor things to come,

39 Nor height, nor depth, nor any other creature, shall be able to separate us from the love of God, which is in Christ Jesus our Lord.

End